D1707128

THE HONG KONG FINANCIAL SYSTEM

THE HONG KONG FINANCIAL SYSTEM

Editors
RICHARD YAN-KI HO   ROBERT HANEY SCOTT   KIE ANN WONG

Contributors
ALLAN K.K. CHAN   DAVID Y.K. CHAN   HELEN W.M. HO
RICHARD YAN-KI HO   SIMON S.M. HO   Y.C. JAO   Y.H. LUI
ROBERT HANEY SCOTT   CLEMENT SHUM   JOSEPH S. WAN
GORDON W. WONG   JIM H.Y. WONG
KIE ANN WONG

With a Foreword by David Li Kwok-Po

HONG KONG
OXFORD UNIVERSITY PRESS
OXFORD   NEW YORK
1991

Oxford University Press

Oxford   New York   Toronto
Petaling Jaya   Singapore   Hong Kong   Tokyo
Delhi   Bombay   Calcutta   Madras   Karachi
Nairobi   Dar es Salaam   Cape Town
Melbourne   Auckland

and associated companies in
Berlin   Ibadan

First published 1991
Published in the United States
by Oxford University Press, Inc., New York

British Library Cataloguing in Publication Data
The Hong Kong financial system.
1. Financial institutions
I. Ho, Yan ki   II. Scott, Robert Haney   III. Wong, K. A.
332.1095125
ISBN 0-19-584998-1

Library of Congress Cataloging-in-Publication Date
The Hong Kong financial system/editors, Richard Yan-ki Ho,
Robert Haney Scott, Wong Kie Ann;
contributors, Allan K.K. Chan ... [et al.].
p. cm.
Includes bibliographical references and index.
ISBN 0-19-584998-1 (hard): $46.00 — ISBN 0-19-584999-X (pbk.)
1. Finance — Hong Kong.   2. Banks and banking — Hong Kong.
3. Financial institutions — Hong Kong.   4. International finance.
I. Ho, Yan-ki.   II. Scott, Robert Haney.
III. Wong, Kie Ann, 1944–.   IV. Chan, Allan K.K.
HG187.H85H66 1991
332'.095125 — dc20   90-25959
CIP

Printed in Hong Kong by Nordica Printing Co., Ltd.
Published by Oxford University Press, Warwick House, Hong Kong

Foreword

COMPARATIVELY few books can honestly be called 'important' or genuinely 'valuable'. As a banker, I feel this is one of those books. Not only does it provide a comprehensive overview of the financial industry, it does so with such clarity, perspective, and depth of analysis that it can serve the needs of Hong Kong and foreign professionals as well as Government policy-makers and students of finance.

Well-written and edited — something not always true of books about finance — it moves deftly from broadbrush to detailed analysis, mixing skilfully the views of scholars and practitioners. It raises issues. It looks at policy. It questions practice. For those of us in the financial sector, this book tells us who we are and, perhaps more important, where we are going.

More than ever before in its history, Hong Kong's future economic success depends on its ability to remain a leading centre for regional and international finance. It is not simply a question of the contribution financial services make to the territory's Gross Domestic Product. It is that the financial sector will ultimately shape the economic role Hong Kong plays in the next century.

Hong Kong was founded a century and a half ago as a safe haven for trade with China, especially southern China. It quickly grew to become something more — an important regional entrepôt, able to service and finance trade throughout much of what we now call the Asia-Pacific region.

Although Hong Kong's economy added an important manufacturing capability after the Second World War, it never lost its role as an entrepôt for trade, services, and finance; and with China's Open Door policy at the end of the 1970s this role has grown steadily more important. Today, as we look ahead, it is clear Hong Kong has gained an important economic hinterland and manufacturing base in southern China, while the potential synergy between Hong Kong, southern China, and Taiwan promises to create a new economic powerhouse in the Asia-Pacific region.

But key to all of this is Hong Kong's ability to provide the financial expertise and mobilize the fiscal resources needed to make promise reality. If Hong Kong loses its position as a major international financial centre, the benefits of synergy will be much harder to come by.

The obvious answer is that Hong Kong cannot afford to lose its position as a major centre of international finance, as the pre-eminent centre for regional finance. A careful reading of this book should help policy-makers and those of us in the financial sector ensure the continued health of the industry.

DAVID LI KWOK-PO
Director and Chief Executive,
The Bank of East Asia, Limited

Preface

WE hope this book, *The Hong Kong Financial System*, will be useful not only to those who work in the financial markets and institutions of Hong Kong, but also to students looking for positions in finance and to foreign businesses that are newcomers to the Hong Kong economy. Our book is far less colourful than most guidebooks for tourists, but in a sense it is designed to be a guidebook for those with a need to know about the availability of financial services in this far eastern financial centre.

A favourite joke of ours about economists goes like this: ask any two economists and you are sure to get at least three opinions. Well, our authors fit this mould, too. No attempt has been made by the editors to try to fashion a uniform expression of opinion. We probably could not do it even if we wanted to. Therefore, the reader should expect to find within these covers expressions of a variety of opinions on policy questions. For example, some authors feel that the fixed exchange rate system introduced in 1983 has worked well; others feel it is deficient, and needs extended government support; others feel it should be replaced with a tie to a basket of currencies rather than to the United States dollar; and one renegade would like to see the whole package tossed in the dust bin to be replaced by a system of freely fluctuating exchange rates and monetary base controls.

Such a wide range of opinion is not found on every issue brought forward for discussion. For example, all authors have agreed to define the term 'billion' in the American way, meaning a thousand million (instead of the British, meaning a million million). They also have agreed that the words 'he' and 'him' apply equally to persons of the feminine gender. There is also uniform concern over the appropriateness of the existence of a banking cartel arrangement for control over domestic deposit rates. Such arrangements seem strangely at odds with the Government's expressions of belief in maintaining a competitive free enterprise environment for business.

Whatever one's views on the variety of policy issues that face Hong Kong's future, it is most important that a plentiful amount of informed discussion of the pros and cons of each policy question comes forward. Such is, after all, the spirit of democratic life.

It is perhaps not too strong to argue that the failure of the existing economic system in communist countries, dramatically displayed in the winter of 1989–90 in Eastern Europe, follows from those systems' rejection of the value of capital in the production process. While celebrating the value of work, those economic systems seem to ignore the workers' needs for tools with which to work. These tools, items of capital equipment, exist as real physical pieces of property, but they are represented in a modern exchange economy by financial instruments in the form of loans, mortgages, bonds, stocks, and other types of equity. Both existing capital and new investments need some source of financing, and only the careful evaluation of the cash flows from investments will guide investors to choose the most efficient investments to make. By rejecting the concept of interest, the return or yield on capital, communist authorities left little or no room for the proper evaluation of investments. Without proper tools, workers' productivity fails to improve and standards of living cannot rise.

China's economy will surely prosper if, in the wake of 1997 when Hong Kong returns to the fold, it opens its doors to the financial sector of Hong Kong. Financial institutions and markets now operating successfully can provide the financing mechanisms needed to bring China's economy into the twenty-first century.

This book was written in 1989. As it went to press in late 1990, the HongkongBank announced on 17 December 1990 that it would move its legal domicile to the United Kingdom by forming a new parent company called Hongkong & Shanghai Banking Corporation Holdings PLC, and that it would suspend further merger talks with the Midland Bank because of difficult economic conditions. The implications of these moves are profound for both the bank and Hong Kong. Regrettably, it is physically impossible to incorporate an analysis of these events in the text. A fuller explanation or discussion therefore has to wait for another occasion.

The editors wish to thank all 10 authors who have contributed chapters to this volume. The range of expertise they bring to their special subjects lends both breadth and depth to this study of the Hong Kong financial system. We also wish to thank the editors at Oxford University Press, without whose thoughtful support, patient assistance, and editorial prowess this book could not have been published. Clerical services provided by Jennifer So, Callie Toh, and Clara Kwong are also gratefully acknowledged.

RICHARD YAN-KI HO, ROBERT HANEY SCOTT, AND KIE ANN WONG
1990

Contributors

Dr Richard Yan-Ki Ho
Head, Department of Economics and Finance, City Polytechnic of Hong Kong.

Professor Robert Haney Scott
Professor, Department of Finance and Marketing, California State University, Chico, California, USA; and Visiting Professor, Department of Finance, Chinese University of Hong Kong.

Dr Kie Ann Wong
Head and Associate Professor, Department of Finance and Banking, National University of Singapore.

Mr Allan K. K. Chan
Head and Senior Lecturer, Department of Marketing, Hong Kong Baptist College.

Mr David Y. K. Chan
Acting Head and Senior Lecturer, Department of Finance and Decision Sciences, Hong Kong Baptist College.

Ms Helen W. M. Ho
Lecturer, Department of Marketing, University of Otago, New Zealand.

Dr Simon S. M. Ho
Lecturer, Department of Accountancy, The Chinese University of Hong Kong.

Dr Y. C. Jao
Reader, Department of Economics, University of Hong Kong.

Dr Y. H. Lui
Senior Lecturer, Department of Economics and Finance, City Polytechnic of Hong Kong.

Mr Clement Shum
Head, Department of Accountancy and Law, Hong Kong Baptist College.

Mr Joseph S. Wan
Senior Lecturer, Department of Finance, School of Business, Hong Kong Baptist College.

Dr Gordon W. Wong
Formerly Vice President and Director, Bank of America Trust.

Mr Jim H. Y. Wong
Formerly Senior Economist, Economic Research Department, The Hongkong and Shanghai Banking Corporation Ltd.

Contents

Part IV Issues and Policies

Tables

Figures

Part I
Depository Institutions

1. The Banking System: An Overview

RICHARD YAN-KI HO

OVER the past decade, numerous changes have taken place in Hong Kong's banking sector. It has effectively been transformed into a functional international financial centre where not only are financial transactions booked but actual operations are carried out. The wave of banking internationalization since the oil crises in the 1970s has also brought about an influx of foreign banks, especially when the Hong Kong Government lifted the moratorium on bank licensing in 1978.[1] Unlike Singapore, Hong Kong is an integrated financial centre with no delineation between offshore and domestic banking business. Thus, foreign banks could always intrude into the domestic market provided that they have been granted a bank licence.[2] This has created intense competitive pressure in the domestic banking sector.

The wave of banking internationalization came in the wake of China's open door policy, which started in 1978. One of the most important effects of this policy is the change in the competitive strategies of the Bank of China (BOC) Group, a group of 13 sister banks owned by the People's Republic of China. Since 1979, this group of banks has gone from maintaining a highly conservative and stagnant position to taking a relatively aggressive and innovative one. Their move has certainly intensified competition in the Hong Kong banking market, which has long been dominated by a locally incorporated but British-managed banking group, the Hongkong and Shanghai Banking Corporation.

Until recently, Hong Kong was well known for its lax government regulations. However, the laxity of the regulations, together with a sudden competitive shock from foreign banks and the 'good' old British tradition of bank secrecy also created an environment that encouraged fraudulent activity and resulted in a banking crisis. One aftermath of the banking crisis has undoubtedly been a stepping up in the regulatory process, giving rise to the Banking Ordinance of 1986 and the many guide-lines issued by the Banking Commissioner of the Hong Kong Government.

The purpose of this chapter is to give an overview of the development and structure of the Hong Kong banking system. A more detailed description of the Hongkong and Shanghai Banking Corporation and the Bank of China Banking Group will be given in Chapters 2 and 3, while a salient analysis of the banking regulations will be presented in Chapter 5. However, before we go into more detailed analysis of the Hong Kong banking system, it is necessary to give a brief introduction to the basic principle of financial intermediation.

Introduction to the Theory of Financial Intermediation

In an economy, there exists a limited amount of productive resources, including land, machines, properties, equipment, natural resources, and manpower. Some of these resources may be used for current consumption, but some may also be needed to 'invest' in activities that will enhance the productivity and hence the future consumption of the economy. In an economy with limited resources, an increase in investment would mean a curtailment in current consumption and vice versa.

Moreover, there also exist many economic units in an economy that includes households, business firms, and government. During a year, each of these units has a certain level of current income and also a certain desired level of consumption. The difference between current income and current desired consumption is called 'saving'.

Besides consumption, the unit may also have a desired level of 'investment' in real assets (such as machines, properties, equipment, and manpower). A unit that has more saving than desired investment is termed a 'saving surplus' unit, a unit that has more investment than saving is termed a 'saving deficit' unit, and a unit that just breaks even is called a 'saving balance' unit.

If all the units in an economy are saving balance units, they are self sufficient financially and there is no need for any form of financial market or institution, or in more technical language, 'financial intermediation'. However, such a case is not at all common in the real world. Some units may be saving surplus ones and some may be saving deficit ones. The surplus units may need to get rid of their surplus by lending their surplus funds and the saving deficit units may need to borrow funds to finance their real investments. Thus, the surplus units create a net supply of funds while the deficit units create a net demand for funds.

In borrowing funds from the lender, the borrower needs to issue a liability item (an IOU) to the lender. To the lender, this item is an asset, usually called a 'financial asset' because no transfer of physical units is involved in the transaction.

Because of the existence of saving imbalance units, the financial market evolves to facilitate transactions between lenders and borrowers. In the financial market, there is a flow of funds from the lenders to the borrowers and a simultaneous flow of securities, that is, financial assets, from the borrowers to the lenders. This is usually called 'direct financing' and the loan involved is called a 'direct loan' because the lenders acquire a claim directly on the borrowers.

However, in the real world, it is very common for a third party to intermediate the transactions between the ultimate borrowers and the ultimate lenders. Such third parties are broadly referred to as 'financial intermediaries'. There are three basic forms of financial intermediary:

1. Brokerage Intermediary.   These are the true middlemen and their major function is to match the lenders with the borrowers and obtain

fees in return for their services. They do not alter the direct relationship between the ultimate lenders and the ultimate borrowers in that they do not acquire claims on the borrowers and they do not issue to the lenders claims on themselves. Stock brokerage firms and money market brokerage firms are good examples of this type of intermediary. Since they do not change the nature of direct financing, they are not usually referred to as 'true' financial intermediaries.

2. Mutual Fund and Unit Trust Intermediaries.   This type of institution usually pools investors' funds and invests them in a portfolio of securities. Mutual fund and trust institutions issue claims on themselves to the investors (the lenders) and acquire claims on the institutions (the borrowers) that issue the securities. The investors have a proportionate claim on the portfolio of assets and the value of the claim varies with the market value of the assets in the portfolio. Mutual funds and unit trusts set up by investment houses such as Jardine Fleming Unit Trusts Ltd., G. T. Management (Asia) Ltd., and Schroders Asia Ltd. are good examples of this type of intermediary.

3. Deposit-taking Intermediary.   This type of institution is similar to the mutual fund intermediary. The difference lies in the fact that the value of the claim offered to the investors is fixed by contract and is independent of the value of the portfolio held by the intermediary. Commercial banks and deposit-taking companies are good examples of this type of intermediary.

There are several reasons for the existence of financial intermediaries, especially the depository and mutual fund types.

1. Transaction Costs.   There are three types of transaction cost and they are detailed briefly as follows:

(a) Identification cost or search cost involves the identification of investment opportunities. In the case of a lender, the identification cost is the cost of finding the appropriate borrower. Verification cost may also be included: this is the cost of evaluating the productivity of an investment or the future cash flow of a borrower once a borrower has been identified.

(b) Monitoring cost involves ensuring that the funds are used for the intended purpose.

(c) Enforcement cost involves ensuring that borrowers fulfil repayment obligations as stated in the borrowing contract.

Financial intermediaries grow large because they enjoy economies of scale. They can handle such costs much better than an individual. Moreover, some intermediaries have a central location, for example, commercial banks and deposit-taking institutions. Both the lenders (the depositors) and the borrowers can easily identify the place to fulfil their needs.

2. Risk Reduction.   This results from the pooling of funds to invest in a portfolio of assets, the return on which is less than perfectly correlated. Thus, investing in a mutual fund is less risky than investing in a single security. Similarly, making a bank deposit is also less risky than making a single direct loan because the bank then uses your funds

together with those of other depositors to lend to a number of borrowers. As long as the default of one borrower would not lead to a default of the rest of the borrowers, the risk is reduced.

Forms of Financial Institutions in Hong Kong

Various forms of financial institutions exist in Hong Kong. They are listed briefly below; a more detailed account will be given in the following sections or in other chapters.

1.   Banking Institutions.   These are the most traditional form of deposit-taking intermediary:
(a)   Commercial banks
(b)   Restricted licensed banks
(c)   Deposit-taking companies

2.   Insurance Companies.   These are close to the deposit-taking intermediary in that the claim offered to the policy holders is fixed by the contract (contingent on the occurrence of an event such as death in life insurance and fire damage in fire insurance).

3.   Mutual Fund Intermediaries.   Investment houses managing unit trusts, mutual funds, or pension funds are typical forms of mutual fund intermediaries. These have become very popular recently as more people are interested in investing in overseas markets, and more corporations offer pension fund schemes to attract or to retain staff.

4.   Brokerage Houses.   These are for the dealing of stocks, foreign exchange, and commodities, and are also getting more popular in Hong Kong.

Categorization of Banks in Hong Kong

The Legal Structure

The banking structure in Hong Kong is a three-tier system which is formed by three types of institutions that are authorized to take deposits from the general public: (1) Licensed banks, (2) Licensed Deposit-taking Companies (LDTCs), and (3) Registered Deposit-taking Companies (RDTCs).

However, on 8 March 1989, the Commissioner of Banking, Mr Nicolle, announced the establishment of a new three-tier system[3] which is composed of: (1) Licensed banks, (2) Restricted Licensed Banks (RLBs), and (3) Deposit-taking Companies (DTCs).

Licensed banks provide normal banking services. They accept deposits of any maturity and size; grant loans and advances; discount trade bills and bankers acceptances; deal in gold, foreign exchange, and other securities; and provide business consultative services. Restricted licensed banks are investment banks or merchant banks. They take deposits of large denominations, underwrite securities, deal in foreign

Table 1.1   The Three-tier Banking System

	Licensed Banks[1]	RLBs[2]	DTCs[3]
Minimum capital	HK$150 million for local banks (for foreign banks there is a minimum asset requirement of US$14 billion but there is not any minimum capital requirement).	HK$100 million	HK$25 million
Minimum deposit for an account	None	HK$0.50 million	HK$0.10 million
Maturity restrictions on deposits	None	None	3 months
Interest rate restrictions	Need to observe the Interest Rate Rule of the HKAB	None	None

Notes: 1. The minimum capital requirement for locally incorporated licensed banks was HK$100 million before March 1989.
2. Formerly known as licensed deposit-taking companies with a minimum capital requirement of HK$75 million.
3. Formerly known as registered deposit-taking companies with a minimum capital requirement of HK$10 million.

exchange and other securities, and provide financial advisory services in issuance of securities and mergers and acquisitions. Deposit-taking companies are finance companies. Their services include taking deposits, granting loans to medium to small businesses, factoring, and leasing.

As shown in Table 1.1, these institutions operate under different restrictions. The licensed banks do not have any restrictions except that they have to comply with the interest rate rule set by the Hong Kong Association of Banks.[4] The RLBs, formerly known as LDTCs, can only accept deposits of not less than HK$500,000 per account; while the DTCs, formerly known as RDTCs, are restricted to accept deposits of not less than HK$100,000 per account with a maturity of not less than three months. All of these institutions must comply with certain minimum capital requirements. The most stringent requirements are on banks and the least stringent are on RDTCs.

In the analysis that follows, the titles of the institutions under the old system will be used, as the historical statistical data still keep such old titles.

Classification by Country of Incorporation

Another common method of bank categorization is by the country of incorporation of its head office. Table 1.2 indicates that a large majority of banks were incorporated outside Hong Kong; banks incorporated

Table 1.2   Authorized Institutions: Parentage

	1989	1986
Licensed banks		
Incorporated in Hong Kong	31	32
Incorporated outside Hong Kong	134	116
Unincorporated banks	—	3
Total number of licensed banks	165	151
Deposit-taking companies		
Registered deposit-taking companies		
Subsidiaries of licensed banks		
Local	30	35
Foreign	76	84
Subsidiaries of foreign banks which are not		
licensed in Hong Kong	46	51
Bank-related	22	17
Others	28	67
Total number of RDTCs	202	254
Licensed deposit-taking companies		
Subsidiaries of licensed banks		
Local	3	3
Foreign	12	14
Subsidiaries of foreign banks which are not		
licensed in Hong Kong	7	9
Bank-related	11	10
Others	3	2
Total number of LDTCs	36	38

in Hong Kong accounted for only about one-fifth of the total number of banks in 1989. However, such a method would not be very meaningful for the DTCs as all these institutions are incorporated in Hong Kong. Instead, the Banking Commissioner differentiates DTCs according to their affiliation with commercial banks. In 1989, a great majority of RDTCs and LDTCs were either subsidiaries of banks or bank-related institutions, leaving only 28 RDTCs and 3 LDTCs free from any form of bank affiliation.

Classification by Country of Ownership

Counting the number of banks by their place of incorporation may not be very meaningful given the wave of mergers and acquisitions in the banking sector which can be traced back to the late 1960s. It is more meaningful to group banks in Hong Kong according to the nationality of their ownership (by majority share holding) or management. Until 1986, there were no official statistics on the number of banks by country of ownership. Both the analysts and the practitioners have

Table 1.3 Analysis of Authorized Institutions by Country of Beneficial
Ownership

Country/Region	Licensed Banks		Deposit-taking Companies	
	1989	1985	1989	1985
Asia Pacific Region				
Hong Kong	15	23	29	61
Australia	5	—	5	9
China	15	13	17	14
India	4	4	4	4
Indonesia	3	2	16	19
Japan	30	20	37	34
Malaysia	3	2	5	6
New Zealand	1	—	1	2
Pakistan	1	1	1	1
Philippines	2	2	7	6
Singapore	4	5	8	10
South Korea	3	3	9	5
Thailand	1	1	8	19
Others	—	—	1	4
Subtotal	87	76	148	199
Europe				
Austria	2	—	—	—
Luxemburg/Belgium	3	2	4	5
France	8	8	11	13
Italy	7	3	—	13
Netherlands	3	3	4	5
Norway	1	—	1	—
Republic of Ireland	1	—	—	—
Spain	3	1	—	—
Sweden	3	—	1	—
Switzerland	3	3	2	4
United Kingdom	7	7	13	18
West Germany	9	8	4	4
Others	—	—	2	3
Subtotal	50	35	42	52
Middle East				
Bahrain	1	1	2	2
Iran	1	1	—	—
Others	—	—	4	6
Subtotal	2	2	6	8
North America				
Canada	6	6	5	9
United States	20	24	34	39
Subtotal	26	30	39	48
Others	—	—	4	3
Grand total	165	143	238	313

Note: Deposit-taking companies include both LDTCs and RDTCs.

Source: Commissioner of Banking, *Annual Report* (Hong Kong, Hong Kong Government
Printer), various issues.

categorized banks in Hong Kong into four groups:[5] the Hongkong and Shanghai Banking Corporation Group, which includes the Hongkong and Shanghai Banking Corporation and a local Chinese bank, the Hang Seng Bank;[6] the Bank of China Group, which includes the 13 sister banks owned by China; the foreign banks; and the local Chinese banks, the number of which has become minimal after the 1982–6 banking crisis.[7]

The Office of the Banking Commissioner started to publish statistics by country of beneficial ownership in 1986 (with data back-dated to 1985). Table 1.3 shows that in 1989, Japan had the largest number of banks (30 banks) followed by the United States (20 banks), Hong Kong (15 banks), and China (15 banks). The United States used to have the largest number of banks in 1985 (24 banks) but their number of banks dwindled over time to 20 in 1989, while those of Japan increased from 20 to 30. This indicates the loss in interest on the part of United States banks in the Hong Kong market, especially in the retail market. The rapid rise in the number of Japanese banks may be attributed to the process of financial liberalization in Japan, and rising Japanese foreign direct investment in and trade with Hong Kong and China.

In the DTC category, Asian and Pacific countries or regions had the largest number of firms — a total of 148 in 1989, but this number was much smaller than that in 1985 of 199. A great majority of RDTCs relinquished their registration voluntarily either because they could not comply with the more stringent capital requirement in the Banking Ordinance of 1986 or because there was a change in the policies of the group to which the companies belonged. Some LDTCs gave up their licence either because their business was absorbed by their parent banks upon those parent banks obtaining bank licences, or else their business was taken into parent banks that were already licensed.

The Structure of Assets and Liabilities of the Banking Sector

The most convenient way to examine the uses and sources of funds for financial institutions is to look at the structure of their assets and liabilities. Tables 1.4 and 1.5 give the balance sheets of licensed banks and DTCs for 1980 and 1989.

Assets and Liabilities of Licensed Banks

Some of the features of bank liabilities are highlighted briefly here:
1. Total Bank Liabilities.   There was a rapid increase in total liabilities from HK$294.98 billion to HK$3,874.35 billion over the nine-year period. The annual compounded growth rate was 33.13 per cent.
2. Liability Item: Due to Banks Abroad.   The most important liability item in 1989 is 'due to banks abroad', which is the amount borrowed by banks in Hong Kong from banks outside Hong Kong. This item

Table 1.4 Balance Sheets of Licensed Banks (HK$ million)

	1980		1989		Compounded Annual Growth Rate (Per cent) 1980–1989
	HK$ million	Per cent in Total	HK$ million	Per cent in Total	
Liabilities					
Due to banks and DTCs in					
Hong Kong	55,760	18.90	410,255	10.59	24.80
Due to banks abroad	118,067	40.03	2,341,970	60.45	39.37
Customers' deposits	86,753	24.41	937,654	24.20	30.28
NCDs outstanding	2,041	0.69	31,019	0.80	35.30
Other liabilities	32,538	11.03	153,448	3.96	18.81
Total	294,979	100.00	3,874,345	100.00	33.13
Assets					
Cash	2,092	0.71	5,467	0.14	11.26
Due from banks and DTCs in					
Hong Kong	47,617	16.14	446,508	11.52	28.24
Due from banks abroad	78,366	26.57	1,979,330	51.09	43.16
NCDs held	4,106	1.39	17,641	0.46	17.58
Loans and advances	124,535	42.22	1,173,005	30.28	28.30
Bank acceptances	5,743	1.95	23,245	0.60	16.81
Floating-rate notes and commercial paper	1,766	0.60	54,679	1.41	46.44
Treasury bills and securities	7,425	2.52	71,763	1.85	28.67
Other assets	23,329	7.91	102,708	2.65	17.90
Total	294,979	100.00	3,874,345	100.00	33.13

Source: *Hong Kong Monthly Digest of Statistics* (Hong Kong, Census and Statistics Department), various issues.

Table 1.5 Consolidated Balance Sheet of Deposit-taking Companies (HK$ million)

	1980		1989		Compounded Annual Growth Rate (Per cent) 1980–1989
	HK$ million	Per cent in Total	HK$ million	Per cent in Total	
Liabilities					
Due to banks and DTCs in					
Hong Kong	31,397	22.37	112,115	30.05	15.19
Due to banks abroad	49,961	35.60	86,408	23.16	6.28
Customers' deposits	42,101	30.00	70,004	18.76	5.81
NCDs outstanding	731	0.52	2,878	0.77	16.45
Other liabilities	16,168	11.52	101,713	27.26	22.67
Total	140,358	100.00	373,118	100.00	11.48
Assets					
Cash	8	*	12	*	4.61
Due from banks and DTCs in					
Hong Kong	38,636	27.53	76,459	20.49	7.88
Due from banks abroad	24,251	17.28	98,630	26.43	16.87
NCDs held	3,648	2.60	10,140	2.72	12.03
Loans and advances	59,392	42.31	98,894	26.50	5.83
Bank acceptances	450	0.32	820	0.22	6.89
Floating-rate notes and commercial paper	2,061	1.47	38,379	10.29	38.39
Treasury bills and securities	4,427	3.15	20,213	5.42	18.38
Other assets	7,487	5.33	29,571	7.93	16.49
Total	140,358	100.00	373,118	100.00	11.48

Source: Hong Kong Monthly Digest of Statistics (Hong Kong, Census and Statistics Department), various issues.

Note: • Less than 0.01 per cent.

accounted for 60.45 per cent of total liabilities in 1989 but contributed only 40.03 per cent of liabilities in 1980, indicating that banks in Hong Kong were increasingly using overseas funds to finance their assets.

3. Other Liability Items.   The other important liability items were 'customers' deposits' and 'due to banks and DTCs in Hong Kong'. Their shares in total liabilities were 24.20 per cent and 10.59 per cent, respectively, in 1989. The first item is just deposits from individuals and non-deposit-taking firms. Since Hong Kong is an integrated financial centre, there is no delineation between resident and non-resident deposits. The second item is the amount borrowed by banks from other banks and DTCs in Hong Kong. This item is usually referred to as 'inter-bank borrowing' (please see Chapter 8 for details). Since foreign banks lack a strong deposit base, it is very common for them to be net debtors in this market. Although both of these items experienced enviable growth rates, they still had to give way to overseas inter-bank borrowing.

4. Liability Item: NCDs Outstanding.   These are negotiable certificates of deposit issued by banks and not yet redeemed. Since most NCDs have a maturity of longer than 15 months and/or a minimum denomination of larger than HK$500,000, banks do not have to comply with the interest rate rule when issuing these instruments.[8] Thus, banks, especially foreign banks, use these instruments as a tool for liability management.[9] Over the past nine years, NCDs enjoyed the tremendous annual growth rate of 35.30 per cent, but because of their small base, their share in total liabilities was still less than 1 per cent.

On the asset side, there are several noteworthy points:

1. Asset Item: Due From Banks Abroad.   'Due from banks abroad' are deposits of banks in Hong Kong with overseas banks. This item was the largest asset item (51.09 per cent of total assets) in 1989. This item experienced rapid growth from 1980 when its share in total assets was only 26.57 per cent, and was in the same order of magnitude as 'due to banks abroad.' This demonstrates well the role of Hong Kong as an international financial centre: funds are channelled from and to countries outside of Hong Kong and such transactions are generally carried out through the local and overseas banking system. In Chapter 17, it will be seen in greater detail that banks in Hong Kong usually get funds from European countries and lend them to other countries in the Asia Pacific region. Since these are offshore transactions,[10] the currency denomination is mostly foreign. It will be made clear later in this chapter that close to 100 per cent of borrowing from and lending to banks abroad is denominated in foreign currencies.

2. Asset Item: Loans and Advances.   'Loans and advances' is the second largest asset item. This includes various types of bank loans to individuals or business firms for various purposes (more detailed analysis will be given later in this chapter). This item was the largest one in 1980, when its share in total assets was 42.22 per cent but gradually dwindled to 30.28 per cent in 1989 even though it also enjoyed a growth rate of 28.30 per cent over the years. This is because

inter-bank transactions with overseas banks had increased at the extremely rapid rate of 43.16 per cent. The rapid increase in the size of the banking sector is thus mainly attributable to international banking activities rather than domestic activities.

3.   Asset Item: Due From Banks and DTCs.   'Due from banks and DTCs' was the third largest item, but its share in total assets declined from 16.14 per cent in 1980 to 11.52 per cent in 1989.

4.   Other Asset Items.   The holding of some of the liquid assets or marketable securities such as NCDs, bankers acceptances, floating-rate notes, commercial paper, treasury bills, and securities also enjoyed very rapid growth, ranging from 17.58 per cent for NCDs to 46.44 per cent for floating-rate notes and commercial paper. However, their share in total assets is still minimal.

Thus it is fair to say that half of all banking activity is related to international banking, which is basically inter-bank borrowing and lending with banks overseas. Other than these international banking activities, the overall activities of licensed banks in Hong Kong are relatively traditional, and include taking deposits from customers and making loans to individuals and business firms. Using more aggressive instruments to attract deposits or investing in other marketable securities does not show up as very significant on the balance sheet. Of course, this may not be a good representation of the foreign banks, especially the new ones, which have their main business in taking funds from the money market and in trading money market instruments. One of the reasons for the insignificance of these items is that Hong Kong's banking sector is rather concentrated and the balance sheet is basically overwhelmed by the large banks. Activities such as swaps, futures, options, and underwriting commitments are neither asset nor liability items and they are simply not recorded on the balance sheet itself, although they may be referred to in footnotes that accompany the balance sheet.[11]

The Asset and Liability Structure of Deposit-taking Companies

Since the Government reports only the aggregate data on both types of DTCs, it becomes impossible to differentiate the asset and liability structure of the LDTCs and the RDTCs.

On the liability side there are several features:

1.   Source of Funds Shift.   Although the share of 'due to banks abroad' in total liabilities was still very large (23.16 per cent) in 1989, it was declining and the share of 'due to banks and DTCs in Hong Kong' was increasing. This indicates that the major source of funds has shifted from inter-bank borrowing from overseas banks to local financial institutions.

2.   Share of Customers' Deposits.   The share of 'customers' deposits' showed a tremendous decline from 30 per cent to 18.76 per cent, and the annual growth rate is just 5.81 per cent over the past nine years.

This might be due to two factors. First, after the establishment of the three-tier system, the RDTCs, especially the independent ones, found it more difficult to attract deposits from the general public because they were not able to offer short-term deposits. Second, the LDTCs might use more aggressive liability management methods, that is, inter-bank borrowing and issuing NCDs, to fund their Hong Kong dollar assets rather than attracting deposits from the general public which, as mentioned earlier, was less flexible. That also explains why 'NCDs outstanding' increased at the very fast rate of 16.45 per cent and its share in total liabilities also increased from 0.52 per cent to 0.77 per cent.

On the asset side, there are also several interesting features:

1. Increase in Largest Asset Item.   The share of 'due from banks abroad' was one of the largest items, and increased from 17.28 per cent in 1980 to 26.43 per cent in 1989.

2. Decline in Loans and Advances.   Another large item is 'loans and advances', which accounted for 26.50 per cent of total assets in 1989. However, this item used to be the largest, as evidenced by its 42.31 per cent share in 1980. Such a rapid decline was due to a decrease in the demand for loans by countries in this region.

3. Decline in Amounts Due from Banks and DTCs.   The share of 'due from banks and DTCs in Hong Kong' also shows a decline, from 27.53 per cent to 20.49 per cent. When compared with 1980, the inter-bank lending item in 1989 was much smaller than the inter-bank borrowing item. This is mainly because after the three-tier system was established, DTCs encountered difficulties in attracting public deposits. Thus they needed to borrow more than they lent to the inter-bank market.

4. Increase in Liquid Assets.   The share of the liquid assets, such as NCDs, bank acceptances, floating-rate notes, commercial paper, treasury bills, and securities showed a very rapid increase over the years. The most striking increase was in the floating-rate notes and commercial paper items. Since these are floating-rate instruments, DTCs may hold them in anticipation of more volatile interest rates ahead.

In general, the DTC sector grew at a much slower rate than the banking sector. This is due to two factors. First, the three-tier system made it more difficult for the RDTCs to attract funds and some of the banks actually closed their RDTC subsidiaries. Thus the DTCs sector is actually in a stage of consolidation. Second, in the 1980s international loans have been out of fashion and creditworthy borrowers have begun to tap funds from the international financial markets using their own names, that is, by issuing bonds, commercial paper, and other direct financing instruments. Thus, merchant banks have begun to buy such instruments from corporations instead of granting loans to them directly. Moreover, merchant banks also started to be more involved in helping corporations and Government in the issuing process. In return, the merchant banks charge the issuer service fees, which provide a risk-free income when compared with the interest income from granting loans. Thus, two points can be concluded from the balance sheet analysis: DTCs have become more dependent on the local inter-bank market to fund their assets, and they have also become more active in the trading of money market instruments.

Currency Composition of Assets and Liabilities

Tables 1.6 and 1.7 give the currency composition of licensed banks and DTCs for 1980 and 1989.

The features of the currency composition for the licensed banks is summarized below:

1. The Foreign Currency Component.   There was a rapid increase in the foreign currency component, from 50.1 per cent in 1980 to about 81.8 per cent in 1989. This may be due to several factors. First, the Hong Kong banking sector has become more international. Second, more foreign currency deposits are rechannelled back to Hong Kong after the Hong Kong Government abolished the withholding tax on

Table 1.6   Balance Sheet Structure by Currency Denomination: Licensed Banks (per cent)

	1980		1989	
	HK$	FC	HK$	FC
Liabilities				
Due to banks and DTCs in				
Hong Kong	74.6	35.4	47.3	52.7
Due to banks abroad	3.3	96.7	3.5	96.5
Customers' deposits	87.8	12.2	38.2	61.8
NCDs outstanding	61.3	38.7	75.7	24.3
Others	75.7	24.5	48.5	51.5
Total liabilities	49.9	50.1	18.9	81.1
Assets				
Hong Kong notes and coins	100.0	0	100.0	0
Due from banks and DTCs in				
Hong Kong	48.5	51.5	44.4	55.6
Due from banks abroad	8.0	92.0	1.1	98.9
NCDs held	4.0	96.0	45.8	54.2
Loans and advances	65.5	34.5	40.4	59.6
Bank acceptances	13.0	87.0	5.6	94.4
Floating-rate notes and commercial				
paper held	26.6	73.4	16.7	83.3
Treasury bills and securities, etc.	88.4	11.6	40.8	59.2
Other	52.5	47.5	22.8	77.2
Total assets	45.2	54.8	19.9	80.1

Note: FC = Foreign Currency.

Source: *Hong Kong Monthly Digest of Statistics* (Hong Kong, Census and Statistics Department), various issues.

foreign currency deposits in 1982. Third, part of the rapid increase in the foreign currency component is due to the currency translation effect because the Hong Kong dollar has been depreciating.[12]

2. Foreign Currency and Banks Abroad.   A great proportion of the items 'due to' and 'due from banks abroad' was in foreign currency (96.5 per cent and 98.9 per cent respectively in 1989). This is understandable as borrowing from and lending to banks overseas is usually denominated in currencies other than the Hong Kong dollar.

3. Foreign Currency Deposits.   Depositors were also making more foreign currency deposits in 1989 than in 1980.

4. Hong Kong Dollar NCDs.   Banks were issuing and holding more Hong Kong dollar NCDs in 1989 than in 1980 as more banks were using NCDs as a means to get local currency funds.

The currency composition of the DTCs' balance sheet is quite similar to that of the licensed banks except:

Table 1.7   Balance Sheet Structure by Currency Denomination: DTCs (per cent, end of year)

	1980		1989	
	HK$	FC	HK$	FC
Liabilities				
Due to banks and DTCs in				
Hong Kong	30.7	69.3	36.3	63.7
Due to banks abroad	1.2	98.8	2.1	97.9
Customers' deposits	83.1	16.9	42.2	57.8
NCDs outstanding	86.0	14.0	33.3	26.3
Others	60.0	40.0	18.9	81.1
Total liabilities	39.6	60.4	25.0	75.0
Assets				
Hong Kong notes and coins	100.0	0	100.0	0
Due from banks and DTCs in				
Hong Kong	71.9	28.1	46.2	53.8
Due from banks abroad	1.0	99.0	0.9	99.1
NCDs held	20.6	79.4	50.6	49.4
Loans and advances	37.5	62.5	51.5	48.5
Bank acceptances	12.6	87.4	5.5	94.5
Floating-rate notes and commercial				
paper	13.7	86.3	7.9	92.1
Treasury bills and securities, etc.	62.1	37.9	8.6	91.4
Other	41.6	58.4	9.1	90.9
Total assets	40.8	59.2	26.7	73.3

Note: FC = Foreign Currency.

Source: *Hong Kong Monthly Digest of Statistics* (Hong Kong, Census and Statistics Department), various issues.

1. DTCs and Inter-bank Borrowing.   DTCs had more inter-bank borrowing from local institutions because DTCs had to borrow Hong Kong dollars from banks or from other DTCs.

2. DTCs and Foreign Currency.   DTCs were issuing more and holding more foreign currency NCDs than licensed banks.

The Use of Loans by Industry

Table 1.8 shows the distribution of loans for use in Hong Kong. In 1989, a great majority of loans were used to finance property-related concerns. Loans to finance the purchase of residential property and property development accounted for 35 per cent of the total loans. Wholesale and retail trade also had a relatively larger share than manufacturing loans. This indicates that Hong Kong has moved from a manufacturing-based economy to a more service-oriented one.

It must also be noted that lending to financial institutions other than banks and DTCs grew very rapidly, and its share increased from 9 per cent in 1986 to 15 per cent in 1989. A substantial portion of this was in loans to leasing companies, reflecting Hong Kong's role as a financial centre for leasing.

The Market Structure of the Hong Kong Banking Market

The term 'market structure' usually relates to the degree of competition in the market. When the market is more competitive, market shares are generally quite evenly distributed among firms. If the market share is concentrated in a few firms the market is said to be less competitive or more 'concentrated'. This has certain economic implications. According to economic theories, firms in a more concentrated market would produce less and at a higher price than those in a more competitive environment.

Banks are also private firms. Like other commercial firms, they buy factors of production to produce products or assets. In the case of a banking firm, the factors of production usually include various types of financial liabilities (such as customers' deposits and NCDs) and real resources (such as machines, computers, and human resources), and the products or assets are various types of financial assets (such as loans, NCDs, and floating rate notes) and other real services (such as cheque-clearing, data processing, and financial consultancy services). In normal commercial banking business, the bulk of financial liabilities and assets should be deposits and loans, respectively. Thus, it is usually predicted by economic theory that in a highly concentrated market fewer loans and higher loan interest rates would result than in a more competitive environment. Similarly, on the deposit side, fewer deposits and a lower deposit interest rate would result. Such an abnormal spread between deposit rate and loan rate induced by a concentrated market

Table 1.8 Loans for Use in Hong Kong: All Authorized Institutions (HK$ billion)

Sector of Financing	December 1986		December 1987		December 1988		December 1989	
	HK$ billion	Per cent	HK$ billion	Per cent	HK$ billion	Per cent	HK$ billion	Per cent
Manufacturing	25	9	30	8	39	8	46	8
Transport and transport equipment	18	7	20	6	23	5	37	6
Electricity, gas, and telephone	5	2	4	1	4	1	5	1
Building, construction and property development	35	13	40	11	59	13	96	16
Wholesale and retail trade	34	12	43	12	60	13	63	11
Purchase of residential property	49	18	65	19	86	19	110	19
Financial concerns (other than authorized institutions)	23	9	34	10	53	12	85	15
Professional and private individuals	29	11	44	12	48	10	55	9
Miscellaneous	53	20	72	20	85	19	88	15
Total	271	100	353	100	457	100	585	100

Note: Individual sector figures for December 1988 are not strictly comparable with those for earlier periods. Arising from a change in the reporting return, institutions are now more correctly classifying loans according to their intended usage rather than by the businesses of the borrowers.

Source: Hong Kong Monthly Digest of Statistics (Hong Kong, Census and Statistics Department), various issues.

would not be beneficial to depositors and borrowers. Thus, in some developed markets such as the United States, any merger or acquisition would not be approved by the government unless it could be proved that the degree of competitiveness would not be unduly downgraded. Although we do not have such a law in Hong Kong, it is in the interest of the general public to have some idea about the market structure of the Hong Kong banking market.

Distribution of Institutions by Size

Tables 1.9 to 1.11 give the distribution of authorized institutions (licensed banks, LDTCs, and RDTCs) by size from 1986 to 1989. Such data are given in the Annual Report of the Commissioner for Banking. The 1989 Annual Report also differentiated banks into two groups according to their principal place of business.

In the licensed bank sector, for banks whose principal place of business is in Hong Kong, 20 out of 38 banks or 53 per cent of the total had assets of HK$10 billion and over in 1989. The distribution for banks whose principal place of business is outside Hong Kong is similar, but there is a slightly larger proportion of smaller banks which may be attributed to the newly licensed foreign bank branches. In terms of deposits, the distribution is quite different for banks whose principal place of business is in Hong Kong from those whose principal place of business is outside Hong Kong. There were relatively more large banks in the former category but more small banks in the latter. Again, it is interesting to note that for banks whose principal place of business is outside Hong Kong, the asset and deposit distributions are quite

Table 1.9 Distribution of Licensed Banks by Size

| | Principal Place of Business | | | | | | | |
| | In Hong Kong | | | | Outside Hong Kong | | | |
	1986	1987	1988	1989	1986	1987	1988	1989
Total Assets (HK$)								
10 billion and over	9	11	16	20	35	44	44	52
5–10 billion	14	15	11	10	24	20	30	24
2–5 billion	9	7	8	4	22	23	17	27
Below 2 billion	10	9	7	4	25	25	25	24
Deposits (HK$)								
7 billion and over	9	12	16	18	6	8	10	11
3–7 billion	15	15	14	13	10	16	17	25
1–3 billion	9	7	5	4	31	30	27	22
Below 1 billion	9	8	7	3	59	58	62	69
Total no. of licensed banks	42	42	42	38	106	112	116	127

Source: Commissioner of Banking, *Annual Report*, 1989.

Table 1.10   Distribution of Licensed Deposit-taking Companies by Size

	Principal Place of Business							
	In Hong Kong				Outside Hong Kong			
	1986	1987	1988	1989	1986	1987	1988	1989
Total Assets (HK$)								
6 billion and over	6	6	6	6	—	—	—	—
3–6 billion	6	5	4	7	—	—	—	1
1–3 billion	14	14	20	16	4	4	3	2
Below 1 billion	7	6	2	3	1	—	—	1
Deposits (HK$)								
1 billion and over	4	7	6	6	1	—	1	1
0.5–1 billion	5	2	7	9	2	2	1	2
0.1–0.5 billion	12	15	12	8	1	2	1	1
Below 0.1 billion	12	7	7	9	1	—	—	—
Total no. of LDTCs	33	31	32	32	5	4	3	4

Source: Commissioner of Banking, *Annual Report*, 1989.

Table 1.11   Distribution of Registered Deposit-taking Companies by Size

	Principal Place of Business							
	In Hong Kong				Outside Hong Kong			
	1986	1987	1988	1989	1986	1987	1988	1989
Total Assets (HK$)								
10 billion and over	5	8	2	—	—	—	—	—
1–10 billion	51	54	53	53	1	1	1	—
0.4–1 billion	42	39	43	46	1	1	1	—
0.1–0.4 billion	68	68	66	55	—	—	—	1
Below 0.1 billion	85	60	50	47	1	1	—	—
Deposits (HK$)								
1 billion and over	8	9	9	6	—	—	—	—
0.1–1 billion	49	41	42	49	—	1	1	—
30–100 million	50	54	48	40	1	1	—	—
3–30 million	73	73	62	52	1	—	1	—
Below 3 million	71	52	53	54	1	1	—	1
Total no. of RDTCs	251	229	214	201	3	3	2	1

Source: Commissioner of Banking, *Annual Report*, 1989.

different: the asset distribution is skewed towards the largest size while the deposit distribution is skewed towards the smallest size. This is because most of the foreign banks do not use local deposits to fund their foreign assets. They may get funds from their parent banks or from other financial centres.

In the LDTC sector, a great majority of institutions had their principal place of business in Hong Kong. On the asset side a majority of institutions fall within the HK$1 to HK$3 billion category, although they are more evenly distributed on the deposit side. However, the entire distribution of the amount in deposits is much narrower than that of assets. This, again, indicates that LDTCs do not use Hong Kong as a funding source.

In the RDTC sector, only 1 out of 202 institutions had their principal place of business outside Hong Kong. For those 201 RDTCs whose principal place of business is Hong Kong, none had assets of HK$10 billion and over, and only 6 out of 201 RDTCs had deposits of HK$1 billion and over. This indicates that the RDTC sector may be more monopolistic than other institutions' sectors.

Distribution of Loans and Deposits Among Three Types of Authorized Institutions

Table 1.12 gives the distribution of loans and deposits among licensed banks, LDTCs, and RDTCs.

It is obvious that the licensed banks have the lion's share of both the loan and deposit markets and they seem to become more and more dominating. Both LDTCs and RDTCs are losers in both the loan and deposit markets, irrespective of the currency.

Distribution of Assets and Deposits by Country of Beneficial Ownership

Table 1.13 gives the distribution of assets and deposits by country of beneficial ownership. In 1989 the Japanese banks had a dominant share of total assets (56.13 per cent) and the share was also higher than that in 1986. However, the share of the Japanese banks in total deposits was only 10.02 per cent. Thus, Japanese banks had to resort to other, non-traditional sources of funds such as inter-bank borrowing and issuing NCDs to finance its asset expansion.

However, Hong Kong banks still had the largest share of the Hong Kong currency denominated asset and deposit market.[13] Their deposit share was also larger than their asset share, indicating that Hong Kong banks had excess funds to lend to foreign banks to buy Hong Kong dollar assets.

A more vigorous measurement of market concentration would be the Herfindahl index,[14] which involves the use of individual bank data of all the banks in Hong Kong. This approach is impossible since foreign banks are not required to publish any information on their operations in Hong Kong. However, judging from the above discussion, it may

Table 1.12 Loans and Deposits by Category of Groups of Authorized Institutions

	Licensed banks including subsidiary deposit-taking companies	Licensed deposit-taking companies not owned by licensed banks	Registered deposit-taking companies not owned by licensed banks	Total
1989				
Loans				
HK$	510	6	9	525
Foreign Currency	726	8	13	747
Total	1,236	14	22	1,272
Per cent	97	1	2	100
Deposits				
HK$[1]	446	4	1	451
Foreign Currency	522	26	9	557
Total	968	30	10	1,008
Per cent	96	3	1	100
1986				
Loans				
HK$	240	4	6	250
Foreign Currency	222	10	18	250
Total	462	14	24	501
Per cent	92	3	5	100
Deposits				
HK$[1]	269	2	2	273
Foreign Currency	255	14	9	278
Total	524	16	11	551
Per cent	95	3	2	100

Note: 1. Including swap deposits.

Source: Commissioner of Banking, *Annual Report*, various issues.

be possible to generate several observations, if not conclusions, on the Hong Kong market structure:
(a) The banking market is generally concentrated and dominated by large institutions, especially in the licensed banking sector and the RDTC sector.
(b) The banking market is heavily dominated by the licensed banks and it seems such a trend will persist in the future.
(c) The Hong Kong dollar denominated markets are heavily dominated by Hong Kong banks. Foreign banks have to borrow from the local inter-bank market or issue NCDs to fund their Hong Kong dollar assets.
(d) The foreign currency asset markets seem to be dominated by the Japanese banks. This is an over-exaggeration, as most of the Japanese banks book their loans in Hong Kong for tax purposes. The foreign currency deposit market seems to be able to reflect the fact that the international banking market is more competitive.

Table 1.13 Assets and Deposits: Country/Region of Beneficial Ownership (HK$ billion)

| | Assets | | | | | | Deposits | | | | | |
| | 1989 | | | 1986 | | | 1989 | | | 1986 | | |
	HK$	Foreign Currency	Total	HK$	Foreign Currency	Total	HK$	Foreign Currency	Total	HK$	Foreign Currency	Total
China	169 (19.40)	160 (4.74)	329 (7.75)	94 (18.80)	69 (4.18)	163 (7.58)	96 (21.29)	100 (17.95)	196 (19.44)	58 (21.25)	44 (15.83)	102 (18.51)
Europe	157 (18.03)	416 (12.32)	573 (13.49)	95 (19.00)	276 (16.73)	371 (17.26)	59 (13.08)	109 (19.57)	168 (16.67)	35 (12.82)	64 (23.02)	99 (17.97)
Japan	147 (16.88)	2,237 (66.26)	2,384 (56.13)	47 (9.40)	934 (56.61)	981 (45.63)	19 (4.21)	82 (14.72)	101 (10.02)	8 (2.93)	46 (16.55)	54 (9.80)
United States	73 (8.38)	183 (5.42)	256 (6.03)	56 (11.20)	144 (8.73)	200 (9.30)	28 (6.21)	72 (12.93)	100 (9.92)	20 (7.33)	43 (15.47)	63 (11.43)
Others including Hong Kong	325 (37.31)	380 (11.26)	705 (16.60)	208 (41.60)	227 (13.76)	435 (20.23)	249 (55.21)	194 (34.83)	443 (43.95)	152 (55.68)	81 (29.14)	233 (42.86)
Total	871	3,376	4,247	500	1,650	2,150	451	557	1,008	273	278	551

Note: Figures in parentheses are percentages of the total.

Source: Commissioner of Banking, *Annual Report*, various issues.

(e) Thus, the Hong Kong domestic banking market is quite traditional in that the indigenous market is highly monopolistic and dominated by a few large banks, while the international banking market, with the participation of many multinational banks, is more competitive. Thus, the local banks or the grandfathered foreign banks can exploit the monopolistic profit by operating in the local currency market, but they have to compete furiously in the international banking market. Similarly, the foreign banks, especially the new-comers, may not be very interested in going into the retail market in Hong Kong. Their major objective of getting a foothold in Hong Kong is to get involved in international banking activities such as foreign exchange dealing, money market activities, and project financing for the surrounding countries, especially China.

Factors Leading to the Current Banking System

The Hong Kong banking system can be characterized by the following features:
(a) It is highly internationalized.
(b) The deposit market is relatively segmented and heavily dominated by the licensed banks.
(c) The domestic market is rather oligopolistic, heavily dominated by several banking groups: the Hongkong and Shanghai Banking Corporation, the Bank of China Group, and the Standard Chartered Bank.
(d) In a society which is predominantly Chinese, there are relatively few purely local Chinese banks.

It is, of course, not easy to find a simple explanation for the evolution of such a system. There is a host of reasons more appropriately left for the detailed discussion in Chapter 5. But before going into greater depth it is useful to mention some of the basic reasons.

Economic Growth and Technological Advances

Hong Kong started to enjoy enviable economic growth in the 1970s (especially late in the decade, from 1976–80, when the average economic growth was 12.3 per cent). Such a growth trend can also be sustained into the 1980s (although at a more moderate rate) and the average growth rate for 1981–88 was 7.1 per cent. There is no doubt that such a strong economy could also lead to a rapid increase in the supply of deposits and the demand for loans. Besides, as the economy becomes more mature, people use more banking services, for example, they use more bank cheques to settle their transactions and they invest more in bank deposits as a means to store their wealth. Thus, the demand for bank intermediation has been increasing. On the other hand, the banking system has adopted various types of advance technology such as automated teller machines and electronic banking, to increase the cost-effectiveness and hence the supply of intermediation services. Thus, both the supply and demand factors favour increasing the size of the banking services industry.

Of course, Hong Kong is not alone in riding the tide of economic growth. Other newly industrialized countries[15] have similar or even better economic performances in the 1970s and 1980s. In order to finance such rapid economic growth, some of these countries needed to borrow heavily from overseas. The two oil crises in the 1970s provided another reason for them to borrow to finance their current account deficit. South Korea, Malaysia, Indonesia, and the Philippines are some of the heavily indebted Asian countries. In the 1970s and early 1980s, Hong Kong channelled funds from European countries and the United States to the Asia Pacific region, notably Korea, which has been a major borrower.

In the 1980s, there were some basic changes in the economic environment that altered the role of Hong Kong as a financial centre. First, the economic reform of China began to take effect, and China changed its attitude about borrowing from abroad. Hong Kong thus became one of the major centres for lending to China. Second, the rising trade deficit and fiscal deficit of the United States made the United States a net recipient of funds and made some of the countries in Asia, notably Japan and Taiwan (and probably South Korea in the more distant future), net suppliers of funds. These basic economic and financial factors made the international banking activities of Hong Kong more important. More detailed discussion will be given in Chapter 17.

Government Policies

The predominant role of the licensed banks in the deposit market is not a natural outgrowth of market competition. From 1966 to 1978, the Government imposed a moratorium on new bank licensing. Foreign financial institutions then wishing to get a foothold in Hong Kong could not incorporate themselves as commercial banks but had to form establishments such as merchant banks or investment banks. At that time, some local firms also set up finance companies to lend money to people investing in the securities market and property market, or to companies doing relatively high-risk business. Because these kinds of institutions were free from any form of regulation, their number increased very rapidly to about 2,000 in the early 1970s. Then the Government introduced the Deposit-taking Companies (DTCs) Ordinance, which required DTCs to have a minimum paid-up capital of HK$2.50 million. These DTCs were not allowed to accept deposits of less than HK$50,000 for any one account. However, since these institutions were not controlled by the interest rate rule, they could still compete for deposits with higher interest rates than licensed banks, and their share in the deposit market had reached almost 30 per cent in 1980.[16] In order to have better control over the interest rate and provide better protection for depositors, the Government then established the three-tier system which, effectively, precluded DTCs from accepting short-term deposits, and also enabled banks to recapture their market share.

The Banking Crises

The evolution of the oligopolistic nature of the banking system, that is, a few banking groups dominating the whole domestic market, can also be traced back to the banking crises of the 1960s. The first serious bank run occurred in 1961 on the Liu Chong Hing Bank. The run was later stopped, after a joint support programme was announced by the Hongkong and Shanghai Banking Corporation and the Standard Chartered Bank. Later, in 1965, a more serious banking crisis occurred. A small, sole proprietorship bank, the Ming Tak Bank, and a medium-sized bank, the Canton Trust and Commercial Bank Ltd. collapsed. Panic soon spread to other local banks, which faced runs by depositors, too. In order to restore depositors' confidence, the largest and the most successful local Chinese bank, the Hang Seng Bank, was acquired by the Hongkong and Shanghai Banking Corporation. Other smaller local Chinese banks also sought an injection of foreign capital in order to maintain depositors' confidence. Foreign banks were more than willing to acquire local Chinese banks simply because no new bank licence was being granted during that time.

Another major banking crisis occurred from 1982 to 1986. Jao (1988) proposed three main reasons for that crisis:
(a) Imprudent management or even fraud was committed by directors or managers of banks or DTCs.
(b) There was a general economic recession, a political crisis, and a rapid fall in property prices and the Hong Kong dollar exchange rate stemming therefrom.
(c) The banking regulations at that time were too lax and inadequate to handle a banking system that was expanding at such a rapid pace. Some of the Government officials were also not well equipped to supervise banks and DTCs.

As a result of the crisis, several DTCs collapsed and the Government had to take over three banks including the Hang Lung Bank, the Overseas Trust Bank, and the Hong Kong Industrial and Commercial Bank. 'Lifeboat' type funds were also supplied by the Government to several problem banks including the Ka Wah Bank, the Union Bank, the Wing On Bank, and the Hon Nin Bank. Later, the Ka Wah Bank was acquired by the China-owned China International Trust and Investment Corporation; the Wing On Bank was acquired by the Hang Seng Bank, which also belonged to the Hongkong and Shanghai Banking Corporation; the Union Bank was acquired by Modern Concepts Ltd., which is a joint venture between the United States and the China-owned China Merchants Steam Navigation Co.; and the Hon Nin Bank was acquired by the First Pacific Group. Thus, after all these crises, only a handful of purely Chinese banks remained.

Problems and Prospects

Although the financial crisis had a short-term damaging effect on the Hong Kong economy, it was also a catalyst for overhauling the quality of financial regulations. The Banking Ordinance of 1986 is a clear example of the result of the banking crisis in the early 1980s, although the international trend of aiming at more uniform supervision also plays an important part, as will be made clear in Chapter 5.

Thus, it can be said that regulations are bred by crises, and such a crisis-regulation cycle can also be found in other markets. Some examples are the linking of the Hong Kong dollar to the United States dollar at a fixed rate of US$1.00 to HK$7.8 after the currency crisis in September 1983 (see Chapter 9), and the formation of the new Securities and Futures Commission after the global stock-market crash in October 1987 (see Chapter 10). In a sense, the development of banking and financial supervision has become more mature, and Government officials have become more knowledgeable. This, coupled with the strong growth potential of the Asia Pacific region and the open door policy of China, has created a more stable growth environment for the financial sector than previously existed.

However, there also exist some worrying elements. Hong Kong is an integrated financial centre because funds can be channelled in and out of the city at will. Indeed, this is one of the advantages of Hong Kong as a regional financial centre, but it also makes the Hong Kong economy very volatile. Moreover, no matter how good the quality of supervision is, bank failures or short-term liquidity squeeze cannot be avoided. This would seriously damage Hong Kong's economy, especially as there is no form of central bank or monetary authority (see Chapter 13). Up to now, the Hong Kong Government does not seem to be very enthusiastic about setting up institutions that carry out central banking functions, as demonstrated by the fact that the Government has repeatedly turned down recommendations to set up a monetary authority or a discount window (a discount window is a place set up by central banks for commercial banks to discount their short term bills). However, several measures have been implemented since 1988 to make the Government more capable of intervening in the financial markets. Such measures include changing the accounting arrangement between the Exchange Fund and the Hongkong and Shanghai Banking Corporation in July 1988, establishing a dealing room in August 1989, and issuing 91-day Exchange Fund bills each Tuesday since 13 March 1990. Thus, it seems that the Government is planning to watch the financial market more closely and is standing ready to carry out some central banking functions, but it is still reluctant to establish a full-fledged central bank. Nevertheless, this is a comforting signal, as Government officials are now more willing to learn from the market-place.

Another worrying element is the political turmoil of China in 1989. This caused a down-turn in China trade and investments, and a slow-down in commercial bank lending to China. This may affect Hong Kong's role as an international trade and financial centre (see Chapter 17). The political turmoil in China has also hastened the emigration trend, which is the most damaging. However, the Government has already increased expenditures on higher education as well as on technical training which, it is to be hoped, can remedy part of the problem.

Notes

1. A moratorium on issuing new bank licences was introduced in 1966 in order to avoid fierce competition among banks, but it was lifted in 1978 in view of the development of Hong Kong as an international financial centre.

2. However, foreign banks that obtained their licence after 1978 can only maintain one office in Hong Kong. This has made it extremely difficult for newcomers to compete in the retail market.

3. These institutions are governed by the 1986 Banking Ordinance and are collectively called the 'authorized institutions' in the Ordinance.

4. The interest rate rule is an interest rate cartel that sets the maximum interest rate on deposits, and has to be observed by all licensed banks. Since the DTCs are not members of the Hong Kong Association of Banks, they are not bound by this rule and can freely set their own deposit rates. See Chapter 5 for a detailed description of the interest rate rule.

5. This is the categorization adopted by Jao (1974).

6. The Hang Seng Bank also acquired 50.3 per cent of Wing On Bank's share holdings in 1986.

7. There are ten fully independent or semi-independent local Chinese banks (with less than 50 per cent capital owned by foreign institutions): the East Asia Bank, Dah Sing Bank, Tai Sang Bank, Tai Yau Bank, Hong Kong Industrial and Commercial Bank, United Chinese Bank, Commercial Bank of Hong Kong, Shanghai Commercial Bank, Wing Lung Bank, and Liu Chong Hing Bank.

8. Deposits with maturities of longer than 15 months are not governed by the interest rate rule.

9. Liability management is a bank management technique which employs aggressive strategies to attract funds to finance bank assets. In this respect, taking regular customer deposits is considered to be a passive strategy because the bank has no control over the volume of fund influx. However, banks are more certain about the amount of funds obtained by issuing certificates of deposit because such instruments are usually purchased by institutional clients and/or underwritten by merchant banks. Besides, banks can also control the timing of fund influx because they can issue NCDs only when funds are needed. However, for regular deposits, it is almost impossible to reject a depositor who wants to put money in the banks.

10. Two conditions must be fulfilled to have a loan qualified as an offshore transaction: (1) the uses and sources of funds have to originate outside of the country where the transaction is executed, and (2) the transaction is normally denominated in foreign currency.

11. The term in financial circles for such transactions is 'off balance sheet' transactions. Since they are not as 'visible' as deposits or loans, and since such items are not without risk, they have created considerable difficulties in bank supervision. Such issues will be addressed in Chapter 5.

12. The Hong Kong dollar has been linked to the United States dollar at a fixed rate of US$1.00 to HK$7.80 since October 1983. Thus, the translation effect would be minimal after 1983. However, in view of the declining United States dollar exchange rate, depositors are shifting their portfolios to non-United States dollar foreign currency deposits, and more international trades are carried out in Japanese yen. The translation effect would thus carry substantial weight in explaining the heavier foreign currency component of the last couple of years. Indeed, it was disclosed in the Hong Kong Government's *1987 Economic Background* that the share of United States dollar deposits in total foreign currency deposits was 67.3 per cent in 1986, but dwindled rapidly to

56.5 per cent in 1987. It is expected that the United States dollar share will decline while the non-United States dollar share will increase further.

13. In addition to the Hong Kong banks, the term 'other banks' includes banks from other Asia Pacific countries (excluding China and Japan), Latin America, Africa, Eastern Europe, the Middle East, and Caribbean countries. It is believed that the share of banks other than Hong Kong banks is extremely small, and this item should be seen as heavily dominated by banks from Hong Kong, especially the Hongkong and Shanghai Banking Corporation.

14. The Herfindahl index is calculated as $\sum S_i^2$ where S_i is the share of the ith bank in the market under consideration.

15. The newly industrialized countries include Hong Kong, Korea, Singapore, and Taiwan.

16. This might be an exaggeration, as some of the DTCs were also subsidiaries of banks.

References

Commissioner of Banking, *Annual Report* (Hong Kong, Hong Kong Government Printer), various issues.

Ghose, T. K., *The Banking System of Hong Kong*, (Singapore, Butterworths, 1987).

Ho, Y. K., 'The Role of Hong Kong and Singapore in the International Financial Intermediation Process', paper presented at the Conference on Research in International Finance, Centre HEC-ISA, Jouy-en-Josas, France, June 19–20 1986.

Hunt, Christopher, 'China's Debt isn't yet a Problem', *Asian Wall Street Journal*, 14–15 July 1989.

Jao, Y. C., *Banking and Currency in Hong Kong*, (London, Macmillan Press, 1974).

—— 'The Rise of Hong Kong as a Regional Financial Centre', *Asian Survey*, July 1979, pp. 674–94.

—— 'Hong Kong as a Regional Financial Centre: Evolution and Prospects', in C. K. Leung, J. W. Cushman, and Wang Gungwu (eds.), *Hong Kong: Dilemmas of Growth*, (Canberra, Australian National University Press, 1980), pp. 161–94.

—— 'Monetary System and Banking Structure', in H. C. Y. Ho and L. C. Chau (eds.), *The Economic System of Hong Kong*, (Hong Kong, Asian Research Service, 1988), Chapter 4.

Jao, Y. C. (ed.), *Hong Kong's Banking System in Transition: Problems, Prospects, and Policies*, (Hong Kong, Chinese Banks Association, 1988).

Lee, S. Y. and Jao, Y. C., *Financial Structures and Monetary Policies in Southeast Asia*, (London, Macmillan Press, 1982).

Lui, Y. H., *The Hong Kong Financial System*, (Hong Kong, Commercial Press, 1989, in Chinese).

Park, Y. S., 'The Economics of Offshore Financial Centers', *Columbia Journal of World Business*, Winter 1982, pp. 31–5.

Scott, R. H., K. A. Wong, and Y. K. Ho (eds.), *Hong Kong's Financial Institutions and Markets*, (Hong Kong, Oxford University Press, 1986).

2. The Role of the HongkongBank

Y. C. Jao

Introduction

The Hongkong and Shanghai Banking Corporation, popularly known as the HongkongBank, provides a case study of a financial entity that combines the roles of a profit-making commercial bank with a quasi-central bank, a phenomenon most unusual in the latter half of the twentieth century. One does not need much perspicacity to realize that such a combination creates many problems and dilemmas. How they can be solved in a sensible manner will be of crucial importance to the future well-being of Hong Kong's financial system and economy.

For ease of exposition, we shall use the Bank's official abbreviation, HSBC; its popular name, the HongkongBank; and its collective name, the HongkongBank Group interchangeably in this chapter.

Historical Origin and Development

The HSBC was founded in 1864 by a group of British and foreign business men in Hong Kong, and opened in the following year for business.[1] Among the British overseas banks, it was the only one that set up its head office in Hong Kong. The ability of its management to make decisions on the spot without referring to London enabled it to outsmart its competitors, build up a special relationship with the Hong Kong Government, win loyal support from local business people, and weather a series of banking crises. By the turn of the century, the bank had become not only the dominant bank in Hong Kong, but also one of the most powerful foreign banks in China, particularly in Shanghai.[2]

During the Japanese occupation of Hong Kong in 1941–5, the bank was forced to evacuate its head office to London, its Hong Kong business being liquidated by the Japanese authorities. After the war, the bank's decision to honour 'duress notes' in April 1946, and its pivotal role in financing Hong Kong's rehabilitation and transformation from a mere entrepôt to an industrial economy from the late 1940s onward again won it widespread goodwill and a loyal following.[3]

As the HSBC began its Hong Kong-based recovery in the early post-war years, it experienced another serious setback: the total loss of its China operations after the Communists came to power in 1949. The People's Republic was then in a phase of virulent anti-Western xenophobia, and the HSBC, seen by the Chinese Communists as a prototype imperialist bank, found it impossible to carry on normal business. By

1956, the HSBC's formerly extensive network in China had been reduced to a small office in Shanghai.

It was not until the late 1950s, therefore, that the HSBC felt strong and secure enough to embark on a course of expansion. In 1959, it made two strategic acquisitions: the Mercantile Bank and the British Bank of the Middle East. At the height of Hong Kong's banking crisis in 1965, it acquired majority control of the Hang Seng Bank, then the largest local Chinese bank.[4] Since the late 1950s, it has also successively formed its own finance companies, merchant banks, and other subsidiaries. The most sensational acquisition was, of course, the Marine Midland Bank, the thirteenth largest commercial bank in the United States, in 1980.[5] Although its bid for the Royal Bank of Scotland in the following year was thwarted by the Bank of England and the Monopolies and Mergers Commission, the HSBC succeeded in acquiring a 14.9 per cent stake in Britain's Midland Bank in November 1987. Today, the HongkongBank Group is a global financial conglomerate that comprises a wide array of financial institutions: commercial banks, merchant banks, finance companies, investment companies, insurance companies, financial services companies, and trustee and nominee companies. It also has significant interests in non-financial entities. In 1987, the HongkongBank Group ranked thirty-first among the world's top 500 commercial banks by assets less contra accounts, twenty-ninth by total deposits, and eighteenth by capital and reserves.[6]

The Composition of the HongkongBank Group

The HongkongBank Group's principal subsidiary and associated companies may be grouped under the following major headings.

Commercial Banks

Company	Ownership (Per cent)	Place of Incorporation
HBSC	parent bank	Hong Kong
The British Bank of the Middle East	100.00	U.K.
Hang Seng Bank Ltd.	61.48	Hong Kong
HongkongBank of Australia Ltd.	100.00	Australia
HongkongBank of Canada	100.00	Canada
Marine Midland Banks, Inc.	100.00	U.S.A.
Midland Bank	14.90	U.K.
The Cyprus Popular Bank Ltd.	21.40	Cyprus
Hongkong Egyptian Bank SAE	40.00	Egypt
International Commercial Bank PLC	22.00	U.K.
Saudi British Bank (owned by the British Bank of the Middle East)	40.00	Saudi Arabia

Of these subsidiaries, the Midland Bank, being one of the four major 'clearers' in the United Kingdom and itself a multinational bank, is clearly the most important. Marine Midland Banks, a major commercial bank in the United States, became a wholly owned subsidiary in 1987. Hang Seng Bank, which acquired a 50.3 per cent stake of Wing On Bank in 1986, is still the largest private ethnic Chinese bank in Hong Kong. The British Bank of the Middle East, which also owns 40 per cent of the Saudi British Bank, is an important regional bank in the Middle East. The HongkongBank of Canada, formerly known as the Bank of British Columbia, was acquired in 1986, and is now the third largest foreign bank in Canada. HongkongBank of Australia was granted a full banking licence in 1986, and the HongkongBank Group's shareholding was raised from 80 per cent to 100 per cent in the following year. The other three subsidiaries, Cyprus Popular Bank, Hongkong Egyptian Bank, and International Commercial Bank, are joint ventures in which the Group has minority interests.

Merchant Banks and Brokerage Houses

Company	Ownership (Per cent)	Place of Incorporation
Wardley Holdings	100.0	Hong Kong
CM&M Group, Inc.	100.0	U.S.A.
Equator Bank Ltd.	83.3	Bahamas
James Capel & Co. Ltd.	100.0	U.K.
James Capel Australia Ltd. (formerly Rivkin James Capel)	100.0	Australia
James Capel Bankers Ltd.	100.0	U.K.
James Capel (Far East) Ltd.	100.0	Hong Kong
Wardley Australia Ltd.	100.0	Australia
Wardley-Thomson Ltd.	67.0	Hong Kong
Korea International Merchant Bank	20.0	South Korea
Utama Wardley Bhd	30.0	Malaysia

The Wardley Holdings is a leading merchant bank in Hong Kong and the Asia Pacific region. It has its own subsidiaries in various countries. James Capel & Co., a leading brokerage house in the United Kingdom famed for its research and investment services, was acquired in 1986 in anticipation of the Big Bang.[7] Like Wardley Holdings, it has its own subsidiaries. James Capel Bankers Ltd., formerly known as HongkongBank Ltd., serves as the European merchant banking arm of the Group. CM&M, the fifth largest primary dealer in United States Government securities, was originally a subsidiary of Marine Midland Banks. Equator Bank and Korea International Merchant Bank are both merchant banks operating in Africa and South Korea respectively.

Finance and Leasing Companies

Company	Ownership (Per cent)	Place of Incorporation
Wayfoong Finance Ltd.	100.0	Hong Kong
Wayfoong Credit Ltd.	100.0	Hong Kong
Wayfoong Mortgage and Finance (Singapore) Ltd.	100.0	Singapore
Mortgage and Finance (Malaysia) Berhad	100.0	Malaysia
Concord Leasing Ltd.	100.0	U.K.
U.S. Concord Inc.	100.0	U.S.A.
Hong Kong International Trade Finance Ltd.	100.0	U.K.

These companies are mainly engaged in housing mortgage, hire purchase, deposit-taking, leasing, and trade financing. Of them, Wayfoong Finance Ltd., being incorporated in 1959 under the then Banking Ordinance, is also a licensed bank, while Wayfoong Credit Ltd. is a registered deposit-taking company in Hong Kong. Hong Kong International Trade Finance Ltd. was formerly known as TKM, an acceptance house in Britain taken over by the HSBC in 1982.

Insurance and Retirement Benefits Companies

Company	Ownership (Per cent)	Place of Incorporation
Carlingford Insurance Co.	100.0	Hong Kong
Gibbs Insurance Consultants Ltd.	100.0	Hong Kong
Carlingford Swire Assurance Ltd.	74.5	Hong Kong
Gibbs Hartley Cooper Ltd.	100.0	U.K.

Carlingford Insurance Co. transacts all classes of non-life insurance business in Hong Kong, while Carlingford Swire is a joint venture with Swire in life insurance and retirement benefits. Gibbs Insurance Consultants is a professional consultancy for corporate and government clients in Hong Kong. Gibbs Hartley Cooper Ltd. is a Lloyd's broker based in the United Kingdom.

Transportation and Communications Companies

Company	Ownership (Per cent)	Place of Incorporation
World Finance International Ltd.	37.5	Bermuda
World Maritime Ltd.	20.0	Bermuda
World Shipping and Investment Co. Ltd.	20.0	Cayman Islands
Cathay Pacific Airways	16.4	Hong Kong
Hong Kong International Terminals	5.0	Hong Kong
Hutchison Cable Vision	6.0	Hong Kong

World Finance International Ltd. is a leasing and shipping finance company formed in 1975 with the Industrial Bank of Japan and Sir Yue-kong Pao's World-wide Group, while both World Maritime and World Shipping are joint ventures with the World-wide Group. In December 1988, the HongkongBank Group reached an agreement with the Pao family whereby the Bank sold shares to the latter and thus reduced its shareholdings in World Maritime and World Shipping from 50 per cent and 45 per cent respectively to 20 per cent each. Earlier, the Group's interest in Cathay Pacific Airways was reduced to 16.4 per cent by the sale of 156.5 million shares to the China-owned China International Trust and Investment Corporation (CITIC) in February 1987. All these transportation companies are indirectly held through Grenville Transportation Holdings Ltd. and Fort Hall Ltd., two investment holding companies wholly owned by the Group.

Apart from the principal core companies listed above, the Hongkong-Bank Group also owns equity interests in other companies. In 1986–7 it disposed of all its shareholdings in the South China Morning Post. However, it retains a 20 per cent interest in Agifel, a Hong Kong-based investment company with Kuwaiti and Saudi Arabian partners, and a 50 per cent interest in Central Registration Hong Kong Ltd., a joint venture with Jardine Matheson, which reputedly accounts for over 95 per cent of the share registration business in Hong Kong. The Group also has numerous trustee and nominee companies all over the world. In December 1988, the Group used the proceeds from the sale of its shares in Pao's World-wide Group to acquire a 5 per cent stake in Hong Kong International Terminals (HIT), a subsidiary of Hutchison Whampoa, owned by another leading Hong Kong entrepreneur, Mr Li Ka-shing.

Geographically, the HongkongBank Group operates through a network of more than 1,300 offices in 55 countries in the Asia Pacific region, the Americas, Europe, the Middle East, and Africa as shown in Table 2.1.

At the end of 1988, the Group employed 52,414 persons — 23,343 by the parent bank; 13,892 by Marine Midland; and 6,011 by Hang Seng

Table 2.1 International Network of the HongkongBank Group (number of offices as of 15 March 1988)

Asia Pacific Region		Americas		Europe		Middle East and Africa	
Australia	19	Argentina	1	Belgium	1	Bahrain	6
Brunei	10	Bahamas	14	Channel Islands	12	Cyprus	104
China	7	Brazil	3	France	5	Egypt	3
Fiji	1	Canada	58	Gibraltar	4	Jordan	6
Hong Kong	425	Cayman Islands	3	Ireland	1	Lebanon	5
India	29	Chile	4	Italy	3	Oman	5
Indonesia	5	Colombia	1	Monaco	1	Qatar	2
Japan	11	Mexico	1	Netherlands	3	Saudi Arabia	32
Macau	6	Panama	2	Spain	1	United Arab Emirates	14
Malaysia	44	U.S.A.	368	Sweden	1	Zambia	1
Mauritius	9	Venezuela	1	Switzerland	2		
New Zealand	4			U.K.	36		
Pakistan	2			West Germany	8		
Philippines	3						
Singapore	24						
Solomon Islands	1						
South Korea	5						
Sri Lanka	1						
Taiwan	1						
Thailand	3						
Vanuatu	3						
Total	613	Total	456	Total	78	Total	178
Grand total	1,325						

Source: The Hongkong and Shanghai Banking Corporation, *Annual Report*, 1987.

Bank. Hong Kong accounted for about 20,000 or 38 per cent of the total staff of the Group.[8]

The HongkongBank as a Quasi-Central Bank

Although there is no formal central bank in Hong Kong, central banking powers and functions do of course exist. Such powers and functions are shared by a number of public and private sector institutions. Thus, monetary policy is the responsibility of the Monetary Affairs Branch of the Hong Kong Government, which also manages the Exchange Fund. As the repository of the foreign exchange reserves for the note issue, as well as the Government's fiscal reserve, the Exchange Fund is both the ultimate guardian of the stability of the currency and the lender of last resort for the financial sector. Prudential supervision of the financial sector is handled by two Government departments: the Office of the Commissioner of Banking and the Office of the Commissioner for Securities and Commodities Trading, which regulate the depository institutions and the financial markets respectively. Under Hong Kong's present governmental hierarchy, both Commissioners are responsible to the Secretary for Monetary Affairs, who in turn reports to the Financial Secretary.[9] Legal tender currency is issued by two private commercial banks.

A significant range of central banking powers and functions is the preserve of the HSBC, as listed below.

(a) The HSBC issues the predominant proportion of legal tender currency.

(b) The HSBC is the Management Bank of the Clearing House of the Hong Kong Association of Banks (HKAB).

(c) The HSBC shares with the Standard Chartered Bank on a permanent rotating basis the Chairmanship and Vice-Chairmanship of the HKAB.

(d) The HSBC is the principal banker to the Government.

(e) The HSBC serves as an agent of the Government in carrying out monetary policy, such as occasional interventions in the money market and foreign exchange market.

(f) The HSBC serves as the financial adviser to the Government, principally, though not exclusively, through its membership in key official committees such as the Banking Advisory Committee and Exchange Fund Advisory Committee.

(g) By tradition, the Chairman of the HSBC is given a permanent seat on the Executive Council, Hong Kong's equivalent to the cabinet in other countries.

Concerning the note issue, Table 2.2 shows clearly that the HSBC regularly accounts for more than 70 per cent of the total currency in circulation. The authority to issue notes has been granted by the Government through successive ordinances of the Bank since its incorporation in 1866. Under the Bank Notes Issue Ordinance of 1895

Table 2.2 Currency in Circulation, Year-end (HK$ million)

	1980	1981	1982	1983	1984	1985	1986	1987	1988
Commercial Bank Issue									
HSBC	7,374 (70.5)	8,634 (70.2)	9,884 (71.0)	11,124 (72.5)	11,754 (75.2)	14,234 (73.1)	17,054 (76.1)	22,504 (78.2)	26,734 (78.4)
Chartered Bank	2,000 (19.1)	2,432 (19.8)	2,762 (19.8)	2,806 (18.3)	2,492 (16.0)	3,732 (19.2)	3,572 (15.9)	4,422 (15.4)	5,092 (15.0)
Government Issue	1,090 (10.4)	1,241 (10.0)	1,282 (9.2)	1,413 (9.2)	1,375 (8.8)	1,493 (7.7)	1,786 (8.0)	1,841 (6.4)	2,262 (6.6)
Total	10,464 (100.0)	12,307 (100.0)	13,928 (100.0)	15,343 (100.0)	15,621 (100.0)	19,459 (100.0)	22,412 (100.0)	28,767 (100.0)	34,088 (100.0)

Note: Figures in brackets indicate per cent of total.

Source: *Hong Kong Annual Report* (Hong Kong Government Printer), various years.

(subsequently revised on many occasions), however, only two banks were authorized to issue banknotes: the HSBC and the Chartered Bank of India, Australia and China (now the Standard Chartered Bank). In 1911, the Chartered Mercantile Bank of India (later renamed the Mercantile Bank) was added to the list of authorized note-issuing banks, though this privilege was withdrawn to merge with that of the HSBC in January 1978. Notes issued by these three banks did not become legal tender until December 1935, when Hong Kong followed China in abandoning the silver standard.

From our present point of view, the more important question is the seigniorage or profit gained by the HSBC from its note issue. It may be useful to distinguish between pecuniary seigniorage and non-pecuniary seigniorage. In this connection one should note that, technically speaking, the note issue is divided into two parts, the 'authorized issue' and the 'excess issue'. The authorized issue was initially confined to the amount of the paid-up capital of the HSBC. Since it was last raised to HK$60 million in 1978, it has remained unchanged, even though the HSBC's capital account has increased enormously. Against this authorized issue, the HSBC need only deposit with the Crown Agents interest-bearing securities. Since there are no opportunity costs (or interest foregone), the pecuniary seigniorage is equal to the interest earned on HK$60 million less the printing and other costs, which the HSBC has to bear. While the net amount is not large, it is not zero either. The excess issue, on the other hand, had to be backed 100 per cent, initially by specie, and since December 1935, by non-interest-bearing Certificates of Indebtedness (CIs). The printing costs of the excess issue are entirely borne by the Exchange Fund. In this case the Bank derives neither pecuniary gain nor loss. It does, however, derive considerable non-pecuniary seigniorage in the form of free advertising through the circulation of its notes. The goodwill and prestige associated with this free advertising is incalculable. The Bank can claim that, in so far as it is required to pay foreign exchange for the non-interest-bearing CIs (from December 1935 to July 1972 in sterling, and since 17 October 1983 in United States dollars), it foregoes interest income that would otherwise accrue to it if it did not issue any notes. But the counter-argument is that the Bank can also use the notes so issued to buy income-earning assets. On balance, the Bank probably still derives some positive seigniorage, though the exact amount is difficult to quantify. It is also interesting to note that the Treasury in London had on numerous occasions put pressure on the Hong Kong Government to take over the note issue from private banks, but on each occasion the latter firmly resisted it.[11] If there is any unfairness in the note-issuing system, it arises less from the HSBC's seigniorage *per se* than from the Government's refusal, implied in the 1895 legislation, to extend the note-issuing privilege to other qualified banks.

The HSBC's other quasi-central banking privileges are less easy to justify. Among the most controversial is its role as the Management Bank of the Hong Kong Clearing House of the HKAB. Under this arrangement, all licensed banks, in effect, have to keep clearing accounts with the HSBC. The HSBC does not pay any interest on the credit balances in the clearing accounts of other banks, but charges a rate on debit balances, normally the prime rate on any debit balance up to a certain amount, but 3 percentage points over the prime rate on any debit balance exceeding that amount. The line of credit varies from bank to bank. There are several inequities in this system, according to the HSBC's competitors. First, the expenses of the Clearing House are shared by all member banks, but income from the free use of the credit balances and the interest charge on the debit balances accrue to the HSBC alone. Moreover, the debit balances do not represent any voluntary borrowing from the HSBC by other banks, but rather fortuitous events beyond the control of other banks (for example, a heavy subscription to a new share offer). Second, although the Management Bank is ostensibly appointed by the HKAB, the HSBC is also one of the two permanent rotating chairmen of the HKAB. It is well known that the Standard Chartered Bank is a much smaller and weaker bank, and hence the real power rests with the HSBC. It is no exaggeration to say that, in effect, the HSBC appoints itself permanently to run the Clearing House. Third, under the rules and regulations of the Clearing House, member banks are forbidden to organize or join any alternative clearing arrangement, thus effectively preventing any opposition from forming. Fourth, as the Management Bank as well as one of the ten Settlement Banks, the HSBC has access to confidential information about the clearing positions of its main rivals.[12]

The Hong Kong Government has never publicly explained why it has given other special privileges to the HSBC: statutory Chairmanship of the HKAB, principal banker to the Government, agent of the Government in monetary policy actions, and permanent seat on the Executive Council, except perhaps on the implicit grounds that the HSBC is the largest and most powerful bank in Hong Kong. The permanent membership of the highest policy-making body is especially unusual: can anyone imagine, for example, the Citibank permanently represented in the United States Cabinet, or the National Westminster Bank accorded the same status in the United Kingdom Cabinet?

Even its role as a *de facto* lender of last resort, which is supposed to be socially desirable, is not immune from criticism. Critics argue that, had the HSBC not customarily acted as the *de facto* lender of last resort, it could not have acquired the Hang Seng Bank at extremely favourable terms during the 1965 crisis. Moreover, the HSBC could act confidently as the lender of funds during crises in the secure knowledge that the Government's Exchange Fund stood fully behind it.[13]

To sum up the HSBC's quasi-central bank status, it is sufficient to note that in virtually all other market economies there is a strict segregation between central banking and commercial banking: the central bank is not supposed to engage in profit-making activities in competition with other commercial banks or non-bank financial intermediaries, and, by the same taken, no commercial bank or financial institution is given central banking powers and privileges. The underlying rationale is, of course, to prevent conflict of interest and concentration of power. In Hong Kong, however, due to its peculiar historical circumstances and institutional structure, central banking and commercial banking are intermingled in a way that gives one private-sector bank a very special status. Such arrangements inevitably give rise to conflict of interest and favouritism.

The New Accounting Arrangements between the Exchange Fund and the HongkongBank

It is against this background that we should assess the significance of the 'New Accounting Arrangements between the Exchange Fund and the Hongkong and Shanghai Banking Corporation' announced by the Hong Kong Government on 15 July 1988.[14] The main points of this monetary package are:

(a) The HSBC is required to maintain a Hong Kong dollar account (the 'Account') with the Exchange Fund, effective from 18 July 1988.

(b) The HSBC must maintain a balance (the 'Balance') in that account which is not less than the net clearing balance ('NCB') of the rest of the banking system.

(c) No interest is paid on credit balances in the Account.

(d) If the Balance falls short of the NCB, HSBC pays interest on the shortfall to the Exchange Fund.

(e) If the NCB is in debit, the HSBC pays interest on the debit amount to the Exchange Fund.

(f) Up to a certain amount, the rate of interest payable by HSBC under (d) and (e) is the Best Lending Rate ('BLR') or Hong Kong Inter-bank Offered Rate (HIBOR), whichever is higher. Beyond that amount, the interest rate payable is 3 per cent over BLR or HIBOR, whichever is higher. In exceptional circumstances, an alternative rate may be determined by the Financial Secretary, after consultation with the HSBC.

(g) The Exchange Fund will use the Account, at its discretion, to effect settlement of its Hong Kong dollar transactions with HSBC.

(h) The Exchange Fund will also use the Account, at its discretion, to effect settlement of its Hong Kong dollar transactions with other licensed banks.

(i) In the case of (h), the Exchange Fund will either credit or debit the Account and the HSBC will correspondingly credit or debit the clearing accounts of banks dealing with the Exchange Fund.

(j) The Treasury of the Hong Kong Government will also maintain a Hong Kong dollar account with the Exchange Fund.

From the point of view of the HSBC, the July package brings about two significant changes in its privileged position. First, the HSBC is in effect required to keep a clearing account with the Exchange Fund, and

Case (a)
HSBC

Assets		Liabilities	
US dollars	+10 m.	Exchange Fund	+10 m.

Case (b)
Banking System

Assets		Liabilities	
		Exchange Fund	+10 m.
		Customers' deposits	−10 m.

Case (c)
Other Banks

Assets		Liabilities	
US dollars	+10 m.		
Balance with HSBC	−10 m.		

HSBC

Assets		Liabilities	
		Other banks	−10 m.
		Exchange Fund	+10 m.

Banking System

Assets		Liabilities	
US dollars	+10 m.	Exchange Fund	+10 m.

thus by a stroke of the pen, its control of the inter-bank liquidity passes to the Government. Having strengthened its own hand in the inter-bank market, the Government finds it much easier to maintain the linked rate system at US$1 = HK$7.8. Suppose that the Hong Kong dollar weakens to 7.9 and beyond, and that the Government is too impatient to wait for the market arbitrage to correct this deviation, so that the Exchange Fund is instructed to sell United States dollars. To make this operation effective, the Hong Kong dollar inter-bank market should tighten. But before 18 July 1988, this would not happen. Whether the Exchange Fund sold United States dollars to the HSBC, or to the public, or to other licensed banks, the result would be the same: the banking system would not experience any loss of reserves denominated in Hong Kong dollars, hence the inter-bank market would not tighten. This can be shown in the T-accounts on the preceding page, where Case (a) denotes the sale of United States dollars worth HK$10 million to the HSBC; Case (b) denotes the sale of the same amount to the non-bank public; and Case (c) denotes the sale of the same amount to other banks.

As these entries demonstrate, the sale of United States dollars by the Exchange Fund would not result in any loss of Hong Kong dollar reserves for the banking system. If the other banks felt that their clearing balance with the HSBC had fallen dangerously low, they could always swap their United States dollars for Hong Kong dollars with the HSBC. Hence, the inter-bank liquidity would not be affected by the sales of United States dollars, and interest rates would not automatically rise to support the Exchange Fund's operation. The crux of the matter was that the HSBC controlled the inter-bank market because not only did it manage the Clearing House, but it did not have to maintain any clearing account with anybody else. On top of that, the HSBC was the principal banker to the Government, including, of course, the Exchange Fund. Note that in Case (c) above, the banking system's T-account is the consolidated account of HSBC and other banks.

Since 18 July 1988, however, the HSBC has had to keep an account with the Exchange Fund, which can use this account for open market operations. Again, let us use T-accounts to show the consequences of the sale of United States dollars worth HK$10 million by the Exchange Fund. Cases (a), (b), and (c) on p. 44 have the same meanings as before. Again, in Case (c), the banking system's T-account is the consolidated account of those of HSBC and other banks.

These entries show that, in all cases, the banking system will suffer a debit to the Account with the Exchange Fund, which, all things being equal, will reduce the supply of funds to the inter-bank market, thus producing a contractionary effect and pushing up the HIBOR. The Exchange Fund's intervention therefore becomes much more effective in moving the market rate back towards HK$7.8 to US$1.

The Exchange Fund, after 18 July 1988, is still a customer of the banking system, notably the HSBC. The important thing, however, is that the Exchange Fund, at its discretion, can use the Account to effect Hong Kong dollar transactions with the HSBC or other banks, and that only it can alter the Balance in that Account. Moreover, the fact that the Treasury also maintains an account with the Exchange Fund provides an additional mechanism for the authorities to influence liquidity in the inter-bank market. Thus, when the Treasury switches funds from its general revenue account with the banking system to the Exchange Fund, in return for interest-bearing debt certificates, the supply of funds to the inter-bank market will contract, forcing up the HIBOR, and vice

Case (a)
HSBC

Assets		Liabilities
US dollars	+10 m.	
Account with		
Exchange Fund	−10 m.	

Case (b)
Banking System

Assets		Liabilities	
Account with		Customers' deposits	−10 m.
Exchange Fund	−10 m.		

Case (c)
Other Banks

Assets		Liabilities
US dollars	+10 m.	
Balance with HSBC	−10 m.	

HSBC

Assets		Liabilities	
Account with		Other Banks	−10 m.
Exchange Fund	−10 m.		

Banking System

Assets		Liabilities
US dollars	+10 m.	
Account with		
Exchange Fund	−10 m.	

versa. This and other operations can also be clarified by the T-account approach, but owing to space limitation, we will not describe them in further detail.

In short, one important effect of the new accounting arrangements is that the Exchange Fund replaces the HSBC as the ultimate provider of liquidity to the inter-bank market, thus making the authorities' interventions in the money and foreign exchange markets much more effective in maintaining the 7.8 link. However, it is to be emphasized that controlling inter-bank liquidity is not tantamount to controlling total money supply, as some commentators tend to imply.[15] As long as Hong Kong remains a small open economy, and its currency is 100 per cent backed by and indefinitely convertible into the currency of a major power at a fixed rate, monetary aggregates in Hong Kong are ultimately determined by the balance of payments. Money supply, in other words, is endogenous, not exogenous.

The second significant change, on which the official announcement did not elaborate, is the transfer of most of the HSBC's monopoly profit from managing the Clearing House to the Exchange Fund. Under the new accounting arrangements, the HSBC undertakes to keep a Balance with the Exchange Fund of not less than the net clearing balance of the rest of the banking system. The Exchange Fund does not pay interest on the credit balance, but charges interest on the debit balance to the extent that the balance falls short of the net clearing balance. Thus, the HSBC loses its privilege of using the interest-free credit balances of other banks. But as long as it does not use such credit balances the HSBC, by virtue of its being the Management Bank as well as a Settlement Bank, still retains the privilege of charging interest on other banks' debit balances. Thus, the HSBC's monopoly profit is reduced, but by no means eliminated. Nevertheless, there is a widespread perception among investors that the HSBC can no longer retain its monopoly profit completely, as reflected in its share price performance after the announcement of the July package.[16]

To sum up, the new accounting arrangements effective from 18 July 1988 have weakened the HSBC's central banking status by depriving it of the control over inter-bank liquidity, and a substantial part of its monopoly profit from running the Clearing House. However, the HSBC's other quasi-central banking powers and privileges remain unaffected. Thus it is premature to argue that the new accounting arrangements represent the first step towards the creation of a formal central bank or monetary authority, as some commentators tend to do. In any case, the Hong Kong Government has repeated its rejection of any proposal for the establishment of a formal central bank or monetary authority, indicating that it has no intention of ending the HSBC's privileged status.

Performance and Strategies of the HongkongBank Group

To assess the HongkongBank Group's performance, one has to rely heavily on the Group's published financial statements. There are two basic problems with this approach. First, the Group's financial statement is a consolidated one without a detailed breakdown. Thus, the balance sheet of the parent itself is a consolidated account of all its branches and offices throughout the world. From the published statements alone, therefore, one is unable to ascertain the amounts of deposits and assets the Group has in Hong Kong, or how much profit it derives from Hong Kong. The regulatory authorities presumably have this information, but on grounds of confidentiality they refuse to disclose information concerning individual reporting institutions.[17] Second, it is well known that the Group regularly transfers part of its after-tax profits to its 'inner reserves', or vice versa. Thus there can be considerable divergence between its published profits and true profits. The question of inner reserves is highly controversial, but is beyond the scope of this chapter: suffice it to say that this accounting practice is still legal in Hong Kong. The HongkongBank Group has long maintained a tradition of impenetrable secrecy about its inner reserves, though there is no lack of speculation about their size.[18]

Because of these problems, analysis based on published financial statements (in the absence of alternative reliable sources of information) cannot hope to be wholly accurate. The reader will appreciate, however, that the deplorable lack of transparency is not the responsibility of the analyst, but is rather the consequence of the HongkongBank Group's accounting policy and Hong Kong's legal system.

With this caveat in mind, let us analyse the HongkongBank's recent performance according to its published accounts. Table 2.3 shows the financial highlights of the Group in 1980–8. As may be seen, most leading indicators — total assets, issued capital, shareholders' funds, capital resources, published group profits, total distribution, earnings per share (adjusted), and dividends per share (adjusted) — all registered double-digit compound annual rates of growth. Although the growth rates on the whole seem impressive, they represent a considerable slow-down compared to those for the longer, earlier period of 1974–88, shown in Table 2.4. The slow-down in growth rates was especially significant for published group profits and earnings per share. Compared to an even earlier period, the slow-down was more striking. Citing figures for the 1969–80 period, the Monopolies and Mergers Commission reports that the compound growth rates for total assets, issued capital, total shareholders' funds, and published group profits were 26.0 per cent, 27.6 per cent, 29.7 per cent, and 24.5 per cent respectively.[19]

The growth slow-down reflects partly the inherent mathematical property that, as the base grows larger and larger, it becomes harder and harder to maintain the same compound growth rate. But it may also reflect the disappointing performance of some of the Group's subsidiaries. In 1987, Marine Midland made an additional provision of US$600 million for its Third World loans, resulting in a net loss of US$408.8 million (though the Group's share of the provision, US$270 million, and the write-off of goodwill amounting to US$389 million, were absorbed by inner reserves). Other units that suffered losses included the James Capel Group, and branches in Fiji, Bahrain, and

Table 2.3 Financial Highlights of the HongkongBank Group (HK$ million)

	1980	1981	1982	1983	1984	1985	1986	1987	1988	Compound Rate of Growth (1980–1988) (Per cent)
Total Assets	242,953	304,293	379,186	470,315	481,607	545,610	715,284	837,400	883,711	17.60
Issued Capital	2,786	3,899	5,200	5,720	7,150	7,865	9,438	11,818	13,102	21.40
Total Shareholders' Funds	10,326	14,147	15,606	19,586	20,863	21,882	26,511	33,299	35,930	16.90
Published Group Profits	1,531	2,116	2,357	2,492	2,591	2,719	3,056	3,593	4,300	13.80
Capital Resources	12,984	19,164	22,754	28,798	31,524	41,218	51,483	54,692	59,927	21.10
Total Distribution	724	996	1,144	1,258	1,316	1,447	1,548	1,795	2,094	13.82
Hong Kong $										
Earnings per Share (adjusted)	0.38	0.51	0.55	0.57	0.59	0.63	0.70	0.78	0.82	10.10
Dividends per Share	0.18	0.24	0.26	0.29	0.30	0.33	0.36	0.38	0.40	10.50

Source: Hongkong and Shanghai Banking Corporation, *Annual Report*, various years.

Table 2.4 Compound Rates of Growth, 1974–1988

	Per cent
Total Assets	24.5
Issued Capital	23.4
Total Shareholders' Funds	23.6
Published Group Profit	19.1
Capital Resources	27.5
Total Distribution	19.2
Earnings per Share	18.1
Dividends per Share	17.9

Source: Hongkong and Shanghai Banking Corporation, *Annual Report*, various years.

some European countries. Lower profits were recorded by the British Bank of the Middle East, Equator Holdings, and Grenville Holdings.

The decline in profitability is also confirmed by the trend in rates of return during 1980–8. As shown in Table 2.5, the rates of return on total assets (less contra items) and shareholders' funds fell from 0.87 per cent to 0.49 per cent, and from 14.83 per cent to 12.15 per cent respectively. In 1979 the Group's rates of return on total assets and shareholders' funds were 1.07 per cent and 29.95 per cent respectively, making the decline in the 1980s even more striking.[20]

Table 2.5 Key Financial Ratios of the HongkongBank Group (per cent)

	1980	1981	1982	1983	1984	1985	1986	1987	1988
Rate of return on total assets (less contra items)	0.87	0.77	0.69	0.59	0.54	0.53	0.44	0.45	0.49
Rate of return on shareholders' funds	14.83	14.96	15.10	12.72	12.42	12.43	11.53	10.80	12.15

Source: Hong Kong and Shanghai Banking Corporation, *Annual Report*, various years.

The HongkongBank Group has, however, a very strong capital base by international standards. In recent years, it has raised considerable additional capital both in Hong Kong and overseas, partly to meet the world-wide trend in the regulatory authorities' demand for a higher capital adequacy ratio, and partly to position itself for more acquisitions. Thus in 1985–6, it raised US$1,200 million primary capital subordinated undated floating notes; in March 1987, it raised HK$3,303 million by a rights issue; and in July 1988, it further raised £150 million by placing long-term subordinated loan capital with a number of international financial institutions. We are unable, however, to calculate the Group's capital to risk assets ratio as defined by either the Hong Kong regulatory authorities or by the Basle Committee, because of the lack of detailed and disaggregated information in the Group's financial statements.[21] In any case, although the Group ranked thirty-first in the world's largest banks by total assets, it ranked eighteenth by capital and reserves. It can also be safely predicted that the Group will have no problem in meeting the internationally agreed minimum capital adequacy ratio of 8 per cent by the end of 1992.

The HongkongBank Group's market share in Hong Kong's banking business is difficult to quantify for reasons already explained. The conventional wisdom that the Group holds about 50 to 60 per cent of total bank deposits can now be shown to be grossly erroneous. The Banking Commissioner began giving annual reports in 1986. While giving no precise figures for the Group, the reports do delimit the maximum market shares of total deposits and assets that the Group can hold. As shown in Table 2.6, the HongkongBank Group is included in the category 'Others including Hong Kong.' From the figures in this table, it can be shown that this category cannot account for more than 20.23 per cent and 16.19 per cent respectively of total assets, and more than 42.10 per cent and 41.19 per cent of total deposits in 1986 and 1987, respectively.

For deposits, the local independent Chinese banks' deposits can be estimated using their published financial statements, though even here there is the problem of inner reserves. However, no information whatsoever is obtainable on the deposits of other foreign banks (such as Canadian banks, Singaporean banks, and so on).[22] If we assume that their market share is trivial, we may deduce that the HongkongBank Group accounted for about 29–30 per cent of total deposits in 1986–7. However, the HongkongBank Group's position in the Hong Kong dollar deposit market is much stronger than the average market share indicates, owing to its extensive branch network and its status as the principal banker to the Government, hence it probably accounted for about 40–2 per cent of Hong Kong currency deposits and about 24–6 per cent of foreign currency deposits. The Group's annual reports indicate, by way of bar charts rather than precise figures, that its assets (less contra items) in the Asia Pacific region were HK$275 billion and HK$340 billion in 1986 and 1987 respectively. Assuming that about 90 per cent of these assets were attributable to Hong Kong, they accounted for no more than 11.5 per cent and 9.5 per cent respectively of total assets in 1986 and 1987.[23] On the surface, these shares were dwarfed by those of the Japanese banks, which were 45.6 per cent and 54.97 per cent respectively.

The phenomenal growth of Japanese banks' assets has of course its special reasons: the marked appreciation of the Japanese yen, the aggressive expansion by Japanese banks abroad after liberalization, and their propensity to book loans in low-tax centres. However, the Japanese banks comprise many independent and competing units which

Table 2.6 Bank Assets and Deposits in Hong Kong: Country/Region of Beneficial Ownership (HK$ billion)

Country/Region	Total Assets						Deposits					
	1986			1987			1986			1987		
	HK$	Foreign Currency	Total	HK$	Foreign Currency	Total	HK$	Foreign Currency	Total	HK$	Foreign Currency	Total
China	94	69	163	112	113	225	53	49	102	73	66	139
Europe	95	276	371	115	367	482	34	65	99	43	88	132
Japan	47	934	981	63	1,706	1,769	8	46	55	10	56	65
United States	56	144	200	56	164	221	15	48	63	18	59	77
Others including Hong Kong	208	227	435	240	281	521	135	97	232	166	125	290
Total	500	1,650	2,150	587	2,631	3,218	245	306	551	310	394	704

Note: Figures in this table pertain to both licensed banks and deposit-taking companies.

Source: Annual Report of the Office of the Commissioner of Banking for 1987.

are grouped together by the Banking Commissioner's Office for convenience only. The HongkongBank Group, on the other hand, is a homogeneous entity sharing a common goal. Hence, on an individual rather than a collective basis, the HongkongBank Group is still the largest bank in Hong Kong. Even so, given that Hong Kong is an international financial centre, the Group is facing stiff competition from other transnational banks, and its market shares in areas where it enjoys no special privileges, such as foreign exchange, syndicated loans, and securitization, are far from dominant.[24]

The HongkongBank Group's business strategy, as it has evolved since the end of the Second World War, can be briefly reviewed as follows:

In financing Hong Kong's post-war recovery and export-oriented industrialization, the HSBC skilfully blended two banking traditions: the British commercial banking tradition and the German universal banking tradition, and successfully applied this flexible combination to the unique circumstances of Hong Kong. On the one hand, the bread-and-butter business of trade financing, and in the context of an export-oriented economy, foreign exchange transactions, being consistent with the real bills doctrine, ensure steady liquidity and profitability. On the other hand, being keenly supportive of Hong Kong's industrialization, the HSBC has not hesitated to provide long-term capital to the industrial sector, and like the German Universalbanken, has often taken equity interests in non-financial firms, though stopping short of the German 'from the cradle to the grave' approach by disposing of these interests when the firms are firmly established.[25] Examples are Cross-Harbour Tunnel, East Asia Navigation, Cathay Pacific Airways, South China Morning Post, World-Wide Shipping, and very recently, Hong Kong International Terminals. It has also often bailed out near-bankrupt firms, nursed them back to health, and then sold them at a profit. The classic case is Hutchison Whampoa, which was taken over by the HSBC in 1975 and resold in 1979.

Although the HSBC is a British-managed bank, it is no longer a predominantly British-owned bank. Indeed, it is believed that a substantial proportion of its shares are held by Hong Kong and overseas Chinese, and even mainland China. It has always been a key element of the bank's strategy to court the Chinese business community and their leaders in Hong Kong. The HSBC has an uncanny gift of identifying promising Chinese entrepreneurs and backing them to the hilt. The best examples are, of course, Y. K. Pao and Li Ka-shing. In several well-known episodes, the HSBC supported the newly emergent Chinese tycoons against old-line British interests. Thus in 1979 the HSBC sold its stake in Hutchison Whampoa to Li Ka-shing at extremely favourable terms rather than to two other British conglomerates, the Jardine Group and the Swire Group. In 1980, during the take-over battle for Wharf Holdings, the HSBC supported Y. K. Pao rather than the British-owned Hong Kong Land. Then in 1985 the HSBC, through its subsidiary Wardley, supported Pao in acquiring another British-owned conglomerate, Wheelock Marden. In recent years, the HSBC has turned its attention to the overseas ethnic Chinese communities, which are increasingly strengthened by Hong Kong immigrants, in the United States, Canada, and Australia. The purchase of the remaining equities in the Marine Midland and the HongkongBank of Australia, as well as the integration of the former Bank of British Columbia into the HongkongBank of Canada, all form part of an overall strategy to serve the needs of the world-wide ethnic Chinese communities.

Although not as original and innovative as its United States counterparts, the HSBC management is highly progressive in the sense that it has been remarkably quick in adopting technological and financial innovations to enhance the quality and range of its services to its customers. Thus, the HSBC is among the first banks to computerize banking operations. It now operates a system of some 550 Automated Teller Machines (ATMs) jointly with the Hang Seng Bank in Hong Kong. It is one of the founders of the Easy Pay System, which is now available in more than 1,100 retail outlets in Hong Kong for cash-free shopping. For the Group as a whole, there are more than 950 ATMs throughout the world. In 1985 the Group launched a new electronic banking system called Hexagon, which delivers a wide range of financial services including market information, documentary credit, fund transfer, and so on, directly to a personal computer installed in the customer's office. Hexagon is carried by the Group's Global Data Network, to which almost all members of the Group are linked. In 1987, the Hong Kong head office introduced a new computerized treasury trading system called TREATS, which uses touch-screen technology to provide a fully automated link between the front and back office by exercising real-time control of exchange, interest, and credit exposures, and improving information on profitability.

Generally speaking, the HongkongBank Group's lending strategy has been much more cautious than strategies of other international banks, resulting in its negligible exposure to Third World debt. Although such exposure has increased following the Group's acquisitions of Marine Midland and the Midland Bank, its aggregate exposure is still smaller than, say, most major United States and United Kingdom banks.

Recognizing quite early on that the global financial revolution of the past two decades has been eroding the traditional demarcations between commercial banks and other non-bank financial intermediaries, the HongkongBank Group during the same period has either created or acquired a considerable number of merchant banks, finance companies, brokerage houses, securities dealers, insurance companies, financial and computer services companies, and so on. Thus by the late 1980s it could claim to have largely achieved its aim, in common with other multi-national giants, of offering one-stop banking products and financial services under one roof.

Within Hong Kong itself, the HSBC (though not the Hang Seng Bank) has ceased to expand its 'brick-and-mortar' branches, relying instead on the extension of ATMs. Emphasis is now being increasingly laid on personal banking and treasury trading and management. The Bank has recently embarked on a programme of branch refurbishment, so that a part of the banking hall is specially reserved for the private banking department. Among the personal banking products now being aggressively marketed are home mortgage loans and credit cards, which provide opportunities for cross-selling other products. Treasury business, involving a whole range of products and services from currency and interest rate swaps to cash management, was systematically introduced in 1985. As mentioned earlier, the Group's capability in this area has been greatly facilitated by the installation of TREATS.

By far the most important strategy pursued by the HongkongBank Group during the past three decades has been its geographical diversification away from Hong Kong. Because of its importance, we will discuss it in greater detail in the next section.

Internationalization of the HongkongBank Group

Although the HSBC opened its offices simultaneously in Hong Kong, Shanghai, and London in 1865, and established branches in major ports in Asia, Europe, and the United States in the next twenty years, it remained essentially a Hong Kong-based, or at most a Far East-based bank until the outbreak of the Second World War. After the end of the war, the HSBC, while rebuilding its Hong Kong business, endured the loss of its China operations. It was not until the late 1950s, therefore, that the HSBC began a programme of overseas expansion and acquisitions, initially on a very modest scale. In 1955 it established its own subsidiary in the United States, the HongkongBank of California, Inc., which for a variety of reasons never flourished. The first successful acquisition occurred in 1959, when the HSBC took over the Mercantile Bank and the British Bank of the Middle East (formerly the Imperial Bank of Persia), thus establishing itself in India and the Middle East. In subsequent years, the Bank acquired a majority interest in the Equator Bank and minority interests in Cyprus Popular Bank, Hongkong Egyptian Bank, and the Saudi British Bank, thus strengthening its position in the Middle East as well as extending its presence to the Mediterranean and Africa.

However, in the mid-1970s, apart from a number of branches and partly owned subsidiaries (such as the 22 per cent owned United Kingdom-based consortium bank, International Commercial Bank), the HSBC still lacked a serious presence in North America, Europe, and Australia. It had already reached the stage where the size of the Hong Kong market could no longer satisfy its growth potential. Increasing competition in international banking and integration of global financial markets also had made it imperative for the HSBC to expand abroad if it was to survive as a major bank. Apart from these considerations, the 1997 issue also began to loom large. Because of its seat on the Executive Council, the HSBC must have known quite early on, certainly much earlier than the general population, about China's intentions for the future of Hong Kong. Thus, an accelerated programme of overseas acquisition and diversification became an urgent priority.

The first tangible result of this programme was, of course, the successful acquisition of 51 per cent of the Marine Midland Bank of the United States, at a price of US$314 million. Because of the legal complexities involved, it took more than two years (early 1978 to March 1980) to complete the acquisition process. On the completion of this deal, the HSBC was required, under United States law, to dispose of its subsidiary in California.[26]

Hard on the heels of the Marine Midland Bank acquisition, the HSBC in the following year (1981) was engaged in a fierce take-over battle with the Standard Chartered Bank for the Royal Bank of Scotland. The Bank of England at that time favoured the Standard Chartered Bank and strenuously opposed the HSBC's bid. In the event, both bids were vetoed by the Monopolies and Mergers Commission.[27] Undaunted by this set-back, however, the HSBC continued to target Europe, especially the United Kingdom, as an important area for its overseas expansion and diversification. Earlier, in 1978, it had acquired a British merchant bank, Anthony Gibbs, and renamed it Wardley London Ltd. In 1982, it acquired an 80 per cent interest in an acceptance house, TKM, which later became a wholly owned subsidiary and renamed Hong Kong International Trade Finance Ltd. In 1984, in preparation for the Big Bang, it acquired a 29.9 per cent interest in the third largest brokerage house in the United Kingdom, James Capel, which became a wholly owned subsidiary in 1986. Meanwhile, Wardley London Ltd. was first renamed HongkongBank Ltd. of London, then renamed James Capel Bankers in 1986, to become the European merchant banking arm of the HongkongBank Group. Finally, the HSBC's ambition of acquiring a commercial bank in the United Kingdom was rewarded when, in November 1987, it was able to purchase 14.9 per cent of the enlarged capital of Midland Bank PLC, one of the four major British clearing banks, for £393 million. This time the Bank of England did not object. The purchase agreement provided for a three-year standstill in any further purchase or sale by the HSBC of shares in Midland, except with the consent of Midland's board. It also provided for integration and rationalization of the two banks' operations: broadly speaking, Midland would take over the bulk of the HSBC's business in Europe (though the HSBC will retain its United Kingdom offices), while the HSBC would take over most of Midland's business in Asia and Canada.

Meanwhile, the acquisition programme in other major geographical areas continued apace. In December 1987, the HSBC used US$770 million (or US$83 per share) to acquire the 48 per cent of Marine Midland it did not already own. The move was partly dictated by regulatory considerations: as the majority owner, the HSBC already had had to bear the risks and responsibility of full ownership, hence increasing its stake to 100 per cent was consistent with the balancing of risks and rewards. Earlier, the HSBC's branch in the United States purchased four branches and deposits of the failed Golden Pacific National Bank at the price of US$6.5 million in 1985, and the Global Union Bank from the Tung family in 1986 at an undisclosed price. The HSBC also acquired 51 per cent of CM&M, a large government securities dealer, from Marine Midland in 1986. Marine Midland, in turn, acquired Westchester Financial Services Corporation in the same year. It also announced a plan to merge, when permissible by law after 1990, with the Philadelphia-based First Pennsylvania Corporation, the holding company of First Pennsylvania Bank. In Canada, the HongkongBank of Canada has made enormous strides in recent years through acquisitions: it first acquired the Halifax and Winnipeg offices of the failed Canadian Commercial Bank in 1985, and then acquired most of the assets and liabilities and a network of 41 branches of another failed bank, the Bank of British Columbia for C$2.6 billion in 1986. In 1990, it expanded its position further by buying Lloyds Bank Canada for C$190 million. In Australia, the HongkongBank Group increased its shareholding in the HongkongBank of Australia to 100 per cent by purchasing the 20 per cent stake formerly held by Victorian Economic Development Corporation.

The HSBC has been extraordinarily lucky for the opportunities presented to it by the misfortunes or mismanagement of other financial institutions. However, internationalization is not an unalloyed blessing. Marine Midland's problems with the Third World debt, and James Capel's losses from the October 1987 Crash, have already been mentioned. The Midland Bank, apart from its disastrous experience with its United States subsidiary, the Crocker National Bank, also has problems with Third World debt. Indeed, investors' perception of the HSBC's international exposure, together with its loss of the monopoly profit from running the Clearing House in Hong Kong, largely explained the below-average performance of its shares in 1988. Nevertheless, the HSBC takes a long view, and will not be deterred by the temporary set-backs, in its view, of its subsidiaries. It is almost certain that after the three-year standstill (which will expire in November 1990), the HSBC will increase its stake in Midland, with the ultimate aim of achieving 100 per cent ownership.

It must not be supposed that the HSBC during the past three decades has embarked on a single path of expansion. Along with its acquisitions, the HSBC has also consolidated and retrenched. Thus, from the mid-1970s onward, it has reduced its branch network in the United Kingdom because of disappointing results. Its disposal of the Hong-kongBank of California has already been mentioned. In 1984 it sold the Mercantile Bank to Citicorp, which resold it to Mitsubishi Bank in 1987. In 1986 the HSBC sold its 83 per cent holdings in Carlingford Australia Insurance Co. at an undisclosed price to CIC holdings. Then in April 1988, it sold its branches in Fiji, Vanuatu, and the Solomon Islands to Westpac Banking Corporation. In Hong Kong itself, the HSBC since the mid-1970s has successively disposed of its shareholdings in the Cross Harbour Tunnel, East Asia Navigation, Hutchison Whampoa, and the South China Morning Post; reduced its stakes in Cathay Pacific Airways and Y. K. Pao's World-wide Group; and sold quite a number of properties, notably the China Building, three floors in Admiralty Towers, and Wayfoong Plaza, as well as residential properties in Clear Water Bay. The HSBC's branch network in Hong Kong was gradually reduced from its peak of 289 in September 1985 to 267 at the end of 1988, though that of the Hang Seng Bank increased somewhat from 103 to 112 during the same period. Between March 1989 and February 1990, the HSBC sold 1 per cent of its shareholdings to each of three Japanese life insurance companies, namely, Dai-Ichi Mutual Life Insurance Co., Meiji Mutual Life Insurance Co., and Nippon Life Insurance Co.

Table 2.7 Geographical Distribution of HongkongBank Group's Total Assets

Year	Asia Pacific	Americas	Middle East	Europe
1981 Assets (HK$ billion)	105	125	10	40
% of total	37.5	44.6	3.6	14.3
1982 Assets (HK$ billion)	140	140	23	54
% of total	39.2	39.2	6.4	15.1
1983 Assets (HK$ billion)	165	195	20	50
% of total	38.4	45.3	4.7	11.6
1984 Assets (HK$ billion)	180	197	24	54
% of total	39.6	43.2	5.3	11.9
1985 Assets (HK$ billion)	218	205	32	82
% of total	40.6	38.2	6.0	15.2
1986 Assets (HK$ billion)	280	260	30	125
% of total	40.3	37.4	4.3	18.0
1987 Assets (HK$ billion)	330	260	30	180
% of total	41.3	32.5	3.75	22.5
1988 Assets (HK$ billion)	390	280	30	160
% of total	45.3	32.6	3.5	18.6

Source: Hongkong and Shanghai Banking Corporation, *Annual Report*, various years.

The HongkongBank Group's geographical distribution of total assets (net of contra items) is shown in Table 2.7. During the period 1981–8, the relative shares of two principal geographical areas, the Asia Pacific region and Europe, increased from 37.5 per cent to 45.3 per cent, and from 14.3 per cent to 18.6 per cent respectively. The relative share of the Americas declined, however, from 44.6 per cent to 32.6 per cent, while that of the Middle East remained virtually the same.

Impact of the HongkongBank's Future Moves on Hong Kong

Given the HSBC's strategic role in Hong Kong's financial system, its future moves, especially in the light of the impending transfer of sovereignty in 1997, will be of great concern to Hong Kong. Not being privy to the HSBC's policy-decision process, we can only speculate, on reasonably plausible assumptions, on its possible courses of action and their implications.

From our previous discussion, it should be obvious that the HongkongBank Group's long-term strategic objective is to build itself up into one of the top transnational financial institutions of the world. One critical aspect of this strategy is to diversify internationally to such an extent that Hong Kong will eventually account for insignificant proportions of the Group's total assets and profits, so that even the total loss of Hong Kong will not threaten the viability of the Group's international status. While opinions may differ as to what constitutes an optimal geographical distribution, one might reasonably surmise that the HSBC management would probably regard its global position as being very safe if Hong Kong's relative weights in the Group's total assets and profits fell to, say, no more than 25 per cent and 15 per cent respectively.

Although this appears to be the long-term objective of the Group with regard to Hong Kong, there are different ways to achieve it. We might envisage three possible scenarios. The first scenario is one of rapid realization of the above targets before the transfer of sovereignty on 1 July 1997. This short-term strategy will call for drastic liquidation of the Group's assets in Hong Kong in the absolute sense, and might even entail a change in the Group's legal domicile. Needless to say, the impact of such a scenario would be catastrophic to general confidence in Hong Kong, since it would be widely (and correctly) interpreted as the Group's determination to get out of the territory as soon as possible. It is no exaggeration to say that any panic move on the Group's part may well cause the breakdown of Hong Kong's financial system.

The Group would be forced to make such a drastic move, however, only under extreme conditions, such as China's repudiation of the Sino-British Joint Declaration, and its atavistic reversion to Maoist policies and practices. These conditions, in short, will make it impossible for the Group to carry on normally in Hong Kong. Even though China's political future is unpredictable, and its modernization and reform programme is fraught with pitfalls, the probability of the first scenario seems very small.

The second scenario is one where the Group tries to achieve its target ratios over the longer period of say, 10 to 20 years. Under this medium-term strategy, the Group's total assets in Hong Kong would not be liquidated wholesale (except for internal reshuffling and readjustments), but they would not increase either. In other words, by expanding only its overseas assets, the Group would hope to reduce Hong Kong's weight in total assets and profits to the desired levels.

The probability of the second scenario is greater than that of the first, and its negative impact on Hong Kong would be much softer. However, this strategy also implies that the Group's market share will shrink further. Since Hong Kong is a major profit centre — it is estimated that Hong Kong still accounts for about 70 per cent of the Group's total published profits — the probability of adopting this strategy is not high unless there is a marked deterioration of the political environment in China and Hong Kong.

The third scenario is one where the Group would try to attain its desired geographical distribution over a period of 20 years or more. Under this long-term strategy, the Group's assets in Hong Kong would still grow, but at a much slower rate than that of its overseas assets. Thus, Hong Kong's relative weight would gradually, almost imperceptibly, fall to the desired levels. The negative impact of this gradual approach would be negligible. Indeed, if the shareholders realize that this strategy is in their own long-term interests, its impact could even be positive.

In this author's considered judgement, the third scenario has the highest probability. The HongkongBank Group's actual behaviour during the past decade, as described in the previous section, is consistent with this judgement. However, this judgement also rests on certain suppositions, namely, that the Joint Declaration will be faithfully observed and implemented by all relevant parties concerned, that China will be able to maintain political stability on a long-term basis, and that its open-door and reform policies will remain unchanged. It goes without saying therefore that if these suppositions do not hold, the probabilities of scenarios one and two will correspondingly increase.

Whatever strategy the HongkongBank Group may adopt with regard to Hong Kong, one thing is certain: any precipitate withdrawal of the Group will have catastrophic effects on Hong Kong's financial system and economy. China is aware of these consequences, and there is considerable evidence that China is trying hard to persuade the Group to stay in Hong Kong. It was reported that when Mr William Purves, Chairman of the Group, went to Beijing in March 1988, he was urged by Premier Li Peng and State Councillor Ji Pengfei to retain the HSBC's leading role as a note-issuing bank.[28] China has also allowed the HSBC to operate three full branches in China (Shanghai, Xiamen, and Shenzhen) — the largest number of branches granted to a foreign bank since 1949. In Hong Kong, the Bank of China Group in recent years has deliberately kept a low profile concerning sensitive questions such as note-issuing and other central banking functions. Thus Mr Huang Diyan, Director of the Bank of China Hong Kong and Macau Office, told the press in late 1986 that the Bank of China Group had no intention of taking over the HSBC's role in Hong Kong's financial affairs.[29] At the same time, it has co-operated closely with the HSBC in stabilizing Hong Kong's financial system: examples are 'life boat' operations for Ka Wah Bank in June 1985 and the Hong Kong futures exchange in October 1987. Indeed, the Bank of China Group has sometimes gone out of its way not to offend the HSBC.[30]

From Hong Kong's standpoint, the ideal arrangement would be for the HSBC to maintain its strong presence in the territory after 1997, but as a private commercial bank without any special privileges. It may retain its note-issuing power provided other qualified banks are given the same right. While the HSBC's quasi-central bank status and other privileges have attracted a great deal of criticism from its competitors and disinterested scholars, they have not caused wide-spread resentment among the populace, largely because of the bank's acknowledged contributions to the stability and development of the economy. Thus one of the most delicate tasks facing Hong Kong is how to phase out gradually the HSBC's special privileges without endangering the stability of the territory's financial system.[31]

Notes

1. For a more detailed account, see the archival history by King (1988a).
2. See King (1988a), and the essays under 'The Hongkong Bank in China' in King (1983a), pp. 230–320.
3. During the Japanese occupation of Hong Kong, senior managers of the HongkongBank in captivity were forced by the military authorities to sign unbacked banknotes for circulation. Although the notes were illegal, the Bank decided to honour them in April 1946 under a compensation scheme whereby the Bank paid £1 million to the Exchange Fund. (The British Government first demanded £3.5 million.) See King (1986). For an account of the HongkongBank's role in the early postwar reconstruction of Hong Kong, see Jao (1983).
4. See Jao (1974), pp. 247–8.
5. For a detailed account of the acquisition of Marine Midland, see King (1983b).
6. See 'Top 500', The Banker, July 1988.
7. 'Big Bang' is a term borrowed from astronomy by financial journalists to describe the agreement between the Conservative Government and the City of London in 1983 that modernized and liberalized Britain's securities industry with effect from 27 October 1986. The main points of the agreement were: (a) to computerize the London Stock Exchange and link-up with New York and Tokyo for 24-hour global trading; (b) to allow foreign financial institutions to enter the securities industries on the basis of fair competition; (c) to abolish the fixed commission system to allow more competition; and (d) to abolish the traditional distinction between broker and jobber.
8. The total employment figure and figures for the principal companies are taken from the Bank's annual report for 1988. The figure for Hong Kong is by private estimates.
9. After the October 1987 crash, the Davison Report recommended the creation of an independent Securities and Futures Commission outside the civil service. This proposal has been accepted by the Government, and was implemented in 1989.
10. Between July 1972 and 17 October 1983, the note-issuing banks did not have to pay any foreign currency in advance to the Exchange Fund. They merely had to credit the Exchange Fund's account with Hong Kong dollar balances to obtain the CIs. Normally, the Exchange Fund used the proceeds to buy foreign currency from them. However, this ex post constraint was less binding than ex ante constraint. For a more detailed discussion, see Jao (1988b).
11. See King (1986).
12. According to Hong Kong's Secretary for Monetary Affairs, David Nendick, the Settlement Banks also have information about the clearing balances of the Sub-settlement Banks. See Eva To, 'David Li Urges End to "Unfair" Clearing Bank Benefits', South China Morning Post Business Post, 21 December 1988. The Deputy Secretary for Monetary

Affairs, Joseph Yam, claimed in a speech on 30 January 1989 that the Settlement Banks can also use the Sub-settlement Banks' interest-free credit balances and charge interest rates on their debit balances. The main point of these assertions is that the HSBC does not enjoy any special privilege. What they forgot to mention is that the HSBC is not only the Management Bank, but also one of the 10 Settlement Banks. According to the latest membership list of the Clearing House, the HSBC has 106 Sub-settlement Banks, or 69 per cent of all licensed banks. Of the other 9 Settlement Banks, the Standard Chartered has 21 Sub-settlement Banks; the Bank of China has 12 (all of which are its own 'sister banks'); the Belgian Bank has 2; the Citibank and Shanghai Commercial Bank have one each; while 4 others, the Bank of East Asia, Overseas Chinese Banking Corporation, Security Pacific Asian Bank, and Wing On Bank, have none at all. Thus it is undeniable that the HSBC has special privileges.

13. See the Monopolies and Mergers Commission Report (1982), para. 9.13, p. 69.

14. The full text of this document is contained in the 'Press Release from Secretary for Monetary Affairs, 15 July 1988', reproduced in *Asian Monetary Monitor*, July–August 1988, Vol. 12, No. 4, pp. 14–20.

15. This is, for example, the gist of the article by Greenwood (1988).

16. See Ho (1988) for an empirical test of investors' reaction.

17. The Banking Commissioner's annual report provides information on the assets and deposits of five groups of banks, namely those from China, Europe, Japan, the United States, and others, on an aggregate basis. No exact information is available concerning the HSBC alone.

18. James Capel (Far East) Ltd. estimated in 1987 that the HongkongBank Group's inner reserves amounted to HK$30 billion. Because James Capel is a subsidiary, and its methodology of estimate is fully described, its estimate has perhaps more credibility than others. Nonetheless, it remains a guesstimate. See James Capel Hong Kong Research, 'The Banking Industry of Hong Kong', April 1987. In 1989–90, there were persistent rumors that the HSBC would in the near future disclose its inner reserves in order to conform to international practices.

19. Monopolies and Mergers Commission (1982), p. 48.

20. For a more detailed study of the earlier period 1971–85, see Jao (1987).

21. For the Basle Committee proposal, see Committee on Banking Regulations and Supervisory Practices (1988). For the Hong Kong authorities' proposal to follow the Basle recommendation, see Commissioner of Banking Hong Kong (1988).

22. Under Hong Kong's Banking Ordinance, banks incorporated outside Hong Kong are exempted from the obligation of publishing their annual financial statements in Hong Kong newspapers.

23. These figures are meaningful because the official statistics on bank assets are also net of contra items.

24. For a more detailed study of the market shares of the major banking groups in Hong Kong for the years 1985–6, see Jao (1988a), Chapter III. Even in the 1960s, when competition from international banks was less severe, the HongkongBank Group's share of total bank loans fell from 41 per cent in March 1966 to 36 per cent in March 1970, as revealed in an archival study in Jao (1983).

25. The real bills doctrine has many interpretations, but one of its precepts, derived from Adam Smith, is that a bank will always be liquid if it confines itself to short-term self-liquidating loans evidenced by real bills of exchange. The German universal banking denotes an approach that involves the total commitment of a bank to its clients, especially industrial companies, all the way from underwriting and equity ownership to management and policy-making. For more elaboration on the successful blending of these two traditions, see Jao (1983).

26. For full details, see King (1983b).

27. For full details, see Monopolies and Mergers Commission (1982).

28. Seth Faith, 'Bank Chief Urged to Boost Role in China', *South China Morning Post*, 19 March 1988.

29. See 'Bank of China to Strengthen Inter-bank Cooperation: No Wish to Replace Hong Kong Bank', *Wen Wei Pao*, Hong Kong, 23 December 1986; and 'BOC denies Intent to "Control" HK', *China Daily*, Beijing, 7 January 1987.

30. In 1986, the Chinese Banks' Association of Hong Kong formed a Study Group, consisting of leading local and foreign banks, to study possible reforms of the monetary and banking system during the transition to 1997 and beyond. The present writer was invited as its convenor. After two years' research, the Study Group's Report, in both English and Chinese, was published in June 1988. See Jao (1988a). The Report contains some mildly critical remarks on the HSBC's special privileges. Although one member of

the Bank of China Group, Nanyang Commercial Bank, was one of the members of the Study Group, and the Report itself specifically states that its views were those of the Study Group and not necessarily those of the individual members of the Study Group or the Chinese Banks' Association, the Bank of China took the unusual step of issuing a statement publicly disassociating itself from the Report.

31. For a list of proposals along these lines, see the Report of the Study Group of the Chinese Banks' Association in Jao (1988a).

References

Commissioner of Banking Hong Kong, 'International Convergence of Banks' Capital Measurement and Capital Standards: A New Hong Kong Ratio', September 1988, mimeo.

Committee on Banking Regulations and Supervisory Practices, 'International Convergence of Capital Measurement and Capital Standards', July 1988, mimeo.

Greenwood, J. G., 'Intervention Replaces Arbitrage — The July Package of Monetary Measures', *Asian Monetary Monitor*, July–August 1988, Vol. 12, No. 4, pp. 1–20.

Ho, Y. K., 'The New Clearing System — A Monumental Change in the Management of the Hong Kong Financial System', *The Securities Bulletin*, August 1988, No. 28, pp. 24–30.

James Capel Hong Kong Research, 'The Banking Industry of Hong Kong', April 1987, mimeo.

Jao, Y. C., *Banking and Currency in Hong Kong: A Study of Postwar Financial Development*, (London, Macmillan, 1974).

—— 'Financing Hong Kong's Early Postwar Industrialization: The Role of the Hongkong and Shanghai Banking Corporation', in King (1983a), pp. 545–74.

—— (ed.), *Hong Kong's Banking System in Transition: Problems, Prospects and Policies*, (Hong Kong, The Chinese Banks Association, 1988a).

—— 'Monetary System and Banking Structure', in H. C. Y. Ho and L. C. Chau (eds.), *The Economic System of Hong Kong*, (Hong Kong, Asian Research Service, 1988b), Chapter 4.

—— 'Intervention Replaces Arbitrage — The July Package of Monetary Measures: A Comment', *Asian Monetary Monitor*, November–December 1988c, pp. 1–6.

Jao, Y. C. and Ho, Y. K., *Xianggang gelei yinhang de diwei he fazhan (The Major Banking Groups in Hong Kong: Their Current Situation and Future Prospects)*, (Hong Kong, ACL Consultants Ltd., April 1987).

King, F. H. H. (ed.), *Eastern Banking: Essays in the History of the Hongkong and Shanghai Banking Corporation*, (London, Athlone, 1983a).

—— 'An Economic Historian's View of the Investment of the Hongkong and Shanghai Banking Corporation in Marine Midland Banks, Inc.', Discussion Paper No. 12, Department of Economics, University of Hong Kong, 1983b.

—— 'The Extraordinary Survival of Hong Kong's Private Note Issue', paper presented to the ESRC Third World Economic History and Development Group Conference, 5–7 September 1986, University of Birmingham.

—— *The Hongkong Bank in Late Imperial China, 1864–1902: On an Even Keel*, Vol. I of *The History of the Hongkong and Shanghai Banking Corporation*, (Cambridge, Cambridge University Press, 1987).

—— *The Hongkong Bank in the Period of Imperialism and War, 1895–1918:*

Wayfoong, the Focus of Wealth, Vol. II of *The History of the Hongkong and Shanghai Banking Corporation*, (Cambridge, Cambridge University Press, 1988a).

—— *The Hongkong Bank between the Wars and the Bank Interned, 1919–1945: Return from Grandeur*, Vol. III of *The History of the Hongkong and Shanghai Banking Corporation*, (Cambridge, Cambridge University Press, 1988b).

The Monopolies and Mergers Commission, *The Hongkong and Shanghai Banking Corporation, Standard Chartered Bank Ltd., The Royal Bank of Scotland Group Ltd.: A Report on the Proposed Mergers*, (London, HMSO, Cmnd. 8472, January 1982).

3. The Role of the Bank of China Group

JOSEPH S. WAN

THE Bank of China Group (the BOC Group or the Group) is a collective name consisting of 13 sister banks from Hong Kong and 1 bank from Macau. This chapter will be confined to the discussion of the 13 sister banks in Hong Kong. The BOC Group is the second largest banking group in Hong Kong (next to the Hongkong and Shanghai Banking Corporation) in terms of branch networks, and the biggest overseas operation of the Bank of China, headquartered in the People's Republic of China (PRC).

Historical Origin of the Bank of China

The Bank of China (BOC), China's oldest financial institution, was established in August 1905.[1] Now it is a state specialized foreign exchange bank under the supervision of the China's central bank, the People's Bank of China (PBOC). It experienced different phases of development since the overthrow of the Qing Dynasty.[2]

Its predecessor was the Bank of Great Qing, a government bank of the Qing Dynasty which was overthrown in October 1911 by National China. In January of the following year, the Bank of Great Qing was reconstructed to become the Bank of China at its old premises in Shanghai under the instructions of Dr Sun Yat-sen, the interim President of the Republic of China. It functioned as a state bank until 1928, then turned into an international exchange and remittance bank for the country.

In 1949, the founding year of the People's Republic of China, the Bank of China moved to Beijing from Shanghai. It was designated in 1953 as a specialized foreign exchange bank with special permission of the state under the leadership of the People's Bank of China.

In 1979, the State Council of China, in accordance with the economic reform and open door policies, approved the Bank of China as an economic entity under its direct leadership. Until 1986, the Bank of China was again under the leadership of the PBOC according to regulations.[3]

Development of the Bank of China Group

The Bank of China's Hong Kong Branch was established in 1917 and experienced a history similar to that of its headquarters in China. Since

Table 3.1 The Total Branches of the Bank of China Group

Sister Banks	Place of Registration	No. of Hong Kong Branches
1. Bank of China	Beijing	19
2. Bank of Communications	Beijing*	25
3. Nanyang Commercial Bank	Hong Kong	39
4. Kwangtung Provincial Bank	Beijing	21
5. Sin Hua Bank	Beijing	40
6. China and South Sea Bank	Beijing	16
7. Kincheng Bank	Beijing	25
8. China State Bank	Beijing	18
9. National Commercial Bank	Beijing	17
10. Yien Yieh Commercial Bank	Beijing	20
11. Po Sang Bank	Hong Kong	17
12. Hua Chiao Commercial Bank	Hong Kong	10
13. Chiyu Bank	Hong Kong	13
Total		280

Note: * The Bank of Communications moved its headquarters from Beijing to Shanghai in 1987.

Source: *Hong Kong Economic Times*, 27 January 1989.

the establishment of diplomatic relations between the new China and Britain in 1950, the Bank of China Hong Kong Branch has been under the direct management of its Beijing headquarters. At the early stage of the Group, the PRC-registered sister banks (see Table 3.1) were naturally under the umbrella of the Beijing BOC, then merged with other locally registered sister banks into the Group, sharing the same political values and ideology. All sister banks originated either in mainland China or in Hong Kong, but they are all managed under the name of the Bank of China Group.

The Structure of the Bank of China Group

The BOC Group consists of nine China-incorporated banks, four Hong Kong-incorporated banks, and one Macau-incorporated bank.[4] They are all under the leadership of the Bank of China, Hong Kong and Macau Regional Office, which reports and communicates with the Beijing head office directly.

At the early stages of the BOC Group, every sister bank was informally assigned different business areas of specialization. This allowed banks to cultivate their respective potentials and to make effective use of limited resources. Though it is not obvious in task assignment nowadays, the specialized traits can still be identified: the Bank of Communications is quite active in the money and foreign exchange

There are 13 sister banks in Hong Kong:

Bank of China (Hong Kong Branch)
Bank of Communications (Hong Kong Branch)
Nanyang Commercial Bank Ltd.*
The Kwangtung Provincial Bank (Hong Kong Branch)
Sin Hua Trust, Savings and Commercial Bank, Ltd. (Hong Kong Branch)
The China and South Sea Bank, Ltd. (Hong Kong Branch)
Kincheng Banking Corporation (Hong Kong Branch)
The China State Bank, Ltd. (Hong Kong Branch)
The National Commercial Bank, Ltd. (Hong Kong Branch)
The Yien Yieh Commercial Bank Ltd. (Hong Kong Branch)
Po Sang Bank Ltd.*
Hua Chiao Commercial Bank Ltd.*
Chiyu Banking Corporation Ltd.*

Note: * Hong Kong-incorporated banks.

market; Nanyang Commercial Bank Ltd. is the pioneer of and overlooks the credit card business; Po Sang Bank Ltd. specializes in gold trading; and Sin Hua Trust, Savings and Commercial Bank, Ltd. is heavily involved in the industrial loan market. On the whole, they all practise traditional retail banking and occasionally participate in the merchant banking business. In 1977, the BOC Group formed the China Development Finance (Hong Kong) Ltd. intending to compete in the merchant banking business which already is very competitive. The process is slow and business is steady in this direction. For management reasons, the China Development Finance (Hong Kong) Ltd. became the wholly owned subsidiary of the Bank of China, Hong Kong Branch, in 1988. In 1985, the BOC Group also established the China Development Investment (Hong Kong) Ltd. to supervise its investment projects in Hong Kong and China as well. Recently, all the sister banks except Nanyang Commercial Bank Ltd. joined hands to form a brokerage firm, the Chung Mao Securities Ltd., to handle securities transactions for bank clients and other investors.

Every sister bank has its fully owned subsidiary finance company and nominee company to provide full service for the bank customers. In some cases, the sister banks also have investment companies to diversify their assets into other non-banking areas.

The Bank of China, Hong Kong and Macau Regional Office (the Regional Office)

As the name implies, the Regional Office is the chief representative office of the Bank of China, Beijing headquarters, which governs the region of Hong Kong and Macau. Its main objectives are to co-ordinate between sister banks, formulate policies, and communicate with the Beijing head office.

The principal functions of the Regional Office are as follows:

(a) To co-ordinate the business between sister banks so as to avoid unnecessary competition between them.

(b) To oversee and evaluate the performance of the sister banks.

(c) To establish banking policies within the Group. For example, one of the policies is that prior permission from the Regional Office has to be sought for large commercial loans or the issuing of certificates of deposit.

(d) To co-ordinate and operate the group-wide computer system.

(e) To provide training for both banking staff and visitors from mainland China.

(f) To collect and analyse local as well as international economic information.

From the functions listed above, it is fair to say that the Regional Office has been assuming the role of leadership and co-ordination, but each sister bank is allowed to maintain its operating style and independence. This definitely facilitates their participation in the local banking sector as well as in international banking.

There are one Chief Executive and four Deputy Chief Executives to manage the Regional Office. The Office is composed of six divisions and one office (see Fig. 3.1). They are:

(a) The Business Division is responsible for overall local banking strategic planning, managing and approving loan portfolios of sister banks, performing treasury functions for the Group, and overall accounting policies.

(b) The Auditing Division is responsible for the internal audit function for the Group, setting guide-lines or policies for internal control, investigating control problems, and recommending solutions.

(c) The Investment Division is responsible for the investments of the head office. On some occasions it also manages investment projects on behalf of the sister banks. It also sets investment policies for the Group and overlooks the investment activities within the Group.

(d) The Personnel Division is responsible for the personnel policies for the Group, running a training centre, co-ordinating the personnel departments between the sister banks, and evaluating the performance of top management executives of each sister bank.

(e) The Economic Research Division is involved in the collection of local and international economic news and in analysing the information and feeding it back to Beijing headquarters.

(f) The Computer Division is involved in the management of the main computer facilities for the Group, advising the computing policies for the sister banks, and centralizing the Group's computerization process.

(g) The Administration Office runs the daily operation of the Regional Office, providing secretarial support for the Chief and Deputy Executives, and co-ordinating and communicating between the sister banks as well as other banking institutions.

Fig. 3.1   The Structure of the Regional Office

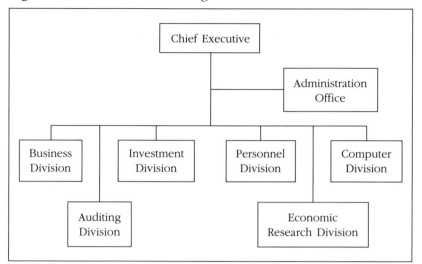

Performance, Operations, and Strategies

The BOC Group has experienced tremendous growth since 1978. The development of the Group in the past decade can be categorized in three stages:

1.   The Growth Stage (1978–83).   The Group followed the changing policies of mainland China's economic reform. It changed from a highly conservative position to a more aggressive one. Since then, the Group has become more aggressive in the retail market. This is evidenced by the tremendous growth in total assets and deposits of approximately 40 per cent.

2.   The Consolidation Stage (1984–5).   As the general banking environment was dismayed by the general economic downturn and concerned for the future of Hong Kong, financially unsound institutions were under enormous pressure to avoid being out-competed or merged with a stronger partner. The BOC Group took this opportunity to review its situation, and its growth of total assets and deposits was levelled off.

3.   Development Stage (1986–8).   The Group diversified its retail banking activity by means of product innovations such as the pioneering launch of retail European Currency Unit (ECU) deposit by Po Sang Bank, telephone deposits by Kincheng Bank, and the fixed mortgage rate loan by Bank of Communications. Meanwhile, it also developed and participated in merchant banking, as in syndicated loans, brokerage services, and even in fund management. Total deposits increased 28 per cent and total assets 33 per cent in 1988 as compared with the previous year (see Table 3.2).

Table 3.2 BOC Group: Assets and Deposits (HK$ billion)

| | Assets | | | | Deposits | | | |
	1988	1987	% Share in 1988	% Growth in 1988	1988	1987	% Share in 1988	% Growth in 1988
China-related Banks*	299	225	8	33	179	139	21	29
Less:								
Ka Wah**	8.31	6.70	—	—	7.84	6.35	—	—
Union**	3.26	2.40	—	—	2.13	1.58	—	—
BOC Group	287.43	215.90	7.8	33.13	169.03	131.92	23.2	28.1

Note: The Ka Wah Bank was taken over by the China-owned China International Trust and Investment Corporation (CITIC) in 1985, while the Union Bank was taken over in the same year by a subsidiary of the China-owned China Merchant Steam Navigation Co. Ltd.

Sources: * Banking Commission's Office.
        ** 1988 Annual Reports.

The Group has injected new capital since 1980 and was further strengthened in 1986 (see Table 3.3). The PRC-incorporated sister banks' capital increased to RMB500 million; the Hong Kong-incorporated sister banks increased to HK$600 million or HK$400 million, except for Chiyu Banking Corporation which had a capital of HK$100 million.

Table 3.3 The Issued Capital Changes of the BOC Group from 1980 to 1986 (HK$ million)

	1980	1981	1982	1983	1984	1985		1986	
BOC*	+600	0	0	0	0	+200	(3,000)	0	(3,000)
Communication*	+200	+100	0	0	0	0	(400)	+200	(600)
Kwangtung*	+120	+100	0	0	0	0	(300)	+200	(500)
Sin Hua*	+120	+100	0	0	0	0	(300)	+200	(500)
South China*	+120	+100	0	0	0	0	(250)	+150	(400)
Kincheng*	0	+120	+100	0	0	0	(300)	+200	(500)
China State*	+100	+100	0	0	0	0	(250)	+150	(400)
China Commercial*	+100	+100	0	0	0	0	(250)	+150	(400)
Yien Yieh*	+100	+100	0	0	0	0	(250)	+150	(400)
Nanyang**	+100	0	0	0	+200	0	(400)	+200	(600)
Po Sang**	+25	+50	0	0	+100	0	(200)	+200	(400)
Hua Chiao**	+20	0	0	0	+100	0	(200)	+200	(400)
Chiyu	0	0	0	0	0	0	(100)	0	(100)

Notes: * = RMB.
        ** = HKD.
        ( ) = Total Issued Capital.
        Chiyu increased its capital to HK$300 million in 1987.

Sources: Annual Reports of various banks.
        Figures for 1986 are from *South China Morning Post*, 31 December 1986.

In March 1987, the Bank of China announced its increase in capital to RMB5 billion and dated back its capital account to 1986.[5] Meanwhile, the Bank of Communications re-established its headquarters in Shanghai and increased its capital from RMB600 million to RMB2 billion,[6] making it the second largest of all the sister banks in terms of capital size. Subsequently, in 1987 the Chiyu Banking Corporation also increased its capital to HK$300 million.

The BOC Group has also had good performance in recent years. In 1987, the Bank of China was the eleventh largest lead manager in the Asian Pacific syndication loan market, with a total value of US$1,465 million.[7] The Bank of Communications was ranked second as the lead manager in Hong Kong's certificates of deposit market, with a total value of HK$700 million. Though the Group only started its merchant banking activities a few years ago, it will become more active in the near future.[8]

The Business Scope of the BOC Group

The BOC Group is still focusing on traditional retail banking business. It covers the areas of savings and current deposits, various loans, trade finance, renminbi remittance, foreign exchange, deposit boxes, travellers' cheques, ATM service, and so on.

Specialization of business among the 13 sister banks has also been developed. Examples include the Po Sang Bank which specializes in gold trading; the Nanyang Commercial Bank which emphasizes credit card business; and the Bank of Communications which is actively involved in foreign exchange. The Group also develops toward and participates in the merchant banking business for diversification and for raising needed capital for China's modernization programme. It includes syndicated loans, trading certificates of deposit, brokerage services, and, more recently, fund management services.

Market Operations of the BOC Group

The lower middle income group, traditional Hong Kong Chinese merchants, and China-related companies comprise the clientele base of the Group. Its market share in loans and deposits accounted for approximately one-fifth of local retail banking business. Judging from the operation of the locally registered sister banks, as their return on assets in 1987 averaged 0.63 per cent in comparison to 1.21 per cent of Hang Seng Bank (see Table 3.4), the BOC Group seems to be scoring behind their main competitor. A survey has indicated that the management perception of marketing effectiveness of the BOC Group is moving from 'fair' to 'good',[9] which means the Group has improved its marketing weakness. In order to consolidate and strengthen its present situation, the Group has done a lot internally to improve their services to customers, setting up a training centre, hiring more university graduates to equip itself with additional managerial talent, opening more branches,

Table 3.4　Comparison of the Return on Assets between the BOC Group Locally Registered Sister Banks and the Hang Seng Bank in 1987 (HK$ million)

	Total Assets	Net Profit	Return on Assets (Per cent)
Nanyang Commerical Bank	24,914	136	0.55
Po Sang Bank	18,505	132	0.71
Hua Chiao Commercial Bank	11,156	82	0.74
Chiyu Bank	7,303	42	0.58
Total	61,878	392	0.63
Hang Seng Bank	107,013	1,294	1.21

Note:　We used the Hang Seng Bank as a comparative bank because its assets size and business scope are relevant to the BOC Group locally registered sister banks.

Sources:　Respective banks' 1987 Annual Reports.

and maintaining a strong staff team of over ten thousand people. Externally, the Group provides a variety of new banking products, such as the pioneering retail ECU deposits, telephoned deposits, fixed mortgage rate loans, and so on.

Strategies

'Being deeply rooted in Hong Kong and supported by the motherland, we are capable of facing overseas challenge' is an internal slogan attributed to a high official of the BOC Group and it can be identified as the main mission of the Group. Because political and cultural values are mixed in its mission, the general strategic objective is to support China's modernization. This is to be achieved with the following strategies:

1. Strengthening Local Banking Activities.　This means that a bigger market share of deposits and loans is to be captured. This also implies all-round services to bank customers, provision of loans of competitive rates in every aspect, and strengthening its position in trade finance both for China and overseas.

2. Developing Merchant Banking Activities.　The Group is relatively weak in this area and intends to develop further by active participation in this sector, either by itself or by joining hands with other merchant bankers.

3. Implementing China's Economic Reform.　By raising capital for China's economic development, the Group intends to introduce local and overseas investors into China, or to participate in joint ventures with potential investors to explore China's market.

4. Developing Further in Electronic Banking Services.　In spite of the fact that the Group is the founding member of Hong Kong's largest

Automated Teller Machine (ATM) network — the system of Joint Electronic Teller Services (Hong Kong) Co. Ltd (JETCO) — and that a second computer centre of the Group has recently been established, full utilization of computing facilities is still in the developing stage. Computerization of banking activities is a must in the banking world, and the Group has to try its best in order to maintain its competitiveness.

5. Expanding the Chinese as well as Overseas Markets.   The BOC Group's services have been extended to the Special Economic Zones and the coastal cities where many foreign banks have already set up their offices. The Group has also expanded its banking activities overseas, in places such as the United States and Canada, through the locally registered sister banks.

On the whole, the implementation of these strategies is quite successful or at least heading that way. The Nanyang Commercial Bank, for example, co-operated with James Capel (a subsidiary of the HongkongBank) to launch a retirement fund to the market. The Standard Chartered Bank also joined the JETCO system; their competitive rate and new banking products are sharpened by the local banking competition.

The BOC Group's Relationship with Mainland China

Strictly speaking, the Bank of China is under the supervision of the People's Bank of China, and the BOC Group in Hong Kong is led by the Beijing headquarters. Therefore, officially the Group actually has the status of an overseas branch. However, historical factors once made the Bank of China the most important financial institution in China, and its Hong Kong branch naturally became the only financial channel communicating with the West, and thus the most influential overseas operation of the BOC. A look at its balance sheets shows that the BOC Group accounted for roughly over 20 per cent of the total assets of the Bank of China,[10] and it is consistently the major source of needed foreign exchange for mainland China.

Internal Operating System of the BOC Group

The BOC Group in Hong Kong has enjoyed a high degree of autonomy in terms of running the banking business. This includes setting up the local banking strategies and bank management. But when it comes to principles and general policies such as political belief, China's economic policies, and major banking policy decisions, the Group has to follow guide-lines or seek advice from Beijing.

Generally speaking, the Group follows Beijing's footsteps in setting its banking policies. Substantial loans or investment projects always have to be approved by the head office through the Regional Office. The sister banks have to obtain permission from the Regional Office in granting loans that exceed a certain limit. In some cases, the Regional Office must seek the approval of the head office if the amount exceeds its authorized limit. Once the loans or investments are approved, the actual loans or project management are given back to the sister banks. In other words, the day-to-day banking operations, bank management, and clientele development are still the responsibility of each of the sister banks, though they still count on the Regional Office for major policy matters.

The Group has been quite successful in this setup: decentralization in operation and central control in policy setting. As a result, it relies heavily on the strong leadership of the Regional Office to guide and to co-ordinate while implementing the internal operating system.

Overseas Operations of the Bank of China Group

The long-term strategic objective of the Bank of China is to penetrate the international banking market from its Hong Kong base. The head office and the BOC Group in Hong Kong are therefore developing overseas operations.

Though the decision of the head office to open new branches is sometimes a political rather than a commercial one, the Bank of China still manages to have the following overseas branches and representative offices: branches in Hong Kong, Macau, London, Luxembourg, New York, Cayman Islands, Singapore, Paris, Sydney, and Tokyo; and representative offices in Frankfurt and Panama, making a total of ten overseas branches and two offices.[11]

The BOC Group in Hong Kong is the biggest overseas operation among the branches, and accounts for approximately 80 per cent of the total overseas assets, roughly over HK$157 billion in 1987.[12] It is also one of the few overseas operations offering full-range banking services. The Group takes advantage of the locally registered sister banks to extend their overseas operations and to set up offices in China in order to maintain its competitiveness among the foreign banks. For example, the Nangyang Commercial Bank has established branches in Toronto, San Francisco, Beijing, Shenzhen, Shehou, and Hainan Island;[13] the Kwantung Provincial Bank has a branch in Guangzhou; the Chiyu Bank opened a branch in Xiamen; and the Bank of China, Hong Kong Branch is planning an overseas operation in Mauritius.

Most of the overseas branches set up by the Beijing headquarters are less involved in full banking business. They perform as a representative office rather than a full-fledged branch. Though their overseas operations are relatively small in scale, generating needed information and establishing an effective banking relationship with those regions is a stepping stone toward further internationalization. This is definitely beneficial to the further development of the Bank of China.

The Role of the BOC Group in the Hong Kong Financial System

The BOC Group is the second largest commercial banking group in Hong Kong. Its contribution to the Hong Kong business community is believed to be substantial and its influence on Hong Kong's financial system is tremendous. Although the BOC is a state bank in China, it has been functioning as a commercial bank for many years. This dual identity has the advantage of being able to attract the confidence of local depositors. However, it also suffers as political decisions sometimes override commercial decisions.

The role played by the Group in the Hong Kong financial system can be described as the Three Bs:

1. Balancing Force in the Hong Kong Financial System.   The quasi-central bank, the Hongkong and Shanghai Banking Corporation, used to be the sole and ultimate player able to carry out central banking activities on behalf of the Hong Kong Government, such as rescuing the Hang Seng Bank from a bank-run in 1965. Now, the BOC Group shares this unofficial obligation with the HongkongBank, as for instance when it joined with the Hongkong and Shanghai Banking Corporation to stabilize the Ka Wah Bank in 1987, and when it provided HK$100 million stand-by credit for the Hong Kong Commodity Futures Exchange to prevent further market collapse in October, 1987. The Group also acted on its own behalf by acquiring the problem-filled Conic Investment Holding Company in 1983; and taking over the loss and binding debts of the China Cement Company in 1985. During 1983, uncertainty over Hong Kong's future ignited the Hong Kong dollar crisis, and the Group, along with the HongkongBank, supported the declining Hong Kong dollar to be pegged with the United States dollar at a fixed rate of HK$7.8 to US$1.0.

2. Banking in Hong Kong.   The intention of the BOC Group's banking in Hong Kong can be identified from its defined mission and is also confirmed by its senior executives. In order to maintain its competitiveness in Hong Kong, the Group has introduced many innovative banking products, including the use of ECU deposits of small denomination, fixed rate mortgage rates, telephone deposit services, preferential industrial loans, and many others. It also increased its capital so as to consolidate its presence in Hong Kong. In reviewing its banking performance of the last decade, we can see a considerable growth in the Group's business rate, an active participation in merchant banking, and growing attention to fund management and brokerage service.

3. Bridging China and the West.   There is no doubt that the BOC Group is the major source of needed foreign exchange for China's modernization. At the same time, it supports the local China-related companies by trade financing or business loans. Yet the most important role is to provide a bridge that enables Hong Kong Chinese, overseas

Chinese, and foreigners to trade and to invest in China. Sometimes the Group even puts itself in the position of teaming up with Hong Kong merchants or foreign investors to invest in China. This happened, for example, when it formed a joint venture with Hopewell Holding Co. in Shaojia Coal Fired Power Plant 'B' Station with a total investment exceeding HK$4 billion, and again when it arranged syndicated loans with other financial institutions for Shanxi Coal Exporation and Guang-dong Province Highway Network. The sister banks also act on their own behalfs, either to invest by themselves or to finance Chinese projects directly (various hotels or factories in China).

Problems

Though the BOC Group has grown tremendously over the last decade, it has also experienced many difficulties, and some of them remain unresolved. Unfortunately the Group, being a state bank of China, inherits many management problems that affect most Chinese enter-prises. A foreigner would probably see the Group as burdened by layers of bureaucracy, seriously short of technical skills and expertise, and with many of its operations continually shrouded in secrecy.[14]

Whether the Group is a politically oriented financial institution or a profit oriented commercial bank is unclear. Since most of its decision makers are sent directly from various parts of China, their connection with Hong Kong's banking circle is very weak and they lack the necessary banking skills. Thus, it is inevitable that they still like to stick to their own way — the mainland Chinese way of banking. In some cases, the 'non-experts' are leading the 'experts' which is one of the common problems that China has experienced in management. Besides, most of the Group's early locally recruited personnel came from pro-China secondary schools, and as they admit their past exposure was limited. Now many of them are employed in the Group's various managerial positions. Other recruits from the colleges may have a hard time adjusting to its system, which leads to a high turnover rate. This could be blamed on the unclear delegation of authority, thus slowing down the managerial decision process. The Group still employs tradi-tional personnel management, counting on individual loyalty rather than systematic performance appraisal.

In fact, all these problems are directly related to the present system of mainland China, but they also occur in the BOC Group. If the Group cannot stand apart from those problems, its contribution to the Chinese modernization programme will unavoidably be hindered. Therefore, localization and systematic control may be the immediate answer. As the Chairman of the Bank of China indicated during indicated The Bank of China Overseas General Managers' Conference in 1987, the organiza-tion of the BOC Group should cut down bureaucracy, effectively delegate authority, and take advantage of local talent for certain important positions of the Group.[15]

Prospects

Nevertheless, despite its political commitment, the BOC Group remains one of the major financial institutions in Hong Kong's banking scene. The public might think that the Group would take over the Hongkong-Bank's role after 1997, but this has been denied by the Chief Executive of the BOC Group Regional Office Mr Huang Diyan, who told the press that the Group had no intention of taking over the HongkongBank's role in Hong Kong's financial affairs.[16]

The Group would continue to strengthen its local position, looking for a bigger market share in retail banking and further developing the merchant banking business. The full support of the China-related companies in Hong Kong is still its main strategy for Hong Kong, along with support of the mainland development. Its active participation in every aspect of Hong Kong financial affairs can be predicted in the near future. Co-operation with the HongkongBank will be usually for stabilizing Hong Kong's financial system, implying more assurance in sailing through the 1997 transition, and benefiting everyone in the long run.

Notes

1. *Ming Pao*, 18 July 1988.
2. *Chung Yuen* (Bank of China, Internal Employee Magazine) 1987.
3. *Law Year Book of China*, (Beijing, Law Publishing House, 1987), p. 295.
4. The Bank of China, Macau Branch, formerly Nantung Bank Ltd. before 1988.
5. *Hong Kong Economic Journal*, 15 March 1987.
6. *Hong Kong Economic Journal*, 23 March 1987.
7. 'Capital Markets Survey', *Asian Finance*, 15 January 1988, pp. 14–23.
8. See note 7 above.
9. T. S. Chan, 'Management Perceptions of Marketing Effectiveness — A Study of the Bank of China Group in Hong Kong', Seminar Paper at the Chinese University of Hong Kong, 10 October 1986.
10. *The Bank of China Annual Report*, 1987, and The Office of Banking Commissioner, 1988.
11. *The Bank of China Annual Report*, 1987.
12. *Hong Kong Economic Times*, 27 January 1989.
13. *Nanyang Commercial Bank Annual Report*, 1987.
14. Kevin Hamlin, 'China's Octopus in Our Midst', *Hong Kong Business Today*, 1 December 1987.
15. *Wen Wei Po*, 24 November 1987.
16. Y. C. Jao, *Hong Kong Banking System in Transition: Problems Prospects and Policies*, (Hong Kong, Chinese Banks Association, 1988).

4. Merchant Banking

ROBERT HANEY SCOTT

MONEY changers in ancient times did business on a table, or counter, called a bank (F. banque, It. banca, G. bank, E. bench). The term 'bank' eventually came to refer to an institution that receives, lends, and safeguards money.

In modern times, however, banks do much more. There are commercial banks, merchant banks, investment banks, savings banks, and in the United States there is even a class of banks called non-bank banks! The point is that there are many different types of banking institutions that have been fashioned out of the web of legal constraints or privileges that governments impose or grant.

In modern exchange economies the management of the financial affairs of a business, or even those of an individual, can be an exacting task. It calls for specialized expertise. In a free enterprise economy such as Hong Kong's, a felt need for a service will induce suppliers of the service to come forward. That is why, in Hong Kong, all forms of financial management services are readily available, and are offered in a highly competitive marketplace.

Like other businesses, banks may offer their services in the pattern either of specialty shops or of department stores or supermarkets. Bank managers are even known to refer to their services as 'products'. One view of a supermarket is that it is a cluster of shops offering special classes of products. Today many banks, regardless of their heritage, have become department stores of financial services. Others have remained specialized.

Merchant Banking and Commercial Banking — Historical Origins

In this very brief description of the origins of merchant banking it is useful to distinguish merchant banks from commercial banks. There is a great deal of overlap in the activities of the two types of financial enterprises in today's world economy. The overlap is so great that Alan Greenspan, Chairman of the Federal Reserve Board of Governors, refers to 'universal banks' that combine commercial bank activities with those of investment banks.[1] To understand the universal banks of today it is useful to spend a few paragraphs on the origins of banking.

The Origins of Commercial Banking

Commercial banks have their early origins in the activities of merchants in the Lombard region of northern Italy at the close of the Middle Ages, around the year 1200. It was in this same period that Venice was a centre of world trade. While the merchants of Venice traded foreign currencies, financed shipping expeditions, and invented double-entry accounting, they did not become bankers. That is, they did not accept deposits of money for safekeeping as a part of their business activities. This activity was, however, a business activity in and near another city in Italy, Milan.

Although the earliest commercial banking activities may have preceded those of the warehousing of gold, it provides an archetypical example. Gold was widely used as a medium of exchange, but was easily lost to highwaymen. It needed safekeeping and the protection of a guarded vault. Merchants would deposit gold with a gold warehouse and would receive a certificate stating that the merchant had, held on deposit in his behalf, a sum of gold. It was signed by the warehouse's owner. Modern day bank issues of certificates of deposit are descendent from those of early times.

Certificates of deposit were held by many merchants. When a transaction between two merchants took place, it soon became common for one to simply turn over the certificate and write a note on the back to the owner of the warehouse saying 'please pay this gold over to ——', and then the certificate was signed by the gold's owner. Since these merchants generally knew each other, and the signatures were known, the owner of the warehouse would accommodate the merchant's request. The 'order to pay' written on the back of the certificate is the same today, except it is now on the face of a cheque.

The certificate of deposit became a 'negotiable' instrument. A financial instrument becomes negotiable when its legal ownership may be transferred by signature, as when signing over the ownership of a deposit of gold to another person. There is, in the financial world today, a huge volume of negotiable certificates of deposit issued by banks and traded on secondary markets. Furthermore, cheques are negotiable orders to pay that are signed over from bank to bank as they are cleared to provide for collection of the funds that are due. It would be impossible for a modern exchange economy to function well without the legal arrangements that provide for negotiability.

Before long it became clear to the manager of the warehouse that the gold just sat in the vault. Since merchants involved in trade simply used the certificates of deposit rather than the real gold, why not lend out some of the gold to credit-worthy merchants and earn interest to help cover the costs of safekeeping the gold? So long as the warehouse had enough gold to redeem certificates of deposit for all those who happened by, no one would ever know that the warehouse held less than enough gold to back all outstanding certificates. Confidence in the ability of the warehouse owners to repay was all that was required, and this confidence was maintained so long as the owners retained a sufficiently large fraction of gold reserves against outstanding certificates.

By issuing more certificates of deposit for gold than there was gold in the vault, the warehouse created paper gold, that is, it created money just as modern banks do. It created money in the process of receiving and lending money. It earned interest on the money it created and lent to borrowers. The business of fractional reserve banking was born.

But safeguarding deposits becomes difficult if rumours abound. Runs on banks make bankers unpopular. Cries of 'there ought to be a law' force governments to impose laws to oversee and regulate those activities involving prudential and/or fiduciary responsibilities. Banking becomes a regulated industry.

The Origins of Merchant Banking

Unlike commercial banking, which grew out of a safekeeping function, merchant banking grew from the need to finance trade. The merchants of ancient Venice were money changers but also made loans to finance shipping. Because of ecumenical laws against the charging of interest (usury), they were forced to cover up interest charges by disguising them in exchange rate calculations.

By the middle of the 1600s, Amsterdam was the centre of world trade and hence the centre of merchant banking. Before the Industrial Revolution, the large merchants were involved in world trade and colonization, so merchant banking concerned the financing of shipping ventures and trading in international exchange. But with industrialization it was the financing of manufacturers's production and sales, both domestic and foreign, that drew the services of merchant banks into play.

A manufacturer may need to borrow funds to establish a production facility and purchase an inventory of materials. If the product were to be shipped abroad, the exporter would want a guarantee of payment by being given an 'acceptance' created by a merchant bank. An acceptance simply indicates that a credit-worthy bank has accepted responsibility for the debt created by the transaction.

Thus, merchant banks became involved in arranging the financing and issuing of securities for governments, public utilities, railroads, industry, and foreign trade.

Changes in the law in the mid-1800s permitted an expanding role for the creation of joint stock companies. Trading partners could form companies and acquire limited liability. The risks in building factories were constrained. Stanley Chapman notes that 'The most enterprising exponents of what we may term the "joint-stock subsidiary"' were undoubtedly Jardine, Matheson & Co., originally a merchant house in the China trade.' He continues:

Jardine Matheson & Co. had begun to explore possibilities in banking, insurance, silk reeling, sugar refining, mining, railways and cotton mills. In thirty years or so of apparently boundless enterprise, they produced . . . varied joint-stock subsidiaries . . . In this way Jardine Matheson maintained its mercantile interests in the Far East, but developed rapidly into an investment house or (in present day terms) an investment group.[2]

Thus, investment banking activities grew out of the need to finance manufacturing and trade, and some traders and manufacturers abandoned their activities and became specialists in finance.

In more recent times consumer finance has grown in importance. Today, not only do manufacturers need their usual financing, but they also need to arrange for consumers to borrow the funds needed to purchase the goods they produce. They say to the consumer, 'Here, wouldn't you like to buy this car? And here's the money to buy it with!' One of the largest consumer finance companies in the United States is General Motors Acceptance Corporation. This institution borrows funds on the capital markets and lends them to car buyers. Thus, today there is financing available at every stage of the economic process.

It is important to recognize that in all of the description of the activities of merchant banks there has been no mention of money creation. Merchant banks do not create money unless they have extended their activities so as to engage in commercial banking as well.

The Commercial Loan Theory of Banking

If banks permit their reserves to fall to very low levels, they may grant many loans, and in the process create lots of money. If they create too much money there will be inflation (too much money chasing too few goods). If they create too little money there will be a depression (too little money chasing too many goods).

Because commercial banks generally play a role in the money-creating business, governments feel a need to maintain some control over them in addition to the control necessary to ensure that they carry out their fiduciary responsibility to the depositing public. The question governments face is, what kind of controls are appropriate?

The answer, held by economists for a hundred years prior to the Great Depression of the 1930s, was found in the Commercial Loan Theory of Banking — sometimes called the 'real bills' doctrine. According to this theory, banks should expand loans to meet the needs of trade, that is, to finance inventories of real goods. Thus, if the crop was bountiful, banks should make loans to finance the farmer's harvest, the miller's wheat, and the baker's flour — real goods in process. The sale of the goods to the next stage of production, and finally to the consumer, would serve to repay the loans the banks had made. And the amount of money created would meet the needs of trade. Loans backed by real goods were both secure and appropriate for trade. Commercial banks were restricted to commercial lending.

The problem with this theory, it turns out, is that in boom times the banks pour money into the economy, causing an inflationary spiral, and in recessions they stop lending and cause depression. Economies would repeatedly swing from financial panic to depression to inflation and panic again. According to the Commercial Loan Theory, panics were supposed to be controlled by a central bank that would reduce bank reserves by setting high discount rates (bank rates) for loans to banks *prior to the development of inflationary conditions*. Lacking the ability to foretell the future, although one would never know it by their bearing, central bankers always played catch-up. Like shutting the barn door after the horse was gone, central bankers would cut off reserve credits after the panic, not before. This resulted in the world-wide depression of the 1930s.

The Great Depression brought on bank failures by the hundreds. The response of government, in the United States especially, was to legislate the clear separation between commercial banks and investment banks. Investments in factories, real estate, construction, trading ventures, and so on, were all too risky and speculative and likely to fail. They should not be part of a bank's business. So, let investment groups finance these risky activities only with their own capital, not with the savings of the depositing public. That was the attitude of the public and it was reflected in the actions taken by legislators.

Commercial banks in the United States were not allowed to underwrite sales of securities or own shares of companies or real estate (except for their own office buildings), and so forth.

The Securities Exchange Commission was established by the United States Federal Government in 1934 to set disclosure standards for the issue of shares to investors and to regulate trading in securities. The Federal Reserve was instructed to establish rules and regulate the extent to which individuals could use borrowed money for investment in securities. So, investment bankers (merchant banks) found themselves swimming in a sea of regulation that they had not experienced before.

Over the past forty years the regulations that separated investment banking from commercial banking have worn away. The morphology of banking in the United States has undergone dramatic change since the enactment of the Depository Institutions Deregulation and Monetary Control Act of 1980, and the Garn-St Germain bill of 1982.

The merchant banks of Britain, West Germany, Switzerland, and other west European countries have not been subjected to such traumatic changes because their activities were not arbitrarily split apart to begin with. Foreign banks with branches located in Hong Kong are not restricted in their activities as they are when they operate in the United States. In Hong Kong they can enter into competition with existing financial intermediaries in any of the wide ranges of financing activities in which they have the appropriate expertise. Except for the obligation to operate under Hong Kong's three-tier system, as described in Chapter 1, they can either be 'universal banks' or specialized institutions.[3]

Merchant Banking Today

Because of the extensive diversification of financing activities that merchant banks engage in today, it is impossible to discuss more than a few of them in these pages. Merchant banks may act both as brokers and as dealers in a wide variety of securities. Income is earned on the spread between the purchase price and the sale price. They may provide research services and give consultation on all varieties of management problems that are caused by financial concerns. For advice and information they will charge fees. They trade money market instruments such as certificates of deposit. They stand willing to underwrite the debt issues of government and manage the sale of corporate debt and stock. They may serve as agents for corporations as trustees to handle the payment of dividends to shareholders, and they may maintain a register of owners of shares to use for mailing official notices. They handle mergers, acquisitions, divestitures, interest rate swaps, leveraged buy-outs, and other fee-earning activities. To the extent that they participate in syndicated loans, they may earn interest on their own capital investments and realize capital gains if shares they purchase should rise in value. And they may establish joint-stock subsidiaries and, indirectly through them, operate production facilities. They may issue credit cards.

Leveraged Buy-Outs

In a leveraged buy-out, a group of the firm's managers may arrange to borrow money, essentially by pledging the assets of the firm as collateral, and then using the borrowed funds to buy the firm's shares. Shares are then held by only a few people and the firm becomes privately held rather than publicly held. (It is the reverse of the situation when managers of a growing firm decide it is appropriate to 'go public', that is, sell shares in the firm to raise funds to finance expansion.)

Raiders from outside the firm, rather than the firm's own managers, may initiate the buy-out.

The funds used to purchase the outstanding shares of stock may be borrowed from banks initially, but are most often borrowed by arranging for an issue of 'junk bonds', that is, bonds that are high-interest bearing and low-rated for quality. Such bond sales are arranged by investment banking firms.

Several effects on the firm's financial status follow from a leveraged buy-out. First, shareholders in the marketplace are offered high prices for their shares of ownership. A raider will purchase a supply of shares and then declare a leveraged buy-out and receive huge capital gains as the price of shares rises. Borrowed money is used to pay the shareholders high prices for their holdings, and this potential for substantial gain pleases existing shareholders. They generally tend not to fight against such a takeover of a firm because of substantial capital gains.

Second, the firm's debt-to-equity ratio increases. Since more of the firm's assets are being financed by debt, and less by equity, there is less of an equity cushion to be absorbed by shareholders in case the firm's earnings should decline. Existing bondholders, those existing prior to the buy-out, find that their bonds fall in value to equal that of the new issues of junk-bonds.

Thus, in the event of a leveraged buy-out, existing shareholders realize capital gains and bondholders suffer capital losses.

Third, because of the higher debt burden, the firm's interest payments take up a much larger part of net income. Fixed obligations allegedly force managers to prune expenses and run a tighter, more efficient, ship than they would have without the buy-out. Frills are no longer be allowed — they can't be afforded.

Fourth, tax laws treat interest as an expense but do not treat dividends as an expense. Thus, the firm realizes some tax saving as a result of the increase in the debt-to-equity ratio.

A company which already has a high debt-to-equity ratio is not a candidate for a buy-out.

It is easy to see that the activities and arrangements involved in a leveraged buy-out would require the expertise of an investment banker.

Widespread use of leveraged buy-outs in the United States in recent years has led to many criminal prosecutions for allegedly violating laws against trading on inside information. Once a group starts taking the first steps toward a buy-out, some individuals in the investment community are bound to learn of the plan. Since the knowledge of the plan is kept confidential, the opportunity opens up to the few who are on the inside. This creates a great temptation to buy some of the shares in the market and wait for the announcement to push up the price of the shares. The person who sells shares to the insider has no information and no opportunity to have the information that the insider is privy to. Thus, the seller of shares has a legitimate complaint.

In this author's view, the problem has its source in the existence of secrecy rather in the trading of inside information: it would be better to expand the requirements for immediate disclosure of plans for buy-outs than it is to create an unstable secret situation that creates temptation for insiders and simultaneously threatens them with criminal charges. The issues regarding the fairness of the markets for securities are complex and cannot be discussed here. Again, however, knowledge of the law as well as of the financial questions involving leveraged buy-outs requires the kind of expert advice that merchant bankers make available to their clients.

Swap Agreements: Interest Rate Swaps and Currency Swaps

In the 1960s, significant advances ere made by academics who studied in the field of finance. They formulated an approach to the measurement of risk. This led to an understanding of the premium that a borrower must pay in order to compensate for risk where risk is measured by the *variation* in the rate of return to an asset or portfolio of assets. Holding other factors constant, the lower the variation in the returns to an asset the higher its value will be. The risk-return relation had always been a subjective element in financing decisions, but now it has become a formal aspect of financial advising.

If risk can be reduced, the value of the firm will be increased. If both parties to a swap can reduce the variation in rates of return on their assets, then both parties benefit. Interest rate swap agreements that allowed both parties to benefit were first introduced into the Eurobond market in early 1982.

Merchant bankers with many business clients recognized that some clients had interest payment liabilities that varied widely over time, while the stream of earnings from their assets was quite steady from year to year. Others had fixed interest payment liabilities but returns from assets that varied widely from year to year. This situation sets the stage for a mutually beneficial swap of interest payment liabilities.

Applying this general frame of reference, consider the differing asset and liability structure of a pair of firms, A and B. A graphic representation of their balance sheets is shown in Fig. 4.1.

Fig. 4.1 Differing Types of Asset and Liability Structure

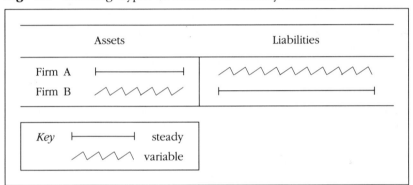

Year by year firm A has steady earnings from its assets as indicated by the straight line. However, interest payments on its liabilities fluctuate widely year by year as indicated by the jagged line. The pattern is the opposite for firm B. If firm A were to assume the straight line pattern of interest liabilities then both its assets and its liabilities would show steadiness. The year to year *variation* in returns to the firm's owners would be reduced, that is, risk would be reduced and this would increase the firm's value.

So the question is, would firm B be willing to trade its steady flow of interest payments on its fixed interest payment obligations with firm A? If the managers of firm B take a close look at the *pattern* of fluctuation in the interest payments on A's liabilities, and if the pattern matches the pattern of returns that it expects to receive, then a swap would leave firm B with the same pattern on both assets and liabilities. For B, earnings on assets would fluctuate in line with its interest expenses. Net returns to the owners of firm B would vary less from year to year.

In this example, the average net earnings for both firms need not change, but the fluctuation in these net earnings would be reduced, and this reduction in risk should improve the prices of shares of both firms. As in all commercial transactions that are freely entered into in a competitive marketplace, both participants in the transaction benefit.

Firm A is said to have 'rate-sensitive liabilities' and firm B is said to have 'rate-sensitive assets'. See Chapter 8, especially Table 8.5, for a description of an interest rate swap that benefits both firms because one firm has good access to floating-rate loans and the other has access to fixed-rate loans. They agree to borrow funds in the market and then swap the interest liabilities. It should be noted that the principals are *not* swapped — only the streams of interest payments.

Needless to say, the details of interest rate swap agreements become quite complicated quite rapidly, and each case must be treated individually. Furthermore, it is nearly impossible for one firm to find another firm whose cash flows meet the criteria for a mutually beneficial agreement. For these reasons investment bankers arrange swap agreements.

Besides understanding the need for similar patterns in the variable cash flows, bankers take care to ensure that the maturity (or the duration) is the same for both of the obligations that are swapped.

There is usually a need to decide on a basic interest rate, such as the United States Treasury bill rate, or the London Inter-bank Offered Rate (LIBOR), or the Hong Kong Inter-bank Offered Rate (HIBOR), as a basis or index for the contract. For example, the contract may call for firm B to pay firm A interest at a variable rate of 0.5 per cent above the HIBOR.

An investment bank may make the arrangements for the swap to occur prior to the time any borrowing takes place. For example, some borrowers are better equipped to borrow floating- or variable-rate funds and others are better equipped to borrow fixed-rate funds. Each firm may enter the market where it can get the best rate and simultaneously swap the contracts with each other. In effect they borrow for each other.

It is quite common for the investment bank to act as the collector and disburser of funds to both firms. Indeed, each of the firms may contract with the bank itself so that the firms need not contract directly with each other. Creditworthiness of the parties to the swap may be evaluated by the bank and the contract with the bank may involve some extension of the bank's backing for one or the other party.

For all of these services the bank will charge fees. For example, a fee may be 0.5 per cent of the face value of the agreement at the time the swap is executed. Since, in essence, it is not engaged in either borrowing or lending, it has no opportunity to obtain some kind of interest earnings as it would if it were to be an investor in a firm.

It is also possible that firms could swap assets with each other, especially if these assets are financial assets rather than plant and equipment. However, given contracts for leasing equipment, and so forth, a large variety of differing arrangements may present itself.

Swap agreements such as those described above are sometimes called debt swaps. In many instances the swap of debt obligations may also involve a swap of currencies in which the debt obligations are denominated. For example, a Hong Kong firm, firm A in the example, may owe a stream of payments in yen to a Japanese firm. This stream is bound to rise and fall in value along with the foreign exchange value of the yen. Another Hong Kong export firm, firm B, may have an asset that brings in a stream of yen which will vary with the value of the yen. Firm A could offer firm B a steady stream of Hong Kong dollar revenues in exchange for firm B accepting A's debt in yen. Firm B will be willing to accept this debt because then its payments in yen will match its receipts of yen. Of course, hedging against fluctuations in the value of foreign currencies can be accomplished in the futures and options markets as well.[4]

The market for swap contracts developed extensively during the 1980s, and there now exists the International Swap Dealers Association. It has developed a standard contract and code of terms that can be used in documentation of swap agreements. The global swap market is now entrenched as a major market for the reduction of risk.

Syndicated Loans and Underwriting

Loan syndication is one of the oldest activities of merchant bankers. Projects that require large capital investments nearly always require syndication. Even if one firm is able to finance an entire project its managers will choose not to because, like all investors, they know that it is desirable to diversify risk. It is customary for investment banks to take a piece of a loan, rather than the entire package.

Legal regulations in the United States limit the extent to which a commercial bank or a savings and loan institution can lend to a single individual or company. These limitations do not apply to investment banks, but prudence dictates that loans be spread among groups of investors. Correspondent relations have grown among investment groups and are carried on informally. But formal contractual relations regarding the issuing of bonds and other financing instruments prevail. Financial difficulties can arise in many ways, especially when several parties are involved.[5]

Mergers, Acquisitions, and Divestitures

Managers of business firms know that the outlook for the firm's future net cash inflows changes every few weeks. It is desirable, therefore, to keep a lookout for opportunities for changes that will enhance the firm's profit position. Often opportunities arise that lead to decisions to abandon operations of a plant or factory. Abandonment may involve selling for scrap or selling to a competitor, or even a supplier, or perhaps someone who has an alternative use for the equipment or the site.

An analysis of cash flows may indicate that replacement of equipment involves an upgrade of quality that requires expensive financing. A look around leads to the discovery that new equipment could be acquired just as efficiently by purchasing an existing firm that already has the equipment in place and operating. Firms may expand into new market areas, which is called horizontal expansion. Or, they may expand vertically by acquiring a supplier or a customer.

Both horizontal and vertical expansion may also occur through the merger of one firm with another. Mergers may take place, however, even if the expansion is not horizontal or vertical. Many firms may merge with others that are in an entirely different line of business. When such mergers take place it is called forming a conglomerate. Conglomerates were popular when financial managers emphasized that firms whose rates of return varied in opposite directions could merge and realize a reduction in risk. Swap agreements, discussed above, could be replaced by a merger if the two firms were agreeable. If both firms could benefit from a swap agreement, they might benefit from a merger as well. Managers rely on the expertise of merchant bankers to help them sort out the many pros and cons of such complicated financing arrangements.

Other Consulting Activities

Merchant banks advise business firms on a wide variety of financing decision making. For example, firms doing business in different countries must be sensitive to tax laws in those countries in order to ensure that no more taxes than required need be paid. There are different classes of common stock that can be issued by a firm. Some portion of the stock may have voting rights while another may have limited voting rights or none at all. Thus, control over the firm's management may depend on the decision made when the stock is first made public.

Merchant Banking and Deposit-taking Companies

As described in Chapter 1, there is in Hong Kong a three-tier system of deposit-taking authorization: banks, licensed deposit-taking companies, and registered deposit-taking companies. Approval was obtained in 1989 for enhancing the status of Licenced Deposit-taking Companies (LDTC). This senior category of deposit-taking company will be renamed 'Restricted Licensed Banks' (RLBs). These institutions will be permitted to describe themselves as 'investment' or 'merchant banks'. The commissioner of banking may permit other descriptions but not 'retail' or 'commercial bank'. Banks from overseas with names that include the word 'bank' will be permitted to use their name in connection with a branch, but will be required to indicate prominently that they are 'restricted licensed banks'.

Registered Deposit-taking Companies (RDTCs) will no longer be required to use the term 'registered' in their names.

In future, therefore, the three-tier banking system will consist of banks, restricted licensed banks, and deposit-taking companies. According to the 1989 Annual Report of the Banking Commission, 'One of the strongest criticisms of the present system was by DTCs, concerned that their standing was not understood internationally by those unfamiliar with the Hong Kong arrangements.' The new system is scheduled for implementation in 1990.

The Hong Kong Government also takes care to follow international guide-lines set by the Basle Committee on measures and minimum levels of capital for international banks (capital adequacy ratios). The minimum capital adequacy ratio is to be raised to 8 per cent by the end of 1992 in order to conform to the international standards.

International banking authorities have taken considerable strides in recent years to set uniform banking standards across international boundaries. Given the internationalization of banking activities, these uniform standards are desirable not only for prudential reasons but also to provide fair rules for all banking competitors to operate under. In a highly regulated industry, one country giving special privileges and a competitive advantage to its institutions will attract business from another. The governments of Hong Kong and Singapore have, at times, directly responded to each other's regulations in the banking field, especially in regard to taxation matters.

Data on Size and Profitability

Merchant banks in Asia find their recent balance sheets and income statements studied and compared each year by journalists who report in *Asia Finance*. The ninth annual study published in its 15 March 1990 issue dealt with 157 merchant banks in Hong Kong, Singapore, Malaysia, the Philippines, and Korea. Many of these banks were, of course, subsidiaries of banks in Japan, the United States, Canada, England, and other countries. Out of this 157, the top 6 in terms of return on equity for the year 1988 were Paribas Asia, BT Asia, United Merchants Finance, First Chicago Hong Kong, Citicorp International, and Jardine Fleming Holdings.

Return on equity is a useful measure to those who own part of a merchant bank. Perhaps of greater interest to those who expect to do business with a commercial bank is the bank's size as expressed in the dollar value of total assets. In 1988 Wardley had assets of over US$6 billion, followed by Dresdner SEA with US$2.7 billion, Daiwa Securities (HK) with US$1.8 billion, and Hang Seng Finance with US$1.7 billion which was the equal of Nomura International (HK).

The problem with the reporting of rankings using financial ratios is that they may cover up more information than they reveal. The five banks listed with the lowest return on equity nevertheless had equity returns that were 15 times greater than their returns on assets. Results such as these could easily have followed from activities in which services to clients were offered at low costs. If the services were satisfactory, then such firms would be good sources of low cost services.

Hong Kong Dollar Debt

As of 7 August 1989 the total volume of Hong Kong dollar fixed interest rate debt in circulation was estimated to be HK$25,919 million.[6] Of this amount, some 43 per cent was due to mature within 2 years. Some 75 per cent was due to mature within 3 years. Only 6 per cent had a maturity that exceeded 10 years. The supply of debt is less than market traders would like.

Political uncertainty plays a role in determining how much debt local corporations will issue. After the troubles in June 1989, the number of new issues per month increased to 12 in July from a typical 3 per month before June. There was also an increase in the number of debt issues in the wake of the crash of the stock-market in October 1987.

In April 1989, the World Bank borrowed in Hong Kong, and in 1990 the Government issued its Exchange Fund Bills which are described in Chapter 13. It is generally believed that the market would work more efficiently if a larger supply of Hong Kong dollar denominated fixed-rate debt securities were made available. The Government has been urged to issue a medium-term bond simply to satisfy the needs for a liquid security that traders could use as a base for hedges.[7]

Summary

As the years go by, there is bound to be a continuation of the development of new ways of financing industrial and commercial activities. Innovation in financing will surely emanate from the merchant banking industry. Readers may keep abreast of developments as they are reported in *The Securities Bulletin, Asia Finance*, and *Asia-money*.

Perhaps the two most important developments in merchant banking that have taken place over the past 20 years are the increased competition from the entry of commercial banking firms into the activities of merchant banks and the internationalization of the financial industry that is principally the result of the internationalization of merchant banking activities. Branches of commercial banks that set up shop in other countries do so principally *not* to engage in deposit taking from the typical customer off the street, but to deal with large corporate or business accounts and arrange financing deals.

In general, large commercial banking firms now offer not only commercial banking services but also merchant banking services. Whereas merchant banks have retained their specialities in arranging financing, only rarely have they turned their attention to competition in the field of services generally reserved for the commercial banks.

That world capital markets have become more and more integrated seems to follow directly from technological innovation in communication that has shrunk the size of the world. Wire transfer of funds around the world twenty-four hours a day means that trading in securities is a continuous process. The location of Hong Kong and its time zone make it a natural transfer point as the trading day passes from New York to Tokyo and on to London. It is the merchant banks along with the exchanges such as the futures markets and foreign exchange markets that keep world financing in progress all day long. Merchant banks are principal players in maintaining the linkage from one domestic financial market to another around the world.

Notes

1. See p. 8 of Mr Greenspan's speech, cited in the references.
2. See p. 142 of Chapman's book, *The Rise of Merchant Banking*, cited in the references.
3. One of the concerns in the United States is that financial power not be permitted to become excessive. Indeed, the heritage of the American Revolution is that power should be divided as in the separation of powers in the branches of government, that there should be no aristocracy, that business trusts are illegal, and so on. It follows that a concentration of financial power is also viewed with suspicion, and, as Mr. Greenspan notes in his remarks on p. 8 of the citation in the references, if there were greater concentration of market power it would increase the cost of capital to the economy as a whole, and threaten economic growth.
4. In Ribeiro's chapter on swaps, he notes that the first widely publicized swap agreement was in 1983 when the World Bank and IBM agreed that IBM would service $175 million of World Bank's long-term dollar debt and the World Bank would service IBM's long-term Swiss franc debt. (See reference citation, p. 340.)
5. See the discussion of the difficulties that arose among three banks when an expansion project ran into trouble on p. 28 of Scott, Wong, and Ho in the reference section. The example there is true, but details were completely changed to retain anonymity.
6. Reported in a feature article by Patrick K. Thomas, 'The Hong Kong Capital Market: Life after Tiananmen Square', *The Securities Bulletin*, No. 41, September, 1989, p. 24.
7. See note 6 above.References

References

Chapman, Stanley, *The Rise of Merchant Banking* (London, George Allen & Unwin, 1984). Unlike histories of individual merchant banks, many of which are cited here, this volume deals with the history of merchant banking as a sector of finance that is important to both the national and international economy. The time period of reference is from the eighteenth century to World War I.

Effros, Robert C. (ed.), *Emerging Financial Centers* (Washington, DC, International Monetary Fund, 1982), pp. 95–114.

Fraser, Donald R. and Kolari, James W., *The Future of Small Banks in a Deregulated Environment* (Cambridge, Mass., Ballinger Publishing Company, 1985).

Greenspan, Alan, 'Commercial Banks and the Central Bank in a Market Economy', *Economic Review*, Federal Reserve Bank of Kansas City, November 1989, pp. 3–13. These are the published remarks made in a speech in Moscow, U.S.S.R., on 10 October 1989. Mr Greenspan describes 'universal banking' as a combination of commercial and investment banking that is found in West Germany, Switzerland, and other countries.

Kuhn, Robert Lawrence, *Investment Banking: The Art and Science of High-Stakes Dealmaking*, (New York, Harper & Row, 1990).

Pauly, Louis W., *Opening Financial Markets: Banking Politics on the Pacific Rim*, (Ithaca, New York, Cornell University Press, 1988). This volume contains a brief discussion of the takeover by the Hongkong and Shangahi Banking Corporation of the Marine Midland Bank in the United States (no relation to Midland Bank of Britain) in 1978. The book describes financial markets in the United States, Japan, Australia, Canada, and developments in western Europe, but does not describe those of Hong Kong or Singapore.

Ribeiro, Frank, 'Currency Swaps', Chapter 14 in Poniachek, Harvey A., (ed.) *International Corporate Finance*, (Boston, Unwin Hyman Inc., 1989). Fourteen contributors wrote chapters for this volume.

Scott, Robert Haney, K. A. Wong, and Yan Ki Ho (eds.), *Hong Kong's Financial Institutions and Markets* (Hong Kong, Oxford University Press, 1986).

Skully, Michael T., *Merchant Banking in the Far East* (London, Financial Times Business Publishing, second edition, 1980).

—— *Merchant Banking in ASEAN* (Kuala Lumpur, Oxford University Press, 1983).

5. The Regulatory Framework of the Banking Sector

RICHARD YAN-KI HO

THIS chapter deals with the regulatory framework of the Hong Kong banking sector. In almost all countries, financial markets, particularly banking institutions, usually belong to the most heavily regulated sector of the economy. There are generally two broad categories of regulation. The first is imposed by the government or by some monetary authority. Then the regulations are spelled out explicitly and rigidly as laws, and the regulated firms have to fulfil certain requirements as stated in the legal documents. Sometimes regulations are more subtle and the regulated firms observe informal rules which are laid down by the authority simply because they respect the authority as a regulatory agency. The European tradition of banking regulation falls in the former category, while the British tradition falls in the latter (at least before the enactment of the 1979 Banking Act). The second category of regulation is self-imposed by firms in the same industry, for example, interest rate cartels and agreements. Although self-imposed regulations are not initiated by the government, they can be treated as government-endorsed (informally or formally) because the government always has power to enact legislation to dismantle cartels or agreements. Thus, the existence of self-imposed regulations may be the result of the government's willingness to accept them as 'regulations' in order to achieve certain objectives. This chapter will explain briefly the rationale for regulation in general, and for regulating the banking sector in particular. The development and evolution of the regulatory process of the Hong Kong banking sector will then be discussed in detail. First, however, a brief introduction to the theories of regulation is in order.

Theories of Regulation

Several bodies of theory related to regulations are summarized here.

The Theory of Public Interest

Basic economic textbooks usually tell us that the market mechanism or the 'invisible hand' always leads to the most efficient allocation of resources. Thus, an unfettered market with unrestrained entry and exit is all it takes for proper functioning of the market, including the financial market. However, inefficient market practices may result from

monopolies or other externalities. Since such inefficiency is not beneficial to the general public, the government 'supplies' regulations to
correct such anomalies.

The Capture Theory

This theory asserts that regulators, as suppliers of regulations, do not
act in the public interest. Rather, they are captured by, and operate in
accordance with, various interest groups who seek to maximize their
own wealth by controlling the regulators.

Stigler's Theory of Regulation

According to Professor Stigler (1971), a Nobel prize laureate in
Economics, there is a market for regulation, which is seen as a right
to tax the wealth of those in the non-regulated group. There is a group
demanding regulations that can increase their wealth. There is another
group that can supply regulations. The suppliers are the politicians who
seek political support by supplying regulations desired by voters.

The Dynamic Theory of Regulation

While both the Capture Theory and Stigler's Theory assume that regulators are sympathetic to the regulated because the number of the
regulated is small with a lower co-ordinating cost than that of the
general mass of consumers, Joskow (1974) asserts that there is a
dynamic interaction between regulators, consumers, and the regulated.
According to Joskow, regulators usually have two behaviour modes. The
first is the equilibrium mode, in which the regulators behave passively
as long as they believe that there is an appropriate balance or equilibrium between the regulated firms and the consumers. However, if
there is an unbearable imbalance or disequilibrium between the firms
and the consumers, the regulators will switch to the innovative mode
and search for new techniques to restore equilibrium.

An extension of the Dynamic Theory is the 'regulatory dialectic'. This
concept is proposed by Kane (1977), who asserts that regulations
change the behaviour of regulated firms because they employ methods
to bypass the imposed constraints. Sooner or later, the regulations
become no longer binding. Such a non-restraining environment coupled
with a particular economic situation induces a financial crisis. As chaotic
conditions are not acceptable to regulators, they establish new
regulations to cope with the new conditions. However, firms always
find ways to get around the new regulations, and the cycle of
regulations–innovations–crisis–regulations continues. Kane's regulatory
dialectic seems to be able to explain the regulatory process of most
countries, and there is no doubt that we will find it useful in explaining
Hong Kong's own regulatory process.

Justification for Regulating the Financial Market

Economies of Scale

Regulations are justified if the market cannot function properly without them. If substantial economies of scale existed, large banks would dominate the market. Small banks would find it difficult, if not impossible, to enter the market. Less competition would result, and the allocation of resources would be less than optimal. For this reason, some may argue that regulation is needed to maintain a competitive environment. However, according to United States evidence, economies of scale in banking seem to lose their effectiveness at a relatively small size (at around US$10 million to US$23 million). Therefore, this does not constitute a strong justification for regulation.

Information

If the free market is to function properly, information must be freely available. Depositors and other fund suppliers must have access to information on the assets, liabilities, and capital structure of the bank. Moreover, the riskiness of such items must also be known. Thus, depositors will be able to judge whether their returns are commensurate with the risk incurred.

However, the functioning of the information market is not perfect. First, information has the nature of public goods. The provision of one specific set of bank information to an individual does not preclude another individual from consuming that information. Moreover, the consumption of data by one individual does not deplete or invalidate its contents. According to economic theories of public goods, there would be an under-production (less than the optimal level) of information on bank activities. Government regulations are thus needed to facilitate the optimal production of information.

Moreover, there also exist economies of scale in the production and interpretation of information. An individual depositor may not have the techniques to digest all the sophisticated financial data available. Some of the more relevant bank information, such as the management style, quality, and integrity of the senior executives and owners, is also qualitative in nature. Such information cannot not easily be made available in a readily digestible and accurate form for general public consumption. Again, this justifies the introduction of government regulations, but it is not unique to financial firms. Information disclosure for non-financial corporations can also be justified on these grounds.

Contractual and Agency Problems

While the aforementioned considerations certainly justify regulation, they cannot explain why financial firms, particularly banking firms, need to be more heavily regulated than non-financial firms. The issue of agency and contractual relationships may provide an explanation.

In a developed exchange economy, transactions are usually facilitated by contracts that specify the obligations and benefits of the parties to the transaction. If one party does not honour the contractual relationship, he or she will be penalized by the other party through legal actions. Of course, fraudulent activities can also occur but they are not usually so wide-spread as to dismantle the whole contractual system. If they were, nobody would transact any business and the whole market economy would collapse. In the context of a banking market, the depositor and the banking firm are the two parties involved, and the deposit account is the contract. If the deposit is a demand deposit, the depositor has the right to withdraw the face value of the funds on demand. If the deposit is a time deposit, the depositor can also get back the face value of the deposit under certain conditions as specified in the deposit contract.

Another important point to note is that the deposit contract is actually an agency contract. The banking firm is not the ultimate user of funds but serves as an agent for the depositor to channel his funds to the borrower. In this connection, another problem of the information market arises. This is the problem of uneven availability of information to the banking firm and to the depositor. The banking firm has accurate knowledge about its financial activities, but the depositor is usually poorly informed. This may cause the expropriation of wealth from one party (the poorly informed) to another party (the well-informed). In a regulation-free environment, the depositor is well aware that the performance of the banking firm (the agent) is practically unmonitored. Under such circumstances, the agency contract is structured to allow the depositor to withdraw from the agreement whenever he or she detects any problem that the bank may have encountered. If a large number of depositors act in this way, the bank is facing a bank run.

External Diseconomies of Bank Failures

Of course, the failure of only one bank or a run on only one bank should not be of genuine concern to the government. There is, though, the possibility that a single failure may trigger depositors of other banks to run on their own banks because of imperfect information. This phenomenon is commonly referred to as 'external diseconomies'. There is ample historical evidence in Hong Kong, as well as in other western countries, to indicate that wide-spread panic occurs during banking crises and some safe institutions may be run unjustifiably.[1]

Macroeconomic Concerns

People may still argue that the government may not need to intervene even though there is industry-wide repercussion. Should regulations be introduced to govern the restaurant industry when the general public loses confidence in eating out? Obviously, the answer is no. One major difference between banking firms and other firms (including financial firms) that makes them subject to heavier regulation is the nature of their liabilities. The bulk of banks' liabilities is its deposits, which are highly liquid assets to the depositors. The deposit with the highest liquidity is, of course, the demand deposit, which can be used directly as a medium of payment and can immediately be converted into real purchasing power. Although other deposits, such as savings deposits and time deposits, are less liquid than demand deposits, they also can be readily converted either into cash or demand deposits, and have an impact on the economy. That is why in most countries bank deposits are counted as money supply. Thus, an expansion of bank liabilities would cause the economy to expand, while a decrease in bank liabilities would cause it to contract. A wide-spread bank run means a very rapid conversion of deposit money into cash-in-hand for the general public. This would cause a rapid contraction of the money supply and hence a drastic contraction in the economy. It is this macroeconomic disturbance caused by bank failures that justifies such heavy regulations and the associated costs.

Forms of Regulations

Edwards (1981) maintained that:

there are two regulatory objectives that must remain firm if we are to have financial and economic stability. First, central banks must have the power to control 'money' or to control relevant monetary aggregates; and second, the solvency of financial institutions in general, and especially that of banks, must be assured by appropriate regulatory safeguards. Economic stability is not compatible with widespread bank failures and 'bank panics' nor with untempered cyclical swings in the money supply.[2]

Thus regulations usually fall into two forms: macroeconomic controls and microeconomic controls or prudential supervision. Macroeconomic controls aim at maintaining stable monetary conditions, while prudential supervision aims at maintaining a safe and sound banking system.

Monetary controls include liquid asset ratios, open market operations, discount operations, central bank lending, and quantitative limits on bank lending.

There are various forms of regulation aiming at the objectives of prudential supervision.[3] They can be grouped into several categories according to the experience of various countries:

1. Entry Control.   This includes the licensing of financial firms by minimum capital size and other non-quantitative standards such as the number of years in operation and relation with the host country. This kind of regulation has existed for a long time in Hong Kong.

2. Price Control.   This includes the control of interest rates paid on deposits or charged on loans, that is, pricing control of assets and liabilities. Deposit rate control is the most common form of price regulation. It can be in the form of a formal, government-imposed

interest rate ceiling or an interest rate cartel. In Hong Kong, this control is in the form of an interest rate agreement between licensed banks.

3.   Product Line Control.   This includes the prohibition of certain types of products such as accepting certain types of deposits, extending certain types of loans, and undertaking other non-banking business. Forbidding DTCs to accept short-term deposits is an example of product line control in Hong Kong. In the United States and Japan, commercial banks are still forbidden to do investment banking business.

4.   Ratio Control.   This usually includes a minimum level of ratio constraint such as the liquid asset to total assets ratio and the capital to total assets ratio control. The purpose of this control is to maintain a sound banking system, as well as to restrain the size of the system. Hong Kong has had a liquid asset ratio constraint for some time but the capital ratio, which has long been employed in the United States and some European countries,[4] has only been recently adopted in Hong Kong.

5.   Other Qualitative Controls.   These include examining the quality and integrity of the top exectives, the adaptability of the management to both outside and inside shocks,[5] management style, the operating procedure for granting loans, and so on. While this type of regulation was not common in Hong Kong, regulators have found it increasingly crucial for an efficient supervision system.

6.   Quantitative Control.   This involves constraining the size of the balance sheet, and is usually imposed on the absolute size of the total loans as was the case in the United Kingdom in the 1950s and 1960s. Hong Kong does not have this form of regulation.

7.   Geographical Area Regulation.   This involves the prohibition of operation outside a firms' geographical area. The purpose of this regula-tion is to avoid an over-concentration of banks. Hong Kong does not have this control.

The Development of the Regulatory Framework in Hong Kong

The evolution of the regulatory framework in Hong Kong is a clear manifestation of both Kane's regulatory dialectic and the Capture Theory of regulation. All the banking ordinances were enacted after a series of crises and some of the structural regulations, such as the three-tier system and the interest rate cartel, are the result of protecting one or another of the interested parties.

Before the enactment of the Banking Ordinance of 1964, banking regulation was almost non-existant. In the Banking Ordinance of 1948, the definition of banking was very vague and there was no liquidity requirement. In 1961, there was a run on a family-owned local bank, the Liu Chong Hing Bank. There were two main reasons for this run. The first was a liquidity squeeze in the market because of a large volume of new issues. The second and most important reason was that the Liu Chong Hing Bank had invested too heavily in the property market and had competed too aggressively in the deposit market. That bank run stimulated the Government in 1962 to invite an expert from the Bank of England, Mr H. J. Tomkins, to advise them on banking regulations in Hong Kong. The famous Tomkins Report resulted, and some of the recommendations in that report formed the blueprint for the Banking Ordinance of 1964.

There are several crucial points in the Banking Ordinance of 1964 that laid the foundations for the current regulations:

(a) Entry requirement: a minimum capital requirement of HK$5 million was established.
(b) Ratio requirement: a minimum liquidity ratio of 25 per cent was established.
(c) Information disclosure: all locally incorporated banks were required to publish their annual reports.
(d) Regulatory authority: the Office of The Commissioner of Banking was formed. The Commissioner grants licences and can inspect bank accounts.

However, the Banking Ordinance did not have time to take effect before another banking crisis occurred in 1965. Two problem banks, the Ming Tak Bank and the Canton Trust and Commercial Bank, were taken over by the Government and were later liquidated because of heavy lending to the property sector and fraud. The panic spread to other local banks including the Hang Seng Bank, the Far East Bank, the Kwong On Bank, and the Dao Heng Bank. In order to stop the panic, both the Hongkong and Shanghai Banking Corporation and the Standard Chartered Bank extended unlimited support for banks that encountered problems. In fact, 51 per cent of the capital of the Hang Seng Bank, the largest local Chinese Bank, was later acquired by the Hongkong and Shanghai Banking Corporation.

After the 1965 crisis, the Banking Ordinance was amended in 1967 to increase the power of the Commissioner and to raise the minimum capital requirement from HK$5 million to HK$10 million.

In the 1980s a series of more serious crises occurred, leading to a basic change in the banking regulations in Hong Kong.[6]

In 1982, a bank run occurred on the Hang Lung Bank, which was then taken over by the Hong Kong Government in 1983. A serious crisis also occurred in the DTC sector in early 1983 when seven DTCs failed, leading to a big loss for the depositors. This shook the confidence of depositors very badly. Later, in 1985, the Overseas Trust Bank also became insolvent and was taken over by the Government. A subsidiary of the Overseas Trust Bank, the Hong Kong Industrial and Commercial Bank, was also taken over by the Government. During the same year, the Ka Wah Bank was acquired by the China-owned China International Trust and Investment Corporation (CITIC). In 1986, three other acquisitions occurred: (1) the Wing On Bank was acquired by the Hang Seng Bank; (2) the Union Bank was acquired by a Sino-

American joint venture, Modern Concepts Ltd.; and (3) the Hong Nin Bank was acquired by the First Pacific Holdings Ltd., and its name was changed to the First Pacific Bank in 1987.

Jao (1988) maintains that there were two main reasons for the 1982–6 crisis. The first is various forms of mismanagement or even fraudulent activities, and the second is the lax regulatory structure or incompetent regulatory authorities. As predicted by Kane's theory, it is natural for the Government to expand its regulatory structure in the wake of these crises. Indeed, in September 1984, Mr Richard Farrant of the Bank of England was invited by the Government as a consultant, to advise on the reform of banking regulations. Later, Mr Robert Fell was appointed Commissioner of Banking and DTCs to replace Mr Colin Martin. A set of discussion papers, drawn up by the joint efforts of Mr Farrant and Mr Fell, was circulated among the banks and DTCs for their comments. Finally, the new Banking Ordinance was enacted in May 1986.

The Banking Ordinance of 1986 marks a monumental change in banking regulations in Hong Kong. The major innovations of the Ordinance are listed here.

(a)   The Ordinance governs both banks and DTCs and the Commissioner of Banking supervises both types of institution.
(b)   The power and the duty of the Commissioner of Banking is enhanced.
(c)   A ratio constraint, the minimum capital to risk assets ratio requirement, is instituted.
(d)   A new liquidity requirement is imposed.
(e)   The Commissioner is also empowered to issue guide-lines for banking operations from time to time.

Thus, it is obvious that the regulatory structure of the Hong Kong banking system has become more modern. A detailed description is given in the next section of this chapter.

Types of Regulations in Hong Kong

As we have seen, banking regulations can be grouped into several categories. In Hong Kong, they are: (1) entry constraint, (2) price control, (3) product line regulations, and (4) ratio constraint.

Entry Constraint

Entry regulations are commonly employed by regulators for various purposes. The most obvious is to restraint 'excessive' competition. Regulators usually believe that more competition is destabilizing because banks would invest in riskier assets. However, a more monopolistic environment will make bank operations less efficient or more costly, which will drive down their profit margin and thus expose them to a higher risk of bankruptcy. Some entry regulations are stipulated in the form of minimum size. This kind of regulation aims at admitting only the larger banks, and has the implicit assumption that larger banks are safer and may, therefore, draw less on the Government's supervision resources.

The two basic forms of entry constraint are minimum capital requirement and the supplementary criteria for authorization. On 8 March 1989, the Commissioner of Banking, Mr Nicolle, announced the new requirements in the new three-tier system. Under the new system, there are three types of authorized institutions: the licensed banks, the Restricted Licensed Banks (RLBs), and the Deposit-taking Companies (DTCs).[7]

The reasons for adopting the new system are three-fold:

(a) To provide a higher status for the LDTCs in the old system since they were not allowed to use the word 'bank' in their promotional materials. Now they are allowed to use the word 'bank,' but with qualifying adjectives such as 'merchant,' 'restricted', or 'investment.'

(b) To facilitate the establishment of RLBs. Previously, it was necessary for an LDTC to become an RDTC first. This was an irrational requirement, as the RDTCs operated mostly in the retail market while the LDTCs operated mostly in the wholesale market. Thus, the experience of running an RDTC would not be beneficial to the operation of an LDTC.

(c) To strengthen the authorization criteria for deposit-taking institutions and to enhance the protection for depositors.

The minimum capital requirement for these three types of institutions are listed below:[8]

	Minimum Capital (HK$ million)
Locally Incorporated Licensed Banks	150
Restricted Licensed Banks	100
Deposit-taking Companies	25

There are other supplementary criteria for licensing or authorization:[9]
1. Licensed Banks.   Parent countries of overseas applicants must make available to Hong Kong banks some acceptable form of reciprocity. Moreover, granting a licence to the applicant would enhance Hong Kong's role as an international financial centre. Local applicants must be in the business of taking deposits from, and granting credit to, the public in Hong Kong for at least ten years. They must have deposits from the public of at least HK$1,750 million and total assets of at least HK$2,500 million.
2. Restricted Licensed Banks.   The applicant, if locally incorporated, must be either an existing (registered) deposit-taking company or at least 50 per cent owned by a bank. An applicant incorporated overseas must be a bank and subject to adequate prudential supervision by the recognized banking authorities of its parent country. An applicant that

is a subsidiary or associate of a licensed bank in Hong Kong must have a separate management structure at the executive level.

3. Deposit-taking Companies.   The applicant must be 50 per cent owned by a bank and the controlling bank must be adequately supervised by the prudential supervisory authority of the parent country. The company must also be in reputable ownership, and the beneficial owner of 10 per cent or more of the voting share capital must be identifiable and reputable.

Price Control

Price control is another common form of regulation. Price control can be imposed either on the asset items, for example, a maximum interest rate on loans; or on the liability items, for example, a maximum interest rate on deposits. Such regulations can either be imposed by the government in the form of interest rate ceiling, as was the case in the United States in the late 1970s; or they can be in the form of an interest rate cartel agreed upon among the institutions, the case in the United Kingdom before 1972.

The intention of the government in imposing an interest ceiling or accepting an interest cartel is to avoid price competition. The regulators usually believe that price competition would increase the cost of operation, which would then induce banks to invest in high yield and high risk assets. However, price control would, in reality, force banks to practise non-price competition by opening more branches and offering more free services. This would also increase the cost of operations[10] and hence lower the profit margin and would thus make banks invest more in highly risky assets. Thus, price control would be more destabilizing than free competition.

In Hong Kong, price control in the banking sector is in the form of maximum deposit rate. This control originated in 1964 as an interest rate cartel aimed at reducing excessive competition among banks. According to the most current interest rate rule imposed by the Hong Kong Association of Banks, commercial banks in Hong Kong are divided into two categories:

Category I Banks

Category I banks consist of:
(a) The note-issuing banks.
(b) Banks not incorporated in Hong Kong or the People's Republic of China.
(c) Banks having more than 25 per cent of the issued share capital held by the note-issuing banks or banks mentioned in (b).

Category II Banks

Category II banks are banks not included in Category I. According to the interest rate cartel:

(a)   All banks should pay no interest on current accounts.
(b)   All banks should pay the same interest rate on savings deposits.
(c)   A basic rate is set on time deposits.
(d)   Banks in Category I should offer deposit rates up to the basic rate while banks in Category II can pay 0.50 per cent higher than the basic rate.
(e)   Deposits over 12 months, Government deposits, and inter-bank deposits are exempted from the cartel rate.

In 1988, in order to facilitate the implementation of a 'negative interest rate' system for the purpose of defending the linked exchange rate system, the Hong Kong Association of Banks made an amendment in the interest rate rule allowing the Association to impose charges on depositors.

The interest rate agreement was changed again on 21 September 1990 when the Hong Kong Association of Banks announced that it had accepted the Government's proposal to end the delineation of banks into two categories. This change was needed because the General Agreement on Tariffs and Trade (GATT) is soon to be extended to trade in services (including banking services). The continuation of the delineation of banks into two categories would invite criticism from foreign banks, which have to offer lower deposit rates on time deposits than their local counterparts.

Product Line Regulation

Product line regulation means that banks are forbidden to offer certain types of liabilities or to purchase certain types of assets. There are many reasons for these restrictions. The government usually restricts financial institutions from receiving certain types of deposits because it may want to dampen the degree of competition or to protect the depositors by preventing them from depositing in the more risky institutions. The government may also want to prevent financial institutions from engaging in certain types of activities, for example, commercial banks are forbidden to underwrite business in many countries because such activities are believed to be too risky for them.

In Hong Kong, the major product line restriction is in deposits. RLBs are not permitted to receive deposits of less than HK$500,000, while DTCs are not permitted to receive deposits of less than HK$100,000 and with a maturity of less than three months.

The main reason for such a regulation is to protect small depositors. In the existing institutional set-up, licensed banks are the most heavily regulated firms and hence (supposedly) are the safest institutions, while other institutions, such as the RLBs and the DTCs, are relatively risky. It is usually more costly for small depositors to collect and to interpret financial information. Thus, it is the view of the Government that small depositors (those with less than HK$100,000) should deposit their money in licensed banks only. Thus, if a small depositor wants to make short-term deposits (with a maturity of less than a year), his or her deposits should fall under the restriction of the interest rate rule of the Hong Kong Association of Banks.

Other than the deposit constraint, there are practically no restrictions on the types of liability that the bank can offer or the types of loans that the bank can make. However, the Banking Commissioner does place some limitations on the holding of certain assets. These limitations are documented briefly as follows:

(a)   A bank or an RLB should not grant any unsecured loans to any of its directors or its relatives in excess of 10 per cent of the paid-up capital and reserves of the bank.

(b)   A DTC should not grant any unsecured loans to any of its directors or its relatives.[11]

(c)   An authorized institution should not grant any unsecured loans to any of its employees in excess of one year's salary for the employee.

(d)   An authorized institution should not acquire or hold any part of the share capital of any other companies or land in excess of 25 per cent of the paid-up capital and reserves of the institution.

(e)   The Banking Commissioner may, after giving notice, prohibit the authorized institution from granting any credit facilities to a foreign bank.

Ratio Constraints

There are two broad types of ratio constraint: the liquidity ratio and the capital adequacy ratio.

Liquidity Ratio

A minimum liquidity requirement is not uncommon in financial regulations, particularly with depository institutions. Most depository institutions have a large dollar amount in very short-term liabilities. Therefore, they should maintain a relatively high liquidity to be able to meet the withdrawal of funds by depositors. However, even for depository institutions that are constrained to accept only longer term deposits, for example, the DTCs, depositors still have the right to withdraw their funds at any time if they choose to forego the interest. Thus, a common liquidity requirement is imposed on all three types of depository institutions.

Before the enactment of the Banking Ordinance of 1986, the concept of liquidity as reflected in the requirement was rather obsolete. The original law required banks to maintain a minimum amount of liquid assets equal to 25 per cent of the deposits. Thus, it reflected that liquidity could only be generated from the assets and only from those parts of assets that are traditionally labelled 'short-term assets.' However, according to the modern concept of liquidity, cash inflow can be generated from both assets and liabilities, and some of the 'seemingly' long-term assets can also produce cash flow. Attracting customers' deposits and issuing certificates of deposit are obvious examples of 'liability-induced' liquidity. Some very long-term assets, such as long-term loans that are very close to their maturity date, can also generate liquidity. Even loans that have a long time to maturity can generate ample liquidity for banks. A vivid case is a new 20-year mortgage, which enables the institution to receive a relatively stable cash payment (both principal and interest) each month.

In the Banking Ordinance of 1986 there is a basic change in the definition of liquidity requirement, which reflects the change of attitude of the regulators towards liquidity management. According to the new regulation, all authorized institutions should maintain a minimum liquidity ratio of 25 per cent and the liquidity ratio is defined as:

$$\frac{\text{Liquefiable Assets}}{\text{Qualifying Liabilities}} \; > \; 25\%.$$

The asset items that can be counted as liquefiable assets can be summarized briefly as follows:

(a)   Net amount of one month inter-bank deposits.
(b)   Hong Kong dollar or (convertible) foreign currency notes and coins.
(c)   Loan repayments which will fall due within one month and which are not expected to have any default.
(d)   Other cash inflow that can be realized within one month (net of cost of realizing such a cash flow) such as export bills, Government securities, negotiable certificates, and other notes and debt securities accepted by the Commissioner.
(e)   Gold.

Qualifying liabilities include:

(a)   Net one month inter-bank liabilities.
(b)   The total of other one-month liabilities.

Although there is an improvement in the calculation of liquidity by admitting cash flow generated from loan assets and other long-term assets, the Government still does not take into account the discretionary power of some banks or institutions to generate liquidity through issuing liabilities. Some institutions, especially the larger ones, are more capable of issuing securities, for example, certificates of deposit, to generate cash inflow than other, smaller institutions. Thus, the more established or more reputable institutions should be given lighter or less stringent liquidity requirements.

Capital Adequacy Requirements

Although capital adequacy requirements have a long history in the United States, their implementation in the United Kingdom is a very recent event. The United Kingdom started a formal capital adequacy ratio requirement in 1979 after the enactment of Banking Act of that year. However, it is the view of most of the central bankers in the developed world that more uniform capital requirements should be adopted. As a major financial centre in Asia, Hong Kong should follow suit. This is one reason that such a regulation was first introduced in Hong Kong in 1986. Another major reason was the 1982–4 banking crisis, which demonstrated clearly that the institutions that encountered problems were all under-capitalized relative to their assets.

The minimum Capital Adequacy Ratio (CAR) as laid down in the Ordinance is 5 per cent and is calculated as:

$$\frac{\text{Capital Base}}{\text{Risk Assets}} > 5\%.$$

The capital base includes:
(a) Paid-up capital, inner reserves, share premiums, and revaluation reserves.
(b) Undistributed profits.
(c) Perpetual subordinated debt.[12]

'Risk assets' are the weighted average of the book value of the asset items. The assets of the institutions are classified into five risk categories, and each category is assigned a weight ranging from 0.0 to 10 depending on its degree of risk.[13]

Category	Weight
I	0.0
II	0.2
III	0.5
IV	10.0
V	1.0

The following example shows how the capital-risk asset ratio is calculated for the ABC Bank Ltd.:

Category	Amount ($ million) (1)	Category Weight (2)	Weighted Risk Assets ($ million) (1) × (2)
I	40	0.0	0
II	300	0.2	60
III	200	0.5	100
IV	10	10.0	100
V	450	1.0	450

Total Assets = $1,000 million.

Total Risk Assets = $(60 + 100 + 100 + 450) million
= $710 million.

Given Capital Base = $35.5 million.

Capital Risk Asset Ratio = $35.5/710 \times 100\% = 5\%$.

Thus, the ABC Bank Ltd. can just fulfil the minimum CAR and if it wants to invest more in assets in Categories II to V, it has to raise more capital. For example, if the ABC Bank wants to lend $10 million more (Category V asset with a weight of 1.0), the total risk assets and the required capital will be as follows:

$$\text{Total Risk Assets} = (\$710 + \$10 \times 1.0) \text{ million}$$
$$= \$720 \text{ million.}$$

Capital Risk Asset Ratio = $35.5/720 \times 100\% = 4.93\%$.

Thus, the ABC Bank does not fulfil the minimum CAR and has to raise an additional capital of:

$$(0.05 \times \$720 - \$35.5) \text{ million} = \$0.5 \text{ million.}$$

Thus, as is made clear from the above example, if the institution cannot fulfil the minimum requirement, it either has to add more capital or reduce its asset size. Either action would boost the safety of the institution and hence the banking system.

In addition to the basic minimum requirements listed above, the Commissioner has also asked institutions to set a safety margin above the minimum CAR. Should an institution's ratio fall below this margin, the institution will be asked to explain the reasons behind such a change and the steps to take to avoid a breach of the statutory minimum CAR.

Although the great majority of licensed banks could meet the requirements, some DTCs still had a capital ratio that was below the minimum of 5 per cent in 1987. Since the minimum CAR requirement was made effective in September 1988, a number of institutions increased their capital base during 1988. Thirty-nine DTCs, especially the Japanese-owned ones, added HK$3.2 billion in cash to their equity while there were five issues of perpetual subordinated debt. Other institutions took a different route to make up for their shortfall in meeting the minimum CAR by reducing their assets. In 1988, the total assets of DTCs decreased by 16 per cent while those of locally incorporated banks increased by 20 per cent. The assets of the Japanese DTCs suffered the greatest fall, of more than 25 per cent. That is why the Japanese banks were the most active opponents of the minimum CAR requirement when it was first announced in 1986.

Although the adoption of the capital adequacy requirement is a big advance in prudential supervision, there is still room for improvement. An obvious point is that a major portion of all the assets fall in the same category, that is, Category V, and thus carry the same weight. It is clear that not all loans bear the same degree of risk. A mortgage fully backed by property is far safer than an unsecured personal loan. Thus, the present scheme has the effect of over-penalizing the more conservative bank. Another point is that off-balance sheet items such as credit line, standby letters of credit, forward contracts, underwriting facilities, swaps, options, and futures contracts are not handled clearly. Moreover, some of the requirements may not be consistent with international standards. However, as will be made clear in the next section, if Hong Kong is going to maintain its status as an international banking centre its regulatory quality should be on a par with that of other developed countries. Thus, whenever there is a major change in the regulations in the major developed countries, Hong Kong should follow suit.

The New Regulations on Capital Adequacy

In December 1987, representatives of the central banks and supervisory authorities of the group of ten countries,[14] Switzerland, and Luxemburg met in Basle and proposed to standardize the measurement of banks' capital and to set minimum levels of capital adequacy. The objectives of the proposal are two-fold. The first is to strengthen the stability of the international banking system; the second is to remove a source of competitive inequality for banks or deposit-taking institutions arising from differences in regulations. Mr Nicolle, the Commissioner of Banking, announced that Hong Kong should follow the Basle format and sent out the Basle proposal in December 1987 to all the institutions for consultation. Subsequently, a new framework of capital adequacy requirement was agreed upon in September 1988 and was made effective in December 1989.

In the new regulations, there are four distinct components which are described briefly below.

1. The Minimum Capital Adequacy Ratio (CAR).   The new minimum CAR is 8 per cent, with possible maxima of 12 per cent for licensed banks and 16 per cent for RLBs and DTCs.

2. The Definition of the Capital Base.   The new definition of the capital base includes a wider range of capital elements and is composed of two tiers: the core capital or Tier 1, and the supplementary capital or Tier 2 (a detailed list of the capital items is given in Appendix 5.1).

Tier 1:   core capital consisting principally of equity and perpetual non-cumulative preference shares.

Tier 2:   supplementary capital includes inner reserves, certain revaluation reserves and general provisions, other preference capital, and debt where repayment is subordinated to the interests of creditors.

In the calculation of the minimum CAR the core capital must account for at least 50 per cent of the total capital base. This wider definition of the capital base enables institutions to have greater flexibility in capital management so as to minimize the cost of capital.

Table 5.1   The Weighting System

Category	Weight (%)	Example
I	0	Notes and coins, gold bullion, loans to governments of developed countries.
II	10	Short-term fixed-interest securities and floating-rate securities.
III	20	Long-term fixed-interest securities and claims on authorized institutions.
IV	50	Residential mortgage loans and mortgage-backed securities.
V	100	Private sector loans, fixed assets, and real estate.

Source: Office of the Banking Commissioner, 1989.

3.   The Weighting System.   There are still five categories of weights (0 per cent, 10 per cent, 20 per cent, 50 per cent, and 100 per cent) but the weighting system for various risk assets is redefined to reflect the creditworthiness of the counterpart. In the new system, discrimination against the RDTCs (or DTCs under the new system) is removed[15] as claims on both licensed banks and DTCs carry the same weight. Another improvement is that there is a concession for residential mortgage loans, the risk weight of which is reduced from 100 per cent to 50 per cent. While a detailed list of the weighting scheme is given in Appendix 5.2, a brief description is given in Table 5.1.

Another novelty in the new weighting scheme is that loans to different countries carry different weights according to the economic strength of the countries. In the Basle framework, countries belonging to the Organisation for Economic Co-operation and Development (OECD)[16] have greater economic strength than non-OECD countries. Loans to OECD countries should thus attract a lighter weight than those to non-OECD countries. Hong Kong does not follow the Basle scheme exactly since Hong Kong does not belong to the OECD and many overseas banks are making their presence here as authorized institutions. In the Hong Kong scheme, there are two tiers of countries, Tier 1 and Tier 2. Tier 1 countries include Hong Kong and OECD countries, and Tier 2 countries comprise all countries are not included in Tier 1. Loans to Tier 2 countries should attract a heavier weight than loans to Tier 1 countries. However, any loans to institutions authorized in Hong Kong and incorporated overseas should be treated in the same way as loans to those incorporated in Hong Kong, that is, Tier 1 countries.

4.   Treatment of Off-balance Sheet Items.   A more comprehensive and standardized treatment for off-balance sheet items is adopted. Under the new proposal, the risk weight for the off-balance sheet items is determined by a two-step procedure:

(a)   Credit conversion: the face value of the item is converted to an amount equivalent to a credit item such as a loan on the balance sheet. This is done by multiplying the off-balance sheet item by a credit conversion factor which ranges from 0 per cent to 100 per cent.[17]

(b)   Risk weighting: the converted credit item calculated in (a) is then assigned to the appropriate risk category similar to the regular balance sheet item.

Other Regulatory Guide-lines and Informal Supervision

One innovative development in banking regulations is that, apart from the rules spelled out explicitly in the Ordinance, the Commissioner can also issue guide-lines for authorized institutions on business practices from time to time to elaborate or clarify certain items in the Ordinance. At the time of writing the Commissioner has issued four sets of guide-lines and proposed one set, which are discussed briefly in the following sections.

The Code of Conduct Guide-line

On 28 November 1986, just about three months after the enactment of the Banking Ordinance, the Commissioner issued a set of guide-lines about ethical standards for authorized institutions. The Code of Conduct containing these guide-lines was issued in accordance with Sections 7(2)(c) and (d) of the Ordinance, which maintains that the function of the Commissioner is to:

7(2)(c) promote and encourage proper standards of conduct and sound and prudent business practices amongst authorized institutions;

7(2)(d) suppress or aid in suppressing illegal dishonourable or improper practices in relation to the business practices of authorized institutions.

The Code of Conduct supplements the Prevention of Bribery Ordinance and section 124 of the Banking Ordinance of 1986 with respect to guarding against corruption in the banking industry. The purpose of the guide-lines is to ensure the adoption of a uniform code of conduct and to set a standard for those institutions that do not have a published code.

Such a guide-line was issued so early because many fraudulent and unethical practices were discovered during the 1982–4 banking and DTC crises. Thus, during the drafting of the new ordinance, the Government considered that a wider statutory provision should be adopted to promote a proper standard of conduct. It was finally decided that guide-lines were a more proper way of achieving this objective.

The Code of Conduct Guide-line has the following major components:

1.   Preparation of Code of Conduct.   Every authorized institution

should prepare a code of conduct for its staff, setting out standards to which the management of the institution expects the staff to adhere. A copy of the code should be sent to the Commissioner for approval.
2. Notification of Staff.   The staff should be notified of standards set out in the code of conduct.
3. Staff Queries.   A senior officer should be appointed to handle queries from staff relating to the code of conduct.
4. Records of Benefits.   A written record of personal benefits received by staff should be kept.

The Commissioner has also prepared a model code of conduct for all authorized institutions to follow. According to the model, a code of conduct should contain restrictions on staff with respect to loans, borrowing from third parties, conduct when obtaining business, personal benefits, use of information related to the bank and its customers for financial gain, dealing of securities using information obtained from the bank, and outside employment.

This code of conduct guide-line was issued at a time when the confidence and the integrity of the Hong Kong banking system was badly shaken by the crises, and it signified that the Government was determined to clean up the mess and to encourage ethical and prudent banking practices in Hong Kong. It should thus be welcomed by local people as well as international investors.

The Loan Approvals, Records, and Provisions Guide-line

On 20 August 1987, the Banking Commissioner issued another guide-line on loan approvals, records, and provisions. Again, the issuing of such a guide-line is in accordance with sections 7(2)(c) and (d) of the Banking Ordinance of 1986. The purpose of this guide-line is to develop a model for the basic systems and records necessary for making and accounting for loans. Such records are necessary for the management of the institutions, for their external and internal auditors, and for the Commissioner.

There are two main reasons for issuing this guide-line:
(a)   The Commissioner needs to give institutions explicit guide-lines on the standard elements of controls and records that can fulfil the expectation of the bank examiners because the Commissioner can ask an institution to take remedial actions should its performance fall short of the Commissioner's expectation.
(b)   The Commissioner has found that some institutions have not reached the minimum standard of control and records which, in the view of the Commissioner, is a crucial element for sound and safe banking practices.

There are nine components in the guide-line:
1. Loan Policies.   Every authorized institution should have a written loan policy detailing the criteria for loan approval, types of acceptable securities, and so on.

2. Loan Approval System.   Every institution should have a formalized and documented loan approval system detailing the lending authorities of individual officers and committees, the information or documents required from borrowers, and documents to be maintained on credit file.

3. Loan Review System.   Every institution should have a formalized and documented loan review system to ensure that the performance of loans is regularly monitored and periodically reviewed.

4. Liability Records.   A central liability record for each borrower has to be maintained.

5. Credit File.   A credit file for each borrower has to be maintained and should contain the following minimum information:

(a) The background of the borrower.
(b) The purpose of the loan.
(c) The terms of repayment and interest.
(d) Details of the collateral security and its current value, and information on the guarantor.
(e) An assessment of the borrower's financial position.
(f) Information on the approving officer(s) and the facilities approved.
(g) A copy of the loan agreement, guarantees, and other related documents.
(h) Updating of records.
(i) Review reports arising from regular monitoring, periodic review, and other incidental intelligence concerning the borrower.

6. Review Procedures.   A standard procedure for reviewing the adequacy of provisions should be adopted.

7. General Provisions.   The maintenance of a general provision for loan loss is strongly encouraged.

8. Internal Audit Policy.   A written policy on internal audit is required.

9. Identification of Advances.   A procedure to identify advances to parties related to the borrowers or guarantors and the directors of the institution is required.

Country Debt Provisioning Guide-lines

Section 76 of the Banking Ordinance of 1986 requires every authorized institution to maintain at all times adequate provision for bad and doubtful debts and for diminution of value of assets. When this clause first came out, some institutions believed this rule to be rather vague as it did not specify how much provisioning is adequate. This has become more problematic for country debt. Thus, on 23 December 1987, the Commissioner sent out a consultative paper detailing a proposal to establish provisions against the debt of countries experiencing repayment difficulties. Two alternative approaches were proposed: the Bank of England approach and the Canadian approach. After thorough consultation, the Commissioner announced on 20 May 1988 that the Bank of England approach would be followed.

According to the Bank of England approach, there are three stages in deciding the level of provision:

(a) Identifying countries with current or potential repayment difficulties.
(b) Identifying the nature of those difficulties and the extent of the country's problems.
(c) Determining what proportion of the debt is unlikely to be repaid.

In order to help make the provisioning decision, a total of 15 factors can be identified and weighted to reflect their relative importance in the repayment of the loan. These 15 factors can be grouped into three categories. Category A includes factors that demonstrate a borrower's inability or unwillingness to meet its obligations, whether at the due date or thereafter. Category B includes factors that show a borrower's current difficulties in meeting its obligations. Category C includes factors that help to assess the likelihood that these difficulties will not be overcome.

A three-step procedure has to be followed before making any provisioning decision:

(a) Deciding if a factor applies to a country.
(b) Assigning a weight or score to a particular factor to reflect the relative seriousness of that factor.
(c) Calculating the total score of that country, which is the sum total of all the scores of the individual factors.

The level of provisioning is then established according to the total score:

Total Score	Provision
10–24	5–15%
25–40	16–25%
41–55	26–40%
56–70	41–60%
71–83	61–100%

A Guide-line to Prevent Money Laundering

Since Hong Kong has one of the most open financial systems in the world, financial institutions may sometimes be used (without the knowledge of the management of the institutions) for the transfer or deposit of money derived from criminal activities. This downgrades the confidence of the general public in the banking system. The Banking Commissioner thus issued a guide-line in March 1989 for the prevention of criminal use of the banking system for the purposes of money-laundering.

According to the guide-line, authorized institutions should implement specific procedures to obtain identification from new customers, and should not offer services or active assistance in transactions that they have good reason to suppose are associated with money laundering. Authorized institutions are also expected to co-operate fully with law enforcement authorities to prevent and to suppress the use of the banking system for criminal purposes.

Proposed Guide-lines for the Supervision of Foreign Exchange Risk

Foreign exchange operations are an integral part of the banking business. It was reported that in 1989 Hong Kong was the world's sixth largest global foreign exchange market, with an average daily turnover of US\$ 49 billion.[18] The 1989 Annual Report of the Office of the Banking Commissioner also disclosed that nearly one fifth of licensed banks' gross income (net of interest expenses) came from foreign exchange transactions.

Foreign exchange operations would expose financial institutions to considerable risk from exchange rate movement when there is a mismatch in the currency exposure on the asset and liability sides. For example, if a bank issues Hong Kong dollar liabilities to purchase Japanese yen assets, a depreciation in the value of the yen against the Hong Kong dollar would jeopardize the bank's capability of repaying its Hong Kong dollar liabilities when they fall due (an appreciation of the yen would, of course, benefit the bank). This type of risk has not been properly taken care of in the capital adequacy requirement which addresses primarily credit risk, that is, risk due to default. Thus, in October 1989 the Banking Commissioner sent out a consultative paper on the supervision of foreign exchange risk with the aim of formulating policies to foster the prudent internal controls of foreign currency risk and to link up such a risk with the capital base of the institution.

According to the consultative paper, the aggregate overnight foreign exchange position of a Hong Kong incorporated institution should not exceed 15 per cent of its capital base and exposures in any one currency should not exceed 10 per cent. The aggregate exposures of less experienced institutions should not exceed 5 per cent of their capital base. The Office of the Banking Commissioner also conducted a survey in 1989 and found that the limits suggested above were also compatible with the internal limits set by the institutions themselves. Thus, adoption of such limits would not impede the trading activities of the foreign exchange market. It is also envisaged that the Office of the Banking Commissioner will issue additional guide-lines on the internal management and control of foreign exchange transactions.

The Supervisory Approach

Before 1989, the Banking Commissioner relied heavily on on-site examinations supplemented by statistical returns given by individual authorized institutions. According to the Commissioner's Annual Report of 1987, the overall establishment of the Office of the Commissioner was meant to have a staff of 196, but only 179 were employed at the end of 1987. This group of officers visited the banks and deposit-taking companies regularly throughout the year. In 1987, it was reported that there were examinations, in Hong Kong and overseas, of 70 banks and 130 deposit-taking companies. The Commissioner admitted that some examinations took considerable staff and management time because of the size and complexity of the institutions. On 17 February 1989, the Commissioner announced that new methods could be used to improve the effectiveness and efficiency of supervision, and outlined the new supervisory approach.

The original system emphasized only statistical returns and data obtained during on-site examinations. Thus, the approach tended to be quantitative and mechanistic. The new approach was intended to increase the dialogue with the management of institutions and the efficiency of supervision. The new approach included:

(a)   Supplementing on-site examinations with other methods.
(b)   Focusing examination efforts on potential or identified prudential concerns.
(c)   Setting priorities for the limited supervisory resources.

To supplement the on-site examinations, off-site reviews and prudential meetings were adopted. These are detailed as follows:

1.   Off-site Reviews.   These involve the use of information provided by the institution. Such information includes statistical returns, non-financial information such as internal policy statements, internal management information (such as financial budgets, forecasts, bad and doubtful loan reports), and other published financial information.

2.   Prudential Meetings.   These are regular meetings to be held twice a year with the senior management of authorized institutions. The objectives of such meetings are:

(a)   To understand the institution's management controls, business situation, prospects, business plan, and strategies.
(b)   To clarify certain queries arising from off-site reviews.
(c)   To decide if a greater focus on on-site examination is needed.

While on-site examinations will continue, they will be less frequent. The Commissioner will shift from an 'across the board' approach to on-site examination to a more selective approach. Thus, if the information gathered from off-site reviews indicates an area of concern or an emerging problem, a selective examination will be conducted on specific areas of business. The management of the institutions will also be informed of the scope of an examination beforehand.

This method is an improvement. Not only does the new approach save supervisory resources, it can also collect more relevant information regarding the future prospects and viability of the institution. Such information is extremely important in identifying potential problem institutions, because it is usually too late when certain problems are detected through balance sheet data.

In 1989, there was a sharp increase in the number of off-site reviews and prudential meetings with top executives of institutions. An off-site review aims at checking compliance with the statutory limits applied under the Ordinance and detecting the underlying trends in the business. In addition to the analysis of regular statistical returns, the review looks at accounting and other management information supplied by the institution. Key areas of concern include liquidity, structure of assets and liabilities, composition of earnings, large exposures and other risk concentrations, and foreign exchange operations. A prudential meeting involves a discussion with top executives on various financial and management topics including changes in key financial ratios, the performance of large exposures, and other current and future changes in the business and its control.

Conclusion

Until the enactment of the Banking Ordinance of 1986, the regulatory policy of the Hong Kong Government was passive and reactive in nature. In most cases, financial crises helped the Government to identify the problems and then enact laws to cope with those problems. In a sense, almost all of the ordinances related to the banking sector are the result of various banking and financial crises. However, such passive regulatory attitudes, which are in accordance with Kane's dialectic, may not be able to accommodate the rapidly changing financial environment.

However, since enactment of the Banking Ordinance in 1986, the regulatory attitude seems to have become more proactive. This is because:
(a) The scale of banking crisis that occurred in 1982–4 has made regulators more cautious of future financial disturbances.
(b) The Hongkong and Shanghai Banking Group may not want to bear the burden of bailing out failing institutions.
(c) The quality of regulators has improved and the Government has put more emphasis on training its examiners through training courses offered locally and in overseas countries. Secondments of staff to and from the private sector and overseas regulatory authorities also help to enrich the experience of staff in the Office of the Banking Commissioner.
(d) The Office of the Banking Commissioner has also become more proactive in detecting financial market developments by establishing an economic research unit in 1989, and tapping services of the expanded legal unit of the Monetary Affairs Branch.
(e) Influence from regulations in the western world helps Hong Kong to modernize and to upgrade its regulatory procedures.

Thus, in the future the Commissioner's Office will watch the banking sector more closely but in a more selective and efficient way.

Appendices

Appendix 5.1   Definition of the Capital Base

A. Core capital — Tier 1
1. Ordinary paid-up share capital
2. Irredeemable non-cumulative preference shares
3. Share premiums
4. Reserves
5. Current year profit/(loss)
6. Minority interests
7. Deduct: goodwill

B. Supplementary capital — Tier 2
1. Inner reserves
2. Reserves on revaluation of own premises
3. Latent reserves on revaluation of securities
4. General provisions for doubtful debt
5. Hybrid capital instruments
    (a) Perpetual subordinated debt
    (b) Irredeemable cumulative preference shares
6. Subordinated term debt instruments
    (a) Subordinated term debt
    (b) Term preference shares
7. Minority interests

C. Deductions from total capital
1. Shareholdings in subsidiaries or holding company
2. Exposures to connected companies
3. Equity investments of 20 per cent or more in non-subsidiary companies
4. Investments in the capital of other banks and financial institutions

Appendix 5.2   Risk Categories

I. 0 Per Cent Weight
1. Notes and coins.
2. Hong Kong Government certificates of indebtedness.
3. Gold bullion held in own vault or on an allocated basis, to the extent backed by gold liabilities.
4. Claims collateralized by cash deposits.
5. Loans to, or claims guaranteed by, central governments and central banks of Tier 1 countries.
6. Local currency loans to central governments and central banks of Tier 2 countries funded by that currency.

II. 10 Per Cent Weight
  1. Holdings of fixed-interest securities with a residual maturity of under 1 year or floating-rate securities of any maturity issued by central governments and central banks of Tier 1 countries, or claims fully collateralized by such securities.
  2. Holdings of fixed-interest securities with a residual maturity of under 1 year or floating-rate securities of any maturity issued by central governments and central banks of Tier 2 countries, where denominated and funded in local currency.

III. 20 Per Cent Weight
  1. Cash items in the process of collection.
  2. Holdings of fixed-interest securities with a residual maturity of 1 year and over issued by central governments and central banks of Tier 1 countries, or claims collateralized by such securities.
  3. Holdings of fixed-interest securities with a residual maturity of 1 year and over issued by central governments and central banks of Tier 2 countries, where denominated and funded in local currency.
  4. Claims on, or claims guaranteed by, public sector entities of Tier 1 countries.
  5. Claims on, or claims guaranteed by, authorized institutions in Hong Kong and banks incorporated in Tier 1 countries.
  6. Claims on, or claims guaranteed or collateralized by securities issued by multilateral development banks.
  7. Claims on, or claims guaranteed by, banks which are incorporated in Tier 2 countries but not authorized institutions in Hong Kong, with a residual maturity of under 1 year.

IV. 50 Per Cent Weight
  1. Loans fully secured by mortgages on residential property.
  2. Mortgage-backed securities and mortgage participations.

V. 100 Per Cent Weight
  1. Gold held not backed by gold liabilities.
  2. Claims on public sector entities of Tier 2 countries.
  3. Claims on, or claims guaranteed by, banks which are incorporated in Tier 2 countries but not authorized institutions in Hong Kong, with a residual maturity of 1 year and over.
  4. Claims on non-bank private sector.
  5. Investments in the capital of other authorized institutions or banks (other than where deducted from capital).
  6. Premises, plant and equipment, and other fixed assets for own use.
  7. Other interests in real estate.
  8. All assets not elsewhere specified.

Notes

1. A study by Rolnick and Weber (1985) indicated that during the Free Banking Era in the United States the bank run panic did not spread to other states because the regulations at that time provided people with adequate information on the health of individual banks. While this may have been true during the old days, rapid technological changes and innovations in the banking industry may make it more difficult for depositors to interpret information on the balance sheet.

2. Edwards (1981), p. 2.

3. In some cases it is difficult to distinguish macroeconomic controls from microeconomic controls. Some of the regulations may serve a dual purpose.

4. This does not include the United Kingdom where a capital ratio control was established after the enactment of the Banking Act of 1979.

5. Outside shocks may include business cycles, volatility in the interest rate, and a sudden increase in competition due to the liberalization process. Inside shocks may include a sudden death or the resignation of some key executives.

6. This section was taken from Jao (1987, 1988).

7. These three types of authorized institutions are equilvalent to those in the old system, namely the licensed banks, the Licensed Deposit-taking Companies (LDTCs), and the Registered Deposit-taking Companies (RDTCs), respectively.

8. The original minimum capital requirements under the old system were: HK$100 million for locally incorporated licensed banks, HK$75 million for LDTCs, and HK$10 million for RDTCs. Foreign banks wishing to obtain a bank licence are not subject to the minimum capital requirement but they have to fulfil the minimum asset requirement of US$14 billion. LDTCs that cannot meet the new capital requirement will be grandfathered as DTCs. The existing RDTCs are given a period of two years to meet the new requirements.

9. A more detailed list of the criteria is given in Appendix 5.1.

10. The cost of non-price competition is higher than that of price competition because the utility derived from a dollar of interest income on the part of the depositors is higher than a dollar's worth of free services. Thus, in order to attract the same level of deposits as that in a freely competitive environment, the bank has to spend more on non-price competition and hence on the cost of operation.

11. The restrictions mentioned in (a) and (b) also apply to: (1) any employee of the institution who is responsible for granting loan application, (2) any relative of such employee, (3) any controller of the institution, (4) any relative of such controller, (5) any firm in which the institution or any of its directors or any relative of any of its directors is interested as director, partner, manager or agent, and (6) any individual or firm of which any director of the institution or any relative of any such director is a guarantor.

12. The amount of perpetual subordinated debt that can be counted as capital base should not be larger than half of the sum total of other capital items.

13. A detailed list of the five categories of assets is given in Appendix 2.

14. The group of ten countries is comprised of Belgium, Canada, France, Germany, Italy, Japan, Netherlands, Sweden, the United Kingdom, and the United States.

15. Under the original system, loans made by the institution to licensed banks or to LDTCs (or RLBs under the new system) carry a risk weight of 0.2 while loans to RDTCs (or DTCs under the new system) carry a risk weight of 0.5. The RDTCs protested at such a differential treatment.

16. OECD countries are Australia, Austria, Belgium, Canada, Denmark, West Germany, Finland, France, Greece, Iceland, Irish Republic, Italy, Japan, Luxemburg, the Netherlands, New Zealand, Norway, Portugal, Spain, Sweden, Switzerland, Turkey, the United Kingdom, and the United States.

17. There are four credit conversion factors: 0 per cent, 20 per cent, 50 per cent, and 100 per cent. Items with 0 per cent conversion, for example, include unused commitments with an original maturity of one year or less. Items with 20 per cent conversion include short-term self-liquidating trade-related contingencies such as documentary credits collecteralised by the underlying shipments. Items with 50 per cent conversion include note-issuing facilities, revolving underwriting facilities, and standby facilities and credit lines with an original maturity exceeding one year. Those items with 100 per cent conversion include financial guarantees, standby letters of credit, and other direct credit substitutes.

18. This is the figure taken from a survey reported by the Bank for International Settlement and quoted in the 1989 Annual Report of the Office of the Banking Commissioner.

References

Commissioner of Banking, *Annual Report* (Hong Kong, Hong Kong Government Printer), 1988, 1989.

Edwards, F. R., 'Financial Institutions and Regulation in the 21st Century: After the Crash?', in Albert Verheirstraeten (ed.), *Competition and Regulation in Financial Markets*, (London, Macmillan Press, 1981).

Jao, Y. C., 'A Comparative Analysis of Banking Crises in Hong Kong and Taiwan', *Journal of Economic and International Relations*, Vol. 1, 1987, pp. 299–322.

Jao, Y. C. (ed.), *Hong Kong's Banking System in Transition: Problems, Prospects and Policies*, (Hong Kong, Chinese Banks Association, 1988).

Joskow, P. L., 'Inflation and Environment Concern: Structural Change in the Process of Public Utility Price Regulation', *Journal of Law and Economics*, October 1974, pp. 291–327.

Kane, E. J., 'Good Intentions and Unintended Evil: the Case Against Selective Credit Allocation', *Journal of Money, Credit, and Banking*, February 1977, pp. 55–69.

Rolnick, A. J., and Weber, W. E., 'Banking Instability and Regulation in the U.S. Free Banking Era', *Quarterly Review*, (Federal Reserve Bank of Minneapolis), Summer 1985, pp. 2–9.

Stigler, G. J., 'The Theory of Economic Regulation', *Bell Journal of Economics*, Vol. 2, 1971, pp. 3–21.

Part II
Non-depository Institutions

6. Unit Trusts and Mutual Funds

Richard Yan-Ki Ho

Introduction

In the 1980s, there were two distinct trends in the development of Hong Kong. One was the rapid accumulation of wealth in the Asia Pacific region, a result of the fast economic growth in the late 1970s and early 1980s. The other was the strengthening of Hong Kong's position as a regional financial centre. In line with this development was very rapid growth in the unit trust industry. Although the unit trust business started in Hong Kong in 1960, the industry really took off in the early 1980s. This was partly due to the rapid economic growth and partly due to the stock-market boom. This chapter discusses the rationale behind unit trust investments, the development and the features of the Hong Kong unit trust industry, and its regulation.

Basic Principles of Portfolio Diversification

A unit trust is a pool of funds managed by a professional investment company, the unit trust company.

It is a form of collective investment through which a number of investors combine their money into a large central pool. The investment company then channels funds from this large pool into a diversified portfolio of financial instruments such as equities, bonds, treasury bills, certificates of deposit, bank deposits, warrants, futures, and options.

The benefit of having a diversified portfolio has long been recognized in the adage, 'don't put all your eggs in one basket'. The basic principle is that with a diversified portfolio, the risk or volatility of returns can be reduced. However, Professor Markowitz (1952), the Nobel prize laureate in Economics, asserts that this is not always the case. He derives, mathematically, the condition under which diversification is beneficial, that is, risk can be reduced. Markowitz finds that risk reduction can only be achieved through combining securities that are not perfectly correlated, that is, their correlation coefficient is less than 1.0. If two securities are perfectly correlated, then the returns of the two securities will go up and down in the same proportion, and it makes no sense to diversify in this way. Combining securities that are not perfectly correlated will lower the risk of the portfolio return. Since most of the securities are not perfectly correlated in the real world, the Markowitz principle does seem to work in practice. Thus, having a portfolio that is composed of many assets would enable us to benefit from portfolio diversification.

Advantages of Investing in Unit Trusts

Before we go into the benefits of investing in unit trusts, it is worthwhile to describe briefly the basic structure of a unit trust. The unit trust is a pool of funds contributed by investors. The fund is managed by professional investment managers who use the cash from the investors to invest in a variety of financial instruments such as equities, bonds, bills, and certificates of deposit. The pool of funds is divided into units, and the value of each unit is the total value of the financial instruments in which the trust has invested divided by the total number of units. In the case of open-ended funds, new units are issued by the management companies when new investors invest money in the fund.

There are several advantages of investing in unit trusts, discussed in the following sections.

Risk Diversification

An individual investor usually does not have enough money to purchase a large number of securities. This is because there is a minimum broad lot size requirement. For example, the minimum broad lot size for The Bank of East Asia Ltd. and for the China Motor Bus Co. Ltd. is 200 shares each. Suppose the price per share for The Bank of East Asia Ltd. and China Motor Bus Co. Ltd. is HK$15 and HK$30, respectively. A small investor with only HK$6,000 can only purchase either two lots of The Bank of East Asia shares or one lot of China Motor Bus Co. Ltd. but not both — the minimum broad lot size requirement precludes small investors from the chance of diversifying their portfolios. If a fund manager collects funds from two small investors each with HK$6,000, the manager can invest the total sum of HK$12,000 in two lots of The Bank of East Asia Ltd. shares and one lot of China Motor Bus Co. Ltd. shares. Thus, each of the investors can own half of a portfolio that has a value of HK$6,000. In other words, each investor can now own one lot of The Bank of East Asia Ltd. shares and half a lot of China Motor Bus Co. Ltd. shares. The investor would not have been able to have access to such a diversified portfolio if he had invested on his own. As the pool gets larger, with a larger number of investors, each of the investors is able to own a more diversified portfolio or a smaller fraction of a broad lot. Given that most of the securities are less than perfectly correlated, the benefit of portfolio diversification will be greater when there is a large number of securities. Although we use Hong Kong stocks as an example in the above discussion, the conclusion is even stronger in the case of foreign stocks or bonds such as United Kingdom stocks or United States bonds.

This is because in some of these developed markets the brokerage fee is higher for small transactions.

Market Access

For most of the developed markets in the industrialized countries such as the United States or the United Kingdom, foreigners can have access to the stock-markets directly. Some of the smaller Asian markets such as Hong Kong, Singapore, and Malaysia are also open to foreign investors, that is, foreigners can purchase stocks directly from these markets. However, in some of the closed markets, such as Korea and Taiwan, foreigners are not allowed to buy shares directly from the stock-markets. Instead, they have to purchase local securities through trust funds. For restricted markets like Indonesia and Thailand, foreign ownership is only allowed up to a certain percentage of the total shares outstanding. In both of these cases, it is more cost effective and viable for investors, especially the small ones, to invest in these markets through unit trusts.

Professional Services

It is not easy to make an investment decision, especially in financial instruments, because of the large number of instruments from which to choose. For example, there are close to 300 stocks in the Hong Kong market, 300 stocks in the Singapore market, 1,500 stocks in the United States market (in the New York Stock Exchange), and 5,000 stocks in the United Kingdom market. In order to be able to make prudent investment decisions, an investor must research the background of the company, its financial performance, its future plans, and its recent price behaviour. It may be possible for an investor to study a few stocks, but it is impossible for one person to study thousands of stocks when the cost of time as well as the cost of acquiring the relevant data to do the analysis is considered. Investment companies managing various unit trusts employ professional investment managers to make investment decisions for their clients. Usually, the investment managers receive a great deal of free information and research reports from brokerage houses which provide brokerage services to the companies. Some relatively well-established firms such as the Wardley Investment Services Ltd., G.T. Management Ltd., and Jardine Fleming, may even have their own research departments to do the analysis to support their investment decisions. Since the investment managers are experienced professionals, they are in a better position than independent investors to digest the information provided by the brokerage houses or by their own research units. Moreover, as the investment house handles millions of investments each day, there is an economy of scale for them to process and digest all the highly technical and complicated financial and economic information.

The Hong Kong Unit Trust Industry

As noted earlier, although the unit trust industry started in 1960, its growth really picked up in the 1980s. In fact, the Hong Kong Unit Trust Association (HKUTA) was set up in 1985. As of December 1989, there were more than 700 trusts authorized by the Securities and Futures Commission, but only about 300 funds had been actively marketed as a number of the authorized funds have not been launched. Moreover, the total number of funds should be much greater than 300, as some of them are 'umbrella funds' under which are many sub-funds.

Types of Funds

The types of unit trust available in Hong Kong are no different from those available in other financial centres. There are two broad categories of funds: the growth fund and the income fund.

A growth fund aims at enhancing capital gain, that is, price appreciation of the assets invested. Cash contributed to these funds is generally invested in equity instruments. The Wardley International Trust, the JF Australia Trust, and the GT Universal Growth Fund all belong to this group. This type of fund usually invests in blue chip stocks. Recently, there has been a growing interest in specialized funds that aim at a very high return but carry a greater risk than general growth funds. They can be organized in the form of specialist country funds such as the JF Thailand Fund, the JF Philippines Fund, the Connaught Indonesian Growth Fund, and the Connaught Malaysian Fund. It is obvious that this type of fund aims at sharing the promising economic growth of the small Asian countries. There is another type of specialized growth fund, that aims at capital growth of a particular industrial sector. Examples are the GT Technology Fund, the JF Japan Technology Trust, and the Thornton Pacific Technology Fund. Some growth funds also specialize in the investment of small companies or under-valued stocks, such as the JF Smaller Company Trust, the GT US Smaller Companies Fund, and the Fidelity Special Situation Trust.[1]

Some growth funds specialize in commodity investment, and most of these concentrate their investment in precious metal, especially gold. This type of fund includes the Connaught Goldmine Fund, the MIM Britannia Gold and Precious Metals, and the CEF Canadian Natural Resources Trust. In most cases, these commodity or natural resources funds do not actually invest in the commodities. Instead, they put their money in purchasing shares of those companies that are involved in the exploration of the commodities. These specialist funds tend to have a more concentrated portfolio of less well-known companies or less developed countries. The returns on these funds are usually more volatile than those on the more diversified growth funds. Recently, some management companies have also offered funds that invest primarily in more speculative instruments such as warrants, options, and futures. Examples are the Gartmore Pacific Warrant Fund, the Gartmore

Japan Warrant Fund, and an option fund newly launched by the Connaught Investment Ltd.

An income fund aims at providing a stable income rather than maximizing capital growth. Generally, income funds will invest in fixed income securities such as government bonds, corporate bonds, convertibles, deposits, certificates of deposit, equities with high dividend yield, and treasury bills. Income funds may also be invested in one country or region, for example, the Fidelity Dollar Bond Fund, the Hambro EMMA Yen Money Market Fund, and the Gartmore Capital Strategy ECU Fund; or they may have an international distribution, for example, Hambro International Bond Fund, Schroders Currency and Bond Fund, and the RBC International Currencies Fund. However, although the objective of the income fund is to achieve a stable income stream, it must be kept in mind that the returns on an income fund are not riskless. This is especially true of the bond funds that are particularly sensitive to interest rate movements, that is, a rise (fall) in the interest rate would lead to a capital loss (gain) for bond funds.

Management houses may also launch balanced growth funds, which are a mixture of growth funds and income funds with a bias in favour of equity investments. International funds that invest in a portfolio of equities and fixed income securities are good examples of this type of fund.

In Hong Kong, the Unit Trust Association has placed the more than 300 unit trusts into 29 categories, mostly according to the type of security or the country in which the funds put their money. Details are given in Table 6.1.

Table 6.1 Categories of Funds

1.	Japanese Equity	16.	U.K. Gilt
2.	Hong Kong Equity	17.	U.S. Bond
3.	Australia Equity	18.	International Bond
4.	Singapore/Malaysia Equity	19.	Bond (Others)
5.	Korean Equity	20.	Currency (US$)
6.	Philippine Equity	21.	Currency (Stg)
7.	ASEAN Equity	22.	Currency (Mixed)
8.	Far East Equity	23.	Currency (DM)
9.	U.S. Equity	24.	Currency (SwFr)
10.	U.K. Equity	25.	Currency (Yen)
11.	European (incl. U.K.) Equity	26.	Currency (European)
12.	European (excl. U.K.)	27.	Currency (Others)
13.	International Equity	28.	Commodity
14.	International Managed	29.	Warrant
15.	Equity (Others)		

Source: *The Hong Kong Unit Trust Yearbook 1990* (Hong Kong, Longman, 1990), p. 9.

The Status of Hong Kong as a Fund Management Centre

The unit trust industry in Hong Kong started when the Hongkong and Shanghai Banking Corporation acted as the trustee for a fund launched in 1960. In the early days, most of the subscribers of unit trusts were expatriates from the United Kingdom. Very few local Chinese subscribed to the unit trust concept. The bankruptcy of an international unit trust company, the Investors Overseas Service (IOS) in the early 1970s, caused serious damage to the image of the unit trust industry. Investors' confidence was badly shaken, and the unit trust industry remained extremely quiet, even stagnant for many years.

It was not until the late 1970s that the unit trust industry made a new start. There are several reasons for this rapid growth. The first is the rapid growth of wealth of people in this part of the world. The second is an increase in Hong Kong's political uncertainty due to the transfer of Hong Kong's sovereignty to China in 1997 — people in Hong Kong are therefore interested in diversifying their investments overseas. The third reason is that the establishment of the Hong Kong Code on Unit Trusts and Mutual Funds in 1978, together with all its subsequent amendments, enhanced investors' confidence in unit trusts. In January 1988 there were a total of 279 funds launched in Hong Kong, with a total of US$8,398 million under their management. In December 1989, the number of funds launched and the total fund size grew to 318 and US$17,724 million respectively.

Table 6.2 compares Hong Kong with other fund management centres. As of June 1987, Hong Kong was ranked second after Japan in the Asia Pacific region in terms of the number of funds, the number of investment managers, and the total fund size. Hong Kong was ranked higher than Australia and its closest competitor, Singapore. However, the average fund size in Hong Kong was relatively small (US$45 million per fund) compared with those managed in the United States or other offshore fund centres. This indicates that competition may be rather intense in Hong Kong. The whole Asia Pacific region was also ranked higher than the United Kingdom. Although the total number of funds managed in the Asia Pacific region was close to that in the United States, the total fund size was about one-third as big as that of the United States. Pearson (1988) identified the following factors resulting in the rapid growth of unit trust in Hong Kong:

(a) Failure of other financial centres in Asia either to promote themselves as viable offshore fund centres or to stimulate their own unit trust activities.

(b) Hong Kong is free from the red tape which is very common in many countries in the region.

(c) Hong Kong has a simple tax system and a low tax rate.

(d) There is no foreign exchange control.

(e) Hong Kong can offer efficient banking and custodial services.

(f) Hong Kong has a good communications network, a stable political environment (relative to some other Asian countries), and a pool of highly efficient administrative and systems personnel.

(g) Hong Kong has a good legal system, a pool of competent lawyers and investment experts, and multinational brokers.

(h) Although property in Hong Kong is expensive, it is still relatively low when compared with Tokyo.

Table 6.2   Fund Management Centres

Centres	No. of Trusts	No. of Managers	Total Assets (US$m)	Average Size per Trust (US$m)
Asia Pacific	2,063	108	275,030	133
Japan	1,520	12	245,000	161
Hong Kong	238	35	10,600	45
Australia	135	23	7,400	55
Korea	112	9	5,300	47
India	18	4	5,200	289
Taiwan	8	4	420	53
Malaysia	8	4	350	44
Singapore	9	4	250	28
Thailand	4	4	230	58
New Zealand	7	5	120	17
Indonesia	1	1	110	110
Philippines	3	3	50	17
United Kingdom	1,070	161	56,000	54
United States	2,200	208	810,000	368
Offshore Fund Centres	730	234	63,000	86

Source: Peter J. Pearson, 'Hong Kong's Attractions for Fund Managers', *The Hong Kong Unit Trust Yearbook 1988* (Hong Kong, Longman, 1988), pp. 4–6.

The Operation of Unit Trusts

As mentioned earlier, the fund of a unit trust is managed by an investment company which combines funds from a number of investors and invests them in a portfolio of securities. It is required by law that investors are protected by having their investment held in trust for them by an independent trustee. All the assets of the fund are held in the name of the trustee. In order to strengthen the confidence of the investors, the trustee is usually a major bank or a large insurance company. Table 6.3 presents the trustees for the top ten funds (by fund size) in 1989, and it is obvious that the trustees are all trustworthy, large institutions. The trustee performs a monitoring function, and one of its major jobs is to ensure that the company is managing the fund according to the terms of the trust deed. A trust deed is a contract which lays down how the money in the fund must be invested; how the price of units is to be calculated; how the income is to be distributed; and how much managers can be paid. The trustee can also monitor all unit trust advertising in order to make sure that the management company does not make extravagant or misleading claims about its performance.

Table 6.3 Trustees of the Top Ten Funds

Fund	Trustee
Internationaler Rentenfonds	Dresdner Bank AG, Frankfurt
Fidelity European Trust	Clydesdale Bank PLC
JF Japan Trust	Hongkong Bank Int'l Trustee Ltd.
Concentra	Dresdner Bank AG, Frankfurt
GAM Worldwide Inc.	Pierson, Heldring & Pierson NV
Fidelity Special Situations Trust	Midland Bank PLC
Schroder Japan Fund	Standard Chartered Bank Hong Kong Trustee Ltd.
NM UK Equity Fund	Lloyds Bank PLC
MIM Britannia Jersey Gilt Fund	NatWest Int'l Trust Corp. (Jersey) Ltd.

Source: *The Hong Kong Unit Trust Yearbook 1990* (Hong Kong, Longman, 1990).

When offering units of the funds for investors to subscribe, the management company needs to quote the price of a unit of the fund to the general public. Usually unit trust prices are quoted as bid-offer prices or Net Asset Value (NAV) price. In the bid-offer pricing, two prices are quoted, the bid price and the offer price.

The offer price is the higher of the two and is the price that investors have to pay for a unit of the fund. The offer price is calculated by the total market value of the assets (calculated by the lowest available market dealing offered price) in the fund, plus dealing expenses and the initial fee (it is usually 5 per cent) charged by the management company minus any liabilities and financial charges incurred by the fund and divided by the total number of units.

The bid price is the lower of the two prices and is the price that investors will get when they sell their units. The bid price is calculated by the market value of the assets (calculated by the highest available market dealing bid price) minus dealing expenses, liabilities, and other financial charges incurred by the fund divided by the number of units. The spread between the bid and offer price for most funds is around 5 per cent.

Some funds may just quote one price, that is, the NAV which is calculated as the net asset value of the fund divided by the total number of units. Investors usually pay this amount, plus the initial charge, for a unit of the fund. When investors sell a unit of the fund, they will get the NAV per unit minus the redemption charges. Usually, the management company just charges 5 per cent of the initial fee to buyers of units and does not charge any redemption fee. Any variations in the valuation method and price quotation are possible, and these details should be spelled out clearly in the trust deed of the fund.

Investors can purchase units directly from a unit trust company such as GT Group Managment (Asia) Ltd., Jardine Fleming Unit Trusts Ltd., Schroders Asia Ltd., and Fidelity International Investment Management (Hong Kong) Ltd. Investors can also buy units through a registered investment advisor. A registered investment adviser provides investment consultancy services to its clients for a remuneration, and has to be registered by the Securities and Futures Commission. Registered investment advisers usually collect information from various fund management companies and prepare proposals for clients on the most appropriate portfolio of unit trusts for clients to buy. Generally, the clients do not have to pay their advisers because when those clients buy units, the management companies pay a commission to the advisers for referring business to them.

Since the management company is a firm that provides professional investment services, it needs to be properly compensated. There is usually an initial charge of about 5 per cent and an annual management fee of around 1 per cent. For example, in the Fidelity Japan Special Situations Trust, the initial charge is 5.25 per cent and the annual management fee is 1.25 per cent; and in the Gartmore Pacific Warrant Fund, the initial charge is 5 per cent and the annual management fee is 2 per cent. Usually, the management companies pay commission to investment advisers out of the 5 per cent initial charge. The common practice is that the management companies get about 2 per cent while the investment advisers get 3 per cent. In a very competitive market, the advisers even give some rebate to their clients. Thus, it is actually more beneficial to purchase units through professional investment advisers than to buy units directly from the management companies. This is because when investors go to an adviser, they pay less initial charge and have access to a larger pool of information about various funds than when they go directly to a few management companies. However, some of the management companies sometimes can reduce the initial charge to about 3 per cent for large investors. This may cause considerable difficulties for some of the smaller investment advisers.

The Performance of Unit Trusts

Performance can usually be measured in terms of return. Table 6.4 gives the median return in United States dollars for each category of fund over a year, for the period ending 31 December 1989. It is noted that the top four funds all belong to the smaller Asian markets. The Philippine Equity had the highest return of 98.74 per cent, and the Singapore/Malaysia Equity's performance was the second best with a median return of 88.08 per cent. The performance of fund managers

Table 6.4 Investment Return and Performance Ranking (Unit: US$)

Fund Sector/Median Return and Ranking[1]	For Periods Ending 31 December 1989, over					Since 1.1.80
	6 Months	1 Year	2 Years	3 Years	5 Years	
1. Japanese Equity	22.29% (6)	18.20% (10)	48.88% (7)	113.90% (4)	379.28% (2)	958.87% (1)
2. Hong Kong Equity	26.59% (4)	8.09% (19)	33.67% (13)	19.45% (25)	171.82% (12)	234.43% (9)
3. Australian Equity	13.91% (14)	8.47% (17)	26.04% (15)	6.29% (28)	33.02% (25)	64.15% (15)
4. Singapore/ Malaysian Equity	31.13% (3)	88.08% (2)	134.77% (2)	136.14% (3)	146.57% (13)	
5. Korean Equity	6.84% (22)	11.87% (13)	82.70% (4)	179.36% (2)		
6. Philippine Equity	50.34% (1)	98.74% (1)	133.02% (3)	255.41% (1)	1803.07% (1)	414.86% (5)
7. ASEAN Equity	31.82% (2)	58.20% (3)	134.98% (1)	84.20% (5)	262.34% (7)	467.15% (4)
8. Far East Equity	25.65% (5)	36.93% (4)	64.83% (5)	83.21% (6)	332.34% (4)	618.42% (2)
9. U.S. Equity	6.08% (24)	19.79% (8)	34.64% (11)	29.31% (19)	72.32% (21)	194.28% (11)
10. U.K. Equity	7.55% (20)	8.04% (20)	8.67% (18)	67.48% (7)	217.33% (9)	533.42% (3)
11. European (incl. U.K.) Equity	18.81% (11)	28.60% (6)	47.68% (8)	31.33% (18)	263.25% (6)	255.82% (8)
12. European (excl. U.K.) Equity	21.65% (7)	34.11% (5)	63.59% (6)	38.06% (13)	283.11% (5)	
13. International Equity	17.09% (12)	22.45% (7)	38.99% (9)	42.10% (11)	175.85% (11)	350.93% (7)
14. International Managed	13.93% (13)	17.51% (12)	32.63% (14)	34.02% (16)	225.17% (8)	
15. Equity (Others)	5.47% (25)	17.57% (11)	34.80% (10)	33.13% (17)	214.61% (10)	371.62% (6)
16. U.K. Gilt	7.07% (21)	−5.66% (27)	−3.13% (26)	39.13% (12)	113.83% (16)	146.32% (13)
17. U.S. Bond	3.20% (27)	8.96% (16)	14.78% (17)	16.81% (26)	61.62% (23)	
18. International Bond	6.14% (23)	6.30% (22)	6.20% (23)	22.99% (23)	93.70% (20)	199.70% (10)
19. Bond (Others)	9.51% (18)	5.69% (23)	8.35% (19)	46.65% (10)	371.55% (3)	
20. Currency (US$)	3.99% (26)	8.41% (18)	16.14% (16)	22.99% (22)	40.46% (24)	150.45% (12)
21. Currency (Stg)	11.41% (16)	0.76% (26)	6.77% (21)	47.34% (9)	127.16% (14)	
22. Currency (Mixed)	7.56% (19)	3.53% (24)	7.10% (20)	35.71% (15)	99.00% (18)	96.50% (14)
23. Currency (DM)	19.83% (10)	10.61% (14)	2.59% (25)	28.78% (20)	123.73% (15)	
24. Currency (SwFr)	12.77% (15)	2.62% (25)	−10.31% (28)	15.94% (27)	97.68% (19)	
25. Currency (Yen)	−2.40% (28)	−9.77% (27)	−8.01% (27)	22.26% (24)	110.76% (17)	
26. Currency (European)	20.09% (9)	9.96% (15)	6.34% (22)	35.8% (14)		
27. Currency (Others)	10.98% (17)	7.57% (21)	34.28% (12)	61.18% (8)		
28. Commodity	21.23% (8)	19.25% (9)	3.15% (24)	27.76% (21)	62.22% (22)	
29. Warrant[2]	—	—	—	—	—	

Notes: 1. Numbers in brackets refer to fund rankings.
2. Performance statistics not available as warrant funds authorized in late 1989.

Source: *The Hong Kong Unit Trust Yearbook, 1990* (Hong Kong, Longman, 1990), p. 9.

seems to be especially good during that period, as it is estimated by the Bankers Trust Securities Research that the total gain in United States dollars for the Philippine market in 1989 was 28.6 per cent, and for the Singapore and Malaysia markets was 49.6 per cent and 58.6 per cent, respectively. Thus, the fund managers were able to out-perform the market by a wide margin.

Apart from return, there is also another dimension to the measurement of performance, and that is risk. In the academic world, risk is usually measured by a statistical concept, the standard deviation, which is actually a measurement of how far each individual outcome deviates from the mean or average outcome. The Unit Trust Association started to employ such a method to measure the riskiness of each of the trust funds in 1989. Based on the relative level of standard deviation, all the funds are then given a volatility rating ranging from low to high:

Standard Deviation	Risk Rating
Highest 20% of funds	High
Next 20%	Medium/High
Next 20%	Medium
Next 20%	Medium/Low
Lowest 20% of funds	Low

Table 6.5 gives the volatility rating of the various categories of funds. It is clear that the top performers in terms of median returns are all ranked in the Medium/High to High risk category. This shows clearly that the high returns are compensation for incurring high risk.

The Regulation of Unit Trusts

The regulation of unit trusts is under the jurisdiction of the Securities and Futures Commission, which controls the unit trust industry through the Committee on Unit Trusts. Apart from the Trustee Ordinance (which controls the appointment of trustees) and the Protection of Investors Ordinance (which controls the promotion activities of unit trusts), the unit trust industry has to comply with the Hong Kong Code on Unit Trusts and Mutual Funds for the day-to-day operations of the funds and for authorization of the funds.

In the process of seeking authorization, the applicant must submit to the Commissioner of the SFC a whole range of documents, including the trust deed, the explanatory memorandum, application form, all sales literature, the trust's most recent annual and quarterly reports, the latest annual report of the trust company, and the most recent report of the management company. Moreover, the management company is required to provide the Commissioner with supplementary information, such as the time of the first sale of units; the investment policy; the method of distribution; the calculation of costs and charges; and the connections

Table 6.5 Return and Volatility Profile, 1 January 1987 to 31 December 1989

Returns in US$ (%)			Fund Category	No. of Funds	Volatility Ratings				
Maximum	Median	Minimum			Low	Low/Medium	Medium	Medium/High	High
222.18	113.90	26.67	1. Japanese Equity	(26)		11	12	3	10
56.34	19.45	−25.94	2. Hong Kong Equity	(10)					9
168.26	−6.29	−43.00	3. Australian Equity	(9)					9
183.30	136.14	120.53	4. Singapore/Malaysian Equity	(4)					4
179.36	179.36	179.36	5. Korean Equity	(1)			1		
367.08	255.41	143.75	6. Philippine Equity	(2)					2
177.71	84.20	65.73	7. ASEAN Equity	(9)				4	5
160.70	83.21	−0.66	8. Far East Equity	(16)		2	5	5	4
57.23	29.31	16.42	9. U.S. Equity	(17)		1	7	8	1
131.72	67.48	45.90	10. U.K. Equity	(9)		1	3	5	
47.04	31.33	24.83	11. European (incl. United Kingdom) Equity	(3)		1	2	1	
184.02	38.06	28.90	12. European (excl. United Kingdom) Equity	(6)		2	3	1	
84.18	42.10	29.28	13. International Equity	(11)		3	3	5	
64.11	34.02	9.51	14. International Managed	(6)		5		1	
66.01	33.13	−35.20	15. Equity (Others)	(4)			1	3	
47.72	39.13	29.19	16. U.K. Gilt	(5)	2	3			
19.77	16.81	13.85	17. U.S. Bond	(2)	2				
41.08	22.99	1.69	18. International Bond	(12)	12				
57.61	46.65	35.70	19. Bond (Others)	(2)	1	1			
23.69	22.99	22.20	20. Currency (US$)	(3)	3				
47.41	47.34	36.19	21. Currency (Stg)	(3)	3				
45.12	35.71	17.87	22. Currency (Mixed)	(7)	7				
29.16	29.78	23.39	23. Currency (DM)	(3)	3				
17.38	15.94	11.19	24. Currency (SwFr)	(3)		3			
22.29	22.26	15.61	25. Currency (Yen)	(3)	3				
36.75	35.86	34.98	26. Currency (European)	(2)	1	1			
72.29	61.18	52.59	27. Currency (Others)	(3)	3				
35.79	27.76	19.73	28. Commodity	(2)					2

Source: The Hong Kong Unit Trust Yearbook, 1990 (Hong Kong, Longman, 1990), p. 42.

between the trustee, the management company, the investment adviser, and the distribution company.

The Committee on Unit Trusts

The Committee on Unit Trusts is established under the Securities and Futures Commission Ordinance of 1989. The Committee is chaired by the Vice-chairman of the Securities and Futures Commission (SFC), who is the Executive Director of Intermediaries and Investment Products. Other members include other officials from the SFC, a person nominated by the SFC, the Chairman of the Hong Kong Unit Trust Association, a representative of the Secretary for Monetary Affairs, persons from companies engaged in fund management and from trustee companies, and actuaries.

The job of the Committee is to administer and amend the Code, to authorize unit trusts and mutual fund companies, to approve prospectuses, to grant waivers from the Code, and to recommend amendments to legislation relating to unit trusts and mutual funds. The day-to-day operation of the Commission is run by the Secretary of the Committee.

Requirements Applying to the Trustee

It is required by the Code that the trustee must not be connected with the management company, the investment adviser, or the distribution company. However, this requirement can be waived provided the Committee is satisfied that the Trustee and Management Company act independently and without prejudice to the unit holders.

Generally, there is no minimum capital requirement but a trust company is normally considered to be acceptable if its issued capital, plus capital reserves, plus guarantee to subscribe equity amounts to HK$5 million.

Investment Limitations and Restrictions

The trust deed must set out the restrictions on the investment of the fund's assets and Committee recommends the following limitations:

(a) Investments in any one company, gold, silver, platinum, or other bullion should not exceed 10 per cent of the net asset value.

(b) Investments in a security of any one class in any company should not exceed 10 per cent of the total nominal amount of all the issued securities of that class.

(c) Investments in unquoted companies, warrants, and options should not exceed 15 per cent of the net asset value.

(d) Investments in physical commodities; futures contracts; and options on commodities, futures contracts, and commodity-based investments should not exceed 20 per cent of the net asset value.

(e) Investments in countries where immediate repatriation rights are not available should not exceed 10 per cent of the net asset value.

(f) Investments in other unit trusts and mutual funds should not exceed 10 per cent of the net asset value.

(g) A fund may invest all its assets in a pool of funds known as a 'Unit Portfolio Management Fund' (UPMF) provided that not more than 20 per cent of the UPMF's assets are invested in unauthorized funds, that it may not invest in another UPMF, that it may not borrow to the extent of 5 per cent of its net asset value, that it may not invest in options or futures, and that it must invest at least five funds and not more than 35 per cent of its total assets should be invested in any one fund.

The Committee also recommends that the following investments be prohibited:

(a) Land or interests in land.

(b) Short sale.

(c) Guarantee in connection with any obligation of any person in respect of borrowed money.

(d) Security of a company of which any director of the management company individually owns more than 0.5 per cent or of which the directors collectively own more than 5 per cent.

(e) Investments of all the fund's assets in one unrestricted investment.

(f) Investments that would involve the trustee in any liability.

(g) Investments in unauthorized funds, except by approval of the commissioner.

Requirements Applying to the Management Company

The management company is responsible for preparing the trust's reports with a statement showing the assets and liabilities of the trust. There should also be one dealing date and one quotation of offer and redemption price per week. For investors who want to redeem their units, the management companies are required to make the redemption within a period that does not exceed one month from the dealing day on which, or prior to which, the request was received. Management companies are not allowed to make any forecasts of the trust's performance or to advertise the trust on radio, television, or in the cinema.

Recent Developments

On 7 September 1990, the Securities and Futures Commission (SFC) revised the Code on Unit Trust and Mutual Funds and sent out consultative documents to seek comments from the industry. The draft code is an outcome of a thorough consultation exercise with the unit trust industry, and contains four minor increases in regulation and nine deregulatory items.

The four increases in regulation are:

(a) An increase in the capital requirement for the trustee or custodian of a fund to HK$10 million from HK$5 million with concessions granted for fund subsidiaries of major financial institutions giving certain guarantees.

(b) Custodians of funds are now required to have a supervisory role over their respective funds.

(c) The trustee or custodian and the management company of a fund have to be independent of each other, although they can be owned by the same umbrella group.

(d) Offer documents have to be translated into Chinese except where the scheme is not to be promoted among non-English speaking investors.

There are also nine deregulatory items:

(a) A 'recognized jurisdiction' scheme which enables funds already under a regulatory jurisdiction comparable or better than Hong Kong to gain substantial exemptions when seeking approval in the territory.

(b) Certain annual filings of fund details aare no longer required.

(c) Financial futures are now permitted for hedging purposes without restriction and, on an unhedged basis, for up to 20 per cent of net asset value.

(d) The 10 per cent limit on bullion investment has been removed but it will now be counted within the overall 20 per cent limit on physical commodities.

(e) The 10 per cent limit on investments in countries without immediate repatriation rights has been removed and the onus is now on the manager of a fund to ensure the fund's liquidity.

(f) SFC approval to invest up to 10 per cent of a fund in unauthorized schemes no longer applies.

(g) Allowance also has been made for consideration of specialized or non-standard funds by providing greater flexibility for approval.

(h) Unit Portfolio Management Funds (UPMFs) in recognized jurisdiction schemes without limit have had their borrowing limit increased to 10 per cent from 5 per cent.

(i) A Hong Kong representative of a fund need no longer be licensed as a dealer or exempt dealer as long as a licensed entity is appointed to carry out the distribution function of the fund in Hong Kong.

The newly revised draft seems to be well received. At the time of writing, there is still one outstanding issue for further consultation, that is, the HK$50,000 minimum level for Hong Kong dollar money funds. The funds industry believes that such a minimum limit should be lowered in order to expand their market for money market funds. However, both the banking sector and the Government may not be in favour of such a move because that would increase competition in the deposit market and make monetary policy more difficult.

Immediately after the SFC released the new draft code, on 16 September 1990, the Hong Kong Unit Trust Association also issued a code of ethics for its members. The purpose of such a code is to boost the confidence of the Hong Kong investors in the fund management industry. There are a total of 14 rules on ethical practices in the code, with which members of the Association are required to comply. Otherwise, they will be liable to disciplinary procedures which are to be incorporated in the association's articles of association. The 14 rules are described briefly as follows:

(a) Members are required to observe and comply with all relevant laws and regulations, and observe and comply with the spirit as well as the letter of the Hong Kong Code on Unit Trust and Mutual Funds.

(b) They are required to co-operate with the SFC and all other responsible authorities in Hong Kong in the achievement of the objectives of the Association and the conduct of their businesses.

(c) They must act in a manner which recognizes that integrity and responsibility are essential to win and maintain the confidence of members of the public in all aspects of the unit trust industry.

(d) They are required to conduct their business in a professional manner and in accordance with sound business practice, and ensure that their staff are thoroughly and appropriately trained, and knowledgeable and competent in all aspects of the unit trust industry.

(e) They are also required to respect and preserve the confidentiality of their clients and investors in their unit trusts and mutual funds.

(f) Members must ensure that the overriding principle in managing their unit trusts and mutual funds is the benefit and interest of investors.

(g) They should also ensure that all offering documentation in relation to any unit trust or mutual fund contains such information as is necessary for the investor to make an informed judgement about investment in that unit trust or mutual fund, and that it is written clearly and simply.

(h) Members must not issue misleading advertisements or intrude upon the privacy of members of the public through door-to-door canvassing or other similar methods. They must provide investors with all requisite documentation promptly in accordance with their stated intentions.

(i) Members should abide by all policies and statements of intention stated in their offering documentation, and must ensure that investors and potential investors are given adequate warning of any proposed change of intention or policy.

It is thus very clear that the SFC is determined to streamline the operations and regulations of the unit trust industry. The industry is also trying to co-operate with the Government and implement a system of self-regulation. Although the Code on Unit Trusts and Mutual Funds is not treated as law, the establishment of the ethical code by the industry itself with enhance proper functioning of the industry. This will certainly be a very good case to examine, to discover if self-regulation in the financial sector is viable.

Note

1. The Fidelity Special Situation Trust invests primarily in undervalued 'special situation' equities, mainly in United Kingdom. Examples of special situations include management change, re-organization, product innovation, companies with new issues or takeover prospects, and stocks that have good potential but the value of which has not been fully reflected in the market, and that are therefore relatively cheap to purchase. Thus, the investment strategy of this type of fund relies on the notion that the market or a portion of the stock-market is not efficient, and the current status of the company can be informative about the future performance of the stock.

References

The Hong Kong Unit Trust Yearbook 1988, (Hong Kong, Longman, 1988).

The Hong Kong Unit Trust Yearbook 1990, (Hong Kong, Longman, 1990).

Lui, Y. H., *Hong Kong's Financial System*, (Hong Kong, Commercial Press, 1989, in Chinese).

Markowitz, H. M., 'Portfolio Selection', *The Journal of Finance*, 1952, Vol. 7, pp. 77–91.

Pearson, P. J., 'Hong Kong's Attraction for Fund Managers', *The Hong Kong Unit Trust Yearbook 1988*, (Hong Kong, Longman, 1988), pp. 4–6.

Perkin, I. P., 'New Unit Trust Code Proposed', *South China Morning Post*, 8 September 1990.

—— 'SFC Deserves Praise for Trusts Overhaul', *South China Morning Post*, 8 September 1990.

—— 'Ethics Code for Unit Trust Firms', *South China Morning Post*, 15 September 1990.

7. Hong Kong's Insurance Industry

JIM H. Y. WONG

Insurance Companies and Types of Insurance

Insurance companies may be defined as business entities engaged in taking calculated risks for which they receive income in the form of premiums. They make risks manageable by combining many loss exposures and spreading the cost of any losses among all participants.

There are two main categories of insurance business — life and general. Life insurance is a long-term business concerned not only with insuring the lives of individuals, but also with providing for financial coverage against contingencies such as illness or disability. In a typical life insurance policy, a policy holder contracts with an insurance company to pay a premium periodically in return for an annuity or a lump sum payment in the event of the maturity of the policy, disablement, or death. The premium of the policy is computed on the health and age of the policy holder, against the average mortality rate of the population. Two basic methods for providing pure life insurance protection to individuals, namely, the yearly renewable term method and level premium method, are discussed below.

Two Basic Methods for Providing Life Insurance Protection

1. Yearly Renewable Term Method.   Yearly renewable term method provides life insurance for only one year. The insured is entitled to renew the policy for successive one-year periods with no evidence of insurability required. The pure premium for yearly renewable term insurance is determined by the death rate at each attained age, and individuals within each age group are required to pay their pro rata share of death claims. For instance, the 1980 CSO Mortality Table (see Table 7.1) shows that the death rate at age 30 is 1.73 for each 1,000 lives. If 100,000 individuals at age 30 are insured for $1,000 for one year, the insurance company will pay 173 death claims, or $173,000. If interest and expenses are ignored, each insured will be required to pay a premium of $1.73 (= $173,000/100,000). As can be seen from the Mortality Table, the yearly renewable term insurance premiums increase as the individual gets older. The premium increase is gradual during the early years, but it rises sharply during the later years and it tends to increase at an accelerating rate. Therefore, if the insured wants lifetime protection, the yearly renewable term method may not be practical because the cost of the premiums can be prohibitive at an older age.

2. Level Premium Method. Under the level premium method, premiums stay constant and do not increase with age, and the insured has lifetime protection to age 100. Under this method, premiums paid during the early years of the policy are higher than the amount required to pay current death claims, when mortality rates are low, while those paid in later years are inadequate for paying death claims, when mortality rates and high. A level premium is possible since the excess premiums paid during the early years are invested to generate earnings, and the accumulated funds are then used to supplement the deficiency in premiums paid during the later years of the policy.

Table 7.1 Commissioners' 1980 Standard Ordinary (CSO) Table of Mortality

Male Age	Rate of Mortality per 1,000
20	1.90
30	1.73
40	3.02
50	6.71
60	16.08
70	39.51
80	98.84
90	221.77
99	1,000.00

Source: Based on 1980 CSO Mortality Table.

Life insurance policies today commonly incorporate an investment as well as an insurance element. They vary considerably, from those linked to the performance of specified portfolios to endowment policies covering house purchase loans. While term and whole life policies providing pure insurance cover continue to constitute the bulk of individual life business, endowment and investment-linked insurance policies have become increasingly popular. Often, in fact, in the case of life policies, the insurers are supplying a hybrid product, which not only provides insurance coverage, but also serves as an investment vehicle and loan facility.

General insurance, on the other hand, covers the risks of all non-life business, such as losses of property through accident, fire, burglary, and other mishaps. General insurance is essentially short-term in nature, and the contract may be reviewed and renewed annually by both parties. Premiums are calculated according to the possibility of loss on the basis of statistical information.

The insurance companies, therefore, provide their clients with financial protection against loss of property, income, or life. In addition, through the acceptance of premiums from their clients, especially in the case of the life insurance business, they accumulate substantial financial assets as contingency reserves to meet the possible claims of their clients. In the life insurance business, such reserves constitute a liability of the insurance company to its clients, as well as being a form of long-term savings convertible to cash if necessary. On the other hand, premiums paid on general insurance do not constitute household savings, in view of the short-term nature of the business. In many countries, insurance companies serve as a stable source of capital, because of the steady inflow of premium and investment income and the foreseeability of claims payments under the law of averages, thus fulfilling a very useful economic function. Equally important, insurance relieves policy holders of many of the uncertainties in life and facilitates their forward planning.

According to the nature of their business, insurance companies in Hong Kong can be broadly classified into four categories: life insurers, general insurers, composite insurers (which engage in both life and general insurance), and specialist reinsurers. The last category of companies accepts the obligation of other insurance companies under a contract of reinsurance. In other words, they are specialized in reinsurance, which involves spreading the responsibility for coverage of life or general risks among insurance companies. Under the Insurance Companies Ordinance 1983, insurance businesses in Hong Kong are grouped into 23 different authorized classes, as shown in Table 7.2.

Table 7.2   Classes of Authorized Business in Hong Kong

Class	Description Long-Term Business	Class	Description General Business
A	Life and annuity	1	Accident
B	Marriage and birth	2	Sickness
C	Linked long term	3	Land vehicles
D	Permanent health	4	Railway rolling stock
E	Tontines	5	Aircraft
F	Capital redemption	6	Ships
		7	Goods in transit
		8	Fire and natural forces
		9	Damage to property
		10	Motor vehicle liability
		11	Aircraft liability
		12	Liability for ships
		13	General liability
		14	Credit
		15	Suretyship
		16	Miscellaneous financial loss
		17	Legal expenses

Source: Hong Kong, Registrar General's Department.

Historical Development

The marine insurance business was originally the most important branch of insurance in Hong Kong, having been introduced to the territory in the early days via the British mercantile agencies in Calcutta. Merchants combined to form syndicates, taking it in turns to act as the agent in charge of the underwriting. One of the earliest underwriting arrangements to emerge on mainland China for the purpose of insuring the China trade was a series of 10 'insurance offices' each formed for a period of three years from 1805 until 1832. These offices were superseded by the Canton Insurance Office (later renamed the Lombard Insurance Co. Ltd.) founded in 1836 by Jardine Matheson & Co., one of the managing partners of the earlier insurance offices. A year previously a second venture, the Union Insurance Society (later to become the Union Insurance Society of Canton Ltd.) had been formed by Dent & Co., the other former managing partner. The head offices of both companies were later transferred to Hong Kong.

With the expansion of the domestic economy in subsequent years and the growing fire insurance business, the Hong Kong Fire Insurance Company Ltd. was formed in 1868, to be the first insurance company incorporated in the territory. All these companies underwrote fire and accident as well as marine risks. In 1867 Lloyd's of London appointed a representative in Hong Kong, and in following years, with the growth of the large export firms who placed their insurance in Europe, more foreign branches and agencies were set up in the territory.

By the early 1970s Hong Kong had established itself as one of the leading insurance centres in the Asia Pacific region. The sustained growth in Hong Kong's economy, foreign trade, and capital investment, together with the development of its service industries, made the territory an attractive growth market for insurance business and served as a magnet for foreign insurance companies. During the past fifteen years, the number of insurance companies licenced to do business in Hong Kong has increased by 42, from 233 in 1973 to 275 in June 1989. Meanwhile, the number of people employed in the sector rose from about 6,380 in September 1980 to more than 16,800 in September 1989, while the total number of insurance establishments operating in the market, including insurance companies and their branches, agents, and brokers, increased rapidly from 632 to 3,795 during the same period.

Regulations Governing Insurance Companies

Legislation and Supervision

Insurance companies in Hong Kong are governed by the Insurance Companies Ordinance 1983 (together with its subsequent amendments), which has been in operation since 30 June 1983. Prior to this, there had been no comprehensive system of control and only companies carrying on life, fire, marine, or motor vehicle insurance in Hong Kong were subject to regulation. This ordinance has extended the legislation to cover all classes of insurance business. It prescribes stringent requirements covering the fitness of directors and controllers of insurance companies and these companies' financial requirements. The ordinance also confers wide powers of investigation and intervention upon the Registrar General in his capacity as the Insurance Authority. Under current legislation, the minimum paid-up capital of an insurance company underwriting either long-term or general business is HK$5 million, and for composite insurers and those transacting compulsory insurance business — that is, employees' compensation, motor vehicles, and pleasure craft[1] — HK$10 million.

The insurance companies are required to maintain a minimum solvency margin (that is, the margin between the value of the assets of the company and the amount of its liabilities), the amount of which is determined by the types of business a company carries on and, in the case of general insurance, the level of relevant premium income written by the company[2], as summarized in Table 7.3.

Currently, the Insurance Authority (the Insurance Division of the Registrar General's Department) is responsible for authorizing insurance companies and ensuring their compliance with the ordinance. However, to allow for increased prudential supervision, it is anticipated that the Insurance Division will be spun off from the Registrar General's Department as a separate Insurance Commission sometime in 1990. Under this plan, a restructured and strengthened Insurance Commissioner's Office will — like the Banking Commission — come directly under the Monetary Affairs Branch and will be responsible for the authorization and regulation of insurance companies.

The Monetary Affairs Branch is responsible for policy matters relating to the insurance industry. In addition, under the provision of the Insurance Companies Ordinance, an Insurance Advisory Committee was established to advise the Governor on matters relating to the administration of the ordinance or the performance of insurance business. The committee, which meets every three months, currently has the Secretary for Monetary Affairs (representing the Financial Secretary) as its Chair, the Insurance Authority as an ex-officio member, and 13 other persons appointed by the Governor.

Further Tightening of Prudential Controls and Self-Regulation

As part of the effort to strengthen Hong Kong's position as a regional financial centre and to improve protection for the public, the regulations governing the operation of the insurance industry have been considerably tightened over the past few years. Most recently, the Insurance Companies (Amendment) Ordinance 1989 ('The Amendment Ordinance') was enacted in March 1989, and a bill is under preparation on the regulation of private retirement schemes. The former, containing four amendments, raises the minimum solvency margin requirements (see Tables 7.3 and 7.4).

The Amendment Ordinance also requires an insurer underwriting long-term business to carry out an actuarial investigation (that is, an investigation into an insurer's financial condition, including a valuation of its liabilities and assets by its actuary) at least once a year, instead of every two years prior to the amendments, and increases the powers of the Insurance Authority by allowing it to require insurers to supply additional information, so as to facilitate closer monitoring of the insurer's financial position. Another amendment modifies the criteria by which a person may be considered as a controller of an insurance company, from the holding of one third or more of the voting power to only 15 per cent. A grace period of up to 1 April 1991 is given for existing insurers who are unable to comply immediately with the new solvency margin provisions.

The Law Reform Commission Report on the Laws of Insurance (Topic No. 9) issued in January 1986 recommended legislation covering two main areas — the interpretation of insurance contracts and the regulation of intermediaries. However, this was opposed by the industry on grounds that such legislation would be unnecessarily bureaucratic and complex. Consequently, the Hong Kong Insurance Industry Self-

Table 7.3 Minimum Solvency Margin Required Prior to the Amendments

Type of Business	Not Handling Compulsory Business	Handling Compulsory Business
Long-term Business	HK$2 million	HK$2 million
General Insurance Business		
(a) The relevant premium income of the company in its last preceding financial year did not exceed HK$10 million.	HK$2 million	HK$4 million
(b) The said income that year exceeded HK$10 million but did not exceed HK$50 million.	20 per cent of the said income in that year.	Or HK$4 million, whichever is higher.
(c) The said income in that year exceeded HK$50 million.	The aggregate of HK$10 million and 10 per cent of the amount by which the said income in that year exceeded HK$50 million.	
Both Long-term and General Insurance	HK$4 million or the amount according to the relevant premium income of its general business plus HK$2 million, whichever is higher.	Or HK$6 million, whichever is higher.

Source: Insurance Companies Ordinance.

Table 7.4   Minimum Solvency Margin After the Amendments

Type of Business	Not Handling Compulsory Business	Handling Compulsory Business
Long-term Business	HK$5 million	HK$5 million
General Insurance Business		
(a) The relevant premium income of the company in its last preceding financial year did not exceed HK$25 million.	HK$5 million	HK$10 million
(b) The said income that year exceeded HK$25 million but did not exceed HK$100 million.	20 per cent of the said income.	HK$10 million or 20 per cent of the said income, whichever is higher.
(c) The said income in that year exceeded HK$100 million.	HK$20 million plus 10 per cent of excess income over HK$100 million.	
Both Long-term and General Insurance	HK$7 million or the amount according to the relevant premium income of its general business plus HK$2 million, whichever is higher.	Or HK$12 million, whichever is higher.

Source: Insurance Companies Ordinance.

Regulation Working Group, a committee comprising representatives from all sectors of the industry, was formed in March 1987 to pursue the development and implementation of self-regulatory measures in the industry.

In March 1988, this committee submitted a statement on self-regulation to the Government, proposing a comprehensive self-regulation system aimed primarily at the issues addressed in the Law Reform Commission Report. The proposals, which reflect and closely follow the United Kingdom system and scope of self-regulation, have been accepted by the Insurance Authority in principle. Subsequent to this and following informal discussions with the Authority, a progress report and a formal proposal for the first stage of self-regulation, which deals with Part I of the Law Reform Commission Report on insurance contracts, were submitted to the Government in November and December 1988 respectively. Detailed measures, relating to Part II of the report on the regulation of intermediaries, will be addressed in the second-stage proposal.

Broadly speaking, the proposed system aims to specify standards for the interpretation of insurance contracts and professional conduct and to provide a framework for guidance and intervention. Under the proposal, agreed standards for the interpretation of insurance contracts, both life and non-life, taken out by private individuals in Hong Kong will be established and regulated based on approved Statements of Practice adopted by insurers. At the same time, all independent intermediaries acting as agents for the buyers and sellers of insurance will have to be registered with an association of such intermediaries approved by the authorities. Through establishing the codes of practice for general and long-term insurance and for all intermediaries, and through an agency agreement, formally approved and supported by the Insurance Authority, these associations will regulate the conduct of their members. An insurance claims appeal board will be set up to handle complaints regarding claims arising out of interpretation of personal insurance contracts, and a proposed insurance complaints office will handle complaints against authorized insurers who are members of the councils. Sanctions will be applied for failure to accept the rulings or for blatant or repeated infringement of standards and codes. As for the monitoring of the system, it is proposed that, in the early stage, this will be the duty of the Hong Kong Federation of Insurers (please refer to the next section of this chapter for a brief account of this federation) but an insurance industry self-regulation monitoring board will be formed at a later stage to perform this role.

For years, the perceived inequalities between the insurer and the insured and the absence of control over the activities of intermediaries have been two main areas of concern. Recent developments represent considerable progress towards resolving these problems and developing a more adequate framework for effective self-regulation.

Performance and Market Structure

Hong Kong's insurance industry has enjoyed strong growth in recent years. The general insurance industry has expanded parallel to the growth in commerce and industry, while rising incomes and a growing awareness of the value of insurance have helped boost the demand for life insurance. Hong Kong's role as a reinsurance centre has also developed, underpinned by an increasingly efficient banking system and the absence of foreign exchange controls. The territory's excellent communications facilities, its favourable geographical location, and its pool of well-qualified insurance professionals have attracted a large number of leading foreign insurance companies to the territory.

Rapid Growth and Strong Profitability

Statistics compiled by the Census and Statistics (C & S) Department indicate the domestic insurance sector expanded at an average annual rate of 17.9 per cent between 1981 and 1987, in terms of gross premium income, compared with an average growth rate of 15 per cent in nominal GDP. Of this total, life insurance premiums grew at an average rate of 27.5 per cent to reach HK$4,012 million in 1987, while

Table 7.5 Performance of the Insurance Sector, 1981–1987

	General Insurers (145)		Life Insurers (38)		Total (183)	
	1987 Value (HK$ million)	Annual Growth Rates 1981–1987 (Per cent)	1987 Value (HK$ million)	Annual Growth Rates 1981–1987 (Per cent)	1987 Value (HK$ million)	Annual Growth Rates 1981–1987 (Per cent)
Gross premiums	8,133.5	14.8	4,012.1	27.5	12,145.6	17.9
Retained premiums	4,656.4	18.6	3,548.2	26.9	8,204.6	21.6
Net claims	2,166.8	18.9	1,483.2	36.5	3,650.0	23.9
Funds and reserves	4,369.4	19.9	13,076.9	29.4	17,446.3	26.4
Investment	6,620.6	19.9	11,762.0	28.9	18,382.6	25.0
Retention ratio (per cent)						
1982	49.0		97.4		58.6	
1983	51.3		87.9		58.4	
1984	48.9		87.1		56.8	
1985	55.1		88.6		62.3	
1986	54.1		91.7		66.2	
1987	57.2		88.4		67.6	
Loss ratio (per cent)						
1982	51.7		n.a.		n.a.	
1983	72.3		n.a.		n.a.	
1984	41.1		n.a.		n.a.	
1985	61.0		n.a.		n.a.	
1986	56.0		n.a.		n.a.	
1987	62.9		n.a.		n.a.	

Note: n.a. = not applicable
Source: Census and Statistics Department, Hong Kong Government.

general insurance premiums grew at 14.8 per cent to HK$8,134 million. Alongside this strong growth in business, there had been a rapid accumulation of insurance funds and technical reserves, which were built up at an annual rate of 26.4 per cent to reach a total of HK$17,446 million in 1987. Although more recent official statistics are not yet available, market sources suggest that there was further appreciable expansion in the industry in 1988 and 1989.

Throughout the first half of the 1980s, the results of general insurance underwriting in Hong Kong compared favourably with other international markets, partly because there were no major fire losses or other catastrophes during the period. In Europe and North America, the industry has suffered heavy losses as a result of over-capacity, intense competition, and slow economic growth. In Hong Kong, however, despite the large number of authorized insurers and the highly competitive environment, underwriting results have been reasonably profitable until recent years when the rapid expansion in underwriting capacity and intensified competition have resulted in a drop in premium rates. In some sectors rates have fallen to uneconomical levels. According to the Census and Statistics Department, the overall loss ratio of the general insurance sector averaged 57.5 per cent during period 1982–7. The results of a survey conducted by the General Insurance Council on the Hong Kong business of 146 insurers indicated a loss ratio of 44 per cent in 1987, while total net underwriting balance was estimated at HK$258 million, equivalent to 9.8 per cent of retained premiums. The overall profitability of the companies also significantly depends on their investment earnings, however. The findings of a HongkongBank survey of the published financial statements of 44 large locally incorporated insurance companies revealed that the average rate of return on shareholders' funds for 26 general insurers, excluding extraordinary items, dropped to 10.6 per cent in 1987, having improved from 10.2 per cent in 1985 to 14.5 per cent in 1986, reflecting the unfavourable investment environment in the latter part of the year.

The Size and Market Structure of the Insurance Industry

It should be noted that the statistics published by the Census and Statistics Department as presented in the preceding sections refer only to the 183 insurance companies covered by the survey and do not reflect the entire domestic insurance market. For instance, the figures on premiums in 1987 refer only to policies written by the 183 establishments, including their local business, as well as business assumed from overseas (that is, exports of insurance services); they exclude policies written overseas by Hong Kong companies and residents (that is, imports of insurance services). Premiums written by the Hong Kong Export Credit Insurance Corporation (ECIC)[3] are also omitted. Adjusted for these elements, but still excluding the business of ECIC, it is estimated that insurance services consumed by the domestic economy, in terms of gross premiums, would have been about HK$12.8 billion in 1987: HK$4.4 billion for life insurance and HK$8.3 billion for general insurance. The corresponding figures for retained premiums were HK$9.6 billion, HK$4.0 billion, and HK$5.7 billion respectively. In 1987, the business which the insurance companies assumed from overseas can be roughly estimated at about HK$3 billion in gross premiums, while premiums paid for policies written overseas by Hong Kong companies and residents totalled an estimated HK$3.6 billion.

Recent Census and Statistics Department statistics do not provide breakdowns by subsector. Nevertheless, surveys carried out by the Insurance Council of Hong Kong and the Life Insurance Council of Hong Kong (a brief description of these associations is given in the following section) estimate that as far as local business is concerned, fire, motor, and employees' compensation were the three major types of general business, each accounting for 20 per cent or more of total retained general business premiums in 1987, while accident and marine cargo each constituted about 15 per cent. In the life insurance category, individual business accounted for 64 per cent of gross premiums written, while group business made up the remaining 36 per cent. More than 90 per cent of this group business was in the form of pension and deposit administration. The market composition is also apparent from the number of companies authorized to transact the various classes of insurance business. Of the 276 authorized insurance companies at the end of 1988, 51 specialized in life business, 197 in general business, and the remaining 28 firms handled both life and general business. Accident, fire and allied risks, and damage to property and goods in transit are the most competitive areas, with about 200 companies active in each of these market segments.

One notable feature of the industry is its high degree of concentration, with the market being dominated by a few underwriters. Although statistics about the shares of gross premiums and retained premiums are not available, the Census and Statistics Department figures showed that 64 per cent of total net premiums (that is, retained premiums less commissions and brokerages paid) for non-life business went to 15 top general insurers, and the 11 largest life insurance companies took up more than 90 per cent of the available business. Together, these 26 largest insurers accounted for about 84 per cent of the total insurance funds of the sector and about 60 per cent of the industry's net income and receipts.

Another characteristic of the Hong Kong market is the high degree of penetration by foreign companies. According to the Registrar General's Department, of the 276 registered insurance companies in December 1988, only 127 were of local origin; the remaining 149 were branches of foreign firms incorporated in 29 countries, mainly in other well-known insurance centres: 40 in the United Kingdom, 28 in the United States, 11 in Bermuda, 8 in Japan, and 7 in both Switzerland and Singapore.

Table 7.6 Structure of the Insurance Market by Sector as of 1987 (per cent)*

	Per Cent Share of	
	Gross Premiums**	Retained Premiums***
General Insurance		
Marine/aviation hull	3.9	1.2
Marine cargo	13.2	14.7
Fire and Allied perils	31.0	19.7
Engineering C.A.R./E.A.R.	3.3	0.9
Motor	17.2	26.1
Employees compensation,	17.0	22.5
accident and others	14.4	15.0
Total	100.0	100.0
Life Insurance		
Individual		
Basic		
Life	38.7	
Investment linked	22.0	
Health	0.6	
Ancillary		
Riders	0.3	
Accident and health	2.0	
Group		
Term life and accident	1.7	
Health	1.9	
Permanent	0.0	
Pension and deposit	32.8	
administration		
Total	100.0	

Notes: * The surveys' results may not represent the entire insurance market as they do not cover all insurance companies in Hong Kong. Specifically, the surveys covered 146 companies in the general insurance sector whereas in the life insurance sector 16 companies were included.

** Including direct premiums and inwards reinsurance premiums.

*** As about 90 per cent of life insurance business was retained, the composition of the life insurance business in terms of retained premiums should be roughly the same as that of gross premiums.

Source: The Life Insurance Council of Hong Kong and the General Insurance Council of Hong Kong.

Table 7.7   Market Share of Top 26 Insurers by Net Premiums, 1987

	No. of Establishments	Net Premiums (HK$ million)	Income and Receipts (HK$ million)	Funds and Reserves (HK$ million)
General insurance with net premiums of:				
Below HK$ 50 million	130	793.8	3,961.4	2,348.4
		(36.3)	(61.2)	(53.7)
HK$ 50 million and over	15	1,395.3	2,509.7	2,021.0
		(63.7)	(38.8)	(46.3)
Subtotal	145	2,189.1	6,471.1	4,369.4
Life insurers with net premiums of:				
Below HK$ 50 million	27	339.9	447.6	467.0
		(9.9)	(9.8)	(3.6)
HK$50 million and over	11	3,108.2	4,101.2	12,609.9
		(90.1)	(90.2)	(96.4)
Subtotal	38	3,448.1	4,548.8	13,076.9
General and life insurance with net premiums of:				
Below HK$ 50 million	157	1,133.7	4,409.0	2,815.5
		(20.1)	(40.0)	(16.1)
HK$50 million and over	26	4,503.5	6,610.9	14,630.9
		(79.9)	(60.0)	(83.9)
Total	183	5,637.2	11,019.9	17,446.4

Notes: Figures in parentheses are per cent shares of subtotals/totals.
The term 'insurers' refers to both insurers and reinsurers.

Source: Census and Statistics Department, Hong Kong Government.

Insurance Associations and Tariff Agreements

The two main insurance organizations are the General Insurance Council of Hong Kong and the Life Insurance Council of Hong Kong, which were formed in 1982 and 1984 respectively. In the interests of industry unity on matters relating to both general and life insurance business, and to enable the industry to present a united front in lobbying for its common interests, the two councils have formed a further joint body, the Hong Kong Federation of Insurers, in 1988. Since the formation of these organizations, they have been consulted by, and have made representations to, the Government on various proposed amendments to the ordinances and new legislations relating to the insurance industry. They have also been active in promoting the image of the industry as a whole.

Tariffs (that is, administered premium rates applicable to all clients) on fire, accident, and motor vehicles insurance business are agreed by members of the Fire Insurance Association, Accident Insurance Association. However, not all companies underwriting these types of business are members of these associations. In fact, because of keen competition, there have been extensive breaches of the tariff systems by member companies and rates are often discounted.

Revenue and Cost Structure

Income and receipts generated by the sector amounted to HK$12,078 million in 1987. Of this, 67.9 per cent was retained premiums; 10.4 per cent reinsurance commissions received; 11.1 per cent investment income, including earnings from financial assets, such as stocks and bonds, and fixed assets; and 9.8 per cent other business receipts, consisting mainly of commissions and brokerage and service fees. Reflecting the different natures of their businesses, there were significant differences among the various categories of insurance companies. Retained premiums accounted for 72 per cent of the income of general insurers and 78 per cent of the life companies' income in 1987, whilst the dominant source of income for insurance agents and brokers was receipts from services rendered (95.6 per cent). For general insurers, reinsurance commissions represented the second largest income source, accounting for 17 per cent of the total. Life insurers, on the other hand, secured less than 3.4 per cent of their income from reinsurance commissions, their second most important income source being investment earnings (16 per cent). The difference reflected the relatively smaller share of reinsurance premiums ceded for life business. For the sector as a whole, the bulk of the investment income (over 97 per cent) was from financial assets, whilst less than 3 per cent was from fixed assets. Details of the revenue structure for 1987 are presented in Table 7.8.

On the cost side, total expenditure amounted to HK$8,830 million in 1987. Net claims accounted for the largest share of total cost (41.3 per cent), followed by payments for insurance intermediary services which included rebates, commissions, and brokerages paid (18.1 per cent); compensation of employees (17 per cent); and operating expenses (12.6 per cent). As in the case of revenue, the cost structure of general insurers differed significantly from that of life insurers. The largest cost item for the former was net claims (accounting for 39.8 per cent of the total cost), followed by payments for insurance intermediary services (27.5 per cent). The principal cost for life insurers was also net claims (56.3 per cent), but payments for insurance intermediary services accounted for only 3.7 per cent of costs. Reflecting the need for extensive personal contact in marketing life insurance, compensation for employees accounted for just over 28 per cent of life insurers' total costs, compared with only 6.3 per cent for general insurers. However, the success of new life insurance marketing methods in recent years, including mass marketing through the media or other financial institutions, is likely to reduce the share of this cost. In the case of

Table 7.8 Revenue and Cost Structure of the Insurance Sector as of 1987

	General Insurers (145)		Life Insurers (38)		Insurance Agents, Brokers and Other Insurance Service (1,242)		Total (1,425)	
	HK$ Million	Per cent	HK$ Million	Per cent	HK$ Million	Per cent	HK$ Million	Per cent
Income and receipts								
Retained premiums	4,656.0	72.0	3,548.0	78.0	n.a.	n.a.	8,204.0	67.9
Reinsurance commissions received	1,100.0	17.0	154.0	3.4	n.a.	n.a.	1,254.0	10.4
Income from investments	618.0	9.6	727.0	16.0	n.a.	n.a.	1,345.0	11.1
Financial assets	605.0	9.3	703.0	15.5	n.a.	n.a.	1,308.0	10.8
Fixed assets	13.0	0.2	25.0	0.5	n.a.	n.a.	38.0	0.3
Receipts from services rendered	58.0	0.9	116.0	2.6	1,011.0	95.6	1,185.0	9.8
Income from other sources	38.0	0.6	3.0	0.1	47.0	4.4	88.0	0.7
Total	6,471.0	100.0	4,549.0	100.0	1,058.0	100.0	12,078.0	100.0
Expenditure								
Compensation of employees	340.8	6.3	739.5	28.1	418.7	56.1	1,499.0	17.0
Operating expenses	474.0	8.7	311.2	11.8	328.3	43.9	1,113.5	12.6
Net claims	2,166.8	39.8	1,483.2	56.3	n.a.	n.a.	3,650.0	41.3
Payments for insurance Intermediary services	1,501.1	27.5	97.6	3.7	n.a.	n.a.	1,598.7	18.1
Reinsurance commissions paid to ceding insurers	966.2	17.7	2.6	0.1	n.a.	n.a.	968.8	11.0
Total	5,448.9	100.0	2,634.1	100.0	747.0	100.0	8,830.0	100.0

Notes: n.a. = not applicable.
Figures in parentheses are the numbers of establishments included in the survey.
The term 'insurers' refers to both insurers and reinsurers.

Source: Census and Statistics Department, Hong Kong Government.

agents/brokers, wages and salaries accounted for 56.1 per cent of total expenditure, other than rebates and discounts, which is consistent with the nature of their business.

Sources and Application of Funds

There are marked differences in the sources of funds of the various classes of insurers. The HongkongBank survey found that, for the 44 companies sampled, life funds and technical reserves constituted about two thirds (64.7 per cent) of insurance companies' liabilities, while shareholders' funds accounted for 22.9 per cent. Reflecting the long-term nature of the life insurance business, life funds constituted 96.8 per cent of the total resources of insurers in that sector, who relied significantly less on shareholders' funds as a funding source: 1.5 per cent of total liabilities, against 52.6 per cent for general insurers, 19.7 per cent for composite insurers, and 16.8 per cent for specialist reinsurers. As for the application of funds, stocks, shares, and bonds constituted 45.8 per cent of total assets while deposits and cash balances accounted for 20.7 per cent. With the exception of one large composite insurer, loans and mortgages generally took up a very small proportion of the investment portfolios of the companies surveyed. Only 3 per cent of the resources were directly invested in properties. Consistent with the nature of their liabilities, life insurers had a larger proportion of their resources in long-term assets, while general insurers tended to hold a higher ratio of liquid and near-liquid investment. According to the Census and Statistics Department Survey, with accumulated insurance funds and reserves of over HK$17.5 billion at the end of 1987, and investments under its administration of HK$18.4 billion, the resources of the sector are substantial. The enormous funds at the disposal of the insurance companies, particularly the long-term funds of the life insurance compancies, accord them an important role in economic growth through the rechannelling of these resources into productive activity.

Prospects

In the past three decades Hong Kong has developed as a major commercial, financial, manufacturing, and shipping centre in the Asia Pacific region. It is on this foundation that the insurance industry of Hong Kong has been built. Most recently, Hong Kong has been emerging as a regional centre for reinsurance. Some 15 reinsurance companies, the majority of them of foreign origin, are now operating in the territory. Most of these are branches, regional offices, or subsidiaries of international operating corporations, and their business covers various countries, predominantly in Asia. An efficient banking system and the absence of foreign exchange controls have provided an environment conducive to both insurance and reinsurance businesses. Additionally, Hong Kong's good communications and geographical location have enabled insurance and reinsurance firms to conduct business conveniently and expand globally. Many international companies have been attracted to the local market, although some of them may have their eyes as much on the Taiwanese and Korean markets as on Hong Kong itself. Some of these companies have also set up offices here in anticipation of moving into China. Their increased marketing efforts have in turn enhanced the existing growth potential. Furthermore, the computerization of the industry, which has improved service efficiency considerably over the past few years, is expected to continue. This should allow the industry to allocate more resources to product research and the development of innovative underwriting skills. Recent Government moves to tighten supervisory control, coupled with the anticipated establishment of a self-regulation system, will have a beneficial effect on the industry's image both at home and abroad, and should contribute to its healthy development. All these factors will continue to support the further expansion of the industry.

Given the prospect of a sustained growth in the Hong Kong economy, the outlook of the insurance industry is bright, although its performance in the short term will inevitably fluctuate with the state of the domestic and global economies. General insurance business is likely to grow at least in line with the economy, but probably at a slightly faster rate as more people come to realize that insurance is an effective means of minimizing certain types of risks. The scope for the further expansion of life insurance business is immense, since this particular insurance potential remains largely untapped. Within this category, group life business, especially retirement benefit schemes, are expected to expand rapidly, as it becomes increasingly popular for employers to provide such benefits as part of the remuneration package for employees. Indeed, given the lack of social security schemes to provide for retirement and old age in Hong Kong, the demand for retirement benefit schemes should continue to be strong. Ordinary life insurance business will also grow as people become better educated and their earning power increases. The ageing of the population and the trend towards nuclear families, together with the growing acceptance in the local community of the concept of insurance, will also raise the demand for life insurance. However, with the sector currently plagued by high staff turnover and difficulties in training and recruitment, the full realization of this potential will depend greatly on the ability of the industry to meet the demand for better qualified, professional personnel by intensifying its training efforts.

Table 7.9 Sources and Applications of Funds — by Classes of Insurers, 1987

	Life Insurers (3)		General Insurers (25)		Composite Insurers (9)		Specialist Reinsurers (7)		All Companies (44)	
	HK$ Million	Per cent	HK$ Million	Per cent	HK$ Million	Per cent	HK$ Million	Per cent	HK$ Million	Per cent
Sources of funds										
Shareholders' funds	79.7	1.5	2,975.5	52.6	2,180.3	19.7	597.3	16.8	5,832.8	22.9
Life funds and technical reserves	5,087.4	96.8	1,578.9	27.9	7,485.0	67.7	2,362.5	66.6	16,513.8	64.7
Amounts due to related companies	17.8	0.3	114.6	2.0	221.8	2.0	181.6	5.1	535.7	2.1
Other liabilities	68.3	1.3	985.6	17.4	1,174.7	10.6	408.0	11.5	2,636.6	10.3
Total capital liabilities	5,253.2	100.0	5,654.5	100.0	11,061.7	100.0	3,549.2	100.0	25,518.6	100.0
Application of funds										
Investments in related companies	145.0	2.8	510.3	0.9	299.8	2.7	336.9	9.5	1,292.0	5.1
Loans and mortgages	0.6	0.0	19.4	0.3	3,541.8	32.0	9.3	0.3	3,571.2	14.0
Stocks, shares, and bonds	3,798.2	72.3	1,833.2	32.4	4,287.0	38.8	1,766.8	49.8	11,685.2	45.8
Amounts due from related companies	10.5	0.2	429.4	7.6	339.3	3.1	144.7	4.1	923.9	3.6
Deposits and cash balances	1,228.6	23.4	1,727.5	30.6	1,318.1	11.9	1,014.8	28.6	5,288.9	20.7
Properties and fixed assets	3.5	0.1	139.7	2.5	606.2	5.5	14.4	0.4	763.8	3.0
Other assets	66.7	1.3	994.7	17.6	669.5	6.1	262.3	7.4	1,993.1	7.8
Total assets	5,253.2	100.0	5,654.2	100.0	11,061.8	100.0	3,549.2	100.0	25,528.4	100.0

Note: Figures in parentheses are the numbers of companies included in the survey.

Source: *Recent Performance of the Insurance Industry*, Economic Research Department, HSBC.

Glossary: Definitions of Some Insurance Terms

A Claim is a demand by an individual or corporation to recover under a policy of insurance for loss which may come within that policy, or a demand by an individual against an insured for the damages covered by a policy held by him.

Earned Premiums equal retained premiums received less/plus the increase/decrease in unearned premium reserve during the accounting year, thus representing the actual amount of premiums fully earned during the accounting year.

Gross Claims equal total claims paid during the accounting year before subtracting claims recoverable from reinsurers.

Gross Premiums equal total premiums received during the accounting year before subtracting reinsurance premiums paid to reinsurers for reinsurance.

Incurred Claims include all net claims paid for the losses that occurred during the accounting period whether or not they have been paid by the end of the period.

Life Insurance Funds (life insurance) usually consist of policy reserves and surplus. Policy reserves are funds that are set aside by an insurance company specifically for meeting its policy obligations as they fall due. They represent a liability to policy holders, backed by assets of the company on the other side of the balance sheet. The funds, together with future premiums, interest, and benefit of survivorship, will be sufficient to pay future claims, provided the valuation assumptions are correct.

Loss Ratio is the ratio of incurred claims to earned premiums.

Net Claims equal total claims paid during the accounting year less claims recoverable from reinsurers.

Outstanding Claims Reserve is the estimated cost of settling claims that have already occurred but have not been paid as of the valuation date.

A Premium is the amount of money which the policy holder agrees to pay to the insurance company for the insurance policy.

Retained Premiums equal gross premiums less reinsurance premiums paid to reinsurers for reinsurance.

Retention Ratio is the ratio of retained premiums to gross premiums.

Technical Reserves (general business) are funds set aside by an insurance company for meeting obligations as they fall due. The reserves consist of unearned premiums reserves and outstanding claim reserves.

Unearned Premium Reserve is a liability reserve that represents the unearned portion of gross premiums on all outstanding policies at the time of valuation. The unearned premium reserve reflects the fact that premiums are paid in advance, but the period of protection has not expired. The reserve is also required to provide for premium refund to policy holders on cancelled policies.

Notes

1. Employees' compensation insurance, which includes cover for common law liability, was made compulsory under the Employees' Compensation (Amendment) Ordinance 1982, which was effective from 1 January 1984. Motor vehicle and pleasure craft insurance covering third party bodily injury is also compulsory under the Motor Vehicle (Third Party Risks) Ordinance and the Merchant Shipping Ordinance, which came into effect in 1951 and 1953 respectively.

2. The relevant premium income of a company in any financial year is calculated as (i) 50 per cent of the gross premium income or (ii) its retained premium income in that year, whichever is higher.

3. The Hong Kong Export Credit Insurance Corporation (ECIC) is the only organization in Hong Kong which protects exporters against risk of monetary loss arising from the failure or inability of overseas buyers to pay for goods and services supplied to them. Created by statute in 1966, the ECIC has a paid-up capital of HK$20 million and is wholly owned by the Hong Kong Government, which also guarantees its underwriting liabilities up to HK$5,000 million. It is autonomous in its day-to-day operations and is required to operate on a commercial basis.

References

Davids, Lewis E., *Dictionary of Insurance*, (Totowa, Rowman & Allanheld, 1983).

HongkongBank, 'Recent Performance of the Insurance Industry,' Economic Research Department, various issues.

Hong Kong Government, 'Annual Department Report', Registrar General's Department, various issues.

Huebner, S. S. and Black, Kenneth Jr, *Life Insurance*, (Englewood Cliffs, N.J., Prentice-Hall, 1982).

Insurance Council of Hong Kong, *Annual Report* 1987–88.

Ka, R. P. T., 'Report on the Growth of the National Insurance Industry and Market Structure, Hong Kong", *Reports and Papers, XIIIth General Conference East Asian Insurance Congress*, 20–25 September 1986, Hong Kong, pp. 17–39.

Steward, W. P., 'The History of Insurance in Hong Kong', *Insurance Asia*, Vol. XVI, No. 6, July–August 1986.

Part III
Financial Markets

8. Money and Capital Markets

Y. H. LUI

A FINANCIAL market is a market for issuing and trading financial instruments, through which the efficient flow of funds is facilitated from ultimate lenders to ultimate users. Efficient financial markets are essential to assure adequate capital formation and economic growth in a modern economy.[1]

On the basis of the original maturity length of the financial instruments traded, financial markets can be divided into two general types — the money market and the capital market. The money market is the market for short-term (one year or less) funds and instruments such as treasury bills, banker's acceptances, commercial paper, and so on. Sometimes it also includes securities originally issued with maturities of more than one year but that now have a remaining maturity of one year or less. The one-year dividing line is arbitrary, but traditional.

In contrast to the short-term or money market is the capital market, which is the market for securities with over one year to maturity such as bonds, notes, stocks, and so on. The primary distinguishing feature of the securities that comprise the capital markets is their life — longer than one year. They may range in maturity from an 18-month certificate of deposit issued by authorized institutions to perpetual bonds that have no specified maturity date.

Although Hong Kong is a major international financial centre, some of its financial markets are not yet very well developed. Apart from the inter-bank market, which may be considered a mature market, other money and capital markets are still developing. The major reason may be the lack of government securities as a bench-mark against which other credit instruments can be ranked and compared. Due to the adoption of conservative budgeting policy and the subsequent existence of continuous huge budget surpluses, the Hong Kong Government seldom borrows, except under unusual circumstances in which unexpected budget deficits are incurred.[2] Very few debt instruments issued by the government are in the market. In the absence of the government's participation and support, both the money and the capital markets in Hong Kong have developed slowly. (However, see p. 291.)

Nevertheless, following the global trend toward securitization of debts, these markets now show vitality and rapid growth. In the near future they will become an important channel of capital for business.

This chapter aims to place Hong Kong's money and capital markets in perspective. The development, structure, and operations of each major market will be examined. Particular attention is paid to the Hong Kong Inter-bank Offered Rate (HIBOR) which is one of the most important economic indicators for financial markets. In addition, various capital market instruments will be described.

The Inter-bank Market

Market Development

Owing to the absence of a central bank type monetary authority and the lack of short-term government securities, Hong Kong's money market consists of only the inter-bank market and the commercial paper market. The inter-bank market is the older and the better established. It has existed since the late 1950s. However, before 1970, the market operated on a very small scale and comprised only the domestic banks, which used it to balance their liquidity position.

Stepping into the 1970s, the inter-bank market gained momentum from the emergence of the Deposit-taking Companies (DTCs) and the influx of foreign banks. In the early 1970s, the booming stock-market encouraged many large foreign financial institutions as well as local corporations to commence business here in the areas of corporate finance, underwriting, investment management, share financing, and so on. Since there was still a moratorium on bank licences at that time, these institutions could only operate in the form of non-bank finance companies (namely the Deposit-taking Companies, DTCs). After passing the DTC Ordinance in 1976, the status of this type of company was widely recognized. Some with strong parent bank backup started to participate in market dealings, and this made the market more active.

In 1978 the moratorium on new bank licences was lifted. This together with the booming local economy encouraged more large international banks to set up branches here. Without a large deposit base, these banks had to resort to inter-bank takings to fund their business. Their activities and expertise promptly stimulated the development of the market.

Although the market has experienced rapid development in the last decade, it is not free of difficulties. From 1982 to 1986, the market suffered a setback which originated from a confidence crisis. After Mrs Thatcher's visit to Beijing in September 1982, the political uncertainty over Hong Kong's future triggered a collapse of the property and stock-markets, which in turn became a financial crisis. Many depository institutions which lent heavily to the property sector suffered serious liquidity problems, and some of them became bankrupt. This caused distrust among participants, thereby dampening the market's activities.

Nevertheless, the crisis also had a positive impact on the market by pushing some unsound and mismanaged participants out. Following the joint declaration of the Sino-British governments and the improvement in the quality of banking supervision, the market soon restored its confidence and has experienced a spectacular growth in recent years.

Structure and Operations

The inter-bank market is a market for short-term unsecured loans between deposit-taking institutions. Like foreign exchange markets (which are described in the next chapter), it is an intangible market, without physical location, for getting participants to trade together. In essence it is formed by a complex and sophisticated network of telecommunication equipment connecting the dealing rooms of different deposit-taking institutions.

Although the inter-bank market is named as such, its participants are not restricted to licensed banks only. DTCs with strong backgrounds may participate as well. Participants with surplus funds (either in local or foreign currency) may, through the market, lend to those experiencing a shortage. In so doing, all participants may adjust their asset portfolios and balance their funding positions.

Deposit-taking institutions participating in the inter-bank market may transact with others in two ways. They may trade with other participants directly by means of telecommunication equipment. One party will contact another for a quote and then hit the price if appropriate. Sometimes participating institutions prefer to deal through money brokers, who are the middlemen between the two parties to a deal. These brokers collect bids, offer orders from various participants, and help arrange transactions. As brokers, they do not speculate themselves but earn brokerage fees from providing services. Under either method, a participant must establish reciprocal credit facilities with its counterpart beforehand, and then can deal up to the limit designated by the facilities.

Money can be lent in the inter-bank market in any currency for periods ranging from overnight call up to six to twelve months. The market in foreign currency is one component of the global Euro-currency market.

All transactions are made at prices set in the free market, and determined by market conditions. The market prices are usually quoted in the form of bid and offer (for example, 8.00–8.125 per cent per annum for overnight money). The bid rate (that is, 8.00 per cent) is the market's borrowing price, at which participants may, through brokers, place (lend) funds to the bidding institution at that price. Participants with a shortage of funds may take (borrow) at the offered price (called HIBOR, or Hong Kong Inter-bank Offered Rate, that is, 8.125 per cent). The difference between the bid and offer is called 'spread', which reflects the market's trading activities. When the market's trading is active with ample placing and taking, the spread tends to be relatively narrow.

The HIBOR is a very important price in the local financial system as it is a free price of loanable funds among deposit-taking institutions and is wholly dependent on market supply and demand. We will examine its implications in the following section.

The Market Activities

Although the inter-bank market is the old established money market in Hong Kong, there are no official statistics on its trading volume. The Government only publishes monthly statistics on outstanding inter-institution liabilities. Given these statistics, we can find a better understanding of the market's activities.

Table 8.1 gives the consolidated inter-institution liabilities of all deposit-taking institutions. For the years 1980–8, it can be seen that the inter-bank market size (in terms of outstanding inter-institution liabilities) has been growing very rapidly. By the end of September 1988, the total volume of outstanding inter-institution liabilities was HK$497.1 billion, about 5.7 times that of 1980. The average annual compound rate of growth was 25.2 per cent. The inter-bank market has been widely recognized as a major channel of liquidity for authorized institutions. A significant proportion, about 13.6 per cent as of the end of September 1988, of their total liabilities was inter-institution borrowings. In particular, more than one quarter of their Hong Kong dollar funds was obtained from the market. This is evidence of the market's significance as a source of funds for deposit-taking institutions as a whole.

Further insight may be gained from Table 8.2, which breaks the total inter-institution liabilities into different components. Several points are worth mentioning here. First, among the four activity components, the inter-bank liabilities have grown in importance. Its proportion of the total liabilities has increased from 30.7 per cent in 1980 to about 60 per cent in September 1988, while the proportion of the other three components (banks' liabilities to DTCs, inter-DTC liabilities, and DTCs' liabilities to banks) has declined. This indicates that banks are more active participants and find it easier to borrow funds in the market than DTCs do. There are two possible reasons for this. One is that many active DTC participants were forced to withdraw from the market in the financial crisis of 1982–5. Another reason is that after the crisis, banks became more selective when dealing. As a result, DTC participants became less active.

A second point is that, in 1980 and 1981, the banks' liabilities to DTCs were greater than the DTCs' liabilities to banks, indicating that the banks were net debtors to the DTCs. This reflects the banks' use of their subsidiary DTCs to compete for deposits. However, the trend started to reverse in 1982. In 1982 the DTCs owed the banks a net amount of HK$21,263 billion (HK$56,494–35,231), and that amount increased to HK$44,070 billion (HK$118,538–74,468) in September 1988. This change was due to the establishment of the three-tier deposit-taking system which made it more difficult for DTCs to attract deposits, and thus more dependent on the banks for funding.

Third, the proportion of the Hong Kong dollar component of the total inter-institution liabilities declined consistently from 1980–6. This decline in proportion may reflect the increasing importance of Hong

Table 8.1 The Consolidated Inter-institution Liabilities of Deposit-taking Institutions (HK$ million)

	Inter-institution Liabilities (amount due to Banks & DTCs in Hong Kong)			Total Liabilities			Per cent		
	HK$ (1)	Foreign Currency (2)	Total (3)	HK$ (4)	Foreign Currency (5)	Total (6)	$\frac{(1)}{(4)}$	$\frac{(2)}{(5)}$	$\frac{(3)}{(6)}$
1980	51,240	35,917	87,157	202,916	232,422	435,337	25.3	15.5	20.0
1981	76,366	57,943	134,310	271,522	361,260	632,782	28.1	16.0	21.2
1982	83,256	87,234	170,490	297,521	565,586	863,107	28.0	15.4	19.8
1983	96,982	129,679	226,660	341,155	774,307	1,115,462	28.4	16.7	20.3
1984	114,276	154,397	268,673	384,723	884,935	1,269,658	29.7	17.4	21.2
1985	129,188	179,179	308,367	437,656	1,117,967	1,555,623	29.5	16.0	19.8
1986	149,319	277,409	426,728	503,172	1,647,119	2,150,291	29.7	16.8	19.8
1987	172,842	312,443	485,286	606,780	2,611,010	3,217,789	28.5	12.0	15.1
1988	179,348	317,758	497,106	649,374	3,006,100	3,655,474	27.6	10.6	13.6
Average Annual Growth Rate 1980–1988 (per cent)	17.5	32.5	25.2	16.2	39.1	31.6			

Note: Figures for 1988 are as at end of September; the other figures are as at end of the year.
Source: Hong Kong Annual Digest of Statistics, various issues.

Table 8.2 Components of Inter-institution Liabilities (HK$ million)

	1980			1981			1982			1983			1984		
	HK$	Foreign Currency	Total	HK$	Foreign Currency	Total	HK$	Foreign Currency	Total	HK$	Foreign Currency	Total	HK$	Foreign Currency	Total
Inter-bank Liabilities															
Demand and Call	4,885	646	5,531	5,622	1,000	6,622	4,528	1,156	5,684	4,060	2,055	6,115	4,904	1,980	6,884
Short Notice	3,325	1,350	4,674	5,117	3,564	8,681	8,793	4,614	13,408	9,829	10,676	20,505	10,564	14,642	25,206
Time Deposits	8,723	7,857	16,579	15,982	14,412	30,394	23,090	20,299	43,389	27,654	30,559	58,213	36,875	44,199	81,074
Total	16,933	9,852	26,785	26,721	18,977	45,698	36,411	26,069	62,481	41,543	43,289	84,833	52,343	60,820	113,164
	(33.0)		(30.7)	(35.0)		(34.0)	(43.7)		(36.6)	(42.8)		(37.4)	(45.8)		(42.1)
Banks' Liabilities to Deposit-taking Companies															
Demand and Call	2,273	800	3,073	11,009	1,474	12,483	6,123	1,590	7,713	7,420	1,650	9,071	7,408	1,017	8,425
Short Notice	9,095	759	9,854	2,328	2,007	4,335	2,717	4,121	6,837	2,724	3,996	6,720	2,473	5,025	7,498
Time Deposits	13,295	2,753	16,048	21,466	4,266	25,732	13,647	7,034	20,681	17,431	13,682	31,113	17,398	14,998	32,396
Total	24,663	4,312	28,975	34,803	7,747	42,550	22,486	12,745	35,231	27,575	19,329	46,904	27,279	21,040	48,318
	(48.1)		(33.2)	(45.6)		(31.7)	(27.0)		(20.7)	(28.4)		(20.7)	(23.9)		(18.0)
Inter-deposit-taking Company Liabilities															
Demand and Call	265	75	340	362	322	684	852	1,229	2,081	398	202	600	326	348	674
Short Notice	924	1,021	1,945	1,630	1,622	3,253	948	1,875	2,823	605	1,790	2,395	600	2,380	2,980
Time Deposits	2,104	5,719	7,823	2,728	8,276	11,005	2,442	8,938	11,379	1,693	8,485	10,178	11,292	8,144	19,436
Total	3,294	6,815	10,109	4,721	10,221	14,941	4,242	12,042	16,284	2,696	10,477	13,173	12,218	10,871	23,090
	(6.5)		(11.6)	(6.2)		(11.1)	(5.1)		(9.6)	(2.8)		(5.8)	(10.7)		(8.6)
Deposit-taking Companies' Liabilities to Banks															
Demand and Call	710	425	1,135	980	378	1,358	1,341	562	1,903	987	396	1,383	615	813	1,428
Short Notice	1,702	1,842	3,543	1,815	1,892	3,707	2,133	2,252	4,385	2,152	5,413	7,565	2,169	5,259	7,428
Time Deposits	3,939	12,672	16,610	7,326	18,729	26,055	16,642	33,564	50,206	22,028	50,774	72,803	19,651	55,594	75,246
Total	6,350	14,938	21,288	10,122	20,999	31,120	20,117	36,377	56,494	25,168	56,584	81,751	22,435	61,666	84,102
	(12.4)		(24.4)	(13.2)		(23.2)	(24.2)		(33.1)	(26.0)		(36.1)	(19.6)		(31.3)
Total Inter-institution Liabilities	51,240 (100.0)	58.80%	87,157 (100.0)	76,367 (100.0)	56.90%	134,309 (100.0)	83,256 (100.0)	48.83%	170,490 (100.0)	96,982 (100.0)	42.80%	226,661 (100.0)	114,275 (100.0)	42.50%	268,674 (100.0)

	1985			1986			1987			1988		
	HK$	Foreign Currency	Total	HK$	Foreign Currency	Total	HK$	Foreign Currency	Total	HK$	Foreign Currency	Total
Inter-bank Liabilities												
Demand and Call	4,635	2,109	6,744	4,142	1,198	5,339	8,177	998	9,175	3,365	6,639	10,003
Short Notice	13,349	14,367	27,716	18,737	25,594	44,331	16,716	32,713	49,429	21,792	44,155	65,947
Time Deposits	39,697	53,863	93,559	47,369	116,622	163,992	64,162	126,979	191,141	82,367	136,670	219,037
Total	57,680 (44.7)	70,338	128,019 (41.5)	70,248 (47.0)	143,414	213,662 (50.1)	89,054 (51.5)	160,691	249,745 (51.5)	107,523 (60.0)	187,464	294,987 (59.3)
Banks' Liabilities to DTCs												
Demand and Call	9,232	1,573	10,804	6,363	2,176	8,540	5,863	1,826	7,689	5,216	1,721	6,937
Short Notice	3,729	7,088	10,817	4,001	7,780	11,781	4,869	8,407	13,275	4,047	9,794	13,841
Time Deposits	19,129	15,228	34,357	20,914	21,714	42,628	24,458	26,643	51,101	24,269	29,421	53,690
Total	32,089 (24.8)	23,889	55,978 (18.2)	31,278 (20.9)	31,670	62,948 (14.8)	35,190 (20.4)	36,876	72,006 (14.9)	33,532 (18.7)	40,937	74,468 (15.0)
Inter-DTC Liabilities												
Demand and Call	443	613	1,057	187	397	584	194	379	574	134	94	228
Short Notice	635	1,870	2,505	823	2,052	2,875	853	1,903	2,756	173	968	1,141
Time Deposits	12,876	9,619	22,495	12,962	6,182	19,143	8,173	5,864	14,037	5,138	2,607	7,745
Total	13,954 (10.8)	12,102	26,057 (8.4)	13,972 (9.4)	8,631	22,603 (5.3)	9,220 (5.3)	8,146	17,366 (3.6)	5,445 (3.0)	3,669	9,114 (1.8)
DTCs' Liabilities to Banks												
Demand and Call	668	3,349	4,017	2,064	2,520	4,585	2,627	995	3,622	434	1,134	1,568
Short Notice	3,134	11,171	14,305	4,536	18,654	23,190	3,798	18,947	22,745	3,724	22,545	26,269
Time Deposits	21,662	58,331	79,993	27,221	72,520	99,741	32,954	86,789	119,743	28,690	62,010	90,700
Total	25,465 (19.7)	72,850	98,315 (31.9)	33,821 (22.7)	93,695	127,516 (30.0)	39,378 (22.8)	106,731	146,109 (30.1)	32,849 (18.3)	85,689	118,538 (23.8)
Total Inter-institution Liabilities	129,188 (100.0)	41.90%	308,369 (100.0)	149,319 (100.0)	35.00%	426,729 (100.0)	172,842 (100.0)	35.60%	485,286 (100.0)	179,349 (100.0)	36.10%	497,107 (100.0)

Notes: * Figures for 1988 are as at end of September, the other figures are as at end of the year.
      ** Figures in parentheses are percentages of component total to total inter-institution liabilities.
      *** Figures in totals have been rounded.

Source: *Hong Kong Annual Digest of Statistics*; and *Hong Kong Monthly Digest of Statistics* (Hong Kong, Census and Statistics Department) various issues.

Kong as an international financial centre. As banks accept more foreign currency deposits from local residents as well as neighbouring countries, they have more excess foreign currency funds to lend in the market. Nevertheless, the decline has reversed in recent years. This may be explained by the fact that the market is quite concerned with the revaluative pressure on the Hong Kong dollar. More investors switched their deposits from foreign currencies to Hong Kong dollars and there was also some speculative money flowing in, thereby increasing Hong Kong dollar liquidity in the market.

Another important feature in Table 8.2 is the term nature of the market activities. It is obvious that market activities have been mainly in time deposits which accounted for more than 70 per cent of the total volume. This evidence indicates that participants relied on this market more to finance longer term assets (such as loans) than to balance their short-term liquidity position.

The HIBOR and Interest Rate Determination

Interest rates are the prices of loanable funds. Because of their considerable impact on both real and financial sectors, they are known to be among the most important prices in the economy. Interest rates have long been recognized as a useful weapon of monetary policy which may be adopted as a method of controlling the quantity of money in the economy, with the ultimate aim of achieving macro-economic objectives. There are many kinds of interest rates (some of the better known being saving rates, time deposit rates, the prime rate, the mortgage rate, and so on), but in Hong Kong the most important one among them is the HIBOR, because of its numerous implications.

The HIBOR as an Indicator of Liquidity

Recall that the HIBOR is the offered rate in the inter-bank market. It is indeed a free price whose movement is entirely dependent on the market supply of and demand for funds. When the economy (or more specifically, the banking system) is flooded with liquidity for whatever reasons, the increase in supply of funds will push down the HIBOR and vice versa. Any change in the market conditions will certainly induce a change in the HIBOR and be reflected therein. For instance, a rising HIBOR reflects declining supply and/or increasing demand for funds in the market. Therefore the HIBOR is a useful indicator of the economy's liquidity.

If the economy is booming and inflation is high, demand for funds will increase. The tight liquidity will drive up the HIBOR. In turn the higher HIBOR will give rise to the reduction of credit demand and consequently cool off the overheated economy. Obviously, the HIBOR and the state of economy are interrelated.

The HIBOR as a Reference Price for Wholesale Business

The HIBOR is the cost of borrowing from the inter-bank market borne by authorized institutions, and accordingly becomes a reference price for their wholesale business. When a bank grants a loan of a large amount, say HK$10 million for three months, to a giant corporation with excellent credit standing, the former usually charges the latter an interest rate calculated on the basis of the relevant HIBOR, for example, 3M (three-month) HIBOR plus 0.25 per cent. The margin (that is, 0.25 per cent) on top of the cost (that is, 3M HIBOR) represents the bank's net profit from the transaction. The margin is that low for two reasons. In the first place, the borrower has excellent creditworthiness and so the default risk is presumably very low. Second, the loan is wholesale in nature. Given the large amount of loan, the bank's relative operating cost is low. Taking these factors into consideration, the loan rate based on the HIBOR is very competitive.

Conversely, when a bank accepts a large deposit (say HK$500,000 or above) from its customer, the bank will also price the deposit on the basis of the HIBOR. The practice is to deduct a margin from the HIBOR of the same duration. In so doing, the bank ensures that a profit can be earned from the deposit by lending it in the inter-bank market even if it cannot find a customer for it.

The HIBOR as a Leading Indicator of Banks' Interest Rates

Since the HIBOR is very responsive to market supply and demand, it may be considered a leading indicator of banks' other interest rates. These rates include deposit rates governed by the interest rate agreement, and prime rate.

In Hong Kong, there is an interest rate agreement that regulates the maximum level of interest rates payable on small amount[3] Hong Kong dollar deposits with banks. The agreement is executed by the Hong Kong Association of Banks, which is responsible for reviewing the deposit rates every Saturday. Though deposit rates are regulated, banks are still allowed to set their loan rates freely. The general practice is to follow the two price leaders (namely the HongkongBank and the Standard Chartered Bank) to set a common prime rate as a reference price for retail loan business (for example, mortgage loan, overdraft, personal loan, and so on). The prime rate is a bench-mark interest rate charged to the most creditworthy borrowers. For borrowers that are either smaller or are deemed to pose greater risk, interest charged is higher (for example, prime plus 1 per cent). The point worth noting lies in the relationship among the deposit rates, the prime, and the HIBOR. For the purposes of simplicity, here we use savings rate to represent deposit rates set out in the interest rate agreement.

Generally, the prime rate is the highest among the three rates and set at a level of about 4.5 to 5 per cent higher than the savings rate. Every time the Association refixes the deposit rates, individual banks adjust their prime rate by more or less the same magnitude at the same time in order to keep a relatively stable difference between the prime and the savings rates. This practice aims at protecting banks' operating profit margins. In normal situations, the HIBOR must lie somewhere between the savings and the prime rates. The rationale behind this is simple. Banks with a shortage of funds have to borrow from the market to fund their business, and so the HIBOR is their cost of borrowing. If the HIBOR is above the prime (loan return), they will suffer a loss and consequently an upward adjustment will occur until the prime is higher than the HIBOR. On the other hand, the HIBOR represents a return to those banks having excess liquidity for lending in the market. If the HIBOR is lower than the savings rate, these banks will operate at a loss. In that case a downward adjustment to the savings rate will be made. Under these two conditions, it is understandable that the prime is above the HIBOR which in turn is above the savings rate.

Since the prime and the savings rates are administered while the HIBOR is freely floating, as determined by market supply and demand, it can easily be seen from the above relationship that the HIBOR is a leading indicator of the savings and prime rates. The HIBOR as a freely floating price reflects and conveys some information of the economy's liquidity, which may be used to predict the direction of change in banks' deposit rates and loan rates. A rule of thumb is to observe the difference between the prime rate and three-month HIBOR, which is normally about 1 to 2 per cent. In case the difference falls to less than 1 per cent, the pressure for an upward adjustment increases. Conversely, when the difference widens, the possibility of a decrease in banks' rates is high.

The Commercial Paper Market

Commercial Paper (CP) is a short-term unsecured promissory note typically issued by large corporations to finance short-term working capital needs. The chief attraction of CP to borrowers is its lower cost compared with bank financing, because funds are directly obtained from investors without involving any markup charged by banks. In recent years some firms have also used CP as a source of interim financing for major investment projects. As maturities on CP are very short, usually ranging from 30 to 365 days, CP is classified as a money market instrument and is issued on an unsecured basis. In other words, the issuer pledges no assets to protect the investors in the event of default. Therefore the issuer must be a large, well-known firm of very high credit standing (low default risk) to gain investors' confidence to subscribe. In some countries with well-developed credit markets, there is a systematic credit rating system that compares and ranks various securities (commercial paper, notes, bonds, and so on) in terms of the credit risk of issuers. For instance, in the United States there are two agencies rating CP: Moody's Investor Service and Standard & Poor's. From highest to lowest, CP ratings run: P-1, P-2, and P-3 for Moody's; and A-1, A-2, and A-3 for Standard & Poor's. The ratings provide a very useful indication of the issuers' credit quality for investors. On this basis, investors can decide what yield is required in order to lend funds to a specific issuer. Generally the higher the credit risk of the rated issuer, the higher its borrowing cost. Since Hong Kong's credit market is still developing, there is at present no such system available here. The burden of credit rating usually falls on the shoulders of the merchant bankers concerned.

Historical Development and Regulation

The history of CP in Hong Kong can be traced back to the late 1970s. The first CP issue appeared in 1977. The issue was made by the Mass Transit Railway Corporation (MTRC) in the form of negotiable bills of exchange with a maturity of 360 days to the value of HK$500 million. Since then, the MTRC and some famous listed companies such as Cheung Kong (Holdings) Ltd., Hongkong Land, and so on have also made many issues to raise money. However, early issuers were few in number and were mainly non-financial business firms.

Despite these early issues, the market did not really start to flourish until 1984, when two sources of momentum emerged. The first came from the introduction of tender panel mechanism to CP issuance facilities, which will be discussed later. The second impetus was the clarification of CP issue's legal position. Before November 1984, raising funds from the public via an issue of securities (including CP) was considered to be similar to taking public deposits and to contravene the DTC Ordinance. Therefore exemption had to be sought from the authorities on an individual basis before any issue. The formality hindered the issuer from launching an issue at the most appropriate time and remained a major obstacle to market development. This problem was not resolved until November 1984, when the Government announced that a CP issue is not regarded as equivalent to taking public deposits, so application for exemption was no longer required. Accordingly, the market was stimulated and began to show much vitality.

At present, the issue of CP is mainly subject to the regulation of the Protection of Investors Ordinance. (See Chapter 16 for further discussion of laws of investor protection.) This ordinance aims to protect investors by prohibiting the use of fraudulent or reckless means to induce investors to buy or sell securities or to take part in investment arrangements, and regulates the information in related publications. Accordingly, prior authorization must be obtained from the Commissioner of Securities before any CP issue. Recall that CP is issued on an unsecured basis. It provides no security to protect investors in the event of default. In view of its high risk, the Commissioner stipulates that a minimum denomination of HK$500,000 is required for each CP in order to prevent unsophisticated investors from participating in this unsecured market.

Owing to the requirement of large denominations and the subsequent lack of small individual investors' participation, the CP market is almost entirely a wholesale primary market. The major investors are professional institutional investors such as banks, finance companies, unit trust funds, insurance companies, and so on, who purchase the CP and hold it until maturity. The secondary market is virtually nonexistent.

Mechanics of CP Issue

Firms issuing CP may sell it to investors directly, using their own sales force or indirectly, using dealers that are financial institutions (mainly merchant banks) responsible for the functions of credit rating, pricing, and marketing the CP. The major incentive for direct placement is that the issuer is able to save the 0.125 per cent dealer's commission. However, as the issuing firms in Hong Kong are mainly non-financial corporations without any expertise in the market, dealer placement is more common.

To sell through dealers, the issuing firm must first grant a mandate to a financial institution (the 'manager') empowering it to arrange the issue on its behalf. Having obtained the mandate, the manager will invite other financial institutions to join in forming a dealers' syndicate (the tender panel or the underwriting group), through which the CPs will be marketed and distributed. The dealers' arrangement for marketing the CP may take two forms: underwriting and best efforts. In the former, the dealers buy all the paper from the issuing company less discount and commission, and then attempt to sell it at the highest possible price in the market. In so doing, the dealers commit to bear any risk of ending up holding an unsold portion. Alternatively, the issuing company may assume all the risk, with the dealers agreeing only to sell on its behalf the issue at their best effort, that is, at the best price available, less commission. In that case such issue becomes non-underwritten.

Marketing arrangements may be on an individual basis or on a rollover basis. Under the former, the dealers' responsibility for marketing the CP is once and for all. Most of the CP issued in Hong Kong is on a rollover basis. A facility is first set up by the dealers' syndicate, which agrees to submit bids continually for any CP drawn by the issuers within a certain period of time, (say, three years). The most popular form is the Revolving Underwriting Facility (RUF). Under this, the (underwriting) syndicate guarantees to discount any amount unsold at a predetermined underwritten margin, subject to the condition that the paper's outstanding amount at any time cannot exceed the limit specified by the facility. The RUF provides much flexibility to the issuer in the form of an undertaking that at any time the issuer may draw short-term CP for sums needed for current liquidity. This releases the firm from using a long-term debt for short-term finance and accordingly improves the efficiency of funds management. Moreover, since funds are obtained directly from investors, the cost of borrowing in this way is less than the cost of traditional bank loans.

Though the maturity on CP is short, there is always the risk that an issuer might not be able to pay off or roll over[4] the maturity paper. Therefore, in most cases issuers need to back up their CP issue with a line of credit from a commercial bank. The backup lines ensure a source of funds in the event that the firm experiences a cash flow problem or credit market conditions become tight. From a practical standpoint, most investors will not buy CP unless it is backed by a bank line. Of course, banks receive a fee for providing backup lines.

Pricing

Like most money market instruments, CP issues are sold at a discount from the redemption price (face value). No interest is paid thereon during the outstanding period, and the discount, which is based on the prevailing HIBOR, reflects the return to the investors as well as the borrowing cost to the issuer.

An example may help to illustrate the pricing of issuing and trading a CP. Suppose a company wishes to issue 30-day CPs of HK$500,000 denomination at an effective cost of 7 per cent per annum. The net proceeds received for each CP will be:

$$\text{discounted price}^5 = \frac{\text{face value}}{1 + \dfrac{\text{effective interest rate} \times \text{days to maturity}}{365}}$$

$$\text{or} \quad = \frac{\text{face value} \times 365}{365 + \text{effective interest rate} \times \text{days to maturity}}$$

$$= \frac{\text{HK\$500,000} \times 365}{365 + 0.07 \times 30}$$

$$= \text{HK\$497,140}$$

An investor who pays this price for the CP will earn the following return if he holds it until maturity:

$$\begin{array}{l}\text{effective interest rate} \\ \text{(return)}\end{array} = \frac{\text{discount}}{\text{discounted price}} \times \frac{365}{\text{days to maturity}}$$

$$= \frac{\text{HK\$500,000} - \text{HK\$497,140}}{497,140} \times \frac{365}{30}$$

$$= \frac{\text{HK\$2,860}}{\text{HK\$497,140}} \times \frac{365}{30}$$

$$= 7\% \text{ p.a.}$$

Assuming that the investor decides to sell the CP on the tenth day after purchasing it, and that the market interest rate at the time of the sale rises to 8 per cent per annum, the sale price of the CP in the secondary market will be:

$$\text{discounted price} = \frac{\text{face value} \times 365}{365 + \text{effective interest rate} \times \text{days to maturity}}$$

$$= \frac{\text{HK\$500,000} \times 365}{365 + 0.08 \times 20}$$

$$= \text{HK\$497,818}$$

To the investor, his effective return for the 10 days is therefore:

$$\text{effective return} = \frac{\text{HK\$497,818} - \text{HK\$497,140}}{\text{HK\$497,140}} \times \frac{365}{10}$$

$$= 4.98\% \text{ p.a.}$$

This yield is lower than the original yield of 7 per cent because he has suffered a capital loss due to the increase in the interest rate after purchase. Should he hold the CP until maturity, he still could get the 7 per cent return.

From the standpoint of the third party who purchases the CP at HK\$497,818, this price assures him a return of 8 per cent for the remaining period of 20 days, which is equivalent to the market interest rate at the time of purchase. The calculation is shown below:

$$\text{effective return} = \frac{\text{HK\$500,000} - \text{HK\$497,818}}{\text{HK\$497,818}} \times \frac{365}{20}$$

$$= 8\% \text{ p.a.}$$

Securitization and the Capital Market Instruments

Besides CP, there are many other securities that have frequently been used as a source of financing by large businesses in recent years. Examples of these include bonds, Floating-rate Notes (FRN), Certificates of Deposit (CD), and so on. As the original maturity of these instruments is longer than one year — the dividing line between money market and capital market — they all are put into the category of capital market instruments.

Capital market became one of the most important components of Hong Kong's financial system in the mid-1980s. Its development is quite similar to the CP market mentioned above. In fact these two markets have been going hand in hand in the past and practitioners often include CP as capital market instrument. The first capital market instrument was issued as early as the mid-1970s, but the market did not really start to grow until recently. The active participation of MTRC together with the global trend towards debt securitization vitalized the Hong Kong capital market in the mid-1980s. Table 8.3 provides some statistics on the Hong Kong dollar denominated capital market issues[6] from 1984 to 1988. It can be seen that the market has shown great vitality in terms of number and value of issues since 1984. Nevertheless, as the market is developing, its course is relatively unstable, being mainly dependent on the interest rate fluctuation. When the interest rate was declining in 1985–6, investors rushed to buy and hold fixed income securities (such as fixed-rate CD, bonds, and so on). The demand-pull in turn drove up the market supply side. However, when the interest rate showed signs of reversing its trend in 1987–8, the demand vanished quickly and so the market activities slowed down. The floating-rate market is more stable than the fixed-rate market as the interest rate risk of floating-rate instruments is less. Among the fixed-rate issues of financial institutions, most are used for interest rate swap purposes.

Classification of Instruments

Basically, there are three major kinds of instruments traded in the Hong Kong market: bonds, notes, and certificates of deposit.

1. Bonds.   A bond is a promissory note evidencing a long-term indebtedness in which the issuer (borrower) commits to pay the holders its face value on maturity plus a fixed amount of interest periodically during its life. It is a debt instrument with very long maturities of at least five years. A bond may be issued either by a corporate borrower, or by a government. The former is called a corporate bond while the latter is a government bond.

In Hong Kong, the corporate bond market is dominant as there are very few Government bond issues. The Government has accumulated a huge budget surplus and so seldom borrows. Even though the corporate bond is dominant in the Hong Kong market, it is noteworthy that bond issues by businesses are still not very popular, so the bond market is very inactive. This may be attributed to the tradition that demand for long-term funds is low and business relies far more on bank loans than on direct finance.

One feature of bonds worthy of mention is their interest. Generally bonds are one kind of fixed income securities. Interest on bonds is fixed at the time of issue for the whole outstanding period, regardless of the movement of the interest rate afterwards. Accordingly, investors holding bonds bear interest risk. When the market interest rate rises above the coupon rate, the bond declines in value and can be sold at a discount (that is, the market price is less than the face value), and vice versa.

2. Notes.   The terms 'bond' and 'note' are often loosely used as synonyms but they are not exactly the same. A note is a medium- to

Table 8.3 Hong Kong Dollar Denominated Capital Market Issues, 1984–1988

	1984		1985		1986		1987		1988*	
	No. of Transactions	Amount (HK$ million)	No. of Transactions	Amount (HK$ million)	No. of Transactions	Amount (HK$ million)	No. of Transactions	Amount (HK$ million)	No. of Transactions	Amount (HK$ million)
Financial Institutions										
Certificate of Deposit										
Floating Rate	7	1,425	6	1,000	7	1,350	9	1,999	6	1,050
Fixed Rate	3	260	36	5,300	85	10,926	33	3,816	36	2,741
Revolving Underwriting Facilities	3	1,050	5	860	—	—	2	600	—	—
Floating-rate Notes	—	—	1	360	—	—	—	—	—	—
Others	—	—	—	—	—	—	3	1,650	3	1,300
Total	13	2,735	48	7,520	92	12,276	47	8,065	45	5,091
Commercial										
Bonds	—	—	3	1,500	2	1,180	—	—	2	591
Floating-rate Notes	1	500	1	200	5	4,100	1	400	—	—
Revolving Underwriting Facilities	3	1,350	15	8,000	9	4,485	6	4,590	4	4,910
Transferable Loan Certificates	—	—	2	2,390	1	1,450	3	2,768	6	4,086
Others	—	—	—	—	—	—	1	500	2	3,500
Total	4	1,850	21	12,090	17	11,215	11	8,258	14	13,087
Grand total	17	4,585	69	19,610	109	23,491	58	16,323	59	18,178

Note: * up to November 1988.

Source: Schroders Asia Limited.

long-term debt instrument. It differs from a bond in that its maturity is shorter, usually ranging from one to five years. Interest rates on notes may be fixed or floating. A Floating-rate Note (FRN) is one whose interest rate will be refixed periodically (usually every one month, three months, or six months) in accordance with the market short-term interest rate (usually HIBOR) at the fixing date. As a result, the interest rate risk of FRN is far lower than that of fixed income securities such as bonds, Fixed-rate Notes (FXRNs), and so on.

3. Certificates of Deposit.   A Certificate of Deposit (CD) is a negotiable, interest-bearing instrument evidencing a time deposit with a deposit-taking institution. In Hong Kong only authorized institutions, namely licensed banks, licensed DTCs, and registered DTCs are permitted to accept deposits from the public. Therefore a CD must be issued by this type of institution.

By nature a CD is a form of time deposit. It differs from an ordinary time deposit receipt in three aspects. First, maturity on banks' Hong Kong dollar denominated CDs is usually longer than 12 months. This is to circumvent the regulation of Hong Kong Association of Banks' interest rate agreement, which sets the maximum rates of interest payable on Hong Kong dollar deposits with a maturity not longer than one year with licensed banks. Second, as a result of maturity longer than the regulated range, the interest rate on CDs is usually set higher than on ordinary time deposits to attract depositors. As with notes, interest on CDs may be fixed or floating. Third, a CD is negotiable in the sense that it can be sold to another party before the maturity date. Therefore the funds invested are not 'locked in' until maturity as with an ordinary time deposit.

Product Variety

As mentioned above, the Hong Kong capital market was stimulated and propelled by the global trend towards debt securitization and the reduction in market interest rates in mid-1980s. With the help of some expert investment bankers, many traditional instruments have been repackaged and designed as a wide variety of more complex products, thereby providing more satisfaction to both issuers and investors. This in turn enhances the growth of the local capital market. To gain further insight into the market development and activities, we now examine the various new products available so far.

1. Floating-rate Instruments with Cap, Floor, and/or Collar.   A Floating-rate Instrument (FRI) is an instrument of which the interest is refixed periodically. Generally, the interest rate is fixed according to inter-bank rate (for example, HIBOR, LIBOR) on the fixing date. Examples of this are FRN and FRCD. The problem of issuing or holding such instruments is the inherent uncertainty associated with interest rate movement. Interest rates may go up or down, and so issuers and investors may suffer from higher cost and lower return respectively. In view of the volatile interest rate fluctuation in recent years, both issuers

and investors face considerable uncertainty. To protect their interests, investment bankers have devised a kind of FRI with an upper and/or lower limit of interest rate. The upper limit (the 'cap') stipulates a maximum interest rate to be paid by borrowers, while the lower limit (the 'floor') limits the minimum interest rate to be received by investors.[7] Accordingly the uncertainty of the interest rate faced by both parties is reduced.

A floating-rate instrument of this type was first issued by the MTRC in March, 1986. The issue was arranged by Manufacturers Hanover Asia Ltd. in the form of FRN with a maturity of seven years[8] to the value of HK$500 million. The cap and the floor of the issue were set at 12 per cent and 7.5 per cent respectively.

Besides the MTRC's issue, two more issues of same type were recorded. One was the Banque Nationale de Paris' four-and-a-half-year HK$50 million FRCD in March 1987, a time when the interest rate was thought to have bottomed. The issue was arranged with a cap of 14.375 per cent in order to fix the maximum obligation of the borrower. Another one was a three-and-three-quarter-year HK$500 million FRCD issued by the Banque Paribas in January 1988. This was a minimax issue, with caps varying from year to year. The caps were 6 per cent for the first year, 7 per cent for the second year, 9 per cent for the third year, and 10 per cent for the remaining nine months. The floor was fixed at 3.5 per cent throughout the life of the FRN. The issue was arranged in a time of considerable speculative pressure on the Hong Kong dollar, with the aim of protecting investors from possible negative interest rate schemes as well as attracting deposits at a lower cost for the issuer.

2.   Fixed Interest Rate Substitute Transaction.   Another means designed to protect the issuer's maximum cost of borrowing is the fixed interest rate substitute transaction. It is composed of two kinds of FRIs: Traditional/Host and Bull/Inverse. Traditionally, interest on FRI is based on the HIBOR plus a fraction of the profit margin. However, the bull/inverse FRI works out its interest by deducting the HIBOR from a fixed interest rate and so offers investors a return which changes in inverse relation to market interest rate.

An example may help to illustrate this. In June 1988 MTRC arranged such a transaction through LBI Finance (Hong Kong) and Manufacturers Hanover Asia. Interests on traditional FRI and inverse FRI were three-month (3M) HIBOR plus 0.125 per cent, and 17 per cent minus three-month HIBOR respectively. By issuing in the same proportion two kinds of instruments and fixing the rates on the same day, the issuer's average cost of borrowing can be fixed at 8.5625 per cent,[9] regardless of market interest rate movement. More importantly, such a transaction offers greater flexibility and attractiveness to investors, who can then make their investment decision on the basis of their view of future interest rates. If they expect interest rates to fall, they can take advantage of this by buying the inverse FRI. Alternatively they can buy both to gain a fixed return. Thus investors have more choices, being no longer limited to the purchase of traditional instruments when predicting an upward trend of interest rates.

3. Bull and Bear Instruments.   Traditionally, capital market instruments are redeemed at a fixed price made known to all investors at the time of issue. A new device is to link the redemption price to an object (which may be a commodity, an index, or an instrument) whose value is fluctuating. That is called a linked instrument. Linked instruments are usually divided into two parts: bull instruments and bear instruments. The redemption price of bull instruments will vary positively with any change in the object's price, while the redemption price of bear instruments will vary inversely. Thus, if the object's price increases, investors holding bull instruments will get a higher redemption price than those holding bear instruments, who will suffer from a lower redemption value.

Table 8.4 exhibits the first issue of linked instruments. The issue was launched in July 1987 by Paribas Investment (Asia) in the form of 'Fixed Rate Index Linked Bull and Bear Bonds.' The amount of issue was HK$1.5 billion, (half bull bonds and half bear bonds) for a duration of four-and-a-half years, in the denominations of HK$10,000 each. The interest rates were fixed at 4 per cent and 10 per cent for bull bonds and bears bonds respectively. Both bonds were issued at par and redeemed at a value linked to the Hang Seng Index. On maturity, holders of bull bonds will obtain from the issuer an amount equal to face value plus HK$7.5 multiplied by the number of points by which the Hang Seng Index at maturity exceeds the HSI at issues, while

Table 8.4   Paribas Investment (Asia)'s Fixed Rate Index Linked Bull and Bear Bonds

	Bull Bonds	Bear Bonds
Amount of issue	HK$75 million	HK$75 million
Face value	HK$10,000 each	HK$10,000 each
Interest*	4% p.a	10% p.a
Issue price	At par	At par
Redemption value	HK$10,000 + HK$7.5 × (HSI at maturity − 3,330**)	HK$10,000 + HK$7.5 × (3,330 − HSI at maturity)
maximum	HK$20,000	HK$20,000
minimum	HK$0	HK$0
Example:		
(1) If HSI at maturity is 1,996, then redemption value =	HK$0	HK$20,000
(2) If HSI at maturity is 4,664, then redemption value =	HK$20,000	HK$0
(3) If HSI at maturity is 3,530, then redemption value =	HK$11,500	K$8,500

Notes: * As at the time of issue the demand for bull bonds is higher than that for bear bonds, interest on the former is made lower to equalize for both.
          ** 3,330 is the HSI base value fixed at the time of issue.

holders of bear bonds will receive a payment representing face value plus HK$7.5 multiplied by the number of points by which the HSI at maturity is less than the HSI at issue.[10] In other words, bull (bear) bondholders will benefit in bull (bear) market and lose in bear (bull) market because of the changes in expected redemption value on maturity.

It should be noted that both bull and bear bondholders may receive a fixed interest until maturity regardless of the fluctuation of the HSI throughout the outstanding period. For investors holding same proportion of bull and bear bonds, the investment is in effect a traditional fixed income one, which provides a return of 7 per cent per annum and a fixed redemption value of HK$10,000 each.

The linked instruments made their debut in Hong Kong as recently as July 1987. So far about five issues of this kind have been arranged. Among them, two are stock index-linked, two gold-linked, and one currency-linked. The increasing popularity of linked instruments in Hong Kong arises from their benefits to both the investors and the issuing company. To the investors, buying linked instruments not only offers a stable annual fixed income as with the traditional bonds, but also enjoys the chance of growth in value. These should particularly appeal to Hong Kong people who love indulging in the excitement of risky investments. On the other hand, owing to the hedging nature of bull and bear instruments, the issuing company does not run the risk of price fluctuations of the object to which the instrument is linked, so long as the amount of bull and bear instruments is the same. However, as the instruments offer investors a chance to see their investments grow, the company may reduce its cost of raising funds accordingly. As a result, it is hoped that such a concept will perform even better in the days to come.

4.   Convertible Instruments.   To strengthen the instruments' attractiveness to investors, sometimes the issuing company will attach an option (the 'sweetener') that enables its holders to convert their investment into equity shares within a certain period of time. This instrument is called a convertible instrument or equity-linked instrument. Usually the terms of the option, such as valid period, conversion price, conversion ratio, and so on, are stipulated at the time of issue. Investors may at any time exercise their option in accordance with these terms.

With the sweetener attached, the issuer not only can reduce its cost of borrowing but also can sell its equity shares at a premium. To the investors, the convertible instrument is a hybrid of debt and equity. Investing in it may provide a stable annual return as well as potential capital appreciation, which will materialize if the equity shares on option grow in value.

The most recent issue of convertible instruments was made by the Bank of Communication in May 1988. This is a five-year HK$2 billion fixed-rate (5.3 per cent) bond in denominations of HK$500,000 each. Each bond attaches five warrants, each of which enables investors to buy from the issuer 10,000 shares of Hong Kong Telecommunications

Ltd. at HK$10 per share.[11] In other words, each bond can be converted into 50,000 shares. The issue differs from previous ones of same type in that the equity shares put on conversion are not directly issued by the issuer. Instead, the shares are part of the issuer's investment holding.

5. Step-up Fixed-rate Instruments.   As mentioned earlier, investors holding fixed-rate instruments bear considerable interest rate risk. To minimize its adverse impact on investors, the MTRC launched an issue of 'HK$200 million seven-year step-up fixed-rate bonds' in February 1988, the first issue of this kind in Hong Kong. The issue is so named because interest rates on the bonds step up as time goes by. Specifically, the interest rates fixed for the first to the seventh years are 5.75 per cent, 6.25 per cent, 7.00 per cent, 8.00 per cent, 9.00 per cent, 10.00 per cent, and 11.00 per cent, respectively. To protect investors, the issuer may obtain funds on better terms than by issuing traditional instruments.

6. Mismatch Floating-rate Instrument.   The salient feature of FRI is its interest rate fixing. Interest on FRI is refixed periodically and obtained by adding a margin (say 0.25 per cent) to the HIBOR prevailing at the fixing date (namely the reference interest rate). Traditionally, the duration of the HIBOR taken as reference is matched to the length of the interval between two fixing dates. For instance, three-month (3M) HIBOR will be taken when the interest rate is refixed every three months. The practice of matching appeals to financial institutions, which are the major investors in the market. These institutions borrow funds in the inter-bank market (therefore at cost of HIBOR) to buy the instruments. By matching, they are assured that the margin, on top of the reference interest rate, can be earned when investing. Nevertheless, the practice of 'mismatching' increases in the capital market. It results from taking the duration of HIBOR, different from the length of the interval between two fixing dates. Generally, interest is calculated on the basis of the three-month HIBOR but refixed each month. Under this arrangement, investors can borrow money of one-month maturity from the inter-bank market at a cost of one-month (1M) HIBOR, and hold the instrument at a return of 3M HIBOR plus margin. As a 3M HIBOR is normally higher than a 1M HIBOR, the investors are able to profit from the difference in rates (that is, 3M HIBOR – 1M HIBOR) in addition to the margin markup. On account of this 'bonus', the investors are more willing to accept a lower spread. A company that uses this method can then reduce its borrowing cost.

In an abnormal situation where on a fixing day 1M HIBOR is greater than 3M HIBOR, the next fixing interval will extend from one month to three months, thereby becoming a matched fixing method.

Issuing mismatch FRIs in Hong Kong has but a brief history. Nevertheless, it is becoming more popular in the capital market. By now many large companies such as MTRC, Security Pacific Credit (Hong Kong), Union Faith Canada Holdings, and Sun Hung Kai Properties have adopted this method.

7. Interest Rate Swap Agreement.   An interest rate swap agreement (IRSA) is a new product that emerged in recent years. It is an agreement between two parties to exchange each other's interest payment liabilities. Under the agreement, one party's floating-rate liability is, in essence, exchanged for another's fixed-rate obligation, with the aim of enabling both parties to obtain a cost saving. A simple example will illustrate this.

Suppose there are two companies B and C. B is a merchant bank and has better credit standing than C, which is a corporation. With better credit standing, B can raise funds more cheaply both in fixed and floating markets. However, since B as a bank traditionally charges their loan and investment on short-term interest rate, it prefers short-term floating-rate funds to long-term fixed-rate finance for hedging purposes. On the other hand, C as a business dislikes interest rate risk and naturally prefers loans payable against a fixed rate of interest. In this situation, B and C can use interest rate swap agreement to obtain cost saving and reduce interest rate risk as follows:

Table 8.5   An Example of an Interest Rate Swap

	Merchant Bank B		Corporation C
Creditworthiness	Very good		Good
Cost of raising direct fixed-rate fund	7.00%	<	8.50%
Cost of raising direct floating-rate fund	HIBOR + 0.25%	<	HIBOR + 0.75%
Transactions arranged Funding	Raising direct fixed rate fund @7.00%		Raising direct floating-rate fund @ HIBOR + 0.75%
Interest rate swap B pays C a floating rate of HIBOR	HIBOR	→	(HIBOR)
C pays B a fixed rate of 7.5%	(7.50%)	←	7.50%
After swap Effective cost of borrowing	7.00 + HIBOR − 7.50% = HIBOR − 0.50%		HIBOR + 0.75% − HIBOR + 7.50% = 8.25%
Funding type	(floating-rate funding)		(fixed-rate funding)
Cost saving	0.75%		0.25%

Notably, an interest rate swap agreement is not a means of borrowing. There is no actual movement of funds regarding the principal. Instead it is a means of reducing interest rate risk in connection with capital market borrowing. It benefits the two parties entering into an agreement and so enhances the capital market development. There is no official figure regarding the turnover of the IRSA. However, its popularity is widely recognized, as can be seen from the fact that the Hong Kong Capital Market Association has spent much effort in working on a standardized IRSA since its inception. Standardization was finally achieved in May 1988, and will certainly be constructive and stimulate more use.

8. Forward Rate Agreement.   Another new product in connection with capital market issues in Hong Kong is forward rate agreement (FRA). This is an agreement to fix an interest rate for a nominal amount of money for a fixed period of time starting at some future date. By entering into an FRA with some financial institutions, borrowers may lock into a future borrowing cost and so interest rate risk may be minimized beforehand. So far the FRA in Hong Kong has been developing slowly and is not as popular as the IRSA.

Obviously, there have been many innovations in the Hong Kong capital market in recent years. Even though most of them are imported from the Euro markets, the local market shows an ability to adopt such innovative products very rapidly and to keep on expanding. This indicates that the market is full of vitality and there is much room for further development.

Problems and Prospects

Despite the rapid growth of the market in recent years, there still remain some major weaknesses to be resolved. Those worthy of mention include:

1. The Lack of a Credit Rating System.   Like commercial paper, capital market instruments are issued on an unsecured basis. In the event of default, investors have no protection at all. Therefore, the market is entirely built upon investors' confidence in the quality of the issuers. Among potential investors, there are many unsophisticated individuals who lack expertise in market dealing. Without a systematic credit rating system which can provide an objective and reliable indicator, they may find it difficult and inconvenient to judge an issuer's creditworthiness by themselves. As a result, their participating interest is reduced and this in turn limits the investor base of the market.

2. The Lack of a Local Clearing System.   Like the stock-market, the capital market has been operating since its inception without a proper clearing system. The lack of a local system has inhibited the market's development, as settlement among participants becomes complicated and costly. Although the Hong Kong Capital Markets Association has taken the lead in promoting development of a clearing system, no concrete proposal has been reached yet.

3. Regulatory Problems.   The capital market in Hong Kong also suffers from regulatory problems. The first lies in the minimum

denomination requirement. According to the Securities Ordinance and the Protection of Investors Ordinance, all issues of securities in Hong Kong must be approved by the Securities Commission. Recall that the capital market instruments are unsecured and consequently provide little protection to investors in the event of default. The Commission therefore requires a minimum denomination of HK$500,000 each for all issues, in order to keep small investors out of the market. The requirement of high minimum denomination reduces the popularity of instruments and hinders the market's development.

Another problem concerns the tax on instruments. Interest income received from holding Hong Kong dollar securities issued by corporations other than authorized institutions must be subject to either interest withholding tax (if the investor is an individual) or profit tax (if the investor is a corporation). However, if the securities are not denominated in Hong Kong dollars and not held on shore, the investors pay no tax. This creates a major incentive for investors to stay out of Hong Kong dollar securities and in turn, together with the requirement of minimum denomination, creates a discrimination against issues denominated in Hong Kong dollars.

4.   Limited Base of Investors.   The most serious problem of the Hong Kong capital market is the limited base of investors. Owing to the above-mentioned weaknesses, investors in the market are almost restricted to financial institutions; small investors are very few in number. Without small investors' participation and the consequent broad investor base, the market turnover cannot be enhanced. In particular, this threatens the fixed-rate instrument markets. At times of rising interest rates or high interest rate uncertainty, the financial institutions may not be so willing to buy or trade fixed-rate instruments among themselves. As a result, the fixed-rate market is very unstable and may quickly fade for lack of buying support.

The industry has explored feasible solutions to the above obstacles. The creation of money market funds denominated in Hong Kong dollars, introduction of a wide variety of products and devices, listing securities in the stock exchange, and so on are some ways to widen the investor base. In addition, the industry formed an association (called the Hong Kong Capital Market Association) at end of 1986 to co-ordinate members' efforts to review market conditions and tackle relevant problems. So far much work (for example, arranging to review the establishment of a clearing house for Hong Kong dollar instruments, standardizing interest rate swap documentation, lobbying Government for a review of regulatory problems, and so on) has been done by the Association. In view of the practitioners' ongoing efforts, it is thought that many of the major obstacles may soon be overcome.

As long as securitization becomes more popular, more companies will be inclined to securitize their debt as opposed to simply borrowing from banks. As a result of greater supply, the market will become more active than before. More importantly, the government has recently stated its intention of issuing short-term bills for open market operations. If in fact it is decided to issue these bills, this would provide a critical stimulus to the activities of the capital market. The issuance of short-term bills would provide an easily recognizable bench-mark for Hong Kong dollar cost of funds. In addition, active secondary market-making for the bills would highlight the liquidity feature, which would in turn increase investor awareness and the attractiveness not only of the bills themselves but also of other debt instruments in the market. In view of these favorable factors, the prospect of the Hong Kong capital market is quite encouraging. It is hoped that the market will become an important component of local financial sectors as well as a major channel of capital for business in the near future.

Notes

1. See Van Horne (1984), Chapter 1: The Function of Financial Markets.
2. In the past, the Government borrowed twice by the issue of government bonds: one of HK$250 million in 1975 and another of HK$1 billion in 1984, both for covering budget deficits resulting from unexpected economic downturn. At the time of writing, the second issue remains outstanding.
3. This refers to deposits of less than HK$500,000.
4. Rolling over paper means that the issue sells new CP to get funds to retire maturing paper.
5. The formula is applicable to all money market instruments (for example, treasury bills, banker's acceptance, and so on) that calculate interest on a discount basis.
6. Due to the lack of data, here we restrict our observations to Hong Kong dollar denominated instruments only. However, it should be recognized that there have also been issues in other currencies, notably United States dollar, Australian dollar, and to a lesser degree, Canadian dollar issues. Issues in these currencies tend to be opportunistic in terms of prevailing exchange rates and perceived investor demand, and as such they tend to be peripheral efforts compared with the ongoing progress of the domestic markets.
7. The technical name for a floating-rate instrument with both cap and floor is 'collar' or 'minimax'.
8. The term of maturity may be reduced to five years at the option of either the holders or the issuer.
9. This is calculated as follows:

$$\text{Average cost} = \frac{(3M \text{ HIBOR} + 0.125\%) + (17\% - 3M \text{ HIBOR})}{2}$$
$$= 8.5625\%$$

10. The HK$7.5 was set arbitrarily by the issuer.
11. The conversion price of HK$10 is far higher than the market price of about HK$6.85. It is obvious that the issuer may dispose of its holding of the Hong Kong Telecommunications Shares at a premium when the option provided is exercised by the investors.

References

Chan, Daniel, 'Hong Kong Bond Market: Difficulties and Feasible Solution', *Securities Bulletin*, Volume 14, June 1987, pp. 32–3.
Cheung, H., 'Capital Market Instruments in Transition', *Securities Bulletin*, Volume 24, April 1988, pp. 19–20.
Ho, Y. K., 'The Money Market and the Foreign Exchange Market', in R. H. Scott,

K. A. Wong, and Y. K. Ho (eds.), *Hong Kong's Financial Institutions and Markets* (Hong Kong, Oxford University Press, 1985), pp. 79–103.

Hurst, M. K., 'A Review and the Prospects for Hong Kong Capital Market', *Securities Bulletin*, Volume 33, January 1989, pp. 20–2.

Lui, Y. H., 'The Information Content of the HIBOR', *Hong Kong Economic Journal Monthly*, Volume 12, No. 4, July 1988, pp. 93–6.

—— 'The Variety of Hong Kong Capital Market Instruments', *Hong Kong Economic Journal Monthly*, Volume 12, No. 8, November 1988, pp. 95–103.

—— *The Hong Kong Financial System* (Hong Kong, Commercial Press, 1989).

McBain, R. E., 'Hong Kong Capital Market Since October 19', *Securities Bulletin*, Volume 24, April 1988, pp. 21–4.

Van Horne, J., *Financial Markets and Flows*, (New Jersey, Prentice Hall, second edition, 1984), Chapter 1.

9. The Foreign Exchange Market

Y. H. LUI

THE existence of a well-developed foreign exchange (FX) market is a major element in determining the importance of a country or region as a financial centre. An efficient FX market attracts foreign banks to engage in exchange transactions and at the same time strengthens the link between domestic and foreign financial markets. Hong Kong has one of the most efficient FX markets in the Asia Pacific region. Its average daily turnover is estimated to be US$30 billion, just behind Japan's turnover of US$50 billion and Singapore's of US$40 billion in the Far East. The market's importance arises from its being a segment of the global market, enabling exchange dealings to continue in the Far East even after the markets in Europe and the United States have closed.

In 1983, Hong Kong confronted a financial crisis which induced radical innovations in the financial sector. The most remarkable of these was a new arrangement for issuing notes. This measure indirectly changed the exchange rate regime from a freely floating to a linked one, with significant implications for both the financial system and the economy. Owing to the international status of the territory, the new measure triggered wide interest and international attention.

This chapter examines the development, importance, operations, and future prospects of the FX market in Hong Kong. Particular attention is paid to the mechanism, implications, and viability of the current linked exchange rate system which results from the revised note-issue arrangement that began 17 October 1983.

Historical Development

The Hong Kong FX market has existed for a long time. However, it did not really start to grow until the mid-1970s, when the exchange control scheme was abolished. Before July 1972, Hong Kong was a member of the sterling area. The Hong Kong dollar was pegged to the pound sterling at £1 = HK$14.55 (see Table 9.1) and an exchange control system existed to prevent a reserve drain from the sterling area. The market was relatively inactive. Participants, mainly banks, were few in number.

In July 1972, as sterling came under heavy pressure and the British government was forced to resort to floating it, the Hong Kong government decided to stop pegging the Hong Kong dollar to the pound sterling. Instead, the local currency was pegged to the United States dollar at a fixed parity of US$1 = HK$5.650. After 1973, exchange

Table 9.1 Historical Changes in the Hong Kong Exchange Rate System

	£1 = HK$	US$1 = HK$	DM1 = HK$	.1 = HK$	SDR1 = HK$	EERI Old	EERI New
Sterling Exchange Standard							
16 Dec. 1946[2]	16.00	3.970					
18 Sept. 1949[3]	16.00	5.714					
20 Nov. 1967[4]	16.00	6.667					
23 Nov. 1967[5]	14.55	6.061					
18 Dec. 1971[6/7]	14.55	5.582			6.061		
6 July 1972[8]		5.650			6.134		
14 Feb. 1973[9]		5.085			6.134		
25 Nov. 1974		5.085					
Floating Rate System[1]							
26 Nov. 1974[10]	11.40	4.900	2.00	0.0164	—	—	
End of 1974	11.60	4.930	2.06	0.0165	6.012	105.1	
End of 1975	10.30	5.040	1.93	0.0165	5.900	107.4	
End of 1976	8.20	4.677	2.00	0.0161	5.434	114.4	
End of 1977	8.94	4.620	2.22	0.0194	5.616	106.6	
End of 1978	9.87	4.810	2.66	0.0249	6.263	93.2	
End of 1979	11.05	4.960	2.88	0.0209	6.534	92.7	
End of 1980	12.32	5.140	2.63	0.0254	6.556	88.2	128.5
End of 1981	10.92	5.690	2.54	0.0261	6.623	85.2	125.3
31 Aug. 1982	10.51	6.100	2.44	0.0235	6.607	88.2	
End of 1982	10.63	6.515	2.74	0.0279	7.187	79.5	117.2
19 May 1983[11]	10.98	7.035	2.86	0.0302	7.607	74.7	
31 Aug. 1983	11.36	7.595	2.82	0.0308	7.934	71.3	
17 Sept. 1983[12]	12.15	8.060	3.05	0.0338	—	66.9	
24 Sept. 1983[13]	14.50	9.600	3.70	0.0425	—	57.2	
Linked Rate System							
17 Oct. 1983[14]	12.50	8.000	3.13	0.0349	8.506	65.9	
End of 1983	11.36	7.790	2.87	0.0338	8.156	68.3	101.1
7 July 1984[15]	10.45	7.900	2.83	0.0328	—	70.9	
End of 1984	9.16	7.833	2.51	0.0313	7.678	75.9	115.4
End of 1985	11.27	7.811	3.18	0.0390	8.580	70.6	112.7
End of 1986	11.48	7.795	4.01	0.0488	9.534	64.8	110.3
15 Dec. 1987[16]	14.30	7.751	4.78	0.0612	10.748	56.8	101.7
End of 1987	14.52	7.760	4.91	0.0637	11.009	55.6	100.5
End of Sept. 1988	13.19	7.810	4.16	0.0582	10.078	—	103.3

Notes:
1. Figures in table are based on closing middle-market T.T. rates
2. IMF parity established; HK$ was pegged to sterling.
3. HK$ devalued *pari passu* with sterling by 30.5 per cent.
4. HK$ devalued *pari passu* with sterling by 14.3 per cent.
5. HK$ revalued by 10 per cent, including against sterling, but continued pegged to sterling at new rate.
6. As a result of USA terminating, in August 1971, the convertibility of US$ into gold, IMF began to adopt the SDR as its accounting unit.
7. As part of the general currency realignment, HK$ and sterling appreciated by 8.57 per cent against US$.
8. HK$ pegged to US$ following the floating of sterling.
9. US$ devalued; HK$ remained pegged at new rate.
10. HK$ allowed to float, that is, the government no longer undertook to maintain a particular rate against any other currency.
11. HK$ fell below 7.00 against US$.
12. HK$ fell below 8.00 against US$.
13. HK$ fell below 9.00 against US$ and touched an all time low of 9.60.
14. HK$ was linked to US$, through a new arrangement in the note-issuing mechanism, at a fixed exchange rate of US$1 = HK$7.80.
15. HK$ was pushed down to 7.90 at the time when the draft agreement between the Chinese and British governments was about to be signed.
16. HK$ appreciated to its highest level against US$ since its linking because of the influx of speculative hot money.

Source: *Hong Kong 1988* and *Hong Kong Monthly Digest of Statistics* (Hong Kong, Census and Statistics Department), various issues.

control no longer existed. On 26 November 1974, following a violent speculative attack against the United States dollar, the Hong Kong government gave up attempting to maintain a fixed parity for the Hong Kong dollar, and the pegging came to an end. After that, the Hong Kong currency was allowed to float and became one of the freely convertible currencies in the world.

The abolition of exchange control and the free convertibility of the currency provided the basic necessary conditions for the development of the FX market. But the major impetus behind its rapid growth was the influx of foreign banks and the development of the Deposit-taking Companies (DTCs). In 1978 the moratorium[1] on new bank licences was lifted, and many international banks rushed to operate in Hong Kong. Without a sufficient Hong Kong dollar deposit base, these institutions had to rely heavily on their expertise in FX and money markets to fund their loan operations (either by means of selling foreign exchange, swap transactions,[2] or inter-bank borrowing) and to make a profit in addition to their lending business. Their activities and expertise promptly stimulated the development of the two markets.

Another major type of financial institution, the Deposit-taking Companies (DTCs, also called finance companies; among them are some merchant banks or investment banks), emerged as a result of the stock-market boom in the early 1970s. The boom gave rise to the businesses of underwriting, corporate finance, investment management, share financing, and so on, and attracted both local business men and overseas financial institutions to commence business here. This new type of financial institution was not regulated until 1976 when the DTCs Ordinance was enacted. Since then, their status has been widely recognized. During the period of moratorium on bank licences, this was a particularly attractive way for foreign financial institutions to do business in Hong Kong. The participation of DTCs and foreign banks enabled both the FX and money markets to develop with great diversity and width in their dealings.

In 1982 and 1983 the Hong Kong financial sector confronted a severe test. Following Mrs Thatcher's visit to Beijing in September 1982, a confidence crisis originated from the political uncertainty over the territory's future after 1997. The lack of confidence first triggered a collapse of the property market. Many property-related companies suffered severe liquidity problems; some were forced to close. The disaster promptly spread into the financial sector, because more than 40 per cent of public companies listed on the stock-market were property-related. The stock-market slumped. The stock index fell from 1035.33 in August 1982 to 690 on 4 October 1983. At the same time, those banks and DTCs which had lent heavily to the property industry suffered great losses from loans that had to be written off. In view of this, other financial institutions began to tighten credit lines to those banks and DTCs. In turn, this worsened the liquidity problems of some financial institutions. People, worried not only about the political future but also about the stability of the financial system, rushed to withdraw money and convert it into foreign currencies. Subsequently some banks suffered runs on their deposits, and several DTCs became bankrupt. Many financial institutions which had been previously active in foreign exchange dealings were forced to withdraw from the market.

Political uncertainty induced significant capital outflows. The FX market became very volatile and the Hong Kong dollar was under considerable downward pressure. The trade-weighted exchange index[3] fell sharply from 88.2 at the end of August 1982 to a record low of 57.2 on 24 September 1983, with the exchange rate of the Hong Kong dollar for the telegraphic transfer of the United States dollar (T.T.)[4] touching an all-time low of 9.6 per United States dollar on the same day (see Table 9.1). Pessimistic sentiment prevailed in both the FX market and the economy.

To revive the exchange value of the Hong Kong dollar, the Government announced two measures on 15 October 1983. The first revised the arrangement for issuing notes, fixing the rate at HK$7.8 per US$1.0. That induced what we call the linked exchange rate system, which will be discussed later in this chapter. The second measure was the removal of a 10 per cent interest withholding tax on Hong Kong dollar deposits. Both of these measures aimed to restore confidence in and attractiveness of the local currency, and they seem to have been effective. Under the new arrangement, the forces of competition and arbitrage have ensured that the market exchange rate fluctuates narrowly around the level of 7.8 most of the time.

The withdrawal of some active participants and the stablization of the Hong Kong dollar reduced the degree of activity of Hong Kong dollar dealings. Most T.T. trades are mainly for position covering rather than speculation. Nevertheless, the T.T. market is still vital to the growing export-led economy because of its large volume of external trade.[5] The market for other currencies was not affected: it is still very active and continues to grow.

In recent years, the Hong Kong FX market has grown very rapidly. A recent survey conducted by a local leading magazine reveals that the market's daily average turnover is about US$30 billion, as compared with US$10 billion in 1984.[6] It ranks only behind Tokyo and Singapore in the Far East.

Hong Kong possesses several strategic advantages that contribute to the rapid development of the market. These include a well-established financial infrastructure, a central geographical location, excellent communication, experienced FX professionals, the local government's non-interventionism, a low tax rates structure, an advantageous time zone, and so on. The well-developed economy itself also has a sufficiently large external trade volume to support FX activities.[7] Of course, this relationship is interdependent: the FX market contributes to the rapid growth of the export-led economy as well. With an efficient FX market, external trade is also facilitated.

The significance of the FX market in Hong Kong arises not only from its internal function but also from its external role. The Hong Kong market is a segment of the global FX market and is integrated with other FX markets in leading financial centres (New York, London, Tokyo, Singapore, Frankfurt, Zurich, San Francisco, and so on). Hong Kong's time zone advantage enables its market to bridge the time gap between the two largest markets, New York and London. In other words, foreign market participants can cover or hedge their positions in the Hong Kong market, even after the markets in Europe and the United States are closed. Exchange dealing is possible virtually 24 hours a day around the world (see Fig. 9.1). Furthermore, the Hong Kong FX market links local financial markets with foreign financial markets, thus forming an integrated world market. For the money markets, its presence ensures that interest arbitrage can be carried out to maintain interest rate parity. For the capital markets, it facilitates the process of international investment, and thus benefits from diversification may result. For the gold markets, arbitrage activities can be done through the FX market, ensuring that the local gold price stays in line with the international one. Its significance understood, it should be no surprise that the FX market of the territory now has international status.

Fig. 9.1 The Working Hours of Leading FX Markets (Hong Kong Time)

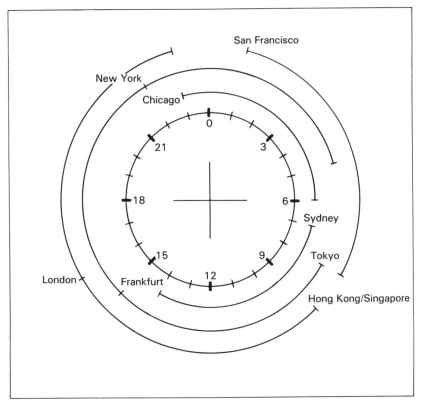

Structure and Operations

Like most FX markets, the Hong Kong FX market has no centralized physical location for FX dealings. In essence it is a complex, sophisticated network of telephone and telegraphic communications between the dealing rooms of financial institutions operating in many financial centres throughout the world. All FX transactions between domestic and overseas parties are made by phone and telecommunication equipment, through which the markets over the world are integrated.

The Market Participants

The major participants of the HK market are licensed banks, licensed DTCs, and registered DTCs. These participants trade on their own accounts and act as either interest arbitragers, speculators, or hedgers. They participate in dealings not only to cover commercial demand but also to speculate. At the end of 1988, the number of licensed banks, licensed DTCs, and registered DTCs was 160, 35, and 216 respectively. Of course, not all of them actively participate in exchange dealings. Since the financial crisis in 1982–3, some DTCs (particularly those without a banking background) have found it difficult to deal in the market because participants have become more prudent in selecting their counterparts.

Among the participants, foreign banks are relatively active in foreign currency dealings. Indeed, the FX is an integrated part of the world-wide payments mechanism. Bank participants may benefit from closer access to the money markets of their country of origin, and so they usually have an advantage in trading their home currency. Therefore, naturally the two commercial note-issuing banks, namely the Hongkong and Shanghai Banking Corporation (HongkongBank) and the Standard Chartered Bank, dominate the Hong Kong dollar dealings in both FX and money markets. Similarly, the Deutschmark (DM) constitutes the overwhelming bulk of transactions for Dresdner Bank and Deutsche Bank, which are the market leaders in this particular area. The Bank of Tokyo has become particularly aggressive in Hong Kong with regard to the Japanese yen. Barclays Bank is the market leader in the pound sterling. But on the broader currency spectrum of the most active currencies such as the United States dollar, the Deutschmark, the Japanese yen, and so on, it is the big American Banks — Citibank, Morgan Guaranty Trust Company of New York, Bankers Trust Company, Chase Manhattan Bank, and Bank of America — which hold an undisputed sway over the Hong Kong market.

Deals among the participants may be done in two ways: directly or indirectly. In direct dealing, which is based on a spirit of reciprocity, participants simply call each other on telecommunication equipment. One dealing bank will make a market, that is, stand ready to buy or sell a currency to another bank on the understanding that the second bank will also make a market for it. Indirect dealing occurs via foreign exchange brokers, who are middlemen between two parties wishing to deal. The job of the broker is to take bids and offers of foreign currencies from the banks and DTCs, communicate them to those other participants who deal through the broker, and help arrange transactions. As brokers, they do not buy or sell currencies for their own accounts, nor do they assume any financial responsibility for the trades they help arrange. Fig. 9.2 shows the relationships among participating brokers and financial institutions in the market. As of late 1988, there were 10 brokerage firms, all of which had to be the members of the Hong Kong Foreign Exchange and Deposit Brokers Association, membership being granted with the official recognition of the Hong Kong Association of Banks (HKAB). Of these 10 brokers, 8 are international brokers. Their presence strengthens the link of the local market with the international ones.

Fig. 9.2 The Relationships Among the Participants in the Hong Kong Foreign Exchange Market

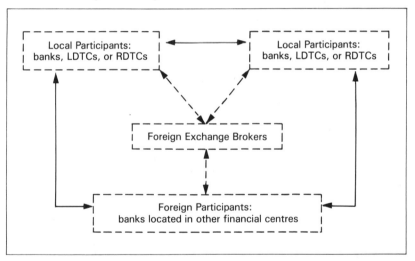

Note: Solid lines represent direct transactions and dotted lines indicate indirect transactions.

About 60 per cent of the deals[8] in the Hong Kong market are done directly, partly because of the existence of a brokerage commission, and partly because direct dealing enables participants to deal a very large amount in a moment of time with less price variation than occurs in indirect dealing. Nevertheless, as the quotation of rates for an indirect deal might combine many quotations from different participants, the spread is probably narrower than that of direct dealing and reflects much more information about market conditions. Thus the two methods of dealing are complementary. Under either method, an institution must establish reciprocal credit facilities with its counterpart beforehand, and transactions between the two parties can then be made up to the limit determined by the facilities.

It is noteworthy that corporations and individuals cannot participate in the FX market directly because it is only an inter-bank/DTC market. Corporations and individuals must go through the banks or DTCs.

Exchange Rate Quotations

An exchange rate is the expression of the amount of one currency (the referred currency) equal to a fixed unit(s) of another currency (the reference or base currency). Theoretically, either of the currencies could act as the referred or reference currency. However, as the medium of exchange in the FX market is the United States dollar, market practice is to quote all rates against the United States dollar, for example:

T.T.	7.8050–60	
$/DM	1.7920–30	
$/¥	126.00–10	where the US$ is the
$/SFR	1.5140–50	reference currency
$/C$	1.1930–40	
$/lira	1356.00–50	
£/$	1.7850–60	where the US$ is the
A$/$	0.8510–20	referred currency
N$/$	0.6270–80	

In other words, prices of all currencies are expressed in terms of United States dollars when the United States dollar is the referred currency.

Most exchange rates shown above are quoted to four decimal places; that is, to 1/10,000 of the basic unit of the referred currency. However, the Italian lira and Japanese yen are given to only two decimal places — that is, 1/100 of the basic unit. This is because the lira and yen are low value units, in fact of the order of 100 times smaller than most currencies. This small division of a currency is called a 'point' or a 'basis point' by dealers. A point therefore means 1/10,000 of a Hong Kong dollar, Deutschmark, Swiss franc, and so on, or 1/100 of a lira or yen. Usually fluctuation in the market price is limited to the last two places, unless the market is highly volatile. Thus the practice in the market is to quote only the last two decimals (for both bid and offer rates) and to leave the big figures unquoted as they are generally understood. For example, the rate for T.T. may be quoted as 50–60 as the round or big figure HK$7.80 is well known to all those who are concerned with the market.

All exchange rate quotations are usually given as two-way rates, that is, bid and offer. The bid rate is the rate at which the dealer quoting the price is willing to *buy* the reference currency and the offer rate is the rate at which he is willing to *sell* the reference currency. Thus, if a bank quotes T.T. as follows:

7.8050–7.8060
(bid)   (offer),

anyone wishing to buy US$1 (the reference currency) from the bank must pay HK$7.8060 and any one wishing to sell US$1 to the bank may obtain HK$7.8050. The difference between the bid and offer rates is called 'spread'. When the market is active with plenty of buying and/ or selling of one currency for another, the spread in the market rates tends to be relatively small (for example, 10 points).

We have already mentioned that the market practice is to trade all currencies against the United States dollar and so to quote dollar rates. That means the United States dollar is either the referred or the reference currency in the market quotations. If we want to get a quotation against currencies other than the United States dollar, we have to work out the 'cross rate' from the respective dollar rates. An example will illustrate the cross rate calculation.

Suppose a bank wants to buy Japanese yen against Hong Kong dollars. The market rates at the moment are:

T.T. 7.8050–60
$/¥ 126.00–10

The bank must first sell Hong Kong dollars for United States dollars, and then use the United States dollars to purchase Japanese yen. Thus it would get the market's selling rate for Japanese yen against Hong Kong dollars with the chain equation:

$$1 \; ¥ = x \; \text{HK\$}$$
$$126.00 \; ¥ = 1 \; \text{US\$}$$
$$1 \; \text{US\$} = 7.8060 \; \text{HK\$}$$
$$x = \frac{7.8060}{126.00} = 0.061952 \; (\text{offer rate}).$$

If the bank wanted to sell, rather than buy, Japanese yen against Hong Kong dollars, the calculation would be:

$$x = \frac{7.8050}{126.10} = 0.061895 \; (\text{bid rate}).$$

Obviously, the bid and offer prices calculated above are just the bank's market costs of selling Japanese yen against Hong Kong dollars and buying Japanese yen against Hong Kong dollars respectively. When the bank quotes the Japanese yen price against the Hong Kong dollar to its customers, a profit margin will be deducted from the above bid price and added to the above offer price to widen the spread, for example:

$$0.061800 \leftarrow 0.061895 - 0.061952 \rightarrow 0.062100.$$

The wider the spread, the larger the dealer's profit margin in the exchange operation.

Types of Transaction

Exchange transactions can be distinguished between spot and forward by the length of time between transaction and delivery (or settlement).
1. Spot Transactions.   A spot transaction is one where delivery of currencies is set for the second working day after the date on which the transaction is concluded. The two-day time lag in settlement is necessary to allow for the administrative handling oı the deal. Since banks in the western world are closed on Saturdays and Sundays, a spot deal made on a Thursday will carry Monday as its value or settlement date. Sometimes, though this is exceptional, transactions may be concluded for delivery one business day after conclusion of the deal (or even value same day). If so, the rates quoted are different from the usual spot market quotations, and depend on the interest rates for the currencies concerned. In Hong Kong, except that delivery for T.T. dealings may be effected on the same day, most transactions in other currencies (for example, United States dollars against Swiss francs, United States dollars against Deutschmarks, and so on) are spot delivery, that is, delivery will occur after two clear working days.
2. Forward Exchange Contracts.   A forward exchange contract is a transaction in which a specified quantity of a stated foreign exchange is bought or sold at a rate of exchange fixed at the time of making the contract, and to be delivered at a future time agreed upon when making the contract. In a forward transaction no currency will change hands between the buyer and the seller until the maturity date of the contract. On the maturity date, the delivery of currencies is effected at the agreed exchange rate irrespective of what happens to the rate in the intervening period.

The rate at which currencies are bought or sold for forward delivery is called the 'forward rate'. Since the forward rate involves future delivery, it is unlike the spot rate, which is purely a reflection of the supply or demand of a currency. What's more, it allows for the interest rate differential in each currency for the period from the transaction date to the maturity date. Therefore forward rates at times move even more dramatically than spot rates. The forward rate is calculated on the basis of the Interest Rate Parity Theory. This theory states that covered interest arbitrage[9] causes the forward exchange rate to adapt to the interest differential between the two currencies concerned.
3. An Example of Interest Rate Parity Theory.   Imagine a bank that can borrow funds in United States dollars or Hong Kong dollars. If it can borrow United States dollars for three months (assuming 90 days) at an annualized interest rate of I_{US},[10] then for each dollar it borrows it must repay $(1 + I_{US} \times 90/360)$. The bank can take the borrowed United States dollar and buy $1 \times \$HK$ at the spot rate (S). If this is

invested at I_{HK} per annum, and if the resulting receipts are sold forward (F), the bank will receive at the end of the 90 days

$$\frac{S}{F}\left(1 + I_{HK} \times \frac{90}{365}\right) US\$.$$

Note that, because of the forward cover, there is no exchange risk and that the bank has begun with no funds of its own. Borrowing United States dollars and simultaneously investing Hong Kong dollars will result in a profit if the number of United States dollars received from the Hong Kong dollar investment exceeds the repayment on the United States dollar loan, that is, if

$$\left(1 + I_{US} \times \frac{90}{360}\right) < \frac{S}{F}\left(1 + I_{HK} \times \frac{90}{365}\right)$$

The reverse activity, borrowing Hong Kong dollars and investing United States dollars, will be profitable if the reverse inequality holds. As long as either inequality holds, it pays to borrow in one market and lend in the other. The covered interest arbitrage constantly taking place helps guarantee that little opportunity for profit remains and that a state of equilibrium will eventually be reached when the following condition holds:

$$\left(1 + I_{US} \times \frac{90}{360}\right) = \frac{S}{F}\left(1 + I_{HK} \times \frac{90}{365}\right)$$

Under this condition, there will be no advantage to borrowing or lending in any particular money market or from interest arbitrage. In other words, lenders and borrowers will be indifferent in regard to choosing a market in equilibrium. Rearranging the equation gives a method for calculating the forward rate:

$$F = S\frac{\left(1 + I_{HK} \times \frac{90}{365}\right)}{\left(1 + I_{US} \times \frac{90}{360}\right)}.$$

Thus if a three-month United States dollar deposit carries an interest rate (I_{US}) of 9.5 per cent, a three-month Hong Kong dollar deposit (I_{HK}) fetches 8 per cent, spot T.T (S) is 7.8050, then the forward rate is calculated as follows:

$$F = 7.8050\frac{\left(1 + 0.08 \times \frac{90}{365}\right)}{\left(1 + 0.095 \times \frac{90}{360}\right)} = 7.77432.$$

There are three possible alternative relationships between the forward rates and the corresponding spot rates. If a currency in the forward is worth as much as in the spot, it is said to be 'at par'. If a currency is cheaper in the forward, it is trading at a 'discount'. When its forward value is more expensive than its spot value, it is trading at a 'premium'. In our example above, the United States dollar is at a discount to the Hong Kong dollar because the United States dollar's forward exchange (7.77432) is worth less than the corresponding spot exchange (7.8050). Notably, a higher interest bearing currency must trade at a discount to a lower yield currency.

It should be stressed that forward rates are not quoted as such in the FX market. Dealers only work with those differences, expressed in decimal points, between spot and forward prices, that is, with the premiums and discounts,[11] for example:

T.T. Spot	7.8050 – 60
3-month discount (points)	306.8–200
6-month discount (points)	650 –500

To obtain forward rates, we have to add the premium to or deduct the discount from spot rates, for example:

T.T. Spot	7.8050	7.8060
3-month discount	306.8	200
3-month forward	7.77432	7.7860
	(bid)	(offer)

Quoting forward differentials (premiums or discounts) rather than forward prices has, of course, its reasons. First, forward differentials very often remain unchanged even when the spot rates experience fluctuations; quoting premiums and discounts rather than forward rates thus requires fewer changes. Second, and more important, the forward rates are of no interest in many cases. For instance, for a swap transaction what matters is the forward differentials while neither the spot rate nor the forward rate are of any significance.

4. Swap Transactions. A swap transaction is a third type of transaction in the FX market. A swap is the combination of a spot purchase of a currency with its simultaneous forward sale (or vice versa). When a bank enters into a swap transaction with another bank, it sells its holdings of one currency to the latter in exchange for another currency, and agrees to repurchase them at a fixed price on a specified future date. Effectively the two parties concerned are swapping one currency for another for that particular period on a hedged basis, thereby involving no exchange risk at all. A practical example will illustrate the procedure.

Suppose spot T.T. (S) = 7.8050:

 3-month T.T. forward (F) = 7.77432

 3-month US$ interest rate (I_{US}) = 9.50% p.a.

 3-month HK$ interest rate (I_{HK}) = 8.00% p.a.

A bank having surplus Hong Kong dollars but lacking United States dollars may enter a swap transaction of buy–sell three-month US$1 million (that is, buy US$1 million spot for Hong Kong dollars and sell US$1 million three-month forward) with another bank to swap Hong Kong dollars for United States dollars.

Spot	Forward	Equivalent Effect
US$1,000,000[+]	US$1,000,000[Δ]	borrow US$ for 3 months
HK$7,805,000[Δ]	HK$7,774,320[+]	lend HK$ for 3 months
@7.8050	@7.77432	

Notes: + = buy (in).
        Δ = sell (out).

Since the United States dollar interest is higher than the Hong Kong dollar interest, it appears on the surface that the bank gains an interest differential as follows:

return on US$ deposit	$= \text{US\$1,000,000} \times 0.095 \times \dfrac{90}{360} \times 7.77432$	= HK$184,640
opportunity cost of HK$ deposit	$= \text{HK\$7,805,000} \times 0.08 \times \dfrac{90}{365}$	= HK$153,962
gain on interest differential		= HK$30,678

However, this gain is just sufficient to offset exactly the exchange loss in the transaction:

$$\text{exchange loss} = \text{HK\$7,805,000} - 7,774,320$$
$$= \text{HK\$30,680} = \text{HK\$30,678}$$

Obviously the two banks concerned do not gain at each other's expense in the swap transaction, but each may adjust its portfolio position and satisfy its need for a particular currency without increasing its exposure to exchange risk.

The Hong Kong FX market is primarily a spot market. A significant proportion of foreign exchange dealings are spot transactions.

Although the FX market is an important segment in the financial sector of the Hong Kong economy, at the time of writing (September 1988), there are no official statistics on the market's trading volume. A recent survey of the Hong Kong FX market conducted by a local magazine reveals that the daily average turnover in 1987 was about US$30 billion, compared with US$10 billion in 1984.[12] All convertible currencies are traded in the market. However, the degree of activity in terms of trading volume for different currencies varies greatly. The most actively traded ones, in order of their turnover, are Deutschmarks (DM), Japanese yen (J¥), sterling pounds (£) and Swiss francs (SFR).[13] The degree of activity of Hong Kong dollar dealing fell following the introduction of the linked exchange rate system in 1983 because the relatively stable exchange rate movement reduced opportunities for speculation. Nevertheless the FX market for the Hong Kong dollar market is still vital to the export-led economy.

It is noteworthy that there are no explicit regulations or guide-lines for the conduct of participants in the market. Basically, the whole market is completely unregulated and is dependent on economic and social incentives for orderly behaviour. It is very important for an operator to keep his own word on the contracts that he has made. Failure to do so will result in elimination from the market. As the industry puts it, 'a dealer's word is as good as gold'.

The Hong Kong Dollar Effective Index[14]

Although it is the market practice to quote dollar rates, exchange rates against the United States dollar alone can no longer indicate the overall changes in the value of a currency. This is because most major currencies have started to float since the collapse of the Bretton Woods Agreement in 1971. It was commonly recognized that, in a period of generalized floating, measurement of the strength or weakness of a currency could better be made in terms of a basket of currencies represented by an index. The Effective Exchange Rate Index (EERI) for the Hong Kong dollar currently published by the Census and Statistics Department is such a trade-weighted index. It is designed to indicate the Hong Kong dollar's overall external value against a basket of currencies, and measure the effect of exchange rate movements on trade flows.

So that the index will be representative, the basket contains 15 currencies of Hong Kong's principal trading partners, selected, and with weights attached to each, on the basis of the territory's merchandise trade pattern. Before 1983, the pattern of merchandise trade of 1972 had been used for selecting the 15 currencies and calculating their weights. In January 1983, the trade weights were updated to reflect Hong Kong's merchandise trade pattern in 1981. Nevertheless, since the Hong Kong dollar was effectively linked to the United States dollar on 17 October 1983, significant changes have occurred in Hong Kong's trade pattern. In view of these changes, a revised EERI was introduced at the end of September 1987. The new EERI has used the average trade weights of the three years 1984–6. A new base period of 24–28

Table 9.2 Comparison of Trade Weights and Base Rates For Old and New EERIs

Selected Trading Partner	Trade Weights			Currencies	Old Base Rate* (Smithsonian Central Rates as at 18 Dec. 1971)	New Base Rate* (Middle-market T.T. Rates as at 24–28 Oct. 1983)
	1972	1981	1984–6			
China	10.61	17.99	27.06	Renminbi	0.445800	0.512105
U.S.A.	27.19	23.14	23.83	US Dollar	1.000000	1.000000
Japan	18.87	16.81	15.09	Yen	0.003247	0.004294
Taiwan	5.49	6.83	6.20	New Taiwan Dollar	0.025000	0.024363
U.K.	10.91	7.15	5.01	Sterling	2.605714	1.496275
Singapore	4.50	7.26	4.43	Sing. Dollar	0.354667	0.469822
F.R. of Germany	7.12	5.19	4.08	Deutschemark	0.310318	0.382987
South Korea	1.72	3.58	4.01	Won	0.002681	0.001262
Australia	3.44	2.74	2.29	Australian Dollar	1.215998	0.920025
Canada	1.97	1.65	1.78	Canadian Dollar	1.000000	0.811520
Switzerland	2.65	2.21	1.62	Swiss Franc	0.260417	0.472515
France	1.31	1.69	1.47	French Franc	0.195477	0.125534
Italy	1.12	1.34	1.32	Lira	0.001720	0.000639
Netherlands	1.63	1.21	1.04	Guilder	0.308195	0.341211
Belgium	1.48	1.23	0.77	Belgian Franc	0.022314	0.019337
				H.K. Dollar	0.179211	0.128226
Total	100.00	100.00	100.00			

Note: * US$ per unit currency.

Source: *Hong Kong Monthly Digest of Statistics*, (Hong Kong, Census and Statistics Department), January 1983 and November 1987.

October 1983 has also been adopted to replace the previous base date of 18 December 1971, in order to reflect the linking of the Hong Kong dollar to the United States dollar. Table 9.2 compares the difference between the old and new EERIs.

The basic formula for compiling the EERI, which is in line with the method advocated by the International Monetary Fund (IMF), remains unchanged:

$$\text{EERI} = \frac{\text{Appreciation/Depreciation of HK\$} \atop \text{against US\$ relative to the base date}}{\text{Appreciation/Depreciation of selected} \atop \text{currencies against US\$ relative to the base date}}$$

However, geometric averaging is adopted to replace arithmetic averaging in the formula for compiling the weighted average of the nominal indexes for the basket of the 15 selected currencies. On each working day, closing buy and sell telegraphic transfer rates in terms of United States dollars are collected for comparison with the new base rates at 24–28 October 1983 to obtain the nominal indexes. The nominal indexes for the 15 selected currencies are geometrically weighted using 1984–6 average trade weights and divided into the nominal index of the Hong Kong dollar to obtain the new EERI. The mathematical formula can be written as

$$\text{EERI}_t = \frac{\dfrac{R_{HK.t}}{R_{HK.B}}}{\prod_i \left(\dfrac{R_{i.t}}{R_{i.B}}\right)^w} \times 100$$

where EERI_t = EERI at time t

$R_{HK.t}$ = US\$ per unit of HK\$ at time t

$R_{HK.B}$ = US\$ per unit of HK\$ at the base period of 24–28 October 1983

$R_{i.t}$ = US\$ per unit of currency of country i at time t

$R_{i.B}$ = US\$ per unit of currency of country i at the base period of 24–28 October 1983

W_i = 1984–6 average trade weights attached to the ith country's currency

$\sum_i W_i = 1$

Although the revised EERI adopts a new base period to reflect the linking of Hong Kong dollars to United States dollars, its effectiveness in indicating the Hong Kong dollar's overall external value is a bit misleading under the current system. We will discuss this in greater detail when considering the implications of the linked rate system in the next section.

The Linked Exchange Rate System

Recall that in September 1982 the British Prime Minister, Mrs Thatcher, visited Beijing. Without the favourable news her visit was expected to bring, people began to worry about the political future of the territory after its lease expires in 1997. The lack of confidence caused by the sovereignty problem first triggered the collapse of the property market and then hammered the stock-market and the FX market. The uncertainty surrounding the political future led to significant capital outflow and this, abetted by a strong United States dollar, unsettled foreign exchange markets worldwide. Speculation created a heavy downward pressure on the exchange value of the Hong Kong dollar. The currency depreciated from 6.10 against the United States dollar at the end of August 1982 (before Mrs Thatcher's visit) to 7.595 on 31 August 1983, nearly 25 per cent in just 12 months (see Table 9.1). Much worse than that, it continued to slump afterwards, reaching an all-time low of 9.60 on 24 September 1983. To support the exchange rate, local interest rates were adjusted upward from 12 per cent to 16 per cent during the period, but given the strength of other factors, these increases in interest rates probably had only a limited stabilizing effect. Against a background of continuing depreciation and increasing instability of the exchange rate of the Hong Kong dollar, the Government decided, effective 17 October 1983, to alter the arrangements for issuing notes and consequently to change the exchange rate system.

The Mechanism of Linked Exchange

The new arrangement centres around Certificates of Indebtedness (CIs), which are issued by the Exchange Fund[15] to the two note-issuing banks, to be held as cover for the issue of Hong Kong dollar notes. Prior to 17 October 1983 the CIs were issued and redeemed against payments in Hong Kong dollars. Under the new arrangement, such payments are made in United States dollars, at a fixed exchange rate of US$1 = HK$7.80. The Exchange Fund promises to issue and redeem the CI at 7.80, and the note-issuing banks agree that they should provide notes to, and accept notes from, other banks on the same basis as they themselves deal with the Exchange Fund, that is, against payments in United States dollars at the rate of US$1 = HK$7.80. In other words, an inter-bank market for Hong Kong dollar notes at the fixed exchange rate was created. A graphic explanation of the mechanism is given in Fig. 9.3. It can be seen that under the new arrangement any rise in note circulation has to be matched by a United States dollar payment to the Exchange Fund, and any fall in circulation is matched by a similar payment from the Fund.

Fig. 9.3 A Graphic Explanation of the Linked Exchange System

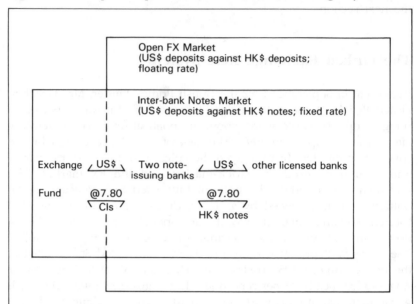

It should be stressed that in the FX market the exchange rate of the Hong Kong dollar is still allowed to float freely, and so theoretically should be determined by market supply and demand. The forces of competition and arbitrage between markets will ensure that the FX market exchange rate stabilizes at a level close to the fixed rate of 7.80 without intervention by the Exchange Fund in the market. An example will illustrate this.

Suppose the Hong Kong dollar is traded in the market at a rate below 7.80 to the United States dollar, say 8.00. Banks will be encouraged to cash in their holdings of Hong Kong dollar notes through the two note-issuing banks for United States dollar deposits at the fixed rate, and then they can turn around to sell the United States dollar deposits for Hong Kong dollar deposits at the market rate for a profit of HK$0.20 per US$1. As a result, in the open market more banks end up buying Hong Kong dollars and selling United States dollar and this puts some downward pressure on the T.T. exchange rate. At the same time, following the redemption of the CI, the Hong Kong dollar notes in circulation are reduced and the liquidity in the banking system is tightened. Local interest rates will rise until they are high enough to attract capital flowing and interest arbitrage. Eventually, demand for the local dollar would boost its market rate close to 7.80.

Of course, the above process will hold only if the market obeys the laws of economics. Political factors might overshadow the normal workings of supply and demand. If people continue to be worried about the future and to withdraw money from Hong Kong, it is inevitable that the Government eventually will have to spend heavily from its foreign exchange fund to buy up Hong Kong dollars in the market in an effort to support the HK$7.80 rate. No government has enough foreign currency on hand to bolster its currency indefinitely. The new arrangement is expected to mitigate adverse political effects. Therefore it was not surprising to see political sensitivity overshadow the function of new system, resulting in pushing the Hong Kong dollar down to a point of 7.90 on 7 July 1984, a time when signing the Sino-British drafted agreement was at hand. Nevertheless, during most of the time since the link, the Hong Kong dollar has held steady against the United States dollar, in contrast to the volatile fluctuations of other major currencies in the world against the United States dollar. This reflects both the effectiveness of the new system and a return of confidence in local currency.

It is worth noting that the market rate is only close to 7.80, but not necessarily exactly 7.80. The rationale behind this is related to the operation of the system's underlying arbitrage mechanism. In the first place, the rate fixed for the CI is not accessible to all parties in the economy. Only banks are capable of dealing at the rate of 7.80 with the Exchange Fund and making arbitrage. Individuals and corporations other than banks (even DTCs) are not allowed to do this with the Exchange Fund. In other words, opportunities for artbitrage are not open to all parties in the economy. Second, in the normal course of business, banks must keep a certain cash ratio to meet customers' withdrawal demands. It is impossible for them to cash in all their holdings of Hong Kong dollar banknotes when arbitraging. Thus, even with their opportunities, banks' ability to arbitrage is not unlimited. Last but not least, the convertibility between United States dollars and Hong Kong dollars is partial only. As the system provides that all licensed banks in Hong Kong have the right to exchange United States dollar deposits for Hong Kong dollar banknotes (but not United States dollar deposits for Hong Kong dollar deposits) or vice versa directly or indirectly with the Exchange Fund, at the rate of 7.80, the fixed rate only applies to note transactions in the inter-bank market but does not apply to Hong Kong dollar deposits. Though both banknotes and deposits are components of money, they are not perfect substitutes for each other in the banking sector. There is no central bank in Hong Kong that can provide the service of changing local currency deposits into cash and vice versa. Licensed banks therefore cannot go to any party (even the two note-issuing banks) in the market to convert Hong Kong dollar banknotes into Hong Kong dollar deposits or vice versa, while, as a service to their customers, they provide for the conversion of Hong Kong dollar deposits into Hong Kong dollar cash at the rate of 1 to 1. It should therefore be no surprise that the open market rate (which is the price of United States dollar deposits in terms of Hong Kong dollar deposits) may sometimes deviate from the official rate of 7.80 (which is the price of United States dollar deposits against Hong Kong dollar banknotes).

Implications

Armed with a basic understanding of the current system, it is interesting to consider its implications for the rest of the economy. These can be summarized as follows.

1. The Adjustment Process.   The new scheme of linking the Hong Kong dollar to the United States dollar transfers the impact of any adjustment to balance of payment pressures away from the exchange rate and onto the banking system, and more specifically onto the liquid reserve base of the banks and onto the level of Hong Kong dollar interest rates. In effect, the exchange rate is no longer an important variable in the economy's adjustment process. Factors such as interest rates, money supply, and the level of economic activity, rather than the exchange rate, now adjust automatically to balance of payment pressure, without government intervention being necessary. For instance, when imports increase and the balance of payments shows a deficit, foreign exchange flows out from the economy and liquidity decreases. The note-issuing banks have less foreign exchange to back the issuance of new Hong Kong dollars. The money supply contracts, interest rates rise, production declines, and the economy slows down, thus reducing the need for imports. On the other hand, when the balance of payments shows a trade surplus, there is a net influx of funds. The banks can increase the money supply. This leads to more credit and a drop in interest rates to fuel investment and consumption, thereby increasing imports and consequently reducing the surplus. Obviously, the adjustment process is automatic. It is interesting to note that there are similarities with a fixed exchange rate system, except that central bank operations are not needed.

2. Monetary Policy.   The effectiveness of the monetary policy has improved. The new measure stipulates that payment for the CIs must be made in United States dollars at the rate of 7.80. First, this strengthens the credibility of the local currency in the sense that all newly issued banknotes are fully backed by foreign exchange assets, similar to the situation when the Hong Kong dollar was pegged with the pound sterling before June 1972. Second, it limits the two banks' ability to issue notes, linking it to the economy's performance in earning foreign exchange. Control of note issue no longer relies on the banks' co-operation nor on human judgement. Instead, it automatically depends on the balance of payments position. Putting it another way, the new system enables the Government for the first time to control the money supply by fixing the rate at which Hong Kong dollars must be backed by foreign exchange.

Further, the role of interest rate as an instrument of monetary policy has altered. Interest rates now assume a more passive role, changing, more frequently perhaps, in response to balance of payments influx and outflow. Under the new exchange regime it is neither so necessary nor so desirable for the Government to influence interest rates through the Hong Kong Association of Banks or by direct intervention in the money market. The importance of the interest rate agreement as a monetary tool is reduced, giving rise to greater pressure for its abolition.

3. Exchange Rate.   Exchange rates are the prices of one country's money in terms of other countries' monies. They are among the most important prices in the economy, since through exchange rates domestic prices are effectively translated into foreign prices and vice versa. Any movement in exchange rates may induce changes in domestic prices, and thus have far-reaching consequences for the economy. Under the linked rate system, as the market exchange rate of the Hong Kong dollar has been stabilized at the level of 7.80 against the United States dollar — the major currency in international trade — external trade is facilitated. The adverse impact of exchange fluctuation on domestic prices, output, employment, and so on can also be minimized. This in turn helps contribute to the buoyant performance of the export-led economy in general.

However, the stabilization of the Hong Kong dollar against the United States dollar also has a side effect on the interpretation of Hong Kong dollar trade-weighted exchange rate index. Under the new system, the EERI can no longer indicate the true performance of the Hong Kong dollar in the market because its fluctuations mainly reflect movements of the United States dollar against other foreign currencies included in the calculation of the index. When the United States dollar rises, the index will naturally rise. When the United States dollar weakens, the index will also follow suit. The strength of the Hong Kong dollar as reflected by the index is likely to misinform. The real performance of the local currency should now be reflected by the money supply and in turn by interest rates as well. When demand for the Hong Kong dollar is greater than its supply (for example, trade surplus, capital flowing in, and so on), money supply will increase because of the increase in foreign exchange in the economy. Increase in money supply may induce lower interest rates which therefore means better performance of the currency now and vice versa.

4. United States Dollar-dependent Economy.   The exchange rate of the Hong Kong dollar under the new system is stable. Without the adjustment in exchange rate as a protecting shelter, the economy is now more at risk to exogenous factors. The link with the United States dollar is equivalent to a United States dollar exchange standard, and the Hong Kong economy has become a United States-dependent economy. The international value of the Hong Kong dollar is now dependent entirely on the performance of the United States dollar and the United States economy rather than its own. When the United States dollar gets stronger, the Hong Kong dollar also gets firmer and vice versa. The United States dollar's performance has a direct effect on our local economy, and so does the impact of United States government policy and its economic and political cycle. Though before the linked rate the relationship between the two economies was quite close, and the United States economy might affect the Hong Kong economy to a considerable extent because of their trade relationship, its influence was

not as direct as it is now. Hong Kong seems to have very little defence against it. Given the very different economic structures and environment of the two places, this may expose Hong Kong's economy to more undue risk. To avoid this, periodic adjustment of the fixed rate seems necessary. However, this will lead to some more serious problems of relinking, to which we now turn our attention.

The Viability of the 7.80 Linking

The linked rate system has been in operation for more than five years. Throughout this period, the system appears to have worked quite well in the sense that it has helped to stabilize the local monetary system and facilitate Hong Kong's external trade. In recent years, the United States dollar has been under considerable downward pressure against other major currencies due to worsening budget problems and trade deficits in the United States. As a result of the link, the prolonged weakness of the United States dollar led to depreciation of the Hong Kong dollar relative to these currencies as well. The depreciation of the Hong Kong dollar not only increases the competitiveness of local export[16] and stimulates the export-led economy to grow rapidly on the one hand, but also fuels the fear of inflationary pressure on the other hand. Some observers are of the opinion that the Hong Kong dollar is undervalued at 7.80 in terms of its improving underlying economic fundamentals, while some blame the linked rate for recent worsening of inflation.

Numerous suggestions have been made to alter or to replace the current system. Among these suggestions, the most remarkable ones are to revalue the Hong Kong dollar, to resume the floating rate regime, or to link the Hong Kong dollar to a basket of currencies. Huge speculative pressure has centred on the linked rate's viability, once in December 1987 pushing the T.T. down to 7.75, its lowest level since the link, and subsequently inducing the Government to adopt the negative interest rate policy (see discussion in Chapter 2). Owing to the significant and comprehensive influence of the linked rate on the economy, great care must be exercised when discussing the issue of its viability. In this connection, several points are worth noting:

First, it should be stressed that the linked rate system was introduced at a time of political crisis and it was obviously a political measure intended to stabilize the Hong Kong dollar. In evaluating whether or not the Hong Kong dollar is undervalued, not only economic fundamentals but also political factors should be taken into consideration. As 1997 approaches, confidence is the most critical factor in determining the prosperity and stability of the territory. No one can predict what will happen during the transition period, or preclude the potential possibility of sharp falls in the currency in response to adverse political news from China or elsewhere. In view of the existence of these political uncertainties, the Hong Kong dollar cannot be said to be undervalued on purely economic grounds.

Second, as the operation of the current linked rate system depends much on private sector arbitrage, it is crucial for keeping widespread confidence that the linked rate not be changed. A change of the rates would give rise to the following unfavourable impacts:

(a) Undermining the willingness of arbitrageurs to engage in arbitrage operations, and consequently destroying the mechanism of the whole system.

(b) Intensifying the speculation on another possible change of the rate, as speculators might believe it could be adjusted in either direction in future, once it is adjusted upward.

(c) Endangering the stability of the local financial system. For instance, depository institutions might suffer an exchange loss as a result of any change in the link.[17] The stock-market would suffer a crash, as there would be a massive sell-off by overseas investors of their holdings in the Hong Kong stock-market. The money market would suffer a drain of liquidity, thus resulting in a jump in interest rates, and so on.

(d) Jeopardizing the normal operation of various sectors in the economy because it takes time to adapt to any new rate or any new system. Furthermore, export competitiveness could be likely dampened as a result of any changes. If so, the export-led economy would inevitably slow down or slump: every sector and everyone would suffer.

Obviously, the consequence of any change is far reaching. Therefore, benefits should be weighed carefully against costs for any alternatives to the present linking.

Finally, it should be borne in mind that inflation may appear under different exchange rate regimes (for example, fixed-rate, floating-rate, and so on) and for various reasons (such as rising import costs because of domestic currency depreciation/undervaluation, rising wages, demand-pull, and so on). Even if the possibility of importing inflation under the linked rate system exists, so far no proof has been offered to support claims that Hong Kong would have been subject to a lower rate of inflation if another exchange rate system had been implemented in the past five years; nor has proof been offered that the linked rate of 7.80 is the main cause for the recent inflationary pressure in Hong Kong. On the contrary, it is evident that the inflation throughout the five years since implementing the linked rate has been less severe than the situation before the link.[18] Similarly, we may note that inflation in mainland China, local rising wages, and demand-pull factors help fuel the recent inflation. As long as the present link is not the main cause for inflation, changing the link on grounds of inflation would be unwise and unhelpful.

Among the various suggestions for changing the current system, linking the Hong Kong dollar to a basket of currencies is a major alternative. This alternative involves selecting a trade-weighted basket of currencies (like the Hong Kong dollar effective index) and linking the Hong Kong dollar to the exchange value of the basket on a particular day. When the values of the basket currencies against the United States dollar fluctuate from time to time, the authorities have to actively intervene and periodically adjust the official exchange value of the Hong Kong dollar against the United States dollar (that is, T.T.) in order to maintain the link.[19] Since non-United States dollar currencies will be included in the basket, proponents claim that the adverse impact of the United States dollar's fluctuation on the local economy may be lessened. Nevertheless, it should be recognized that the basket system is very complicated and will have significant practical drawbacks. In the first place, it is only workable in a system within which a central bank style of monetary authority exists to set the exchange rate, and then actively intervene on a daily basis in the FX market to enforce the chosen rate. Second, the weighting itself will also have to be reviewed continuously with the ongoing changes in the trading pattern of a dynamic economy like Hong Kong's. Undoubtedly these drawbacks will discourage cash arbitrage by the banks, stimulate unproductive speculation by the public, and disturb the various sectors in the economy. Even if a central bank is established in future, extensive intervention seems to be highly undesirable in such a small and open economy as Hong Kong's. Moreover, the less the Government intervenes, the lower the possibility of human error which may ruin the system.

As we all know, the United States dollar is the dominant international reserve currency, which is well-trusted by the Hong Kong public. The United States is also the territory's major trading partner. To a very considerable extent, the local business cycle is influenced by the climate in the United States economy. As such, it is indeed appropriate to link the local currency to the United States dollar. Of course, no exchange rate system can be perfect in all situations. The most important criterion is whether the benefits outweigh the costs of maintaining a particular system. Despite some of its inherent weakness, the present linked rate system has so far proven beneficial to the prosperity and stability of the local economy. Although possible alternatives may have various economic merits, none is better equipped to handle situations emanating from crises of confidence. Thus no radical change in the present system is desirable in the near future. In view of its excellent track record and the political uncertainty as 1997 approaches, the linked rate system is such a measure as we need to stabilize the local monetary system, and so should be sustained throughout the transition period until 1997.

Concluding Remarks

Hong Kong has established its status as a major regional financial centre in the Asia Pacific area and is gaining wide recognition as the third largest international financial centre. Owing to its status, its financial markets have drawn much attention. The foreign exchange market, as an essential determinant of the role and importance of any international financial centre, is the major focus of the financial market. In this chapter we have examined the market's development, significance, structure, and operations. It can be seen that the market is well-developed in terms of turnover. Domestically, it facilitates the development of the territory's economy and strengthens its role as an international financial centre. Internationally, its link with other foreign exchange markets and financial markets makes information flow smoothly, thus providing more precise signals for the efficient allocation of resources for the world as a whole.

We have also delineated the mechanism of its current linked exchange rate regime, which may be considered a hybrid of fixed and floating exchange rate systems. On the one hand, an exchange rate for the note issue is fixed and guaranteed by the Government. The currency is 100 per cent backed by foreign exchange. On the other hand, the open market exchange rate is still allowed to float without any limit, determined by supply and demand. The regime combines the salient features of two completely different systems. Its implications for the economy are far-reaching.

Although the Hong Kong FX market has experienced tremendous growth in the last decade, there still remain problems to resolve. In the first place, the market's rapid growth within such a short time has meant a shortage of well-trained and experienced FX professionals. This phenomenon has been worsened by the braindrain of the recent years. Second, product variety in the market is still relatively limited, mainly focusing on traditional products such as spot dealing, forward dealing, and so on. New instruments such as currency futures,[20] currency options,[21] cap, collar, and so on have either not been developed or are still in their infancy. Last but not least, the Hong Kong market is mainly an inter-bank market. About 90 per cent of the transactions is inter-bank dealing while 10 per cent is for commercial position.[22] Without a significantly high proportion of commercial base as in the leading FX markets of New York, London, Tokyo, and so on, it is not easy for Hong Kong to catch up. It is hoped that the development of mainland China's economy will help the market in this respect. All in all, the prospect of the market is encouraging, even if not free from difficulties. For the market's development not to be hindered, the above problems cannot be ignored and must be resolved.

Notes

1. A moratorium on the granting of bank licences was imposed in 1965 after the banking crisis.

2. For the nature of swap transactions, see the discussion in the section on Types of Transactions in this chapter.

3. This index, also called the Effective Exchange Rate Index (EERI), is an indicator of the average performance of the the Hong Kong dollar against a fixed basket of other currencies. See the section on the Hong Kong Dollar Effective Index in this chapter.

4. The exchange of the Hong Kong dollar against the United States dollar is commonly called 'T.T.' in the market because it is the rate for telegraphic transfer of the United States dollar.

5. The values of total external trade (that is, exports plus re-exports plus imports) during the last decade were:

	78	79	80	81	82	83	84	85	86	87
HK$ (billion)	116.96	167.77	209.89	260.54	270.28	336.14	444.81	466.57	552.49	755.98

Source: Hong Kong, Census and Statistics Department.

6. *Source*: 'Survey of the Hong Kong Foreign Exchange Market 1988', *Sing Tao Business Magazine*, p. 3.

7. See note 5.

8. *Source*: 'Survey of the Hong Kong Foreign Exchange Market 1988', *Sing Tao Business Magazine*, p. 8.

9. A covered interest arbitrage refers to the transfer of funds to take advantage of the interest differential, accompanied by a simultaneous forward cover to eliminate exchange risk.

10. Following the market practice, we will calculate the United States dollar interest on a 360-day basis and the Hong Kong dollar interest on a 365-day basis.

11. Another market term for that differential is 'swap rate'.

12. See note 6.

13. Of course, the United States dollar is the most actively traded currency because of its nature as a medium of exchange in the market. All currencies must be traded against the United States dollar.

14. This section is heavily drawn from two sources: 'Special Review — Updating the Trade Weights for the Effective (Trade-weighted) Exchange Rate Index', *Hong Kong Monthly Digest of Statistics*, January 1983, pp. 99–104; and 'Special Review — Revision of the Effective Exchange Rate Indexes (EERI) for the Hong Kong Dollar', *Hong Kong Monthly Digest of Statistics*, November 1987, pp. 99–109.

15. The Exchange Fund is the official organization responsible for maintaining the stability and covertibility of the Hong Kong dollar and managing Government assets placed in the Fund. The Fund is under the control of the Financial Secretary and is used for such purposes as the Financial Secretary thinks fit, affecting, either directly or indirectly, the exchange value of the currency of Hong Kong and for other incidental purposes.

16. The domestic exports in the 1980s were:

	Value (HK$ million)	Annual (%)
1980	68,171	+22
1981	80,423	+18
1982	83,032	+3
1983	104,405	+26
1984	137,936	+32
1985	129,882	−6
1986	153,983	+19
1987	195,254	+27
1988	217,664	+11.5

Source: Hong Kong, Census and Statistics Department.

17. As at end of September 1988, the open foreign currency position of all authorized insitutions in Hong Kong was a net asset of $31.9 billion.

18. The inflation rates as represented by the Consumer Price Index A during the last decade were:

	79	80	81	82	83	84	85	86	87	88
(%)	11.6	15.5	15.4	10.5	9.9	8.1	3.2	2.8	5.5	7.0

Source: *Hong Kong Annual Digest of Statistics* (Hong Kong, Census and Statistics Department), various issues, and the 1988–9 Budget.

19. For the detailed mechanics of linking the Hong Kong dollar to a basket of currencies, see Chiu (1988).

20. Currency futures are standardized contracts for delivering specific quantities of given currencies; the exchange rate is fixed at the time the contract is entered into, and the delivery date is set by the Futures Exchange. For the nature of futures, see Chapter 11.

21. A currency option is a financial instrument that gives the holder the right — but not the obligation — to sell (put) or buy (call) a specific quantity of a given currency at a set exchange rate and expiration date. The seller of the put option or call option must fulfil the contract if the buyer so desires it. Because the option not to buy or sell has value, the buyer must pay the seller of the option some premium for this privilege.

22. See note 6.

References

Chiu, Y. W., 'A Prediction of Changes in HK$'s Exchange Value After a Basket Link', *Hong Kong Economic Journal Monthly*, Volume 11, No. 12, March 1988, pp. 33–41.

Ghose, T. K., *The Banking System of Hong Kong* (Hong Kong, Butterworth, 1987).

Greenwood, J., 'How to Rescue the HK$: Three Practical Proposals', *Asian Monetary Monitor*, Volume 7, No. 5, September–October 1983, pp. 11–40.

—— 'How to Tighten Up the Linked Rate Mechanism', *Asian Monetary Monitor*, Volume 12, No.1, January–Feburary 1988, pp. 2–13.

—— 'Unrealistic Alternatives to US$ HK$ Peg', *Securities Bulletin*, Volume 22, February 1988, pp. 14–15.

Ho, Y. K., 'The Money and Foreign Exchange Markets' in R. H. Scott, K. A. Wong, and Y. K. Ho (eds.), *Hong Kong's Financial Institutions and Markets*, (Hong Kong, Oxford University Press, 1986) pp. 79–103.

Hong Kong Government, 'Government Measures to Stabilize the Exchange Rate: Explantory Note', Monetary Affairs Branch, October 15, 1983.

Jao, Y. C., *Banking and Currency in Hong Kong* (Hong Kong, Macmillan Press, 1974).

Lui, Y. H., 'Empirical Properties of Foreign Exchange Rates Before and After the Linked Exchange Rate System in Hong Kong', *Hong Kong Journal of Business Management*, Volume IV, 1986, pp. 1–29.

—— 'A Perspective of the Hong Kong Foreign Exchange Market', *Hong Kong Manager*, June/July 1987, pp. 26–40.

—— 'The Linked Rate Must Be Sustained Until 1997', *Hong Kong Economic Journal Monthly*, Volume 12, No. 10, January 1989, pp. 51–4.

—— *The Hong Kong Financial System*, (Hong Kong, Commercial Press, 1989).

Lui, Y. H., and Peasnell, K. V., 'Time Series Behaviour, Predictability and Speculation in the Hong Kong Foreign Exchange Market', *Journal of Business, Finance & Accounting*, Volumn 16, No. 2, Spring 1989, pp. 145–63.

Magnuson, R., 'New Rules Seem to Steady Colony Dollar', *Asian Wall Street Journal*, 24 October 1983.
Swiss Bank Corporation, *Foreign Exchange and Money Market Operations*, 1978.

10. The Hong Kong Stock-market

KIE ANN WONG

THIS chapter describes how stock-markets operate and examines the development and control of the stock-market in Hong Kong. It also discusses the October 1987 market crash and the reforms of the stock exchange as well as the problems and prospects of the stock-market.

The Role of a Stock-market

A stock-market is an elaborate structure geared to bringing together buyers and sellers of securities. It consists of a new issue market and a secondary market. The former is essentially a group of financial institutions which facilitate the distribution of new securities, while the latter consists of stock exchanges and brokerage firms which facilitate the trading of existing securities.

The performance of a stock-market influences the financial affairs of a considerable proportion of the population. Many people are engaged directly in buying and selling securities, and many more people are affected since their retirement funds and insurance schemes are largely invested in corporate securities. The performance of a stock-market also affects the national economy, since this market provides information to facilitate effective decisions in production activities. The economic characteristics of this market have a profound influence on the allocation of capital resources.

First, the secondary market of a stock-market is a primary source of information for corporate managers on the cost and availability of capital funds. Managers need this information in order to determine the appropriate amount of investment that their companies should undertake. Companies whose share prices are high in relation to their expected earnings are encouraged to obtain more equity capital for expansion. Moreover, the market promotes the demand for new securities, since it provides a means through which subscribers can dispose of their holdings in future if they so desire.

Second, the secondary market permits long-term investment to be financed by short-term funds. Many savers wish to make their funds available for investment for a short period only, or to be able to withdraw them at will. Without a secondary market, the funds available for subscription to new shares would be very limited, since any subscription would mean a long-term 'lock in'. Thus a secondary market that functions well enables companies to raise capital funds at a lower cost than would otherwise be possible.

Third, through the trading activities of its stock exchanges, the secondary market offers a simple mechanism for the transfer of security ownership and hence of funds. The transfer needs only a minimum amount of administrative effort by buyers and sellers of securities. Prices are determined by matching buying orders and selling orders, and the actual transactions and quotations are continuously reported by the stock exchanges. Moreover, the exchanges require the release of financial information by listed companies, so that investors are able to evaluate the performance of a company before making an investment decision.

Finally, the stock-market as a whole encourages the growth of enterprises, since it offers numerous entrepreneurs access to funds. Many of these entrepreneurs possess only relatively limited capital and yet, by selling securities through the market, they can obtain funds to carry out large investment projects and mass production plans to achieve economies of scale.

Corporations are important economic institutions in a free enterprise economy, and they require large amounts of capital to finance their activities. An effective stock-market makes funds more readily available to those companies that can make the best use of them. Because of this, we say that such a market is efficient.

Although a large stock-market is not necessarily effective, the breadth and absorptive capacity of a market are the principal facets of efficiency. If a stock-market is narrow and shallow, its efficiency in allocating capital funds will consequently be reduced. This is because activity in the secondary market cannot provide reliable guide-lines for investment decisions in production activities. In recent years, the Hong Kong stock-market has developed rapidly in terms of trading volume and absorptive capacity. However, it is, of course, still relatively small by comparison with the New York, Tokyo, and London markets.

Development of the Stock-market

Although formal stock-trading activities began in Hong Kong as early as 1891 (the year the Hong Kong Stock Exchange was founded), the stock-market has only been an important source of capital funds for business enterprises since about 1969. During Hong Kong's industrialization in the early 1950s, most firms started as modest sole-proprietor ventures, which gradually changed into partnerships or private companies. Firms that were incorporated or controlled from abroad also formed an important part of the business community. Public corporations were not common until the late 1960s.

There was a minor boom in the stock-market during the years 1946–8 as political changes in China drove many Shanghai business men to look for a foothold in Hong Kong. However, as shown in Table 10.1, the Communist seizure of control in China created uncertainty in

Table 10.1   The Value of Stock Turnover, Selected Years (HK$ million)

Year	Turnover	Year	Turnover
1948	159	1973	48,217
1950	60	1975	10,335
1955	333	1977	6,127
1958	150	1980	95,684
1960	876	1981	105,987
1961	1,414	1983	37,165
1965	389	1985	75,821
1967	305	1988	199,181
1970	5,989	1989	299,147

Source: Hong Kong Statistics 1947–67 (Hong Kong, Census and Statistics Department); *Hong Kong Monthly Digest of Statistics* (Hong Kong, Census and Statistics Department), various issues.

Hong Kong and thus caused the prices of all shares to fall rapidly until 1950, when the outbreak of the Korean War brought new trade opportunities to Hong Kong.

Rapid industrial development during the late 1950s brought a massive influx of foreign capital to Hong Kong, part of which flowed to the stock-market for temporary investment. This temporary investment stimulated the participation of local investors and led to a major boom in the market during the years 1959–61. The value of stock turnover reached its highest post-war peak during this period, and share prices, on the average, doubled between 1959 and mid-1961, bringing dividend yields to levels similar to those of the United States and the United Kingdom. This situation was checked soon after a local bank went into difficulties in June 1961.

In 1965, over-speculation by some banks led to a banking crisis. During the crisis the share price fall was sudden and severe, since some banks called in loans secured by quoted shares while others disposed of their own shareholdings. The share prices were further depressed by the unstable political situation in China (specifically the activities of the Red Guards). In 1967, share prices and turnover fell to the lowest point since 1961 as a result of the political disturbances which occurred in Hong Kong in that year. During the disturbances, the Hong Kong Stock Exchange twice suspended operations for periods of about 10 days to prevent panic selling.

The rapid industrialization of Hong Kong had added few industrial companies to the stock exchange list in the period 1957–67. During these years, the number of companies listed on the Hong Kong Stock Exchange fluctuated between 50 and 70, but active dealings were confined to the shares of fewer than 25 of these companies. Of the most active stocks, 8 were the stocks of utility companies.

Several factors were responsible for the narrowness of the stock-market in Hong Kong before 1969. Undoubtedly, the uncertainty over Hong Kong's future, which was due to the special political relationship with China, restricted the development of the stock-market by discouraging equity investment. The dominance of Chinese family firms in the Hong Kong economy also contributed to the short list of quoted companies. There was considerable reluctance to release the tight family control to a board of directors elected by shareholders. Furthermore, the development of the stock-market was also affected by the ready availability of facilities for Hong Kong investors to invest in foreign securities.

Table 10.2 shows the movements of Hang Seng Index in selected years. There was a major boom in the stock-market during the period 1969–73. From December 1971 to March 1973, the Hang Seng Index rose by 5.3 times or at a compound rate of over 13 per cent per month to 1,775.0. Stock prices then fell sharply by 91.5 per cent to 150.1 toward the end of 1974, reaching the lowest level since 1969. The Index began to recover gradually and rose by 3.1 times by March 1976, but it was still only about one-quarter of the 1973 peak level. By November 1978, a new boom started which pushed the Index up by about 4 times to 1,810.2 on 17 July 1981. This was the highest level recorded for the Hong Kong stock-market since 1965.

Table 10.2 The Hang Seng Index of Share Prices, Selected Years

Year	High	Low	Closing
1965	103.5	78.0	82.1
1967	79.8	60.2	66.9
1970	211.9	154.8	211.6
1973	1,775.0	400.0	433.7
1975	352.9	160.4	350.0
1980	1,654.6	738.9	1,473.6
1981	1,810.2	1,113.8	1,405.8
1983	1,102.6	690.1	874.9
1985	1,762.5	1,220.7	1,752.4
1987	3,949.7	1,894.9	2,302.8
1988	2,772.5	2,223.0	2,687.4
1989	3,309.6	2,093.6	2,836.6

Note: 31 July 1964 = 100.
Source: Hang Seng Bank Ltd.

A number of favourable factors were responsible for the major boom in the stock-market during the period 1969 to 1973: the restoration of business confidence after the political disturbances of 1967; the remarkably consistent performance of the Hong Kong economy; the impressive growth of profits in most listed companies; the extreme liquidity of the banking sector, which was caused by an inflow of overseas funds due to the international currency crisis; the opening of three new stock exchanges; and most important of all, the repeated indications by China that Hong Kong was not regarded as a priority issue, but as an issue to be dealt with when the time was ripe. These indications enabled Hong Kong to measure its future in decades rather than years. This change in thinking led to a big boom in the property market.

The establishment of three new stock exchanges (Far East, Kam Ngan, and Kowloon) during the years 1969–72 was partly stimulated by the sharp upsurge in stock-market activities. Their establishment also enhanced market development because they brought in several hundreds of new stockbrokers, thus stimulating interest among the public in share trading. Though these new stock exchanges quoted mainly the same stocks as those of the Hong Kong Stock Exchange, they were all recognized by the Government shortly after their formation. However, a bill was passed early in 1973 to stop the establishment of further stock exchanges. The boom also led to the establishment of the Securities Commission and the Office of the Commissioner for Securities, in order to 'curb questionable practices' on the stock-market.

In the buoyant stock-market between 1969 and 1973, a total of 251 new companies were listed. Many of them were very small and not traded after listing, especially those listed on the Kowloon Stock Exchange. Although about half of these new companies were property firms, there was also a significant increase in the number of textile, shipping, banking and finance, and industrial and commercial companies. The growth of the market seems to have been induced partly by the modern financial concepts introduced by the major financial institutions from Europe which began operating in Hong Kong,[1] and partly by the extremely high share prices which lowered the cost of raising capital. Investors, on the other hand, were attracted by the handsome short-term capital gains as new issue prices were usually set below the market price.

The Stock-market Slump of 1973–1974

The great boom in the stock-market was followed by a slump during the years 1973–4. The slump was initially caused by the discovery of forged share certificates in certain companies and was intensified later with the introduction of a profit tax on stock-trading, rent control imposed by the Government (which undermined the profitability of real estate companies), and the tightening of credit conditions. The Hang Seng Index halved in six weeks before falling more gently to 433.7 by the end of 1973. The fall in stock prices was further aggravated by the international oil crisis and economic stagnation in 1974, in which both company profits and dividends fell, while output and total exports were contracting.

Economic Recovery and the Stock-market Boom

During the years 1975–9, the economic recovery and subsequent inflationary growth resulted in greater company profits and dividends. Stock prices rose gradually to 879.4, about the level of December 1972. This situation was further stimulated by the open-door policy of China, which led to an expansion of its western contacts in trade and investment, and altered investors' perceptions of Hong Kong's political risk. This favourable factor, together with impressive economic growth — an average increase of 11.3 per cent in real Gross Domestic Product (GDP) for the five years 1976–80 — led to a great property market boom, which in turn caused a stock-market boom in the years 1979–81. This was because a very large proportion of listed Hong Kong stocks were stocks of property and property-related companies. Moreover, the open-door policy of China encouraged many foreign companies to set up offices in Hong Kong, and this not only stimulated the demand for residential and office space but also caused an influx of capital from various countries, particularly from Southeast Asia. Property prices in general more than trebled in about five years as a result of excessive speculation.

The Collapse of the Property Market and Political Uncertainties

The collapse of the property market in the second half of 1982 brought the Hang Seng Index down by about 40 per cent. The slump was enhanced by uncertainty about the political future of Hong Kong and the world-wide recession which depressed Hong Kong's key export sector. Several finance companies and property groups became insolvent. Moreover, the first visit of the British Prime Minister, Mrs Margaret Thatcher, to Beijing in September 1982 for talks about the future of Hong Kong after the expiry of the lease of the New Territories in 1997 made it increasingly apparent that the only solution was the return of Hong Kong to China. The Hang Seng Index crashed to 676.3 towards the end of 1982. It recovered by over 40 per cent before the value of the Hong Kong dollar plunged to its lowest figure in September 1983. This fall was largely caused by the slow progress of the negotiations between Britain and China on the settlement of the lease, so that Hong Kong people lost further confidence in the future of Hong Kong. The Index plummeted to about 700 again in October 1983. When the more concrete proposals which were put forward to maintain the stability and prosperity of Hong Kong after the expiry of the lease were accepted by the people of Hong Kong, stock prices began to recover again in January 1984. The settlement of the lease issue, which was announced in September 1984, was favourably received by the stock-market and, during 1984, the Index achieved a net gain of about 40 per cent, closing at 1,200.4.

The collapse of the property market in 1982 had resulted in a series of financial collapses in several banks and finance companies which had invested heavily in the property market. The Hang Lung Bank went down in October 1983 and several finance companies failed around the same time. The Hong Kong Government took over control of Hang Lung Bank and had to do the same thing not long after with the Overseas Trust Bank. In the following two years, the Government had to devise various rescue operations for a number of other local Chinese-owned banks as public confidence fled them.

The unification of the four stock exchanges in 1986 had led the stock-market to a new era. The average daily turnover had increased by about four times. The Hang Seng Index rose to an all-time high of 3,950 on 1 October 1987 before it plummeted to 2,241.7 on 26 October 1987, a fall of 43.2 per cent after the suspension of the market for four days.

As shown in Table 10.3, the number of listed companies has declined marginally over the past 14 years. However, the total issued capital of these companies has grown by about 4 times and the total market capitalization over 10 times. These rates of growth were due largely to the increase in corporate profits and the expansion of

Table 10.3 Number and Capitalization of Listed Companies

Year	No. of Listed Companies	Total Issued Capital (HK$ million)	Market Capitalization (HK$ million)
1976	295	23,257.50	56,674.94
1977	284	23,427.13	51,277.87
1978	265	24,915.61	65,938.58
1979	262	26,853.48	112,809.31
1980	262	33,080.48	209,752.50
1981	269	59,273.61	232,331.28
1982	273	63,560.69	131,639.82
1983	277	67,940.79	142,093.77
1984	278	69,944.56	184,641.57
1985	279	72,234.65	269,511.35
1986	253	73,106.35	419,281.38
1987	276	90,712.97	419,612.06
1988	304	106,213.58	580,378.02
1989	298	103,403.60	605,010.44

Source: Stock Exchange of Hong Kong, *Fact Book*; *The Securities Journal*, various issues.

corporate assets. The levels of share prices and dividend yields seem to fluctuate within an acceptable range by international standard.

The Stock Exchange of Hong Kong

The unification of the four stock exchanges in 1986 brought about a new era in share trading in Hong Kong. The negotiation process took nearly ten years before the unified Stock Exchange of Hong Kong Limited (SEHK) commenced operation on 2 April 1986. The SEHK was recognized under the Stock Exchanges Unification Ordinance (Cap. 361) to have the exclusive right to establish, operate, and maintain a stock-market in Hong Kong. Since unification, average daily turnover had increased from a total of about HK$250 million to over HK$1 billion. The turnover was as high as about HK$4 billion a day immediately preceding the October 1987 crash.

After unification of the stock-market and the introduction of computer-assisted trading, the SEHK attracted more business from international investors. Thus, the market has quickly transformed from an essentially domestic market into one assuming international attributes. Corporate brokers, who were for the first time formally admitted as members of the Exchange, increased their share of turnover from about 20 per cent to over 60 per cent in a period of three years. It is believed that a significant proportion of trading is attributed to international investors.

The SEHK is basically a private company with limited liability incorporated under the Companies Ordinance. This had allowed its management to be dominated by a small group prior to the market crash in October 1987. This was not satisfactory, due to the Exchange's monopoly position and its self-regulatory role. The SEHK should operate as a public utility as it provides securities trading service to the community. As such, it must act in the interests of members, investors, and securities issuers alike. It should be a non-profit-making organization.

The management of the SEHK was vested in a Committee of 21 members. The Committee may exercise all such powers and do all such acts as may be exercised by the Exchange. The Committee members were elected by members of the Exchange, and the Chief Executive of the Exchange was excluded from the Committee. The reform after the 1987 market crash has included the Chief Executive in the Council. Thus, the Council (formerly Committee) has a total of 22 members. Other principal components of the Council are individual and corporate members elected by members of the Exchange and appointed independent members. The Council Chairman acts as the principal spokesman and representative of the market and the person responsible for developing the market.

The Chief Executive is responsible for the employment of staff, day-to-day management of the Exchange, and supervision of the market.

While the Council has ultimate responsibility for policy matters, execution of policy is the responsibility of the Chief Executive and his staff.

There are two categories of membership in the SEHK: individual and corporate. Members may trade as sole traders or form dealing partnerships with other members or non-members. Each member must hold at least one share in the SEHK, which entitles him to a seat on the exchange floor. Shares are transferable in accordance with the rules of the Exchange. The authorized share capital of the Exchange is 1,200 shares of HK$100,000 each. In 1988 there were 661 individual members and 98 corporate members. Dealers registered under the Securities Ordinance are eligible to become SEHK members. An individual member must be of good character and satisfy residence requirements. A corporate member must, among other things, be incorporated in Hong Kong, be of good financial standing, and be only in the business of dealing in securities and related activities.

In the past, the SEHK played an active role in pricing new issues and organizing a queue of listing applicants. This role might lead to significant under-pricing of new issues which would make an issuer receive much less than the company was worth. The queuing system also has the effect of rationing access to the market, which might cause a company to miss an opportunity to raise capital funds in good market conditions. As such, the Exchange might act as a disincentive to companies meeting their capital needs via the stock-market. Now the issue of new securities has been left to issuing companies and their professional advisers. The SEHK's role is to lay down listing requirements and ensure that these are being complied with by the issuing companies.

The SEHK's listing requirements are, among other things, that the company concerned must be a public company; its business should be of sufficient public interest; its market capitalization must be at least HK$50 million; normally at least 25 per cent of the class of securities concerned should be offered to the public; the company must have a trading record of adequate duration; and there should be no conflict of interest arising from the relationship between the company and any substantial shareholder.

The prospectus to an issue of new securities provides the information needed for investors to assess the securities and will be kept up-to-date by on-going disclosure in accordance with market rules. In addition to regular reports, any price-sensitive developments will have to be reported to the market when they occur.

Dealing and Settlement Systems

In the SEHK, dealers perform as dual capacity broker-dealers. Trading of securities is continuous and order-based through a computer-assisted trading system. Deals are generally struck by telephone. However, broker-dealers continue to operate from the stock exchange floor, and trading is therefore occasionally face-to-face. This system is simple and of low cost and has not failed, even in the events of October 1987.

Settlement is a process involving mainly settling money against securities, transferring legal ownership, and entering changes on a register. In Hong Kong, the settlement system has been based entirely on physical settlement of individual trades. No part of the process is centralized or automated and there is no netting of trades between brokers before settlement. If a buyer wishes to exercise shareholder's rights, transfers must be registered. The registration process may take up to 21 days. Shares cannot be sold pending registration because of the 24-hour settlement rule, the prohibition on short selling, and the lack of stock-lending arrangements.[2] For this reason, many shares are held in street names, being endorsed in blank and accompanied by a signed transfer form.

The present settlement procedure, which requires small board lots with individual transfer forms to be delivered physically to different brokers and three weeks for share registration, is not efficient and creates risk to the parties involved. Many of the problems can be effectively addressed by the introduction of a central clearing and settlement system. A centralized clearing system would move away from a paper-based face-to-face settlement procedure towards a paperless, computerized system based on book entry transfers of uncertificated shareholdings.

The Hang Seng Index and the Hong Kong Index

Since there are about 300 stocks listed on the Stock Exchange of Hong Kong, an indicator is needed to reflect the general trend of share price movements for investors as a reference. In Hong Kong, there are two indices which are widely quoted as market indicators by public investors: the Hang Seng Index and the Hong Kong Index.

The Hang Seng Index

The Hang Seng Index is intended to give investors and other interested parties a general idea about share price movements in the Hong Kong stock-market. It is computed by comparing the current total market value of the issued shares of the constituent stocks with their corresponding value on 31 July 1964, the base date. The Index consists of 33 constituent stocks and is weighted by market capitalization. The index at a specific date is obtained by the following simple formula:

$$\text{Index at date } t = \frac{\text{Sum of market capitalization of constituent stocks at date } t}{\text{Sum of market capitalization of constituent stocks at the base date}} \times 100$$

where market capitalization of individual stock is equal to market price per share times total number of shares issued. Adjustments in the sum of market capitalization of constituent stocks at the base date will be made if there are changes in the constituent stocks or rights issues.

The 33 constituent companies can be broken down into four industry groups. There are 4 in the finance sector, 5 in utilities, 9 in properties, and 15 in commerce and industry. As the Index is weighted by market capitalization, it is thus strongly influenced by large capitalization stocks such as Hongkong and Shanghai Bank, Hong Kong Telecommunications, Hutchison Whampoa, and Cheung Kong.

Although the number of companies listed on the Hong Kong stock-market has increased by about four times since the introduction of the Hang Seng Index in 1969, the 33 index constituent companies have consistently represented between 65 per cent and 75 per cent of the market in terms of both market value and turnover. The Hang Seng Index is computed and released once a minute through the Teletext system of the Stock Exchange of Hong Kong and Reuters Monitor Equities Investment Service. It is also published in the Hang Seng Index Daily Bulletin which records the level of the index at 15-minute intervals and high, low, and close for each trading day.

It has been suggested that the movement of the Hang Seng Index is dominated by the movement of the few largest constituent stocks. Thus, a broader-based index would better reflect the price movement of the market. The Hong Kong Index developed by SEHK on unification covers 49 stocks, with 31 stocks overlapping with the constituent stocks of the Hang Seng Index.

The Hong Kong Index

From the time when trading started at the unified Stock Exchange of Hong Kong, the Exchange introduced the new Hong Kong Index. The Index is calculated every 15 minutes and at the close of each trading session. The base date was 2 April 1986 with the Index set at 1,000. The total daily turnover of the constituent stocks accounts for more than 75 per cent of total market turnover and their market value about 80 per cent of the total market capitalization.

The 49 constituent stocks include six industry groups: 6 in finance, 5 in utilities, 14 in properties, 10 in consolidated enterprises, 9 in industrials, and 5 in hotels. The stocks selected for the purpose must be actively traded, issued by large corporations with good financial performance, and listed on the Exchange for at least two years. Thus, the Hong Kong Index has a broader base than the Hang Seng Index, which mirrors the movement of the 33 'blue chips' only.

However, the broader-based Hong Kong Index would not significantly reduce the impact of sharp price movements in major stocks. As the inherent structural features of the Hong Kong stock-market are the dominance of a few largest companies and extensive cross-holdings of the few largest groups, the above two indices are reasonably good indices available to track price movements on the market.

Types of Stocks Listed on the Exchange

In Hong Kong, the stock exchange has not been used significantly for raising capital funds for the manufacturing sector which has been the main driving force behind Hong Kong's economic growth. This is largely due to the small size of the average manufacturing firm, the easily available bank loans for fixed asset investment, and the family control type of manufacturing firms preferring money borrowed from within rather than outside the family. Thus, the trading of equities tends to be dominated by major firms in the business areas of banking, public utilities, trading, and property holdings and developments.

The under-representation of the manufacturing sector of the Hong Kong stock-market continues to be reflected in the structure of total market capitalization. As shown in Table 10.4, the industrial shares accounted for only 5.8 per cent of the total market capitalization by the end of 1989. Some electronics companies have come to the market in recent years, but they have not proved to be a stunning success either in terms of operating results or stock-market popularity. Even the textiles industry, which has been the backbone industry in Hong Kong since the 1950s, has only one substantial firm (Windsor Industrial) listed. In general, Hong Kong's manufacturing industry base remains under-represented in the stock-market.

The Hong Kong stock-market is very 'top heavy'. As of the end of 1989, just 20 out of the total 298 companies listed on the SEHK accounted for about 65 per cent of the total market capitalization. The Hong Kong Telecommunications was the biggest, at just under 9 per

Table 10.4 The Stock Exchange of Hong Kong, Distribution of Market Capitalization by Sector

Sector	1986 per cent	1987 per cent	1988 per cent	1989 per cent	HK$ million
Finance	16.9	16.3	13.8	14.8	89,397.6
Utilities	19.0	17.4	17.3	18.1	109,364.6
Properties	24.8	26.1	28.4	26.2	158,602.3
Consolidated Enterprises	31.0	29.6	29.4	30.1	182,191.2
Industrials	5.4	6.4	6.6	5.8	35,099.9
Hotels	2.8	4.1	4.3	4.0	24,128.9
Others	0.2	0.1	0.2	1.0	6,226.0
Total	100.0	100.0	100.0	100.0	605,010.4

Source: The Securities Journal and Fact Book of SEHK, various issues.

cent, and the Hongkong and Shanghai Bank accounted for just under 6 per cent. Hutchison Whampoa, Swire Pacific, and Cathay Pacific Airways each weighted in something over 4 per cent. Three property companies, Hong Kong Land, Cheung Kong, and Sum Hung Kai Properties each accounted for 3–4 per cent. Listed companies in the property and finance sectors together with consolidated enterprises accounted for a fraction of about 71 per cent of total market capitalization.

Utilities represented about 18 per cent of total market capitalization, but industrials made up only under 6 per cent by 1989. The relatively low representation of industrial companies in the Hong Kong stock-market has made it difficult for Hong Kong to present a picture of a diversified market to international investors. This is due largely to the relatively small number and size of industrial companies listed on the SEHK, not to the over-valuation of major listed stocks. In fact, for all their large capitalizations, Hong Kong's major listed companies are by no means over-valued on fundamentals. An average price-to-earnings ratio of around 11 as of end of 1989 for the Hong Kong Index constituent stocks was not really high. The corresponding average dividend yield was 6.1 per cent. These seem remarkable in international terms.

Regulations Governing the Stock-market

Regulation of the securities industry in Hong Kong has its main impetus from the stock-market boom and collapse of the early 1970s. Prior to 1971, the industry was only loosely regulated under the relevant provisions of the Companies Ordinance and the Stock Exchange Control Ordinance. The latter ordinance was enacted in 1973 to prevent the increase in number of stock exchanges in Hong Kong. (See also Chapter 16 for further information on ordinances and regulations.)

The business of dealing in securities and of giving related investment advice has, since 1971, been regulated by the Stock Exchanges Unification Ordinance (Cap. 361), the Securities Ordinance (Cap. 333), the Protection of Investors Ordinance (Cap. 335), the Companies Ordinance (Cap. 32), and the Rules and Regulations of the Stock Exchange of Hong Kong. These legislations and rules made provisions for the establishment of a three-tier regulatory structure for the supervision of the securities industry: the Securities Commission, the Commissioner for Securities and Commodities Trading and his Office (now both are replaced by the Securities and Futures Commission), and the Stock Exchange of Hong Kong Ltd.

The Securities Ordinance arose out of the 1971 Report of the Companies Law Revision Committee. It provided for, among other things, the establishment of a Securities Commission and brought all four stock exchanges under its supervision. (The unification of stock exchanges took place in 1986). The Ordinance also provided for the creation of a Commissioner for Securities and his Office as the executive arm of the Securities Commission. The Commissioner had certain direct powers, including the licensing of dealers, investment advisers, and portfolio managers. The Ordinance requires dealers to keep proper accounts and records, and obliges the stock exchanges to provide funds to compensate persons who suffer from defalcations by stockbrokers. It provides that investors may be compensated for losses occasioned by improper trading practices such as creating false markets. It also contains provisions for the inquiry into suspected insider dealing by an Insider Dealing Tribunal, though it does not make insider trading a criminal offence.

The Securities Commission was established in 1974 under the Securities Ordinance. Its functions included:

(a)   advising the Financial Secretary on all matters relating to securities;
(b)   implementing the Securities Ordinance and the Protection of Investors Ordinance;
(c)   supervising the stock exchanges (now the SEHK); and
(d)   protecting investors and ensuring fair practices in securities trading.

The Commission has various committees dealing with, among other things, the compensation fund, discipline, mergers and takeovers, and the licensing of unit trusts. The constitution and rules of the SEHK have to be approved by the Commission. The Commission may, after consultation with the SEHK, make rules in respect of listing of securities, new public offers of securities, suspension of trading, and membership of the Exchange. The Governor of Hong Kong may give directions to the Securities Commission or Commissioner in the exercise of their powers, duties, and functions.

The Commissioner for Securities was appointed to carry out the directions of the Securities Commission. He was given a wide range of statutory responsibilities in connection with dealings in securities and licensing of dealers and investment advisers. He also had the power to order a suspension of dealings on the Exchange. As recommended by the Securities Review Committee, the Commissioner's Office and the Securities Commission as well as the Commodities Trading Commission, which was established in 1976, were replaced by a single independent statutory body, the Securities and Futures Commission, in 1989. The new commission is headed and staffed by full-time regulators and funded largely by the market.

The Stock Exchanges Unification Ordinance was enacted in 1981 to provide for the operation of the unified Stock Exchange of Hong Kong which came into being in 1986 on the amalgamation of the four previous stock exchanges. The SEHK is owned by its members. The Unification Ordinance governs the relationship between the Exchange, the then Commissioner for Securities, and the Securities Commission.

The Unification Ordinance governs the Memorandum and Articles of Association of the SEHK. It sets out the rules for minimum eligibility of individual and corporate members of the SEHK and confers powers on the SEHK to make rules with regard to listing, capital requirements of members, and other matters relating to the operation of Exchange. However, the Commission has the power to direct an amendment to the Rules of the Exchange.

The SEHK has prescribed rules to govern the official listing of securities on the Exchange and to regulate the administration of the Exchange. The rules of administration set out the provisions relating to membership, financial and accounting requirements of members, trading rules, code of conduct, disciplinary matters, and payment of fees and charges.

The 1987 Crash and the Reorganization of the Exchange

The Hong Kong stock-market, along with other major stock-markets around the world, had been on a strong uptrend for some time before the crash on 19 October 1987. To compare the peak level of stock prices in 1987 with the same data one year earlier, the increase was about 50 per cent for the London, New York, and Tokyo stock-markets. As for the Hong Kong, Singapore, and Australian stock-markets, the increase over the same one-year period was as high as over 80 per cent. On 19 October 1987, following a week of set-backs on the New York stock-market by more than 10 per cent in the Dow Jones Industrial Average, news of sharp declines spread around the world, culminating in a further 22.6 per cent drop on Wall Street. This was the sharpest one-day decline the Wall Street had ever experienced, surpassing the 1929 crash. Other major markets followed suit, with London, Tokyo, Australia, and Singapore showing record declines over the next few days.

The Hong Kong market was no exception; the Hang Seng Index fell by 11.1 per cent on a turnover of HK$4,176 million on 19 October 1987 alone. When news of the record fall in New York reached Hong Kong in the morning of 20 October 1987, the SEHK Committee held an emergency meeting and decided to suspend trading for four days under its powers to administer affairs of the Exchange given by the Rules of the SEHK. The Committee's decision was based on concerns regarding the possibility of panic selling, confusion and disorder in the market, · the liquidity of members, the possibility of bank runs, and uncertainty caused by the settlement backlog.

Following the SEHK's decision to suspend trading, the Hong Kong Futures Exchange (HKFE) also decided on the same day to suspend trading of Hang Seng Index Futures contracts for the same period. After the suspension of trading, futures brokers were having difficulties in margining contracts as a result of clients walking away from their commitments. A very large number of the short positions contracts were held against physical stock holdings by arbitrageurs and hedgers. If the futures markets collapsed, these persons would be forced to liquidate their physical holdings and create a massive downward pressure on the stock-market. This could cause significant economic disruption and damage to Hong Kong's reputation as a financial centre.

Having regard to the different views of the various parties involved on the HKFE and the complexity of the issues, the Hong Kong Government engaged Hambros Bank Ltd. as its adviser on 22 October 1987. After a series of meetings with the various participants in the market and an analysis of the options available to the Government, a HK$2 billion rescue package was assembled by the Government, in conjunction with major brokers and banks, to save the futures market from bankruptcy and to minimize the effects of massive defaults by futures brokers on Hong Kong's financial system. When the SEHK and HKFE reopened on 26 October 1987, the markets plunged by about 33 per cent. A further HK$2 billion support package was put together overnight by the Government, the Hongkong and Shanghai Banking Corporation, the Bank of China, and the Standard Chartered Bank, though later this facility was found not to be needed.[3]

The rescue package included undertakings from arbitrageurs not to sell any stocks held against short futures contracts until the end of 1987 unless they closed out an equivalent short position in the futures market. They also undertook not to sell any securities matched against November Hang Seng Index contracts until the day when the November contracts became spot contracts. Moreover, the HKFE reorganized its top management with the appointments of a new Chairman and a new Executive Vice-chairman. On 28 October 1987, the SEHK also an-nounced the appointment of a new Senior Chief Executive of the Exchange.[4]

In January 1988, Ronald Li, who had by then retired as Chairman of the SEHK but was still a member of the Committee, was arrested by officers of the Independent Commission Against Corruption. He was charged under the Prevention of Bribery Ordinance with unlawfully accepting an advantage in connection with an allotment of new shares in a construction company. Mr Li and six other members of the Committee, who had not been charged, agreed to distance themselves from the administration affairs of the Exchange. Thereafter, the Committee, by a resolution, delegated all its powers to a Management Committee which was composed of the remaining 14 members of the SEHK Committee.

The Securities Review Committee[5]

On 20 October 1987, the stock and futures markets were closed for four trading days. As discussed above, massive defaults by futures brokers followed and rescue packages were assembled to save the futures market from bankruptcy. From early 1987, the stock-market had been on a strong uptrend; the Hang Seng Index rose by 55 per cent to an all-time high of 3,950 over the first nine months with turnover almost trebling. For the futures market, turnover had grown at a rapid pace since its inception in May 1986, an increase of almost twenty-fold over the first 17 months. The rapid growth of the stock and futures markets had made the market infrastructure and regulatory systems unable to keep pace.

It was against the above background that the Governor of Hong Kong on 16 November 1987 appointed the Securities Review Committee to review the constitution, management, and operations of the stock and futures exchanges and their regulatory bodies. The Securities Review Committee was directed to examine structures and systems critically rather than to conduct an inquiry into the causes and events of the October 1987 crash.

The Committee found that, while the Hong Kong system had originally been based on self-regulation by the Exchanges with the support of an authoritative and impartial supervisory body, the system of self-regulation and self-discipline had failed to develop adequately to cope with the expanding securities industry. Facing this situation, the supervisory bodies charged with overseeing the markets also lost their effectiveness. The defects in the then arrangements may be summarized as follows:

(a) at the SEHK, an inside group treated it as a private club rather than a public utility for the benefit of members, public investors, and securities issuers. Its management was not effective, settlement system not functioning properly, and surveillance of members and listing arrangements were cursory;

(b) at the HKFE, the management system was not built on a strong foundation. The agencies involved in the futures market confused lines of responsibility and obstructed the development of an adequate risk management system;

(c) at the Securities and Commodities Trading Commissions, they had not played an adequate role of direction. Rather than being hiqh-powered watchdogs, they had often been relegated to a passive and reactive role; and

(d) at the Office of the Commissioner for Securities and Commodities Trading, the requests for additional resources to cope with the rapidly developing markets had not been sufficiently supported by the Government. The Office had often not been able to take the initiative on active surveillance and monitoring of markets and brokers.

The Securities Review Committee, after due analysis and consideration, recommended that Hong Kong should strengthen its existing systems and regulatory arrangements in order to become a primary capital market for the Southeast Asian region. Practitioner regulation should continue but safeguards should be introduced at every level. They have, among other things, recommended the following:

(a) a revision of the constitution of the SEHK: there should be proper representation on the governing body for individual and corporate

members, combined with an independent element to ensure that
it works in the interests of all members and users;

(b)   a staff of professional, independent executives in the Exchanges
to implement policies set by governing bodies;

(c)   an extension of the stock exchange settlement period from 24
hours to three days and an early development of a central clearing
system;

(d)   a continuation of the HKFE and its stock index contract but with
the clearing and guarantee system restructured to strengthen the
risk management arrangements; and

(e)   a single independent statutory body outside the Civil Service to
replace the two Commissions and the Commissioner's Office. The
new statutory body should be headed and staffed by full-time
regulators and funded largely by the market. It should ensure the
integrity of markets and the protection of investors.

Almost all of these main recommendations were accepted and
implemented or are now, at the time of writing, in the process of
implementation. The Securities and Futures Commission Bill was passed
in 1989 after much discussion by various relevant bodies. The Bill
largely dealt with the last recommendation stated above.

By October 1989, the new Listing Rules of the SEHK had been
settled after much effort. There remain, however, a number of other
things which still need to be completed. The Securities (Disclosure of
Interests) Ordinance will be brought into operation shortly. The Insider
Dealing Bill is still with the Legislative Council. A draft revised code
on Takeovers and Mergers is at an advanced stage of preparation.
Progress has been made towards preparing a revised and updated
legislative framework for the securities and futures industries. More
legislative changes are expected to complete the implementation of the
recommendations by the Securities Review Committee and to deal with
issues in related areas.

Problems and Prospects

The unification of the four stock exchanges in 1986 was a major event
in the recent development of Hong Kong. Since then the SEHK has
experienced substantial growth both in its business and its regulatory
role. The latter has been especially true since the reforms carried out
after the October 1987 crash. The securities industry is an important
element in Hong Kong's economic infrastructure. It has employed more
than 25,000 people in different capacities, including trading of securities
on the SEHK and internationally as well as investment management
operations in international firms.

A sound regulatory framework is a prerequisite to long-term and
stable growth of securities markets. The main purposes of regulating
securities markets are to protect the investing public, maintain market
integrity, and improve market efficiency in performing capital-raising

and financial intermediating roles. The art of regulation largely lies in maintaining the right balance between the need for control to protect investors and the need to give markets the freedom and flexibility to grow and innovate. The new regulatory framework that has been developed to serve these purposes after the market crash of 1987 has improved the confidence of investors and market users in Hong Kong and internationally. Although the June 1989 events in China seriously damaged investors' confidence in the political environment of Hong Kong, there is evidence that the market institutions of Hong Kong are now capable of withstanding major political shocks without encountering serious problems.

Although investors would get more competence and fairness from financial intermediaries under the new regulatory framework, much improvement is needed in the field of intermediary supervision. The Securities and Futures Commission had started to examine the system for establishing capital requirements for intermediaries. Another vital task for the improvement of investors' confidence in market mechanisms should be the early implementation of a central clearing and settlement system. Further legislative changes also need to be made to implement other recommendations of the Securities Review Committee and to deal with other problems, including those arising from the rapid qrowth in the number of Hong Kong listed companies re-incorporating overseas.[6]

The June 1989 events in China were expected to reinforce the trend of slow-down in Hong Kong's economic growth in the short term. However, given its strategic location, well-established infrastructure and business contacts, and a capable workforce, Hong Kong will remain a viable city for doing business. As the maintenance and development of Hong Kong's financial markets are specifically provided for in the Joint Declaration of China and the United Kingdom, Hong Kong has the potential for becoming a key element of the financial infrastructure of China, and to continue its development as a significant international financial centre.

Since the institutional structure, regulatory system, and efficiency of the stock-market have been enhanced considerably through the implementation of the principal recommendations of the Securities Review Committee, it is perhaps timely actively to consider the plan to establish a second market for the securities issued by young, less mature corporations. This second securities market is to stimulate the supply of venture capital to meet the demands of young innovative enterprises as well as to encourage China-related companies to seek a listing in Hong Kong.

Notes

1. The first merchant bank, Schroders & Chartered Limited, formed by the Chartered Bank, Schroders Limited of London, and Sir Elly Kadoorie Continuation Limited, opened for business in early 1971. This was followed by, among others, Jardine Fleming &

Company Limited, a joint operation between Jardine Matheson & Co. Limited and Robert Fleming Holdings Limited, and by Wardley Limited, a wholly owned subsidiary of the Hongkong and Shanghai Banking Corporation.

2. Short selling in securities is not allowed in Hong Kong as stated in the Securities Ordinance. The penalty for an offence is a fine of $10,000 and imprisonment for six months.

3. In addition, in an effort to support the stock and futures markets, the banks in Hong Kong made two successive 1 per cent cuts in the prime rate, from 8.5 per cent to 6.5 per cent in the two-day period, 26–7 October 1987.

4. The new Chairman and Executive Vice-chairman appointed by the HKFE were Wilfrid Newton and Phillip Thorpe. The new Senior Chief Executive appointed by the SEHK was Robert Fell.

5. This section is largely taken from the Report of Securities Review Committee, *The Operation and Regulation of the Hong Kong Securities Industry* (Hong Kong, Government Printer, May 1988), Chap. 1.

6. As the development of a strong debt market would enhance Hong Kong's attractions to investment managers and its status as an international financial centre, the Hong Kong Government should review and remove any unnecessary regulatory impediments to its development and should stimulate and perhaps sponsor the development of debt markets.

References

Jao, Y. C., *Banking and Currency in Hong Kong: A Study of Post-War Financial Development*, (London, Macmillan, 1974).

Rowley, A., *Asian Stockmarkets: The Inside Story*, (Hong Kong, Far Eastern Economic Review, 1987).

Scott, R. H., K. A. Wong, and Y. K. Ho (eds.), *Hong Kong's Financial Institutions and Markets*, (Hong Kong, Oxford University Press, 1986).

Securities Review Committee, *The Operation and Regulation of the Hong Kong Securities Industry*, (Hong Kong, Government Printer, May 1988).

Stock Exchange of Hong Kong, *Fact Book*, 1987 & 1988.

—— *The Securities Journal*, various issues.

—— *Rules of the Exchange*. English Edition, May 1988.

11. The Hong Kong Financial Futures Markets

GORDON W. WONG

THE past decade has been marked by a substantial increase in the volatility of financial asset prices. The need to provide some protection against the wide range of risks relating to security prices, interest rates, and exchange rates has led to the emergence of new financial markets dealing in 'financial futures'. Financial futures markets are some of the most powerful instruments available in modern portfolio management, offering extra flexibility and allowing portfolio strategies to be implemented more efficiently, at both a significantly lower cost and higher speed.

The concept of financial futures began in the United States; the success in financial futures trading there tempted other world markets to follow, and to introduce their own innovations of the same concept. The Share Price Index of Sydney Futures Exchange, FT–SE 100 Index of London Stock Exchange, and Nikkei 225 Stock Average Futures of Singapore International Monetary Exchange are examples. The growth of usage and the diversity of users of the markets can be interpreted as evidence both of the need for these markets and of the efficiency with which they fulfil their role. Hong Kong has had its own futures market since 1977 when the Government authorized trading in commodities futures. In 1986 trading of financial futures contracts began.

What does the Hong Kong futures market set out to achieve? Is the Hong Kong futures market directly or indirectly useful to investors? What are the drawbacks of using futures contracts in portfolio management? The information in this chapter offers some answers to these questions.

What is a Financial Futures Contract?

A financial forward or futures contract is a commitment to buy or sell a standardized quantity of a particular item for a specific future settlement date at a currently agreed upon price between the trading parties. Such a forward or futures contract does not represent a purchase or sale of an asset, but rather an obligation to accept or make delivery at some later date. This obligation may be and frequently is discharged prior to the expiration of the contract. Both forward and futures contracts perform a vital economic function: risks transfer. Entering a forward or futures contract, one may transfer all or part of the risk exposure, involved in security and commodity prices, interest rates, and exchange rates, to others who are willing to assume that risk in exchange for the opportunity to earn a profit. Forward and futures contracts are, of course, not means of insuring that their prices at a future date will be what they are now, but they are means of ensuring that they can buy or sell the relevant assets at known prices without concerning the true market prices in the future. The price of the futures contract reflects the current expectations of its value at some specified future date. Thus buyers and sellers, who want to hedge the price uncertainty of their current asset holdings, would use either forward or futures contracts to establish or 'lock-in' current prices against late transactions. This phenomenon is known as 'price discovery'.

The principal advantages of a futures contract, as opposed to a forward contract, are its uniformity, liquidity, leverage, and simplicity. All futures contracts are uniform in terms of the quantity, quality, and delivery time for the specific underlying financial instrument. Contract terms are standardized, which leaves only price and number of contracts to be negotiated. Since a regulated futures exchange is involved rather than a specific person or bank, futures contract buyers or sellers do not have to go through a lot of negotiation. Traders can normally close out positions before contracts expire by arranging offsetting transactions. In fact, settlement of gains and losses on open positions can be made daily.

The futures market provides a way for the investors to leverage their assets. Initial margin deposits on futures contracts are modest. This high degree of leverage can generate substantial profits or losses from relatively small price changes. In addition, futures markets allow speculators to participate in broad market price moves in a simple way. If the market price of the financial instrument concerned should be higher at the date when it has to be delivered than the price specified in the contract, the buyer will gain and the seller will lose the difference. Likewise, if the market price of the financial instrument should be lower, the seller will gain and the buyer, in effect, undertakes to meet the difference.

The Hong Kong Futures Market — Historical Development

The trading of futures contracts has a long history in the United States. In the early nineteenth century, the futures markets started as extensions of the spot agricultural markets, allowing the producers a greater degree of certainty about the prices that they could obtain for future deliveries. As international trade has become more and more important, the opening of futures exchanges has also become more common. These exchanges provide the hedger with a place to buy and sell futures contracts and to protect them from loss due to any fluctuation of prices.

The price protection methods, traditionally afforded by the commodity markets, have been extended to a variety of securities, other financial instruments and currencies, providing investors protection against the risks involved in the variable costs of exchanging one asset for another. After four years of careful research and planning, the Kansas City Board of Trade launched a dramatic and innovative futures contract based on the movements of the stock index. The contract, known as the Value Line Index, is based on an equal-weighted return average of approximately 1,500 stocks covered by the Value Line Investment Services. It not only provided a broadly based indicator of movement in the stock-market but also fulfilled a need in the financial community.

The success of the contract trading immediately bred many imitators. The Standard & Poor 500 (S&P500) index futures, which is based on the prices of the 500 common stocks trading on the New York Stock Exchange, American Stock Exchange, and over-the-counter trading, started to trade in 1982. In the same year, the New York Futures Exchange introduced the New York Stock Composite Index futures contract. This contract is based on the weighted average of all common stocks traded on the NYSE.

In 1976, the Hong Kong Legislative Council passing of the Commodity Trading Ordinance led to the establishment of a commodity futures exchange, the South East Asia Commodity Exchange Hong Kong (Holdings) Limited. The Exchange was owned by a consortium which was comprised of Woo Hon Fai, Li Fook Siu, Peter Scales, Rudolf Wolff & Co., and General Management (HK) Ltd. This private company was responsible for setting up the Hong Kong Commodity Exchange Limited (HKCE). The Exchange established rules which provide assurances of proper and consistent performance. The integrity of the market price has been insured by the Clearing House, the International Commodity Clearing House (Hong Kong) Ltd. The Clearing House registers futures contracts and deals with the clearing of all transactions of the Exchange.

A Guarantee Corporation, which guarantees the performance of all contracts registered with the Clearing House, was set up. The Guarantee Corporation was jointly formed by Barclays Bank, Credit Lyonnais Corporation, the Hongkong and Shanghai Banking Corporation, Standard Chartered Bank, the Wing On Bank Ltd., the Chase Manhattan Bank, N.A., and the International Commodity Clearing House (Hong Kong) Ltd. Due to the existence of the Clearing House and the Guarantee Corporation, buyers and sellers of contracts need not concern themselves about each other's identity or financial integrity. Instead, the traders of futures are made with each other in the Exchanges, concentrating on the daily operation of trading. The traders' activities are also guaranteed by the Exchange. This is crucial because it enables traders to cancel their position at any time with any trader in the Exchange. Hence little delivery is ever called for.

In May 1977, trading in cotton futures began. Because of the competition from established hedging systems, primarily in New York, and the lack of local support, the market failed to take off. Later, at the request of several prominent local sugar trading houses and brokers, the sugar futures market was started in November 1978. At the beginning, this market did not meet with immediate success because of a sugar bear market at the time and lack of sustained volume level and international support. In the 1980s, however, sugar futures enjoyed high trading volumes as international interest developed.

In November 1979, the soy bean futures market was launched with support mainly from the Japanese brokerage houses. Trading was conducted in a group trading method, similar to the Japanese futures markets, which favors particularly the Japanese traders. Despite the volume recorded, the open interest — the outstanding contracts — developed was disproportionately small. In August 1980, gold futures started trading, but again at the wrong time, when the precious metal markets were in a major downward trend. Because of fears that local traders would be taxed, while other local gold markets could be traded tax-free, the gold futures market did not attract enough support from either local or international interest.

During the course of 1982, the Hong Kong Commodity Exchange Limited worked on detailed proposals for financial futures markets including stock index, currency and interest rate contracts, and in 1984, the Hong Kong Government finally decided that a major reorganization of the Hong Kong Commodity Exchange had to be done. The new Exchange was to handle all commodities and financial futures trading. In May 1985, the Exchange was renamed the 'Hong Kong Futures Exchange Limited'.

As a result of the reorganization, the South East Asia Commodity Exchange (HK) Ltd. placed itself into voluntary liquidation and a series of committees were formed under four divisions. The four divisions were precious metals (gold), agricultural commodities (soy beans and sugar), stock index (Hang Sang Index), and financial futures (currencies and interest rates). The restructure represented a new era of the financial markets in Hong Kong.

The year 1986 marked two important financial developments: the beginning of a major bull market in Hong Kong equities and the successful introduction of futures contracts on the Hang Seng Index. The development of the stock index futures market is particularly significant, because it represents an integration of equity and futures trading. This integration has important implications for both branches of the investment business. Brokerage firms and investment houses have been quick to incorporate Hang Seng Index futures into their market operations. New and effective trading strategies have been developed to trade the stock index futures exclusively or in combination with physical stocks. This has added a new dimension to equity trading in Hong Kong.

However, like other stock-markets in the world, Hang Seng Index futures trading has been blamed for the 1987 Crash. Daily turnover on the Hang Seng Index futures market had fallen. There were pressures on restructuring the futures markets and protecting investors' interests from the public. According to the proposed changes to the constitution of the Exchange in November 1988 by the Securities Review Committee, chaired by Mr Ian Hay-Davidson, all members of the Exchange are entitled to trade in all the markets operated by the Exchange from 1989.

Members who trade on the floor of the Exchange are to be classified into four major categories. The first category is that of the floor traders, who trade for their own accounts only and have capital of not less than HK$2 million. The second category is that of the floor futures brokers, who book not only their own house trades, but also trades executed on behalf of clients who are also members of the Exchange; they must have capital of not less than HK$2.5 million. Neither floor traders nor floor futures brokers are allowed to trade for non-members of the Exchange. The third type of member is the futures commission merchant, who can trade for not only his own account and other members, but also for third party clients. Such an increase in status means the capital requirement is raised to HK$5 million. The last category is that of the merchant trader, who has the right in the financial or commodity field underwriting the various contracts traded on the Exchange.

The Securities Review Committee also proposed a new Clearing House, HKFE Clearing Corporation Limited, which is a subsidiary of the Exchange. The Clearing House is the counterpart to every trade and is liable as principal on the contracts registered with it. Recourse to a guarantee corporation is longer be relevant. The funds to support the Clearing House come from part of members' deposits and the proceeds of bank guarantees and insurance policies taken out for this purpose.

The Exchange has been seeking to introduce a revised constitution and set of rules. To perform its clearing function, HKCC has contracted ICCH (HK) Ltd. to be the managing contractor for the important functions of trade entry, registration, order processing, and margin control. The new clearing house, HKCC, became operational by 13 March 1989.

HKCC is capitalized in the form of share capital of HK$1,000,000 and a subordinated loan facility from the HKFE of HK$6,000,000, which is adequate on a continuous basis to assure the integrity of soy bean, sugar, and gold contracts. The Government renegotiated the existing support facility and provided support for the Hang Seng Index market until 31 October 1989 by means of a revolving loan facility of HK$100 million. HKCC also had available to it HK$50 million of insurance beginning 13 March 1989 and was consulting bankers with the intention of arranging a HK$50 million bank guarantee or facility.

At the outset of HKCC's operation, ten very significant member brokerage firms had pledged to contribute HK$50 million to the Reserve Fund by 31 October 1989, and, in addition, it was expected that a further HK$40 million would come from other clearing members by the same date. These funds were be deposited over the period March to October and were available until 31 October 1989 to support only new products such as the proposed new interest rate contract. From 1

November 1989 this HK$100 million replaced the Government support for the Hang Seng Index contract referred to above and was used to support all the Exchange's contracts.

At 1 November 1989, the reserve fund totalled HK$200 million made up of three branches: HK$100 million in cash (members' deposits), HK$50 million in insurance, and HK$50 million in bank guarantees or facilities.

The Exchange considered that these resources, together with the margin deposited by clearing members, would provide robust support for HKCC to carry out the important function of being a counter-party to each cleared trade in all of HKFE's markets.

The Operations of the Hong Kong Futures Exchange

The Hong Kong Futures Exchange maintains facilities for continuous trading of all futures contracts. The contracts can be satisfied by one of two markets: delivery or offset. In reality, delivery occurs in less than 10 per cent of futures transactions. Most futures contract holders liquidate their positions before contract expirations by arranging offsetting transactions. In other words, buyers sell out their positions, which sellers buy into at some time prior to the time of delivery. If buyers and sellers do hold their positions until contract expiration, then they must satisfy the requirements of the Hong Kong Futures Exchange for contract settlement. Traditional commodity futures contracts will call for actual delivery of a commodity. Unlike other commodity futures contracts, stock index futures settle in cash rather than in delivery of the stocks in the index underlying the futures contract. Some financial futures, such as bond futures, do call for delivery, however. Cash settlement is carried out by transferring funds into or out of the contract holders margin account in an amount based on the settlement price of the contract. Cash settlement is used because of the cost and logistical problems of buying the component stocks in the index in exactly the right amounts to carry out physical delivery.

The value of Hang Seng Index futures contract is a multiple of its quoted price. The contract value is 50 times the quoted price. The minimum trading increment is 10 points or $500 (10 × 50). A list of the futures contract specifications is shown in Table 11.1.

Buyers and sellers of futures contracts are required to make an initial margain deposit when they enter into futures transactions. The margin on futures is not a down payment, as ownership of the underlying financial instrument is not transferred when a futures position is established. Instead, a futures margin is more like a good faith security deposit that serves as collateral for the contract commitment. The level of initial margin deposit represents only a small fraction of the value of the outright position, and it is designed so as to be prudent against

Table 11.1   Contract Specifications: The Hang Seng Index Futures

Unit of trading	Valued at HK$50 per full index point
Expiry months	Spot plus March, June, September, December
Last trading day	Second last business day in the delivery month
Settlement day	First business day after last trading day
Delivery	Mark-to-market at closing value of the actual Hang Seng Index on settlement date
Prices	Contract quoted in terms of Hang Seng Index
Minimum price fluctuation	One index point on the Hang Seng Index
Minimum price move	Tick size: 1 point Value: HK$50
Initial margin	15% of contract value
Trading hours	10.00–12.30, 14.30–15:30
Contract standard	Cash settlement at the Exchange delivery settlement price

short term intra-day position risk. The leverage ratio was 8.5 per cent when the margin requirement was HK$15,000 for index level at 3,500 on 19 October 1987, and up to 40 per cent when the margin requirement was HK$50,000 for index level at 2,500 on 27 October 1987. At the time of writing, the margin requirement is HK$20,000, representing a leverage ratio of 14 per cent for index level at 2,900 on 18 January 1989. Consequently the initial margin deposit will be subject to change in line with trading conditions in the market, being dependent particularly on historic volatility. The initial margin quoted on contract specifications is for clearing members only; individual brokerage houses and investment firms may make futher demands on clients.

A futures margin does not involve an extension of credit. Thus, no interest is charged on the remaining balance. In fact, futures traders in the United States can earn interest because treasury bills, instead of cash, can be used for collateral in meeting initial margin requirements. In that instance, interest earned on the securities accrues to the investor.

Since a futures contract is a commitment to perform, every position is marked to market at the close of each business day. This means that after a contract is bought or sold and the initial margin deposited, net gains or losses resulting from any change in the market value of the contract are calculated daily and credited to, or debited against, the account. Futures traders and investors have immediate access to their gains without closing out or borrowing against their positions. They can withdraw gains above the initial margin requirement at any time. If the value of the margin deposit in their accounts falls below the maintenance margin level, they must add cash to bring the account value back up to the initial margin level. This is known as 'variation margin' and represents the full loss that an investor has incurred during that day's trading.

For example, assume Investor A bought or went long a December 1988 Hang Seng Index futures contract quoted on 1 September 1988 at a price of 2,400, and Investor B sold or went short the same contract at the same price. Each deposited the HK$15,000 initial margin. At the end of that day, the contract has increased to 2,450, an increase of 50 points, or HK$2,500 (50 × 50). After that day, their accounts would look like Table 11.2. To trade stock index futures is to trade the closing value of the underlying index of a future date (in the example, the end of December of the coming year). The difference between the closing index of that month and the index at which one bought or sold represents his gain or loss. It would be a mistake, however, to regard trading in stock index futures as the same as stock trading. In fact, stock trading is a transfer of assets, but futures trading is a transfer of price risk. The former involves the changing of stock ownership, while the latter is simply an agreement between the buyer and seller.

Table 11.2 Trading Stock Index Futures

	Investor A	Investor B
Initial	HK$15,000	HK$15,000
Mark-to-market change, day 1	+2,500	−2,500
Current equity	17,500	12,500
Excess equity withdrawable	2,500	
Equity loss		2,500
Margin call		2,500

If position is held until expiry such that on delivery date, the index and futures prices converge, buyers' and sellers' positions will be settled by a cash transfer at the Exchange delivery settlement price. The price for cash settlement is declared by the Clearing House and is the Hang Seng Index at the closing of the last trading day. There will then be a movement in the variation margin accounts representative of the change in the future price from the previous day's settlement price. Hence cash settlement never results in the transfer of the underlying value of the Index, only in the transfer of the difference between the price at which the contract was struck and the delivery settlement price. In this way transaction costs are minimized.

Futures contracts have a tradition of trading by 'open outcry' whereby the members stand around a stepped 'pit' or 'ring' quoting prices verbally and when the market is also busy with hand signals. In this way a deal can be struck for an agreed number of contracts at an agreed price between a willing buyer and seller. Everyone in the market has an equal chance to fulfil all or part of each offer or bid. Every best bid and offer competes in an auction market, with no priority as to the time or size. This gives the participant the same market price for one contract as for a multi-contract deal.

At present, Hong Kong Futures Exchange Limited adopts two trading methods: board price system and open outcry system. Nevertheless, all the contracts concluded will be shown on the price board and monitor screen with the price and quantity given. Customers can also obtain the latest price information through brokers or the financial media. The details of the transaction, price, and number of contracts are passed through the Exchange to the Clearing House by the buyer and seller so that they can be checked and matched. Once the 'initial margin' on the transaction is paid, the Clearing House steps between the buyer and seller, becoming a buyer to the seller and a seller to the buyer. Each of the original parties is thereby relieved of any concern over the creditworthiness of the other and is able to reverse, or 'close out', a position at any time independently of the other original party.

The financial integrity of the market relies to a large extent on the guarantee by the Clearing House, which has assumed the risk of the failure of either party. Its power to withstand this risk rests upon the net worth of the Exchange Guarantee Fund, the initial margin payments from contract buyers and sellers, the daily limits on futures price movement, and the strength and power of the Clearing House on margin setting. If a buyer of a contract chooses to settle contractual obligations by making delivery, the Clearing House selects the seller who will send the delivery. The buyer is then notified of the name of the seller. The final invoicing and payment procedures are conducted between the buyer and seller under the Rules of the Exchange and under the supervision of the Clearing House.

Hang Seng Index Futures

Among the fundamental causes of change in the stock price of an individual firm are events and factors unique to that firm. The desire of investors to minimize firm-specific (or unsystematic) risk was the prime factor in the development of mutual funds. Firm-specific risk can be greatly reduced by holding a large portfolio of diversified stocks. In such a portfolio, unexpected decreases in the price of one stock is likely to be offset by unexpected increases in the prices of other stocks, with the result that the portfolio as a whole will exhibit less price variation. Total portfolio risk declines rapidly as the portfolio increases in the number of issues, but it is never eliminated completely.

The risk-reduction potential of diversification is not without limit. Many stocks are affected by global events that may have either a positive or negative impact on the economic well-being of the entire market. Such events — for example, a change in monetary policy — affect more than one stock or even a small group of stocks. This type of variability is called market risk or systematic risk, and is much more important to purchasers of large portfolios of stock than unsystematic risk.

The Hang Seng Index is designed to reflect overall stock movements in the Hong Kong stock-market. Historically, trading in the Hang Seng Index constituent stocks accounts for more than 80 per cent of the market activity. According to modern investment theory, a stock-market index can represent a market portfolio. Investors who wish to perform in line with the Hong Kong stock-market as a whole can try to structure portfolios equivalent to the Hang Seng Index.

Futures on the stock-market index represent contractual obligations to have sufficient funds on deposit at delivery to buy or sell the stocks in the market index at a predetermined price. This price is the value of the futures contract when the futures postion was initiated. Therefore, trading Hand Seng Index futures will be, imitatively, trading a Hong Kong stock market portfolio. Stock index futures provide portfolio managers with a method of adjusting the impact of systematic risk on stock prices. A portfolio manager, who has a Hong Kong stock portfolio, may maintain the value of his portfolio from market fluctuation by selling an appropriate number of futures contracts, thus eliminating systematic (market) risk. The value of the portfolio would be insulated because the losses suffered by the portfolio would be offset by futures market gains. Likewise, if prices rise the portfolio profits would be offset by futures losses. In using the Hang Seng index futures, the sensititivity of the portfolio can be adjusted quickly to assist the manager to achieve his other objectives.

In buying the Hang Seng Index futures, the benefit of the dividend income is sacrificed until the delivery date. Instead, the leverage nature of the futures provides interest income on the balance of the funds that would have otherwise been invested in the market, by placing the funds on deposit in the money markets. Consequently, the theoretical price of the Hang Seng Index futures contract would be determined by the Hang Seng Index, dividend yield, and deposit rate. Given the Hang Seng Index of 2,900 at the time of writing, dividend yield of 4 per cent and deposit rate of 9 per cent, the theoretical price of Hang Seng Index futures would be shown below as 2,935.

Assumptions:

AD = Stock Exchange account days to expiration : 90 days
T = Days in the year : 365 days
R = Deposit rate : 9%
D = Dividend yield : 4%
H = Current Hang Seng Index : 2900

$$\begin{aligned}
\text{Theoretical futures price} &= \text{H} \times (1 + (\text{R} - \text{D}) \times \text{AD/T}) \\
&= 2900 \times (1 + (9\% - 4\%) \times 90/365) \\
&= 2935
\end{aligned}$$

Since dividend payments are not constant but concentrated at certain points in time, the theoretical futures price may be based upwards or downwards on various account dates.

Interest Rate Futures

A futures contract on the three-month Hong Kong Inter-bank Offered Rate (HIBOR) was introduced in February 1990. Like Hang Seng Index futures, interest rate futures have standardized specification in size, maturity month, minimum fluctuation (see Table 11.3). The interest rate futures contracts are traded in terms of an index, which is listed by subtracting the interest rate from 100.00. If the interest rate is 9 per cent, the index price becomes 90. One basis point is represented by 0.01 per cent in the index price.

The basic function of interest rate futures is to provide an efficient risk management tool for bank and financial companies to hedge interest rate uncertainty. Fluctuation in interest rate can have a

Table 11.3 3-Month HIBOR Futures Contract Specifications

Contract size	HK$1,000,000
Delivery or trading months	March, June, September, December, up to two years ahead
Minimum fluctuation/tick size	HK$25.00
Trading hours	09.00 to 15.30 Hong Kong time; trading in the spot month ends at 12.30 Hong Kong time on the last trading day
Last trading day	12.30 two business days prior to the third Thursday of a month in which cash settlement of a spot month HIBOR futures contract is required
Settlement method	Cash settlement
Maturity period	Three months
Daily fluctuation limit	125 basis points
Expanded fluctuation limit	200% of the daily fluctuation limit (that is, 250 basis points)
Expanded limit period	Three business days
No limit	Last five trading days of the spot month

tremendous impact on earnings and cash flows. Hence any companies with a substantial interest rate exposure can transfer this risk by using interest rate futures. For these hedgers, interest rate futures contract prices do not represent their expectations of future interest rate. The prices reflect the cost of carrying debt securities or the differential between yields on the security versus short-term holding cost.

Table 11.4 Interest Rate Futures

	Cash Market	Futures Market
March 13, 1988	Plan to issue 90-day CDs in 3 months at a yield of 11.75%, with a face value of $100 million, to realize $97,062,500.	Sell 100 June interest rate futures at 89.00, with a yield of 11%.
June 11, 1988	CDs are issued at 12.25%, and the bank realizes $96,937,500.	Buy 100 June interest rate futures at 88.75, with a yield of 11.25%.
	Shortfall: $125,000	Profit: $62,500

To illustrate this concept, an example is presented (see Table 11.4). A corporation plans to issue 90-day CDs (Certificates of Deposit), but wishes to hedge the CD issuance against a rise in interest rates. On 13 March 1990 the bank finalizes its plans to issue CDs of $100 million face value in mid-June at a rate of 11.75 per cent. This issuance provides the bank with $97,062,500. It does not account for other costs associated this issuance. The bank hedges this transaction by selling 100 three-month Interest Rate Futures contracts at a yield of 11.00 per cent. By 11 June, interest rates have risen, just as the bank feared when the hedge was established. Then the CDs are issued at a yield of 12.25 per cent, bringing $96,937,500 to the bank. This represents $125,000 less than originally anticipated. However, this shortfall is partially offset by the hedge in the futures market. Over the same period, the Interest Rate Futures contracts yield rose from 11.00 per cent to 11.25 per cent (that is, 25 basis points). The tick size of one basis point is 25 dollars. Thus the profit gained in futures market is 100×25 basis point $\times$ $25, that is, $62,500. This means that CDs are issued at an effective rate of 12 per cent, instead of the desired 11.75 per cent and the unfavourable 12.25 per cent.

Financial Futures Trading Strategies

A wide range of strategies is possible with financial futures. Basically, financial futures provide a means of adjusting, acquiring, or eliminating exposure to the fluctuations in values of the underlying financial instruments. Futures can be used in many diverse applications — hedging, arbitrage, and speculation. These futures can be an extremely flexible risk management tool because of their liquidity and low transaction cost.

Financial futures markets offer a means to hedge the risk of unexpected price changes because they permit the future purchase or sale of an asset at a price set today. The hedging concept can best be illustrated perhaps by an example (see Table 11.5). Suppose Investor A has HK$50 million of Hong Kong equities spread over a few fairly diversified issues on Day 1. He senses that the market is likely to take a significant drop. He wants to protect himself against any adverse price change but is unwilling to sell his portfolio away. On the advice of his broker, he considers hedging the Hang Seng Index futures contract. He knows that if stock prices were to descend quickly, his short futures position would benefit and offset the loss on his stocks. He acts accordingly on the same day. Five days later, the Hang Send Index drops by 10 per cent; the general value of his stocks is substantially lower. But the hedge position leaves his investment value unchanged.

Table 11.5 Portfolio Hedging Strategy

Day 1	
Value of stock portfolio	HK$50,000,000
Portfolio beta	1.0 (same movement as the index)
Hang Seng futures priced at	2500
Value of one futures contract	HK$125,000
No. of contracts for a hedge	400
Day 6	
Hang Seng Index declined by	10%
Value of stock portfolio	HK$45,000,000
Hang Seng futures priced at	2250
Value of one futures contract	HK$112,500
Hedge Result	
Loss from stocks	HK$5,000,000
Gain from futures	HK$5,000,000
Net hedge result	HK$0

Like Hang Seng Index futures, interest rate futures have standardized specification in size, maturity month, minimum fluctuation, and so on. A distinct feature in interest rate futures is its quotation method. The interest rate futures contracts are traded in terms of an index which is listed by subtracting the interest rate from 100.00. If the interest rate is 10.50 per cent, the index price becomes 89.50. One basis point is represented by 0.01 per cent in the index price. Therefore an inverse relationship holds between the interest rate and the index price. If interest rate moves higher, the index price declines. If interest rate moves lower, index price increases.

The users of interest rate futures are securities dealers, bankers, insurance companies, fund managers, corporate financial managers and individual investors.

The purpose of the hedge is not to generate a profit but to help offset realized or unrealized losses (gains) on the cash security with gains (losses) on the futures postion. To establish an offsetting position in the futures market, hedgers must consider the relationship between the value of the security being hedged and the price at which the corresponding futures contract trades. The benefits of financial futures depend on how well the security's cash price follows the futures price. The difference between the cash and futures price is called the 'basis'. The basis can be positive or negative. When market sentiment is bullish, futures are priced at a premium to the cash security, and distant month contracts may sell at increasingly greater premiums. Conversely, when sentiment is bearish, the futures generally trade at a discount, and the discount may become increasingly deeper the further contracts are from the expiration.

The basis is not time-invariant. In fact, the basis can change due to unexpected changes in the cost of carry (short-term interest rate) as well as unexpected changes in the price relationship between the cash security and the futures contract. In reality, investors, who hedge their cash security with futures, are exchanging price risk for basis risk — the risk that basis will move against them despite a favourable change in the price of the cash security. Basis risk is certainly preferable to outright price risk, but unfortunately it cannot be completely eliminated.

Since basis changes ultimately determine whether a hedge produces a profit or a loss, basis is a crucial factor to evaluate in hedging transactions. For a hedge to be successful, the price variation of the hedge position should be less than the price variation of the cash instrument; and the characteristics of the cash instrument and futures contract should be sufficiently similar to result in a high degree of positive correlation in their respective price changes during the hedge period.

Arbitrage is the near simultaneous purchase and sale of the same or related futures contracts and/or cash market instruments in the hope of making a profit through a difference in markets. Trades are made based on observations and expectations. Graphs and mathematical models are used to recognize price abnormalities. The common form of arbitrage strategy in Hong Kong is the spreading strategy.

A futures spread involves establishing a long (short) postion in one futures contract and a short (long) position in a different month contract in the expectation of profiting when the price difference or spread between the two contracts widens or narrows back to normal. Spreaders are not concerned with absolute up and down price changes but with relative price changes. Spreaders who are optimistic about the market would arrange what is known as a bull spread. When the stock market is in an upward trend, prices on contracts in more deferred settlement months are apt to rise faster than nearby month contract prices. Hence a bull spread involves selling a nearby month contract short and buying a distant month contract (see Table 11.6). Similarly, spreaders who expect stock prices to fall would use a bear spread: buying a nearby month contract and selling a distant month contract. Another way of arbitrage is to establish a long positions in the cash market and a short position in the futures markets when the market is bullish. The bullish sentiment tempts a lot of speculators to take long positions in the futures market, so that the futures contract is persistently at premium over the cash market. The extra premium contributes the profit earned by arbitrageurs. However, such an arbitrage between the cash and futures markets cannot be operated in bearish markets because it is illegal to sell short in the cash market. With stock index futures, speculators can go short the market or sell a contract as easily as they can go long or buy a contract. That means they may be able to profit regardless of the direction of the market, without breaking the short sell prohibition law in the stock-market.

Table 11.6 Spreading Strategy

Opening position	Sell one January index contract at 2700; buy one March index contract at 2710.
Spread	10
Closing position	Buy one January index contract at 2710; sell one March index contract at 2750.
Spread	40
Net spread profit	HK$1,500

Program Trading in the Stock-market

The underlying asset of the stock index futures is an index that is itself not traded. As arbitrage requires the purchase or sale of the individual stocks that comprise the index, the index cash price and the index futures price are linked together by arbitrage activities. The purchase or sale of a portfolio of stock pursuant to a single order is called 'program trading'. Although program trading is used for a number of reasons unrelated to index futures, much of it is associated with the index futures arbitrage process. To monitor program trading, sophisticated arbitrageurs can make use of some computer services. These computer services assess and monitor the transaction cost, dividend yield, and tracking risk factors on a continuous basis and give out buying or selling signals for the arbitrageurs.

Index futures call for cash settlement at expiration, rather than for delivery of the underlying asset as is typical in traditional futures contracts. This means that arbitrageurs must unwind their positions in the stock-market on the expiration day. At expiration, the futures contract is settled at the closing price of the underlying index. As a result, the arbitrageur is unaffected by the manner in which the position in the index stocks is unwound, so long as the closing price on each of the stocks is received. Because the arbitrageur is perfectly hedged, the loss on the stocks is offset by the gain on the short futures postion. To assure execution of each index stock at the closing price, the arbitrageur places with the broker market-on-close orders. If many arbitrage programs are being unwound in the same direction late on the expiration day, the result may be an order imbalance that can cause closing prices to move in one direction or the other — 'price effect'. It is this unwinding process that has been blamed for the abnormal stock price movements during the last day of futures trading.

Index futures are cash settlement contracts. For every long in the futures market there is a short. It is thus possible that short futures positions may sell stock while long futures positions buy it, so that there is no imbalance. But investors in long positions may be reluctant to take delivery from the shorts when there is some uncertainty about quality and time of delivery. Then imbalance will arise. In addition, spreaders, who have bought the expiring contract and sold the next maturity, would then buy stocks to replace the long futures position in the expiring contract; this might or might not offset the sales of the stock by the long arbitrageurs depending on the uncertainty. Thus a large open interest on expiration day could portend a large unwinding of arbitrage positions in the stock-market. As open interest figures are public, the stock-market can predict the potential source of volume generated by expiring futures contracts. However, the degree of imbalance between buyers and sellers of stocks remains uncertain. Volume is substantially higher than normal in the stock-market on that day. Analysis of stock- market price changes indicates that the volatility of price changes of those stocks in the index is significantly higher on expiration days. Stocks not in the index exhibit no price effects.

The abnormal price movements of index stocks on the expiration days are undesirable, as the price effects are usually associated with large block transactions. However, the price effects are concentrated in a very short period of time, sometimes in the last 15 minutes of trading. Traders who appear with market orders to sell when an expiration is pushing prices down, or who arrive with market orders to buy when an expiration is pushing prices up, may be hurt. The expiration day phenomenon has the advantage of occurring at a predictable time, giving investors the option of staying away. Unfortunately, predictability of the expiration has not been accompanied by predictability of the direction and magnitude of order imbalances on expiration day. Cost-effective operational procedures for handling unexpected order imbalances on the stock-market are needed.

Selected References

Chan Suk Han, Lui Man Chi, and Sum Mei Lin, 'Financial Futures', *Business Administration Academic Bulletin*, (New Asia College, Chinese University of Hong Kong, 1984), pp. 47–56.

Drabenstott, M. and McDonaley, A. O'M., 'Futures Markets: a Primer for Financial Institutions', *Economic Review*, (Federal Reserve Bank of Kansas City, November 1984), pp. 17–33.

'How Financial Futures Trading Works', *Asian Money Manager*, August 1982, pp. 27–9.

Journal of Futures Markets, Center for the Study of Futures Markets, Columbia University, New York.

Kopprasch, Robert W., 'Exchange Traded Options on Fixed Income Securities' (New York, Salomon Brothers Incorporated, February 1982).

— 'Introduction to Interest Rate Hedging' (New York, Salomon Brothers Incorporated, November 1982).

Leibowitz, Martin L., 'The Analysis of Value and Volatility in Financial Futures' (Salomon Brothers Center for the Study of Financial Institutions, Graduate School of Business Administration, New York University, 1981), No. 3.

Scott, R. H., 'The Financial Futures Markets', *Hong Kong's Financial Institutions and Markets*, (Hong Kong, Oxford University Press, 1986), pp. 104–22.

Stoll, H. R. and Whaley R. E., 'Program Trading and Expiration-Day Effects', *Financial Analysts Journal*, March 1987, pp. 35–42.

Telser, Lester G., 'Why There Are Organized Futures Markets', *Journal of Law and Economics*, April 1981, pp. 1–22.

12. The Gold and Commodities Markets

David Y. K. Chan

Historical Development

The Chinese Gold and Silver Exchange Society

The Chinese Gold and Silver Exchange Society was formed in 1910. Gold, silver, and foreign currencies have been traded at different times throughout the eight decades of its operation. Members of this Society are very active and dominate the physical gold trade of Southeast Asia.

The Society began informally when people engaged in gold and silver coin trading among themselves. Trading was then done under the counter, with a handshake between the two parties involved.

It was not known how many members were in the Society during World War I as all records were lost during the turmoil of the war. On the advice of the Hong Kong Government's Secretary for Chinese Affairs, Mr E. R. Halifax, the Society applied for registration as 'The Chinese Gold and Silver Exchange Society' in 1920, and a series of by-laws were drawn up. Re-registration of members at that time showed more than 200 members.

Business flourished and reached its zenith in 1934 when United States President Franklin Roosevelt replaced the tariff system by fixing the price of a gold coin, weighing 0.89 tael (32.89 grams) at US$20. To avoid losses in foreign exchange fluctuations, big firms in Hong Kong booked gold coins at the Society in advance against their trading in United States dollars in anticipation of future settlement.

The Society was closed during the Japanese occupation of Hong Kong in 1941, but business resumed immediately after the conclusion of the Pacific War. Foreign currencies and gold continued to be traded side by side until 1962 when the Society encountered difficulties in the physical deliveries of foreign currencies and trading had to be dropped. Business has since been done only in gold bars.

At present, the affairs of the Society are run by the Executive and Supervisory Committees of 21 members elected at the Members' General Meeting, held on 15 June every alternate year.

The Hong Kong Futures Exchange Limited

Futures trading has a very long history and its origin is unknown. It is believed that the early futures market developed from deals of tangible agricultural products. In the early nineteenth century, producers, manufacturers, and consumers had already started making agreements on future deliveries. Following the development of international trading, the establishment of futures markets became popular as they provided a place for hedgers to deal in order to avoid losses brought about by adverse price movements.

In 1976, the Hong Kong Legislative Council passed the Commodities Trading Ordinance after three years of intense study by the Government and commodity experts, and paved the way for the establishment of a commodity exchange. It was on 17 December 1976 that the Hong Kong Commodity Exchange was incorporated.

The first futures contract traded was cotton, in May, 1977. This was followed by sugar futures in November, 1977, soy bean futures in November, 1979 and gold futures in August, 1980. The proposal for a Hang Seng Index Futures contract gained Government approval and trading started on 6 May 1986. While the Hang Seng Index Futures market is covered in Chapter 11, this chapter concentrates on the commodity futures market.

In order to expand its membership and introduce new contracts of different natures, the Hong Kong Commodity Exchange Limited began to reorganize its structure in mid-1984. It has now changed its name to the 'Hong Kong Futures Exchange Limited'.

The Chinese Gold and Silver Exchange Society

The Nature of the Market

The society has a limited membership of 193, restricted to ethnic Chinese. It is a principals market and the Exchange Society acts as a monitor. Dealings are based on spot gold with undated delivery. A daily premium/discount rate establishes the carrying charges for either the buyer or seller of gold. Transactions are made through open outcry as well as privately between members.

As a rule, balances between members are settled on a daily basis before the market is closed, based on the morning and afternoon settlement prices.

The Society is self-governing and no default has ever marked it in its history of operation. A variable safe-guard rule is in effect, which limits the gain or loss of each open position from the previous day's close.

Membership

The 193 members are all corporate members with unlimited liability. According to the Constitution of the Society, no new members can be accepted unless the existing membership drops to below 150. Therefore, interested parties can only gain membership through a transfer from an existing member if both parties agree. To apply to the Society for a change of membership, the applicant must secure recommendations from two members altogether, drawn from the Executive and Supervisory Committees. The Society will first examine the applicant's qualifications and then put up a notice for ten days to allow for objections. The matter will then be put to a vote by the Committee and the applicant will be admitted and the change of the firms' name on the Society register is granted.

Each member may have four floor traders and four messengers. No person is allowed to enter the trading hall except those aforementioned. The Society has ruled that members who were admitted into the Society after 1 April 1979 can be represented with only three floor traders and three messengers.

Trading Methods

The trading hall of the Chinese Gold and Silver Exchange Society is packed with gold traders. Whether the price of gold is up, down, or stable, that the bidding is hectic is evident by the shouts and cries among traders on the floor.

The method of trading is like playing catch for a fortune. Verbal quotations and hand signs are used to illustrate gold prices and the first trader to touch a seller's body wins the deal. This explains the phenomenon that all the traders on the floor are men. We call it the 'Open Outcry System', which is fascinating to strangers to gold trading, and it is why women do not become traders although there is no particular legislation in the Constitution of the Society which prohibits this. This trading method, though it appears old-fashioned and obsolete, has existed ever since the days when the Society was still in its embryonic stage. Time has proven that the system is sound and reliable.

Gold Fixing

The fixing prices are determined twice a day, based on the approximate market price (correct to the nearest HK$5) at 12.00 noon and 4.00 p.m. These prices are used by member brokers to settle their accounts. An example will illustrate this: Broker A has a long buying position of 100 taels against Broker B's short selling position at HK$4,000. If the price fixing is HK$4,010, Broker A will receive Hong Kong dollars from Broker B.

Through this mechanism, the brokers do not build up big unsettled payments between themselves, and the healthy condition of the local market is therefore maintained.

The Daily Premium/Discount Rate

The Daily Premium/Discount Rate is variable and is determined at 11.00 a.m. each day by the relative demand for physical gold. This daily rate quoted is based on 10 taels of gold, and by rule cannot exceed 2.1 per cent of contract value on a monthly basis.

By accepting or paying this rate a buyer or seller of gold in the

Hong Kong Market can defer delivery of gold indefinitely. Thus, the Hong Kong gold contract is actually a futures contract with an undated delivery.

Tael bars can be physically transacted every day at 11.00 a.m. when the daily premium/discount rate is established.

Determination of Interest

Interest is determined once a day at 11.00 a.m. Monday to Friday and 10.00 a.m. Saturday. Interest can be positive, negative, or even.

Positive interest arises when the demand for physical gold is greater than its supply. Buyers who cannot get hold of gold are awarded 'interest' which is paid by sellers who cannot make physical delivery.

Negative interest arises when the supply of physical gold is greater than demand for it. Sellers flood the market with gold but cannot find buyers for it. As a result, sellers who do not get sale proceeds have to be awarded 'interest' which is paid by buyers, who do not have sufficient cash to pay the entire amount to sellers.

When we say today's interest is positive 50 cents, we mean that those who have a long position to carry forward to the next day receive from seller 50 Hong Kong cents per 10 taels of gold per day.

Particulars of the Market

The trading hours of the market are as follows:

Monday–Friday: 9.30 a.m.–12.30 p.m.
                         2.30 p.m.–4.30 p.m.
      Saturday: 9.30 a.m.–12.00 noon

Settlement Price:

Monday–Friday: 11.00 a.m., 4.00 p.m.
      Saturday: 11.00 a.m.

Unit of Trade

A contract lot is 100 taels of 99 per cent fine (pure) gold made up of 20 bars of 5 taels of gold with approved brand names and assay marks. One tael of Hong Kong gold is equivalent to 1.191336 troy ounces of 99.99 per cent pure gold.

An example will make this clear. A trader went long in five lots of Hong Kong gold at a price of, say, HK$3,570 per tael on 15 July 1989. Let us assume the interest factor to be a negative HK$17 per 10 taels of gold on the day of purchase.

1. On the Day of Purchase. Assuming an original margin of, say, 10 per cent, the trader would have to furnish a sum of 10 per cent of HK$(3,570 × 5 × 100), that is, HK$178,500. In addition, he would have to pay a commission of HK$50 per lot.

$$\text{Total Commission Payable} = \text{HK\$50} \times 5$$
$$= \text{HK\$250}$$

$$\text{Total Amount Payable on 15 July 1989} = \text{HK\$}(178{,}500 + 250)$$
$$= \text{HK\$178,750}$$

The amount of HK$178,750 would be credited to the trader's account with broker.

Furthermore, as the interest factor was negative (that is, the longs had to pay interest to the shorts) on 15 July 1989, an interest amount would be debited to the trader's account.

$$\text{The Negative Interest Amount} = \text{HK\$17} \times 10 \times 5$$
$$= \text{HK\$850}$$

2.   One Day After the Purchase If the Price Rose.   If the price rose to, say, HK$3,600 per tael on 16 July 1989 and the interest factor became a positive HK$10 per 10 taels of gold, the following entries would be made to the trader's account:

Excess Equity (Excluding Interest)

$$\text{HK\$}(3{,}600 - 3{,}570) \times 5 \times 100 = \text{HK\$15,000}$$

As the interest factor was positive (that is, the shorts had to pay interest to the longs), interest would be credited to the trader's account.

$$\text{The Positive Interest Amount} = \text{HK\$10} \times 10 \times 5$$
$$= \text{HK\$500}$$

On 16 July, the trader could actually withdraw an amount equal to HK$15,000 + HK$500 − HK$850, that is, HK$14,650.

3.   One Day After the Purchase If the Price Fell.   If the price fell to say, HK$3,500 per tael on 16 July 1989 and the interest factor remained the same as above, the trader would have to pay a maintenance margin:

$$\text{Maintenance Margin} = \text{HK\$}(3{,}570 - 3{,}500) \times 500$$
$$= \text{HK\$35,000}$$

The interest factor remained the same, that is, HK$500 credit. On 16 July, the trader would have to pay in an amount equal to HK$35,000 + HK$850 − HK$500, that is, HK$35,350.

Factors Affecting the Gold Market

Before we examine the Hong Kong gold market performance of 1988, we should consider the factors affecting gold prices. Some factors have gained world-wide attention, and they are regarded as the leading reasons for the change of gold prices. Each of them has different degree of influence on price fluctuation.

Demand and supply: gold trading is under a free market system in which the price is simply influenced by the 'invisible hand' of the market. If there is an increase in demand, the price of gold will be bid up, while an increase in supply will pull down the market price. Another factor in the volatility of gold prices is speculation. Speculators tend to buy when inflation is expected to increase and sell when it is expected to decrease. Therefore, in a time of high inflation, gold prices will rise due to the increasing demand for gold.

Political instability in the world contributes to the increasing demand for gold. Investments are liquidated into the gold market, which is seen as a 'store of value' asset.

Official holding of gold leads to instability of the demand for gold. Private and official reserves are large relative to current production — official holdings alone are probably about 35 times larger than current production. As a result, the gold market is quite different from that of most other commodities, as only slight changes in expectation concerning adjustments in stock levels can have profound effects on the speculative demand for bullion.

A Review of Hong Kong's Gold Market in 1988

To illustrate how some factors affect the market, major movements during 1988 are here reviewed briefly. In the first month of 1988, the price of gold was quoted at around HK$4,450, slightly down from its closing level in December 1987. The most substantial decrease in price came in the second month of that year, when gold dropped almost five hundred Hong Kong dollars to close at HK$3,994 in February. Thereafter, gold traded in the range of HK$4,000 to HK$4,300 for the following four months. Starting in mid-June, gold prices continuously dropped from HK$4,322 to the year's lowest level of HK$3,702 in late September. After this wave, there was a major technical rebound for HK$300 which is almost 50 per cent of the previous downward wave from HK$4,322 to HK$3,702.

In January 1988, gold prices moved sharply downwards. It could not breach the psychologically important level of HK$4,525 which is a strong resistance when compared with the previous Double Top of HK$4,850 in January 1980 and HK$4,750 in September 1983 (see Fig. 12.1). Fundamentally, this movement was due to a smaller than expected United States trade deficit of US$13.20 billion for November 1987, which put gold on a technically bearish track. The market was influenced by the United States dollar's volatility and also by easier crude oil value.

Gold prices dropped steadily during February 1988. This was due to the news of gold selling by the Soviet Union. This bearish trend was influenced by weak petroleum prices and heavy selling of gold by producers, including Australia and South Africa.

Fig. 12.1   Hong Kong Gold Monthly Price Chart

High, Low, Closing
(2 January 1974–31 December 1988)

Source: *Hong Kong Economic Journal*, 1989 (in Chinese). Trans. David Y. K. Chan.

In March 1988, gold prices rose dramatically to reach a high of HK$4,258 from HK$3,994. Technically, it was a major correction of more than 50 per cent of the previous downward wave. In fact, this trend was supported by a fall in the United States dollar and by the inflationary implications of a jump in crude oil prices. The political instability of tension between Panama and the United States also contributed to the positive sentiment.

In April and May 1988, a lack of substantial news caused gold to fluctuate around HK$4,162 and HK$4,288. Many investors kept out of the market as it seemed to have no clear direction. Gold prices became firmer because of the co-incidence of the clashes between United States and Iran and growing selling pressure.

But in June, the price of gold renewed its downward trend, though it failed to break the HK$4,000 level. This trend was supported by the expectation of inflationary pressure in the United States and the backing of commodities prices. The continuing United States dollar appreciation and decreasing oil prices also contributed to the downward trend.

In early July, buying pressure from the profit takers caused gold to rally. Afterwards, prices continued to drop and tried to break the supporting level of HK$4,000. This downfall was due to the sharp rise of the United States dollar after the report of a smaller-than-expected United States May trade deficit, and the possibility of an end to the Iran–Iraq conflict.

Gold prices consolidated within the narrow range of HK$4,069 to HK$3,992 due to a lack of substantial news in August. Usually, there is either a continuation of decline or a reversal after a consolidation.

In this case it was a continuation, with the year's lowest price at HK$3702 in September. The downturn in the price of crude oil made gold vulnerable to selling in the market. Moreover, the continuing United States dollar's appreciation reinforced the downward trend of gold market.

From October till early December, prices continuously moved upward. This was mainly due to the depreciation of the United States dollar, caused by the United States Presidential election. Reduction of the trade deficit, which is a long-standing problem in the United States, was one of the election promises made by President Bush. He won the election, not keeping the United States dollar too strong in order to stimulate domestic exports to maintain a good trade deficit figure.

The major trend for the year was therefore upwards, but for most of the year gold traded in a fairly broad and constant range, when compared with previous years, of between HK$4,525 and HK$3,702. If the United States economy continues to improve and United States debt decreases, then gold might fall through the HK$3,531 or US$380 level in the next year.

The Hong Kong Futures Exchange Limited

The Structure of the Exchange

The Hong Kong Futures Exchange Limited is managed by a Board of Directors with 12 members. The Chairman and three Vice-chairmen have executive functions and they are vested with specific power to cope with contingencies in the market. As a whole, the Board formulates rules and regulations and sets the policies of the Exchange. In addition, it has the power to appoint members to the various committees of the Exchange, as well as the power to discipline members.

The commodity futures markets of the Exchange are grouped under different divisions according to the nature of the markets. Currently, there are four market divisions: Agricultural Products, Metals, Indices, and Currency and Interest Rates. Each market division has its individual characteristics and practices.

The Exchange is supported by four staff departments: the Audit and Surveillance Unit, the Training Unit, the Market Section, and the Membership Section. The Audit and Surveillance Unit supervises members' financial positions in order to protect the financial integrity of the market. The Training Unit undertakes training programmes for members and the general public through seminars and courses. The Market Section is responsible for the orderly conduct of the market, while the Membership Section is responsible for the registration and administration of membership. In case of queries, members are encouraged to approach the Membership Section for clarification of the Exchange rules as well as other regulatory matters.

Membership of the Exchange

Members of the Exchange can be divided into three categories. They are either Full Members, Market Members, or Trade Affiliated Members. Full Members must be either individuals ordinarily resident in Hong Kong or limited companies incorporated in Hong Kong. They must hold at least one Ordinary Share (of HK$100,000 par value) in the capital of the Exchange. Full Members are entitled to trade on the floor in all market divisions upon application. They must contribute to the Compensation Fund as shareholders of the Exchange. Full Members should have a capital or paid-up capital of not less than HK$2,000,000 in October 1987.

Market Members must also be individuals ordinarily resident in Hong Kong or limited companies incorporated in Hong Kong. They must hold at least one Standard Share (of HK$25,000 par value) in the capital of the Exchange. They are entitled the right of trading in one market division only. They may be granted the right to trade in other market divisions by special approval of the Board. As shareholders of the Exchange, they also must contribute to the Compensation Fund. Market Members should have a capital or paid-up capital of not less than HK$1,000,000 in October 1987.

Overseas companies can apply as Trade Affiliated Members. Such members will not be granted the right to trade in any market. Therefore, all of their trading orders are placed through a Full Member or a Market Member. Since they are not the shareholders of the Exchange, they are not required to contribute to the Compensation Fund.

The Trading Systems of the Futures Exchange

All trading at the Hong Kong Futures Exchange is centralized in a market place, where facilities such as booths, trading rings, price quotation boards, and audio and visual devices are installed.

Futures markets are traded under various systems. The soy bean market is traded under the One Price Group Trading System. This system is popular in Japanese futures markets, with its special feature of using hand signals to indicate the quantities of buy and sell orders.

Trading is carried out by members' floor representatives standing around a trading ring under the control of a chairman. Trading is not continuous but is held in separate sessions. All business in one session for one month of delivery is recorded at one price.

The gold market is traded under the Open Outcry System. The tempo of this system is quicker than the other two methods of trading. It is known as the 'double auction method' with declining offers meeting rising bids, until an acceptable price is reached. This method is very popular in Chicago, New York, and London and is extensively used in these centres. The sugar market uses both the Group Trading and the Open Outcry Systems.

The Board Trading System is used for the Hang Seng Index Futures. This is a system which is similar to that of the Hong Kong stock-market, whereby members actually write their bids and offers on a trading board located in the front of the trading area.

There are four kinds of product traded in the Exchange nowadays. They are gold (see Fig. 12.2 and Table 12.1), soy beans (see Fig. 12.3 and Table 12.2), sugar (see Fig. 12.4 and Table 12.3), and the Hang Seng Index Futures (this market is covered in Chapter 11). The futures market of cotton has closed and not been reopened, due to an insufficient demand since 1982.

Hong Kong Futures Exchange Limited issues reports daily and weekly to provide information about all transactions made in the market. This information is also disseminated to the public through Reuters and other media channels.

A newsletter is published every month, giving a monthly review together with graphs and statistics of the market.

The Financial Integrity of Futures Markets

The financial integrity of futures markets is protected by the Guarantee System and the Compensation Fund.

In Hong Kong, the International Commodity Clearing House (ICCH) acts as the manager of the Hong Kong Commodities Guarantee Corporation and handles day-to-day affairs. The Guarantee Corporation, owned by a consortium of banks, guarantees the due fulfillment of contracts. The corporation calls each day for original margin and variation margin when prices move adversely. This has a disciplinary effect upon clearing members, and is a major component for maintaining the financial integrity of the futures markets.

On the other hand, private investors are protected by a Compensation Fund. This is used for compensating the losses incurred from improper conduct of any member of the Exchange. Every member of the Exchange is required to make an initial contribution of HK$50,000 to the Compensation Fund, which is administered by the Government. A flat rate levy is collected from members for each contract traded on the Exchange. An investor who has a legitimate complaint against a member may bring it to the attention of the

Fig. 12.2 Trading Volume for Futures Contracts in Gold

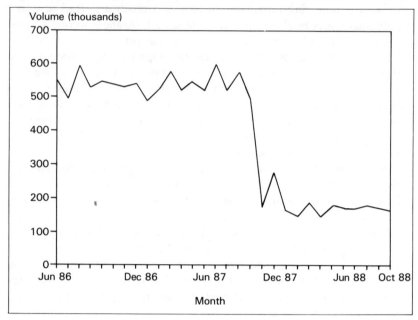

Table 12.1 Gold Futures Contract Specifications

Standard Grade	:	Refined gold of not less than 995 fineness
Trading Units	:	100 oz. fine gold
Tenderable Grades	:	Bars of 100 oz., 50 oz., and 1 kg.
Delivery Point	:	Hong Kong
Price Quotation	:	United States currency
Min. Fluctuations	:	10 cents per oz.
Trading Months	:	Even months, spot month and the following two months
Trading Method	:	Open Outcry
Original Margin	:	US$1,500
Daily Limits	:	US$40*+

Notes: * No limit is imposed on the spot month.
        + Market is closed for 30 minutes and reopened without limit on price movement.

Fig. 12.3 Trading Volume for Futures Contracts in Soy Beans

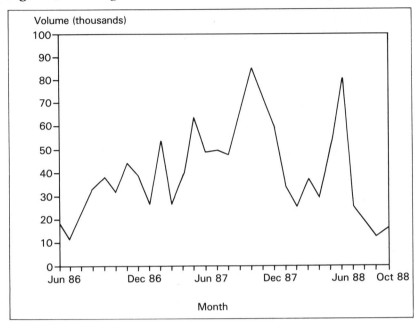

Table 12.2 Soy Bean Futures Contract Specifications

Standard Grade	:	Unselected China yellow soy beans
Trading Units	:	100 bags of 80 kg each
Tenderable Grades	:	US I.O.M. soy beans
Delivery Point	:	Tokyo or Kanagawa, Japan
Price Quotation	:	Hong Kong currency
Min. Fluctuations	:	10 cents per bag
Trading Months	:	Each consecutive month up to six months ahead
Trading Hours	:	09.50, 10.50
		12.50, 14.50
Trading Method	:	Group Trading
Original Margin	:	HK$7,500
Daily Limits	:	Nil

Fig. 12.4 Trading Volume for Futures Contracts in Sugar

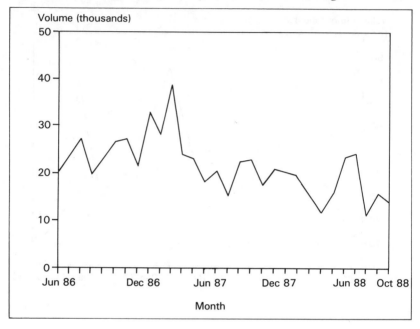

Table 12.3 Sugar Futures Contract Specifications

Standard Grade	:	Raw cane sugar of 96 polarization
Trading Units	:	50 long tons (112,000 lbs.)
Tenderable Grades	:	Growth of S.E. Asian countries
Delivery Point	:	F.O.B., S.E. Asian countries
Price Quotation	:	United States currency
Min. Fluctuations	:	1/100 cents per lb.
Trading Months	:	January, March, May, July, September, October
Trading Hours	:	10.30–12.00
		14.25–18.00
Trading Method	:	Group and Open Outcry
Original Margin	:	US$1,350
Daily Limits	:	US 1 cent*+

Notes: *   No limit is imposed on the spot month.
        +   Market is closed for 30 minutes and reopened without limit on price movement.

Exchange. The complaint will be investigated, and the member advised whether the party should receive compensation.

The Exchange sets rules and regulations that lay the framework for floor trading and brokerage practices. All traders have to apply for membership before they can trade on the Exchange floor.

A Review of Commodity Futures Markets

The futures markets in Hong Kong were very volatile in 1986 and 1988. This section reviews the commodity futures market. The soy bean market was obviously experiencing an upward trend from mid-1986 to late 1987, with its highest trading volume in October 1987 (see Fig. 12.3). Then prices became firmer. The trend was partly attributable to the fall in both the Japanese and Chicago markets, and partly due to the weak United States dollar. After October 1987, the trading volume steadily dropped during the following four months. This was due to the poor crop in eastern Europe and the short supply of soy bean oil in India. The trading interest largely concentrated in December 1987 and April 1988 deliveries. Another rally occurred in July 1988 with strong prices, sparked by the continued forecast of dry weather in the major midwest growing areas in the United States.

In the sugar market, prices dropped steadily and led to a increasing demand for sugar from early May 1986 onwards. Trading volume then steadily increased, to 38,850 lots in March 1987 (see Fig. 12.4). It was believed that the market had over-reacted to the Soviet nuclear accident, and the uncertainty over the extent of its damage to the Soviet crops pushed prices lower in the second half of the year. In April 1987, buying orders made prices firmer and market sentiment gained support from reports by Cuba that sugar cane production in that country was running some 8,000,000 tons behind estimates. Under a firmer price market, the trading volume dropped rapidly during the following three months. Thereafter, due to different market sentiments which made market prices firmer, the trading volume was consolidated at a lower level, forming a downward movement of the market in terms of trading volume.

The Loco-London Gold Market

The History of the Loco-London Gold Market

The success of the Hong Kong gold markets has given rise to opportunities for investors, brokers, and overseas bullion dealers to trade, hedge, or arbitrage gold in Hong Kong with local bullion dealers and each other.

The London bullion dealers have established offices in Hong Kong and have created a market in gold, creating, in effect, basic London vaults parallel to the Hong Kong gold markets.

The Nature of the Loco-London Gold Market

The Loco-London gold market is basically an extension of the London gold market into Hong Kong and other major gold market time zones. Transactions are based on spot market prices, with settlement within two business days of the transaction. However, extension of settlement dates can easily be arranged with the payment of a daily interest factor. Delivery of gold takes place in London and payment is in United States dollars in New York (see Fig. 12.5). Most transactions are made via telex or telephone between dealers.

Fig. 12.5   The Loco-London Gold Market, 1988

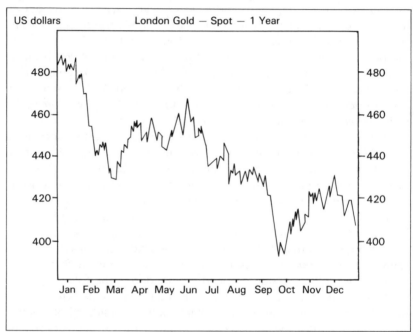

Source: *Hong Kong Economic Journal*, 1989 (in Chinese). Trans. David Y. K. Chan.

In Hong Kong, the Loco-London gold market is an alternate market running parallel to the Hong Kong gold market and has become very important because business can be transacted on international terms. The arbitrage between these markets is so frequent that both markets express a fair market value for gold, as determined by both local and international dealers.

Arbitrage between the Loco-London gold market and the Chinese Gold and Silver Exchange has been very active at times, primarily due to the differences in size of the weight contracted (for troy ounces versus taels), the quality of the gold, and the currency (United States dollars versus Hong Kong dollars). However, since the Hong Kong dollar was pegged to the United States dollar in 1983, arbitrage possibilities have been less attractive.

The Inter-relationship Between the Loco-London and the Hong Kong Gold Markets

By understanding the relationship between the Hong Kong and Loco-London gold markets, investors can exercise arbitrage between these two markets. (See Chapter 13 for a discussion of the gold standard.)

Since 1 tael equals 1.2033 ounces, to convert 1 tael of 99 per cent pure gold to ounces of 100 per cent pure gold, the factor we use is 1.1913 (1.2033 × 99/100). We then come to two variables, the Hong Kong dollar/United States dollar exchange rate (T.T.) and the market price of Hong Kong gold. For example:

HK$4,000

T.T. = US$1.00 = HK$7.80

The equivalent of Hong Kong gold in United States dollars per fine ounce:

$$\frac{\text{Hong Kong gold market price}}{\text{T.T.} \times \text{factor}} = \frac{4,000}{7.8 \times 1.1913}$$
$$= \text{US\$430.47}$$

	Purity of Gold (Per Cent)	Unit of Trade	Currency Per Unit
Hong Kong gold	99	Tael	Hong Kong dollar
Loco-London	100	Ounce	United States dollar

Gold Fixing

Gold fixing is done twice a day in London. At the start of fixing, the Chairman suggests a price midway between bid and offer of the pre-fix price. The five London gold dealers then indicate their net buying, selling, or nil interest at that price, together with the number of bars they want to trade. If the buying interest matches the offers, the gold is fixed. If not, the Chairman changes the suggested price, gets figures from the five dealers again, and fixes the price at which a balance is reached. According to London Gold Market Rules, no commission is paid by sellers at fixings. Buyers are charged commission of 30 United States cents per ounce on the fixing price. However, most clients here enjoy concessionary rates for deals done at the fixings.

	London Standard Time	Hong Kong Time	London Summer Time	Hong Kong Time
Morning Fixing	10.30 a.m.	6.30 p.m.	10.30 a.m.	5.30 p.m.
Afternoon Fixing	3.00 p.m.	11.00 p.m.	3.00 p.m.	10.00 p.m.

Conclusion

Various gold markets are situated in different parts of the world, and each of them operates during different time periods on a world-wide basis (see Table 12.4).

Table 12.4 Round the Clock Trading Hours for Gold

Hong Kong Time		
Summer	Winter	
	07.30	Australia Open
	08.30	Tokyo Open
	09.30	Hong Kong Open
	12.30	Hong Kong Morning Close
	14.30	Hong Kong Afternoon Open
15.30	16.30	London Open
	16.30	Hong Kong Afternoon Close
17.30	18.30	London Morning Fixing
20.20	21.20	New York Comex Open
22.00	23.00	London Afternoon Fixing
02.30	03.30	New York Comex Close
02.30	05.30	United States West Coast

The three major gold markets, New York, London, and Hong Kong operate on a continuous basis in that one opens just before the closing of the preceding one. This arrangement enables gold traders to reduce their risk.

Hong Kong is one of the largest gold trading centres in the world, ranking after New York and London. It was further enhanced when the Government lifted restrictions on gold imports in January 1974.

Activity at the Chinese Gold and Silver Exchange Society appears chaotic as there is a lot of shouting, pushing, and general physical contact. But this is the traditional way of transacting business at the Gold Exchange. Therefore, Reuter and other sophisticated facilities that report gold trading information are able only to collect statistics and other data, but not the tangible, palpable information evident or visible in the interaction and contact between traders on the floors.

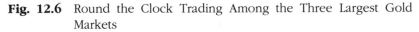

Fig. 12.6 Round the Clock Trading Among the Three Largest Gold Markets

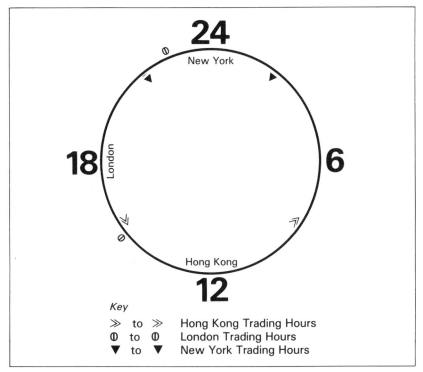

The trading traditions of Hong Kong gold and the Society members' esteem have always been highly regarded. In fact, it is because of the members' rigorous self-discipline and integrity that the exchange's trading system has been functioning well, without a hitch, these past 79 years. The virtue of trustworthiness among members has indeed become the most valuable asset for those involved in gold trading.

For centuries the London market has been considered the gold capital of the world. This market has been increasingly used by producers, industrial consumers, and dealers. In recent years the number of trading firms, investors, and speculators using this market has grown substantially. Consequently, the volume of transactions processed in this market has reached new heights. Today London gold market prices serve as bench-marks for private gold dealings throughout the world.

All authorized banks in the United Kingdom may deal in gold, but activity is concentrated in the hands of the five members of the London Gold Market, namely, Mocatta Goldsmid, Johnson Matthey, Samuel Montague, N.W. Rothschild & Sons, and Sharps Pixley. All five members of the London Market have operating subsidiaries in Hong Kong.

The gold market in New York has been usually called the COMEX gold market. The daily volume of transactions in the COMEX is very large, surpassing any other gold futures market in the world. All economic or political decisions announced during market hours tend to increase its market activity significantly. Over the years, the COMEX gold market has established itself as a market leader in setting gold prices within the North American time zone. Even though physical transactions in COMEX are only a fraction of those of other major gold centres, future prices on this market are carefully monitored by gold traders throughout the world.

References

Dealer Training Course Manual, Training Section, (Hong Kong, Hong Kong Futures Exchange Ltd. and ICCH, 1985).

Green, Timothy, *The World of Gold Today*, (New York, Walker and Company, 1973).

Jastram, R., *The Golden Constant*, (New York, John Wiley & Sons, 1977).

Lam, C. M., *Gold and Commodity Investment*, (Hong Kong, Man Yuen Publication, 1988).

Man, K. Y., *Bullion Dealings in 24 Hours*, (Hong Kong, Kam Ling Publisher, 1987).

Research Department, *Hong Hong Futures Exchange Quarterly Bulletin*, Hong Kong Futures Exchange Ltd., March 1988.

Research Department, *Indices and Financial Futures Market Bulletin*, ICCH (Hong Kong) Ltd., October 1988.

Research Department, *Monthly Newsletter* Nos. 116–43, Hong Kong Futures Exchange Ltd.

Sherman, Eugene J., *Gold Investment Theory & Application*, (New York Institute of Finance, Prentice Hall, 1986).

Sun Hung Kai Securities, *A Survey of the Hong Kong Gold Market*, (Hong Kong, Sun Hung Kai Securities Limited, March 1981).

Tan, Ronald H. C., *The Gold Market*, (Singapore, Singapore University Press, 1982).

Woo, W. F., *The Hong Kong Gold Market*, (Hong Kong, Joint Publishing (HK) Co. Ltd., 1988).

Part IV
Issues and Policies

13. Monetary Policies and Central Banking

ROBERT HANEY SCOTT

AN integral part of every modern exchange economy is, of course, its monetary system. The existence of a monetary system guarantees the existence of a monetary policy. It is never accurate to say 'We have no monetary policy since the money supply is market determined' because to allow the market to determine the money supply is itself a monetary policy.

A central bank is an institution established by government for the purpose of acting: as banker for the government, as banker for commercial and merchant banks that operate in the economy, as the issuer and manager of the economy's currency, and, usually, as the institution responsible for the formation and implementation of monetary policies. While Hong Kong does not have a central bank as such, it is clear that the functions usually performed by central banks in other economies are carried out by a hodgepodge of institutions in Hong Kong. As described in Chapter 2, the Hongkong and Shanghai Banking Corporation is a principal participant in activities that are characteristic of central banks generally. Because the HSBC frequently acts as the agent of government, casual observers sometimes say that it is Hong Kong's central bank. Although this is understandable, careful observers stop short of making this characterization because the Monetary Affairs Branch of government and the Exchange Fund also participate and, as arms of government, appear to direct the activities of the HSBC.

Having evolved principally in response to perceived emergencies, Hong Kong's monetary system is jury-rigged. But temporary solutions often work better than elaborately planned and instituted ones. Many central banks have performed poorly, and since Hong Kong's system has worked well in comparison there is little or no pressure to establish a central bank. However, in July 1988 the Monetary Affairs Branch of the Office of the Financial Secretary responded to a perceived demand for more stable interest rates by introducing a process for supplying or absorbing Hong Kong dollar funds into and out of the Hong Kong Inter-bank Borrowing Market. Thus, the Branch has assumed yet another activity usually performed by central banks (as discussed at some length in Chapter 2 and again, later in this chapter).[1]

This chapter has four major sections. The first section contains a very brief introduction to the theory relating to the importance of monetary policy. The second section contains a description of the measures of money compiled for Hong Kong. The third section describes how the

Exchange Fund operates to control the circulation of Hong Kong dollars and the monetary base. Using the theory and institutional details of the first three sections, the fourth section contains a general discussion of issues in monetary policy facing Hong Kong.

Monetary Theory: A Brief Statement

David Hume's essay 'Of Money' appeared in *Political Discourses*, 1752. In it he articulated the relation between money and prices in literary form, a relation that later became known as the Equation of Exchange:

$$MV = PT$$

where M is the amount of money in circulation, V is the velocity of money expressed as the average number of times a unit of money changes hands during a given period, P is the average price of all items exchanged during the period, and T is the number of transactions during the period.[2]

This equation is an accounting identity and must always hold by definition, but it provides a framework for analysis. Assume that T represents principally the final goods produced in an economy and offered for sale to consumers (domestic or foreign), investors, or government. This output of goods depends upon the resource base of the economy, the vagaries of nature, and the efficient operation of a free-pricing system. Assume that V, the velocity of money, is also given. It depends upon the institutional structure of the pricing system — whether wages are paid weekly or monthly and how much cash a person routinely wants to have on hand.

With V and T both fixed, it follows that changes in M will accompany changes in P. If M increases, P rises. If M rises 6 per cent, then P rises 6 per cent, too, so long as V and T remain fixed. Alternatively, assume that the economy's output level represented by T grows 6 per cent during the year. In this case the 6 per cent increase in M will accommodate the 6 per cent increase in transactions and prices will remain unchanged.

When the average level of prices rises, people call it inflation. Some economists prefer to reserve the term 'inflation' to mean not a single jump in the price level itself but rather to a rate of increase in the level of prices over time. Inflation is usually expressed as an annual rate.

By putting the Equation of Exchange in logarithmic form all four variables can be expressed as rates of change. Thus, if the rate of growth in M exceeds the rate of growth in T while V holds steady, then the inflation rate will simply be the difference or excess growth of M. For example, if M grows at 6 per cent while T grows only at 2 per cent, the inflation rate will turn out to be 4 per cent. Inflation follows when 'too much money chases too few goods'.

In its original form, therefore, what is called the 'Quantity Theory of Money' begins with the Equation of Exchange, and adds the assumptions that V and T tend to be imposed by outside forces and can be considered fixed. The principal implication of this theory is that the price level in any economy depends upon the quantity of money.

Almost without exception, economists agree that the Quantity Theory holds empirically *over the long run*. But when the level of business activity fluctuates, both V and T record dramatic changes. When V and T change, economists *cannot* predict how price levels will respond to changes in M. Thus, events forced economists to amend the Quantity Theory in order to improve its predictive content.

The Modern Quantity Theory of Money

Over the past 250 years the Quantity Theory has evolved into what today's economists call a 'theory of the demand for money'.[3] By re-arranging terms in the Equation of Exchange and adding other relevant variables, the demand for money can be expressed as an equation in functional form:

$$\frac{M}{P} = f(i,\ Q,\ X).$$

In this equation M is the amount of dollars that people wish to hold. When this is divided by the price level, the term on the left becomes the amount of purchasing power people wish to have on hand. M/P is called 'real money balances' to distinguish the term from 'nominal balances of money' measured by M alone. The variable i represents the general level of interest rates. The variable Q represents the real quantity of output produced by economic activity. Since output and income are simply two sides of the same coin, Q could be called real income. In this equation Q is a proxy for transactions. The variable X represents a catch-all set of other factors that may importantly affect the quantity of money that people wish to hold.

The demand for money equation reads as follows: the quantity of real balances of money that people wish to hold is related to interest rate levels, the amount of output the economy is producing, and other factors such as the availability of money substitutes, political stability, and so on.

Graphs help interpret this equation. In Fig. 13.1 the general level of interest rates, i, is measured on the vertical axis. Real balances of money, M/P, is measured on the horizontal axis. The levels of Q and of other X factors do not appear explicitly, but the effects of changes in Q and X can be described.

Let the catch-all variable X be ignored at this time in order to simplify the equation. The downward sloping curve in Part (a) of the figure represents the demand for money relation expressed as $f(i,\ Q_0)$ where the subscript attached to Q indicates that this Q is the fixed amount in an initial period. Since Q is fixed, the curve shows the

Fig. 13.1 Money Demand Functions

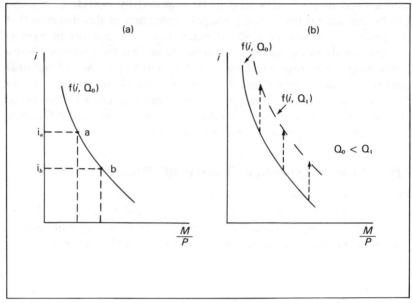

relation between i and M/P for that amount of Q. At lower interest rates people will hold a larger quantity of real money balances. Thus, as i falls from i_a to i_b, the quantity of M/P on the horizontal axis increases. The relation between i and M/P in the equation $M/P = f(i, Q)$ is negative.

The concept of 'opportunity cost' helps explain the negative relation between interest rates and the quantity of money people wish to hold. Instead of holding money, a person has the opportunity to lend the money and earn interest. Thus, the opportunity cost of holding money is the value of the interest that might be earned. The higher the interest rate, the higher the cost of holding money, so at higher rates people hold less money.

In Part (b) of the figure the dashed curve indicates how the demand for money shifts up or to the right when Q increases from Q_0 to Q_1. At each and every level of interest the quantity of money that people wish to hold increases. This is because more money is needed in the economy to accommodate the increased level of transactions that occurs as economic output expands.

If output were to decrease, the curve would shift down or to the left instead of to the right. Thus, the relation between output as measured by Q and M/P in the equation $M/P = f(i, Q)$ is positive. Output and the quantity of money demanded increase and decrease together.[4]

In the two panels of Fig. 13.2 the money supply is combined with the demand for money curve. In Part (a) of the figure the money

Fig. 13.2 Shifts in Money Supply Functions

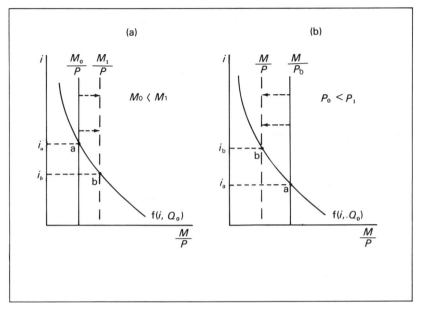

supply is a vertical line and a given initial amount of dollars is indicated by M_0. When the quantity of money demanded equals the quantity supplied, the two curves intersect as indicated at point a. This indicates that the equilibrium level of interest rates is i_a.

If the money supply increases from M_0 to M_1 the vertical line shifts right as indicated by the dashed line. Interest rate levels fall as indicated by point b.

In Part (b) of the figure the vertical line represents the supply of money for a given price level designated by P_0. Should the price level increase from P_0 to P_1, the line shifts to the left. This is because the ratio M/P declines if the denominator P increases. The higher price level results in a higher interest rate level as indicated by the move from point a to point b on the demand for money curve.

To summarize, the graphs show nearly all interrelations among all of the four variables in the equation $M/P = f(i, Q)$. If the catch-all variable X were included, the demand for money curve would shift right or left depending on just what it is that X represents. For example, if X represents a substitute for money, then an increase in X would cause the demand for money to decline, that is, for the demand curve to shift to the left.

If X represented political stability and an unstable political situation were to develop, then people would try to exchange their dollars for goods. The demand for money curve would shift to the left. But as people exercised their spending power, they would push up the price level so that the supply of real money would decrease and the vertical line representing this supply would shift to the left. The variable X may have an effect on *both* the demand curve *and* the supply curve.

Although the curves as drawn do not illustrate the *complete* interaction among all the variables, they do provide a frame of reference to use in analysing Hong Kong's monetary circumstances. But before employing these graphs it is important to examine Hong Kong's money supply — how it is measured and how it comes into circulation.

Defining and Measuring Money in Hong Kong

Money is what people use to discharge debt in an exchange economy. With this *definition* of money in mind it is easy to see that part of the money supply consists of currency that is passed from hand to hand. Ownership passes to the holder. Another part of the money supply is in the form of demand deposits in banks. Through cheque clearing, ownership of the deposit passes from buyer to seller. Thus, the *measure* of money supply in an economy, consistent with the definition above, is the sum of cash in the hands of the public and the spendable demand deposits (current accounts) that the public hold in banks.

The Monetary Affairs Branch of the Hong Kong Government publishes monthly data on the money supply, with a one-month time lag. Forms are sent to all banks and Deposit-taking Companies (DTCs) and must be filed according to the Ordinance governing monetary statistics. Tables 13.1 and 13.2 show the compilation of money supply data in the format in which they are published.

Since, in an exchange economy, people buy things with currency *and* by cheque written on their demand deposit accounts in banks, to arrive at a *measure* of the supply of money the level of demand deposits must be added to currency in the hands of the public.

Currency available for spending consists of all currency issued less the amount that sits in the vaults of banks. Figures in Table 13.1 show the issue of Hong Kong dollars by the two note-issuing commercial banks and by government as a total of 'Legal tender notes and coins in circulation'. From this figure the holdings of notes and coins by banks and DTCs is subtracted, to arrive at a measure of currency available for spending called here 'Legal tender notes and coins in hands of public'.

The demand deposit portion of the money supply appears in the figures in the top line of Table 13.2. The sum of these two items appears in Table 13.1 as 'Money supply (definition 1)'.

It is often useful to draw a distinction between *definitions* and *measures*. The items in Table 13.1 indicate three definitions of the money supply. Perhaps some confusion could be avoided if they were called 'measures' instead. If money is carefully defined, there is only one appropriate measure. In this case it is 'definition 1' and it is usually called M1. The other measures include items other than money *per se* and are called M2 and M3. M2 includes all of M1 plus savings and time

Table 13.1 Currency Circulation and Money Supply as at the End of January 1990 (HK$ million)

	HK$	Foreign Currencies	Total
Legal tender notes and coins in circulation			
Commercial bank issues	45,976	—	45,976
Government issues	2,587	—	2,587
Total	48,563	—	48,563
Banks' and DTCs' holdings of legal tender notes and coins	6,752	—	6,752
Legal tender notes and coins in hands of public	41,811	—	41,811
Money supply (definition 1)	92,014	11,554	103,568
Money supply (definition 2)	412,321	608,851	1,021,172
Money supply (definition 3)	442,867	647,517	1,090,384

Source: Monetary Affairs Branch, Hong Kong Government.

Table 13.2 Deposits from Customers as at the End of January 1990 (HK$ million)

	HK$	Foreign Currencies	Total
Demand deposits with licensed banks	50,203	11,554	61,757
Savings deposits with licensed banks	135,758	58,861	194,619
Time deposits with licensed banks	173,250	533,020	706,270
Total deposits with licensed banks	359,211	603,434	962,645
Deposits with licensed DTCs	8,844	26,398	35,242
Deposits with registered DTCs	20,842	11,784	32,626
Deposits with all DTCs	29,686	38,181	67,868
Deposits with all authorized institutions	388,897	641,615	1,030,512

Source: Monetary Affairs Branch, Hong Kong Government.

deposits. The problem is that no one buys things with a savings deposit. Although an individual may think of himself as holding 'money' in a savings deposit, it is nearly always necessary to transfer funds out of a savings deposit before spending them. An exception occurs when banks permit individuals to pay certain bills out of a savings account by telephone. Such accounts, which permit telephone transfer, are part of the money supply and are part of M1.

M3 includes all of M2 plus deposits in DTCs — deposits that cannot be spent. Thus, M2 and M3 are measures of money plus selected other liquid assets — selected non-money assets that can readily be traded for money.

Technical Treatment of DTC Vault Cash and Deposits

When an individual deposits cash in a bank (not a DTC) in exchange for a cheque deposit, the deposit counts as money but the cash in the bank's vault does not because it is no longer available for spending. To count both vault cash and the deposit would be to double-count. Because of this, when measuring money reporters subtract vault cash, that is, 'bank's and DTC's holdings of legal tender', from all issues of currency as noted in Table 13.1.

But what happens to the money supply when someone deposits currency in a deposit in a DTC? If the DTC deposit is not spendable because it is not a cheque account, then the vault cash in the DTC should not be subtracted when measuring M1. Including the DTCs' vault cash in the measure of money would not be double-counting M1 money since the deposit itself is not directly spendable. DTC vault cash should be treated as money just like cash in any shopkeeper's cash register. Thus, if M1 is the proper measure of money as defined, DTC vault cash should not be deducted. However, if M2 is the measure of money used, then DTC vault cash should be deducted. Since the data are readily available, it would be appropriate to amend their presentation.

Technical Treatment of Government Deposits

It would also be appropriate to remove all government deposits in banks from the money supply figures. To see why, simply assume that the government minted a large amount of coin and held it in a government vault. This coin would not be part of the money supply because it would not be available for people to spend. Measures of the money supply would be infinite if potential amounts that governments could mint and print and pump into an economy were counted as part of the money supply. Thus, it is appropriate to include in measures of money only amounts of money that government has spent and that individuals now hold. It is *not* appropriate for the Monetary Affairs Branch to include, in its measure of deposits, as it now does, government deposits of less than seven days to maturity. It could also remove government time deposits from the M2 measure of money for consistency.

Technical Treatment of Foreign Currency Deposits

Prominently displayed in Table 13.2 are figures on foreign currency deposits held in Hong Kong banks. These are added into the money supply figures presented in Table 13.1. It is interesting to note that, measured by total deposits, the foreign currency deposits exceeded Hong Kong dollar deposits by about 65 per cent on the date in question.

It is useful to keep track of foreign currency asset holdings in the form of deposits in local banks. But foreign currencies are not part of Hong Kong's money supply, and it is misleading to add amounts of the two types of money.

One reason it is misleading is that not all foreign money held by people in Hong Kong is included. For example, Hong Kong citizens and institutions hold large amounts in deposits in banks in other countries. Such deposits are not included here even though they are foreign deposits, too. A second reason it is misleading to pool the two currencies is that, as exchange rates change, the valuation of foreign currency changes while the number of units of foreign currency holdings does not change. Thus, changes in the money supply figures that include foreign deposits must be interpreted with care.[5]

As long as data on money are reported consistently over time, they can usually reveal trends in money growth. Therefore, it is not necessarily crucial to re-do the measures to conform to the technical issues just mentioned. But it is important that analysts be aware of the technical issues. For example, if a sudden change in DTC deposits, or in government deposits, or in foreign deposits, were to occur, analysts might mistakenly interpret these changes as changes in Hong Kong's money supply when in fact Hong Kong's money supply remained constant. Thus, flaws in Hong Kong's money data may not be substantial so long as analysts are aware of the technical issues surrounding the publication of measures of money.

Currency Issue and the Monetary Base

The monetary base of any country consists of those things issued and controllable by the government that provide the basis for money creation. Since a government can control what it issues, it can also control the growth of the money supply by controlling the monetary base. Governments usually provide currency through the minting and issue of coin, and the printing and issue of notes. When governments spend, currency goes into circulation. Individuals deposit currency in banks and use chequing accounts. Banks need only hold a fraction of the deposited currency in their vaults to meet withdrawals. Thus, on the basis of the deposit of currency, banks can make loans and create additional deposit money. This is called the 'fractional reserve' banking system. What banks bank on is not having to pay all their deposit liabilities at once, since vault cash is only a fraction of outstanding deposits. In this case the monetary base is the government issue of currency, part of which is held in the hands of the public and part of which is vault cash held by banks.

When a country has a central bank, banks hold deposits in the central bank. In this case the monetary base consists of the currency that is issued as noted plus the deposits that banks hold as reserves in the central bank.

Turning back to Table 13.1, Hong Kong's monetary base appears as the total of commercial bank issues and Government issues of legal tender notes and coins in circulation. The base also appears as the total of banks' and DTCs' holdings of legal tender notes and coins, and those in the hands of the public. Thus, the base appears twice — categorized once by issuer and once by holder.

It was noted above that the monetary base consists of those items controlled by government. Yet the accounts referred to in Table 13.1 indicate 'commercial bank issues' of legal tender notes. Does government control commercial bank issues of currency? The answer is yes. It does so through special arrangements between the two note-issuing banks and the Exchange Fund, involving an accounting for certificates of indebtedness.

The Exchange Fund and Certificates of Indebtedness

Turbulence in the world economy in the 1930s precipitated many changes in the structure of financial institutions. In 1935 the Government of Hong Kong responded to that turbulence by establishing the Exchange Fund.

The principal reason for the establishment of the Fund, as noted in Section 3 of the Exchange Fund Ordinance, was that it 'shall be used for the purpose of regulating the exchange value of the currency of Hong Kong.' The Fund is held in Hong Kong currency, other currencies, gold, and silver, and may be invested in interest-earning securities such as the gilt-edged securities of the United Kingdom or United States Treasury bills. Through this Fund, the Financial Secretary can buy or sell Hong Kong dollars for foreign exchange in the market and, if the amounts are large enough, push up or down the market value of Hong Kong's currency relative to other currencies.

No data on the Fund's holdings are found here because the Fund does not publish its accounts. Economists believe that more information is preferred to less, and have criticized the Government for keeping the Fund's accounts secret.[6]

A second function of the Exchange Fund may be of greater

importance than the ability to enter the market for Hong Kong dollars. According to Section 4 of the Ordinance, the Financial Secretary may issue certificates of indebtedness to any note-issuing bank. These certificates represent obligations of the Fund. They are held by the note-issuing banks as backing for bank notes that circulate as currency. At the same time, the Financial Secretary requires the bank to pay '... to the account of the Fund the face value of such certificates to be held by the Fund exclusively for the redemption of such notes.'

Thus, the banks hold Certificates of Indebtedness (CIs) as backing for circulating issues of bank notes, and the Fund, in turn, holds assets such as gold, silver, and securities as backing for the CIs.

A sample of changes in selected accounts on the balance sheet of the note-issuing bank demonstrates how the accounts reflect the issue of CIs.

Fig. 13.3   A Sample Note-issuing Bank Balance Sheet

Assets		Liabilities	
3. Certificates of indebtedness (CIs)	+100	1. Notes payable	+100
4. Gold or interest earning assets	−100	2. Demand deposits	−100

Item 1 indicates that the bank pays out 100 worth of bank notes to someone who withdraws equivalent funds from a demand deposit account, item 2. Since there is an increase of 100 in the amount of bank notes outstanding, the note-issuing bank must request additional CIs from the Fund. Item 3 indicates the issue of the Fund's CIs to the bank. Item 4 indicates that the bank gives the Fund assets worth 100 to equal the face value of the certificates issued by the Fund. Thus, highly valued assets that back the currency issue are now held by a government agency, the Exchange Fund.

Presumably the Fund is a more secure place for holding the backing for the currency than the bank. But, security aside, the principal effect of having the Fund hold the backing is that the Fund now earns interest on the assets that the bank has given it. It also serves to gain or lose if the market value of gold fluctuates. With proper management of these assets, however, the Exchange Fund has the ability to earn a great deal of money. The Fund does *not* pay any interest to the banks that hold certificates of indebtedness. Thus, the Exchange Fund earns the *seigniorage* on the outstanding issue of bank notes in Hong Kong. So long as bank notes circulate continuously, the interest earnings on the Fund's holdings of backing generate revenues for Government. Seigniorage is an ancient source of revenues for governments.

Fig. 13.4 A Sample Exchange Fund Balance Sheet

Assets		Liabilities	
2. Gold or interest- earning assets	+100	1. Certificates of indebtendness outstanding	+100

As the items for the Fund's balance sheet indicate, the Fund now has a liability in the form of CIs it has issued to banks and on which it pays no interest. It also has assets in the form that the note-issuing banks provided.[7]

Returning now to the concept of Hong Kong's monetary base, it is understood that the volume of commercial bank issues of legal tender notes will equal the volume of CIs outstanding. Since the Fund, an agency of Government, has control over the issue of CIs, it also has the authority to control the monetary base.

Controlling the Growth of the Monetary Base: A Proposal

Under current procedures, the Fund issues CIs at the request of the note-issuing banks. The Fund's role in the issue of CIs is passive. The interest-earning asset that the Fund receives from the note-issuing bank is simply a deposit account denominated in United States dollars *in the note-issuing bank*. The Fund can use these United States dollars to purchase investments of its choice for backing the currency. But what matters is that the Fund exercises no limit on its willingness to issue CIs. The monetary base expands at the banks' behest. Thus Hong Kong's money supply expands whenever a bank manager considers that the extra value of a loan to the bank's profit position exceeds the extra cost of the liabilities created by the lending activity. This is the loose link in the money creation process under current institutional arrangements. There is no direct control over the extent of monetary base creation.

In years past many economists believed that money growth should be adjusted to counteract cycles or fluctuations in business activity. Thus, if business was depressed, money should be made to grow so that interest rates would fall and investment spending and consumer spending would create employment opportunities. And if the economy suffered from inflation, the money supply should contract so that interest rates would rise and inhibit borrowing and spending. Thus, through tight money and high interest rates, economic activity and inflation would be brought under control. But many monetarists have argued that, although a contra-cyclical monetary policy may be desirable in theory, in practice it would be better to follow a monetary growth rule.[8]

If one can expect real growth of 5 per cent per year, on the basis of experience of saving behaviour and productivity generally, then a 5 per cent growth in money would accommodate the 5 per cent real growth without inflation. For example, assume the demand curve in Fig. 13.2 shifted to the right by 5 per cent as a result of economic growth. If the supply of money also shifted to the right by 5 per cent, the two curves would intersect at the same height as before. Both the interest rate level and the price level would remain unchanged.

Large economies, with a large government sector and a considerable portion of the economy subject to regulation, may need to regulate not only money growth but also spending and taxing. But a small economy characterized by a small government sector is precisely the sort of economy that could achieve a large measure of economic stability through the imposition of a policy of steady money growth.

It would be simple for the Exchange Fund to announce a policy of allowing the issue of CIs to grow at the rate of 0.5 per cent per month, or at 6 per cent per year compounded monthly. Limiting the growth of this part of the monetary base would limit the growth of the supply of Hong Kong dollars. Inflation would be brought under control.

As it stands now, all banks other than the two note-issuing banks must maintain sufficient reserves to meet withdrawal demand in the form of base money or in the form of inter-bank deposits that can be redeemed in base money. Under a steady growth of CIs, the two note-issuing banks would be brought under the same constraints. If they needed more CIs than they had on hand, they would enter the inter-bank market to buy Hong Kong dollar notes so they could meet withdrawals, just as other banks now must do when necessary. Also, special provisions could be made for supplying CIs in case of some unforeseen contingency.

The Operations of Typical Central Banks

Historical circumstances guide each central bank into its own unique methods of operation. But basically central banks have four means of controlling money.

1. Changes in Required Reserve Ratios.   Banks and other financial institutions that issue cheque deposit money must have an account with the central bank. The funds in this account must be kept at some minimum ratio of the bank's outstanding deposit liabilities, say 10 per cent. An administered increase in this ratio reduces the ability of a bank to make loans and create money on the basis of any given volume of reserves on deposit with the central bank. A reduction in the required reserve ratio encourages banks to lend and create more deposit money.

2. Changes in Loan Interest Rates.   A central bank can lend reserve funds to a bank. Such loans enable the bank, in turn, to expand loans to its customers, creating deposit money in the process. Thus, by

reducing the interest rate charged on loans to banks, the central bank can encourage borrowing and money creation. When the central bank raises the interest cost to banks it discourages bank lending and money creation.

3. Changes in the Volume of Bank Reserves. A central bank can buy an item, usually a financial security of some type, in the market-place. The seller of the security is given a cheque on the central bank. To collect the cheque, the seller must deposit it in a bank. The bank then sends the cheque to the central bank, where the individual bank's reserve account is increased by the amount of the cheque. With larger bank reserves available to meet reserve requirements, banks can lend and create money. When a central bank buys something in the open market, bank reserves are increased and money expansion is possible. When it sells something bank reserves fall. Such activities are called 'open market operations'.

4. Moral Suasion. A central bank may simply tell managers of banks to limit their deposit creation to certain amounts. Banks must respond if they are to remain in the good graces of the government. It is assumed that the government acts in the interests of the people and the economy.

Even if Hong Kong's Exchange Fund were to set limits on the issue of certificates of indebtedness, it would hardly be a central bank. However, it would be limiting the creation of reserves just as central banks have authority to do.

Issues in Monetary Policy and Central Banking

Individual prices that are free to fluctuate relative to other individual prices are the *sine qua non* of a free enterprise economic system. High prices encourage supply. Low prices discourage supply. Resources move away from low-priced endeavours into high-priced ones. Thus, fluctuating prices provide information used to guide resources into their most productive activities. So long as resources are free to move and relative prices are free to guide, economic activity will be efficient, productivity will be high, standards of living will grow, and people will prosper.

While individual prices must be free to fluctuate, it is important *not* to let the general level of prices fluctuate. Inflation and deflation reflect changes in the purchasing power of units of money used as a medium of exchange in the economy. By controlling the total quantity of units of money that circulates in the economy, a severe constraint is placed on the extent to which inflation or deflation can occur. Thus, free enterprise economies work best when relative prices are free to fluctuate and guide resource allocation while the average level of prices remains steady. Free enterprise flounders when money is out of control.

It is important to remember that the *purpose* of the architects of Hong Kong's fixed exchange rate system *was to bring the money supply under control.*[9] Economists nearly all agree that exchange rates are relative prices and should be free to fluctuate like other individual prices if resources involved in international trade are to be allocated efficiently. However, under special circumstances it is possible to bring the money supply under control by fixing an exchange rate.

Controlling Money under a Fixed Exchange Rate System

On 17 October 1983, the Government had the Exchange Fund fix the price of CIs. A bank must pay US$100 for every HK$780 it receives in CIs from the Fund. The Fund will also redeem CIs at the same rate of exchange — US$1 for every HK$7.80 turned in to the Fund. This system of fixed exchange rates is sometimes called a 'pegged system' or a 'linked system' in which the Hong Kong dollar is linked to the United States dollar. Under a pure pegged system the Fund would stand ready to buy and sell unlimited amounts of United States and Hong Kong dollars at the going rate in the market for foreign exchange. The current system involves less direct intervention in the foreign exchange market because the Fund is a passive actor, and the market price of United States dollars varies slightly within a narrow range before banks approach the Fund for accommodation. Thus, the term 'linked system' is perhaps more accurate. It is a matter of detail only.

The classical example of a fixed exchange rate system is the *gold standard*. Therefore a very brief review of the working of the gold standard is in order (see also the discussion of the gold standard in Chapter 12).

Under the gold standard a unit of currency is defined in terms of an amount of gold, and gold either circulates in the form of coin or is used to back the government's issues of notes and/or the reserves of the banks that issue notes. Institutional arrangements varied greatly in the past, but the basic economic forces that propelled the gold standard as a device to regulate the money supply worked as follows.

When, for whatever reason, goods are cheap at home, more goods will be exported. Exports will exceed imports, and exporters will accept gold in exchange for their exported goods. Since gold either is money, or backs money, the supply of money increases as gold flows into the economy. Banks have more reserves and more lending ability. As they compete for loans they will lower interest rates. With more money and more loans, people will increase spending. This will only lead to inflation if the economy is at, or near, full employment.

But inflation means that foreigners who earlier bought goods from exporters will now find the prices too high. They will buy less. Inflation also means that foreign goods are cheaper than domestic goods. Importers buy more goods and use gold to pay for them. The gold flow is reversed. Gold flows out of the country. Since gold is money, the outflow of gold pushes interest rates up and, eventually, prices are pushed back down.

The unpalatable part of this system is that the money supply goes through cycles — first expanding and causing inflation and then contracting to cause unemployment and depression. On top of this, gold discoveries cause the base of the money supply to increase, thus introducing instability in price levels and foreign trade. Instability drives governments to 'sterilize' or vitiate the impact of gold flows on the domestic economy. Gold standards are not viable politically over the longer term.

The gold standard mechanism shows, by analogy, how Hong Kong's fixed exchange system is intended to control Hong Kong's money supply.

Hong Kong's exporters sell goods to the United States and earn United States dollars. But in order to pay their workers, exporters must sell United States dollars to banks to obtain Hong Kong dollars. Banks in Hong Kong turn United States dollars in to the Exchange Fund for CIs and issue Hong Kong dollars. Hong Kong's money supply increases.

As shown in Fig. 13.2, an increase in the money supply leads to a decline in interest rates. Spending then increases, and eventually the general level of prices begins to rise. Inflation means that exporters cannot compete any longer and they sell less to the United States. Importers find United States goods cheaper and import more. The supply of United States dollars declines and demand for them increases. The price of United States dollars is fixed and does not respond to supply and demand forces. Instead, local people turn in Hong Kong dollars, and, through the banks, obtain United States dollars that are in great demand. The supply of Hong Kong dollars falls, interest rates rise, spending is dampened, and inflation stopped.

In this fashion, Hong Kong's money supply is controlled through fixing the exchange rate to the United States dollar. The balance of trade rather than the rate of exchange absorbs shocks to the system, and the entire economy swings in order to keep the money supply constant. Surely it would be better to fix the money supply and let it be an anchor to hold the economy in place.

Speculation and the Importance of Relative Interest Rates

The classical analysis of money control under fixed exchange rates presented above pays inadequate attention to the importance of international capital flows. An attempt to remedy this inadequacy follows.

Above, the supply of United States dollars depended on exports. But, if interest earnings on Hong Kong dollars lie above interest earnings on United States dollars, people who hold United States dollars will turn them in for Hong Kong dollars so they can invest them and earn higher yields. The supply of Hong Kong dollars increases and interest rates on Hong Kong dollar deposits and other investments fall back into a position in which further shifts of funds into and out of United States dollars are no longer attractive. Thus relative interest rates play an important role in the money control process in Hong Kong.

The anticipated yield on a United States dollar denominated security depends not only on the interest rate being paid, but also on the anticipated foreign exchange rate expected to prevail when the security matures. If people expect the Hong Kong dollar to appreciate in value against the United States dollar, they will turn in United States dollar holdings and demand Hong Kong dollars. The Exchange Fund will take the United States dollars that are offered and issue CIs, and so the note-issuing banks can expand the supply of Hong Kong dollars. These will be offered as deposits to banks, and banks will be flooded with deposits and lower the interest they are willing to pay depositors.

Fig. 13.5 illustrates the situation. As more and more investors switch out of United States dollars, the Hong Kong dollar supply increases since the Fund accommodates the demand at the fixed exchange rate. The vertical money supply curve shifts rightward steadily and interest yields on Hong Kong dollars decline.

Fig. 13.5   Increasing Supplies of Hong Kong Dollars

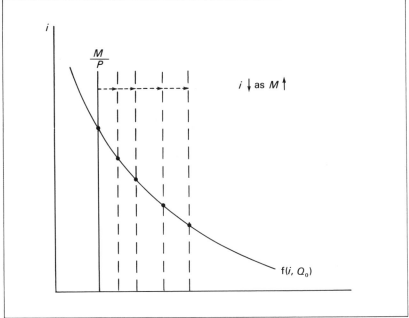

The situation just described has occurred more than once. In September 1985 the United States, in association with other countries, indicated that the value of the United States dollar on foreign exchange markets was too high and should be lowered. A steady decline of the foreign exchange value of the United States dollar against the Japanese yen and German mark began, which continued until the decline reached over 30 per cent. Of course, Hong Kong's dollar, tied to the United States dollar, declined as well. But Hong Kong's dollar was not as weak as the United States dollar, so the people of Hong Kong believed the Hong Kong dollar should appreciate in value relative to the United States dollar. It would have appreciated had the fixed exchange rate system not been in place. Anticipating that the Government might lower the pegged price of HK$7.80 for US$1, people turned in United States dollars and got Hong Kong dollars. If the price of a United States dollar fell, say, to HK$6.80, those people would be able to buy back United States dollars for a great deal less.

In January 1988 trade representatives from the United States and Europe strongly suggested that Hong Kong should revalue the Hong Kong dollar upward against the United States dollar. In response, people continued to turn in United States dollars and the Fund kept creating Hong Kong dollars. Hong Kong's money supply expanded, interest rates on Hong Kong dollar deposits fell to 1 per cent. People would accept only 1 per cent on Hong Kong dollar deposits and give up 6 per cent on United States dollar deposits. The interest rate differential was not large enough to compensate, given the probability that Hong Kong's dollar would appreciate.[10]

Interest rates got so low that in 1988 a proposal to permit a tax to be levied on certain types of Hong Kong dollar deposits was adopted. Having a tax on deposits would essentially mean that the yield or interest return on a Hong Kong dollar deposit would become negative. As it turned out the tax was not imposed, but remains available as a tool should the need arise again.

Negative interest rates are an anomaly. Hong Kong's money supply grew rapidly. Monetary statistics for August 1988 indicate that 'During the twelve months ending August HK$M1 . . . grew by 28.1 per cent.'[11] Inflationary pressures followed.

All of this turbulence was the expected outcome of a system that is designed to control the money supply over the long term through fixing the price of foreign exchange.

What would have happened had the price of United States dollars been permitted to fluctuate freely? The price of United States dollars would have fallen to, say, HK$6.80 each on the local market. The Hong Kong dollar would have strengthened relative to the United States dollar as did the yen and mark. With the new lower price, holders of United States dollars would have suffered a capital loss, but would have had no reason to sell them after the loss was recognized. Hong Kong's money supply would not have increased. Interest rates would not have fallen to bottom levels. Inflation would not have followed.

A caveat is in order at this point. Hong Kong's money supply would not increase in the scenario as described *provided money growth had some anchor.*

Intervention in the Hong Kong Inter-bank Borrowing Market

In July 1988 the Monetary Affairs Branch began a process of intervention in the Hong Kong inter-bank market. The procedures are described in Chapter 2 where the focus is upon the role of the Hongkong and Shanghai Banking Corporation in Hong Kong's financial system. The reader may wish to review the appropriate section in that chapter before continuing. Here intervention is approached from the point of view of the Exchange Fund's role in injecting or withdrawing liquidity from the inter-bank borrowing market.

Before proceeding it is important to note that these intervention arrangements are designed precisely in order to bring more stability to interest rates in Hong Kong. That is, Government authorities recognized that the linked exchange rate system generated undesirable side effects in the form of gyrating interest rates. The fundamental question is whether linking the currency's value *and* controlling interest rates will be compatible with the goal of controlling the money supply. Economic theory suggests that it is not possible to control both the exchange rate and interest rates simultaneously.

Before elaborating on this concern it is important to extend the discussion of the mechanics of intervention into the inter-bank borrowing market beyond that found in Chapter 2.

The Market for Exchange Fund Bills

On Tuesday, 3 March 1990, the Exchange Fund conducted its first weekly auction of Exchange Fund bills. The amount auctioned was HK$300 million. The three-month bills mature in 13 weeks and have a life of 91 days except that the life may be 90 or 92 days in case a holiday should happen to fall on the usual date of maturity. The plan is to sell between HK$200–300 million each week so that after 13 weeks there will be an outstanding volume of approximately HK$3–4 billion. In the first offering, over HK$2 billion in bids were received and the average accepted yield was 8.04 per cent. On the day of the offering HIBOR was 9 per cent on three-month funds. Given the default-free quality of Exchange Fund bills it is reasonable to expect that they would pay lower yields than any other security of the same maturity. In finance literature in future the yield on Exchange Fund bills will be used as a proxy for the 'risk free' interest rate.

Out of approximately 100 recognized bills dealers in Hong Kong, an exclusive group of 14 were selected by the Government to be market makers in the secondary market. While all dealers can bid in the auctions for their own account and as agents for their customers, at this time the Government plans to trade regularly only with the group of 14.

When a government issues securities to borrow money it usually does so in order to obtain the funds needed to make expenditures, that is, to deficit spend or to debt-finance a project. In this case, however, the purpose behind the creation of about HK$4 billion of Government debt was merely to provide a security to be used as a medium for Exchange Fund intervention. Individuals and businesses will find that a default-free investment medium is useful, and it can be argued that government should provide such a debt instrument to the market just as it provides the useful debt instrument we call money. But in this case the issues of Exchange Fund bills were to give the Government something to buy when it wanted to inject funds into the inter-bank market, and something to sell when it wanted to absorb funds out of the market. It could have bought and sold anything else — gold or securities or foreign exchange. But it wanted to have something it could buy and sell that would have only indirect effects on the prices of other commodities or securities. The Government does not want to be accused of speculating in gold or foreign exchange so it now has a market for its own bills to speculate in.

The Mechanics of Intervention Using Exchange Fund Bills

By examining changes in various balance sheet items on the accounts of the Exchange Fund and on the accounts of the Hongkong and Shanghai Banking Corporation one gains insight into the intervention process. Since the Government does not publish the Exchange Fund's balance sheet, a precise description of items is not possible. Therefore, the author is forced to invent account names, so that what follows here is only a caricature that tries to bring out the essence of intervention activity.

In Fig. 13.6 there appears a selected sample of items that would appear in the balance sheet of the HSBC. Similarly, Fig. 13.7 shows relevant items that appear on the Exchange Fund's balance sheet.

Fig. 13.6 A Sample HSBC Balance Sheet

Assets		Liabilities	
Certificates of indebtedness		Notes payable	
Foreign assets		Demand deposits	
		Treasury deposits	
Domestic assets		Exchange Fund deposits	
Loans			
and others		Inter-bank clearing deposits	
		Bank A	−100
THE ACCOUNT at the		Bank B	
Exchange Fund	−100	Band C	
		and others	
			____
		Net clearing balance	−100

Fig. 13.7 The Exchange Fund's Intervention Accounts

Assets	Liabilities	
Foreign assets	Certificate of indebtedness	

Domestic assets
  Deposits in HSBC
  and others
	Treasury deposits
	(Debt certificates issued to
	the Treasury)	

	THE ACCOUNT	−100
	Exchange Fund bills outstanding	+100

The Clearing House of the Hong Kong Association of Banks is managed by the HSBC. There are 10 settlement banks in Hong Kong that maintain clearing balances at the HSBC and about 140 sub-settlement banks that maintain accounts with the settlement banks. The Clearing House is the only institution allowed to provide clearing service in Hong Kong. Therefore, the net clearing balance of the rest of the banking system is reflected in the balance sheet of the HSBC. In Fig. 13.6 the bank clearing balances are represented on the liabilities side of the balance sheet.

A large positive net clearing balance indicates there are lots of funds available to banks. Banks will offer their surplus funds into the inter-bank borrowing market and the Hong Kong Inter-bank Offered Rate, HIBOR, will fall. If there is a shortage of liquidity in the net clearing balances, there will be a tendency for HIBOR to rise.

If liquidity is too high and HIBOR is falling, the Government may wish to absorb some of the liquid funds. With an outstanding supply of Exchange Fund bills in the market the Exchange Fund can add to the supply by selling some to individuals, businesses, or banks. If it sells HK$100 in bills to an individual, that individual will give the Exchange Fund a cheque on, say, Bank A. On the Exchange Fund's balance sheet, Fig. 13.7, the liability account recording Exchange Fund bills outstanding will an increase by 100 as shown. The Fund will collect the cheque by reducing THE ACCOUNT, maintained by the HSBC according to the new rules, by 100 as shown. The HSBC will be notified and in Fig. 13.6 THE ACCOUNT showing an asset with the Exchange Fund will be reduced. Since the cheque was drawn on Bank A, its account will be reduced, and barring other offsetting changes the net clearing balance will also fall. In this fashion a sale of the new Exchange Fund bills will reduce net clearing balances and the liquidity of the inter-bank borrowing market. With this reduced liquidity HIBOR may rise, may not fall, or may not fall by as much as it otherwise would have fallen.

In case the Exchange Fund should wish to add liquidity to the banking system it would enter the bill market and buy some of its bills. The change in the accounts for the HK$100 sale of bills now shown in Figs. 13.6 and 13.7 would simply have their signs reversed if the Fund bought bills instead. If the Fund bought bills and retired them from the market it would give a cheque for HK$100 to the individual from whom it bought them, and the individual would deposit this cheque in the bank, say Bank A. The net clearing balance would increase. The HSBC would see the cheque was on THE ACCOUNT and would increase it by 100. Then it would send the cheque to the Exchange Fund where it would record the increase along with the decrease in the amount of its bills outstanding of 100.

So far the new procedures seem straightforward. However, another provision dictated by the new procedures is that THE ACCOUNT should not fall below the net clearing balance. In the examples above both balance sheet items increased and decreased together. Thus, equality of the two accounts was maintained. However, a problem could arise as in the following example.

Assume that the HSBC makes a loan to a local business so that the domestic asset item shown as loans on the HSBC balance shows an increase of, say, 100. (To avoid clutter in the balance sheet and to save the space required to provide balance sheets for every example, the reader is asked to follow through the discussion of the appropriate entries and imagine the outcomes.) Assume the loan was originally made in the form of a demand deposit so that that liability item increases by 100. However, assume that the individual spends this deposit and buys a machine from someone who banks in Bank B. Upon receipt of the cheque, seller of the machine will deposit the cheque in Bank B and it will enter the clearing process. Demand deposits in HSBC will fall and Bank B's clearing balance will increase by 100. Thus, by expanding its loans the HSBC was sometimes unwittingly pumping reserves into the inter-bank borrowing market. According to a spokesman from the Exchange Fund, this is where a slippage in control permitted wide swings in liquidity positions of banks.

The solution was to require that THE ACCOUNT be kept at or above the net clearing balance. In this example, THE ACCOUNT would not increase along with the net clearing balance. In this case the HSBC has two choices. It may deposit an interest-earning asset into THE ACCOUNT at the Fund so that the Fund will have an additional liability and an additional asset.

THE ACCOUNT at the Fund does not pay interest — THE ACCOUNT at the HSBC does not earn interest. Therefore, with the transfer just described the Fund will now have interest-earning assets. This interest represents seigniorage to the Fund.

If the HSBC does not deposit additional assets with the Fund, it is required to pay interest on the difference between THE ACCOUNT and the net clearing balance, that is, on the shortfall. The interest levied will be either the best lending rate or HIBOR, whichever is highest. Provisions exist for the rate charged to be 3 per cent over these rates after the deficiency of funds in THE ACCOUNT exceeds a certain level.

Other factors will also affect the state of balance between THE ACCOUNT and the net clearing balance. Important among these is the activity of the Treasury. Assume that the Treasury has a considerable balance of funds in its account in Bank C. The Treasury may be asked to place these funds with the Exchange Fund in return for a debt certificate shown as a liability on the Exchange Fund's balance sheet. THE ACCOUNT in the Fund will be reduced and it will also be reduced on the books of the HSBC along with Bank C's balance as part of the net clearing balance. Thus, a transfer of funds from Treasury accounts in banks into the Fund will result in a decline in liquidity in the inter-bank market. Such changes may support the Fund's policy at times and work against the Fund's policy at other times. With the new procedures in place the Fund can offset effects on liquidity from other sources if it wishes to do so.

The Hongkong Inter-bank Offered Rate (HIBOR) is the bell-wether rate that is watched carefully by financial market participants in order to gain a sense of direction about interest rate movements. The Monetary Affairs Branch may buy securities in order to inject funds into the market. This injection of funds will either push HIBOR down or at least prevent HIBOR from rising more rapidly than it otherwise would.

The authorities will announce that their trades in the market are to stabilize a disorderly market. They will not claim that they are trying to set interest rates in the market. Claims like this are important because everyone agrees that disorderly markets are bad. Most also agree that setting interest rates by government intervention is bad, too. So, for political acceptability, intervention must be explained as necessary for correcting disorderly conditions in the markets.

If the Monetary Affairs Branch wants to absorb liquidity from the inter-bank market it will sell securities to dealers in the newly established Exchange Fund bills market. This action will push HIBOR up. Most attacks against the linked exchange rate system have been directed toward increasing the value of Hong Kong's dollar against the United States dollar. In these instances everyone wants to hold Hong Kong dollars so the supply increases and interest rates fall to very low levels. To prevent such declines in the future, the Monetary Affairs Branch now considers that it has in place an arrangement for absorbing the liquidity that leads to such drastic declines in interest rates.

Unfortunately, in a free economy it is always the case that when one price is fixed economic forces make it necessary to fix another and another and yet another price. Both exchange rates and interest rates are prices. Fixing one makes it necessary to fix the other. But holding interest rates fixed means abandoning the automatic control mechanism that is supposed to regulate the money supply under the linked exchange rate system. Absorbing reserves of banks in order to keep HIBOR up means reducing the money supply. Domestic inflation will not occur. Exports will expand. Earnings of United States dollars will increase. Most people will want to turn their United States dollars in for Hong Kong dollars. To hold interest rates up in Hong Kong the Fund will have to absorb even more reserves — and so the cycle goes. The automatic adjustment mechanism has been switched off. The new system may *appear* to be operating smoothly so long as the Fund only enters the market to correct disorderly conditions. The difficulty will be in distinguishing orderly from disorderly movements in interest rates — an impossible task.

The Fixed Exchange Rate Myth

People argue that abandoning the fixed exchange regime, and replacing it with a system of control over the growth in the supply of Hong Kong dollars, will permit great instability in the value of the currency. They argue that even though growth is controlled, speculation against the Hong Kong dollar will surely drive down its value in the run-up to 1997. They are promoting a myth. The reason is that the value of the Hong Kong dollar, like the value of any currency, is represented by its power over the purchase of goods and services in the domestic economy, not its power over the purchase of United States dollars. Over the longer term it is only when the money supply expands and inflation follows that a currency becomes worthless. There is no reason for the government of Hong Kong to run up excessive amounts of Hong Kong dollars as 1997 approaches. Therefore, if Hong Kong takes direct control of its money and prevents inflation there is no reason to believe that speculation against the Hong Kong dollar will occur, let alone succeed in damaging the Hong Kong economy.

To address the issue specifically let us consider alternative scenarios. First, assume that the people of Hong Kong have full faith and trust in the new government and expect both economic and political stability after 1997. There is then no reason to expect speculation against the Hong Kong dollar.

Second, consider a money supply control regime as outlined above, with no fixed exchange rate, and assume that the people of Hong Kong do not trust in the future. Those who can leave will do so. Those who have property will offer it to the market. Prices will fall. Deflation follows. As prices fall the Hong Kong dollar *rises* in value — in its purchasing power. After selling their property, people will offer Hong Kong dollars to buy foreign exchange. The price of United States dollars and other foreign currencies will rise. This makes Hong Kong property even cheaper in terms of United States dollars as the Hong Kong dollar depreciates against foreign exchange, but appreciates in purchasing power in Hong Kong.

These changes in the purchasing power of the Hong Kong dollar will discourage those who might otherwise wish to leave Hong Kong. Foreign exchange is expensive, so it is costly to leave. Those who have foreign exchange to sell find that their exchange buys lots of Hong Kong dollars — dollars that go far in Hong Kong. Foreign investors who have faith in the future of Hong Kong will be encouraged by the low price and high purchasing power of the Hong Kong dollar in Hong Kong. Those who must remain in Hong Kong will also find that they are able to acquire property on very reasonable terms and thus others will be encouraged to remain.

There is a limit to the deflation in Hong Kong and also a limit to the decline in the foreign exchange value of the Hong Kong dollar.

On the other hand, consider a third scenario. Let the fixed exchange rate system continue. As before, as 1997 approaches those people who lack faith in the future of Hong Kong will sell their properties. Prices will tend to fall. Deflation results, as before. But now, under fixed exchange rates, the situation changes. As people turn in whatever Hong Kong dollars they accumulate they are paid United States dollars at the fixed rate. In these circumstances, those who lack faith in Hong Kong's future will benefit from a guaranteed rate of exchange.

Hong Kong's money supply will dwindle as those who leave turn in Hong Kong dollars for foreign exchange, and as the Exchange Fund pays out the reserves of foreign exchange. Interest rates will sky-rocket with the decline in the money supply and the Government will be hard pressed. The longer it resists a run-up in the value of the United States dollar the more difficult it will be. People who wish to leave simply sell their properties and turn in Hong Kong dollars in order to take United States dollars with them. Property prices may collapse. Hong Kong dollars will be in such scarce supply they will soon become valuable as currency always does in a deflation.

Thus, the fixed exchange rate will assist the transfer of wealth out of Hong Kong and thereby assist those who are able to leave. As the supply of Hong Kong currency is redeemed with the Exchange Fund through the retirement of CIs, the Fund will pay out its holdings of securities and other valuable assets. All of this is sure to happen under the fixed exchange regime unless the people of Hong Kong come to believe that mainland China will, in fact, leave Hong Kong alone for another 50 years.

Commentators frequently remark on the wonder of the fixed exchange rate system and give it credit for saving Hong Kong's dollar in October 1983. The argument presented here is that it could have been saved just as well with a program for control over money supply growth through control over the growth in the monetary base. This control could exist with or without a central bank.[12]

The argument here is also that the economics of the two means of ensuring that the Hong Kong dollar remains valuable suggests that the two means serve different groups. Those who plan to leave Hong Kong in 1997 are best served by the fixed system because it assures their abilities to take their wealth with them. Those who want to leave but are unable to, and who hold United States dollars, would be better served by a system of control over the money supply that permits the price of foreign exchange to rise. They could then sell their holdings of United States dollars for high prices in Hong Kong dollars to those who want to leave.

Summary

The government of Hong Kong does not have a central bank. It does not need a central bank in order to control Hong Kong's money supply. However, the fixed exchange rate system has led the Monetary Affairs Branch to begin acting as though it were a central bank when, for instance, it enters the inter-bank borrowing market to stabilize interest rates.

The principal objective of a central bank, or equivalent monetary authority, is to control the supply of money. Control over the money supply is needed to prevent inflation and to provide for efficiency in the exchange of goods in a market economy.

It is often said that under the fixed exchange system that Hong Kong adopted in 1983 the money supply is 'market determined'. This also implies, of course, that the money supply varies at the whim of the market, and that interest rates in Hong Kong are subject to swings in level as the money supply swings. The graphs of Figs. 13.1, 13.2, and 13.5 were used to describe the relation between interest rates and the money supply.

If control over money is the principal objective of a central bank, it is important to know precisely what money is and what money does. Money is defined as anything used to discharge debt in an exchange economy. It is measured by adding currency and demand deposits in banks.

Different economic policies affect different groups of people in different ways. Under the fixed exchange system, interest rates tend to be relatively unstable. In general, under a system of control over money supply growth, interest rates will be more stable but the price of foreign exchange will be variable. Since a market economy is guided by fluctuating prices that absorb shocks to the system, it is more efficient to allow both interest rates and foreign exchange prices to vary.

But the fixed exchange rate system helps provide passage for those individuals and businesses who plan to leave Hong Kong during the first six months of 1997. They will be able to take with them a good portion of the foreign exchange reserves that the Exchange Fund holds.

Space does not permit a complete analysis of Hong Kong's future under different possible monetary policies implemented by a central banking authority or by the patchwork of controls instituted by Government. But one item missing from all the discussion concerns who stands to benefit from one type of policy or another. This author hopes that, in Hong Kong's free society, people will begin to discuss forthrightly the effects of different policy stands on different interest groups.

Appendix

Hong Kong's Monetary Base

The purpose of this appendix is to describe the components of the monetary base and the relation of the base to the money supply, and also to indicate the utility of increasing the Exchange Fund's authority to allow it to control Hong Kong's money supply.

The volume of CIs issued by the Exchange Fund as backing for the currency issued by the two note-issuing banks, along with the volume of coins issued by the Government, comprise Hong Kong's monetary base. A very small change in the wording of the Exchange Fund Ordinance would give the Fund discretion in the issue of CIs. With such authority, the Exchange Fund could announce a policy of allowing Hong Kong's currency supply to grow at a given rate each month. It is assumed that the Government would issue coins in response to demand and that coin issue would grow proportionally with CIs. Steady control over the growth of the monetary base would provide control over the growth of the money supply in Hong Kong.

The terms to be used in this discussion of the components of the monetary base are listed in Table 13A.1.

Table 13A.1 A List of Monetary Terms

Abbreviation	Meaning
M	Money
C	Currency in circulation in public hands
D	Demand deposits of all licensed banks
S	Savings deposits
T	Time deposits
B	Monetary base
R	Bank reserves (equals vault cash)
V	Vault cash
CI	Certificates of indebtedness
GI	Government issue of coin

The total money supply is some multiple of the base, that is:

$$M = mB, \quad \text{or} \quad m = \frac{M}{B}.$$

Money consists of currency in circulation in the hands of the public plus demand deposits, that is:

$$M = C + D.$$

The monetary base consists of currency in public circulation plus bank vault cash reserves $(R = V)$, that is:

$$B = C + R = C + V.$$

Therefore:

$$m = \frac{M}{B} = \frac{C + D}{C + V}.$$

Let $C = kD$, or $k = C/D$, where the ratio k is called the currency ratio and reflects the preference of the public for holding cash as compared with deposits.

Let $R = r(D + S + T)$, or $r = R/(D + S + T)$, where the ratio r is called the reserve ratio and reflects the preference of banks for holding vault cash reserves against all their deposits.

Let $S = sD$, or $s = S/D$, where the ratio s is simply called the savings deposit ratio and reflects the preference of the public for holding part of their spending money in savings deposits.

Let $T = tD$, or $t = T/D$ where the t ratio reflects the preference of the public for holding time deposits.

By substitution of these ratios into the equation for m we have:

$$m = \frac{kD + D}{kD + r(D + S + T)}.$$

Dividing all terms in both numerator and denominator by D gives:

$$m = \frac{k + 1}{k + r(1 + s + t)}.$$

The ratio of currency in circulation in public hands to demand deposits was .83 at the end of 1990. That is, out of every HK$100, about HK$45.4 was in the form of currency and HK$54.6 was in the form of cheque accounts.

The ratio of bank vault cash to total deposits in licensed banks was much less. It was only .019. Thus banks held only about HK$1.90 in cash in their vaults as reserves against the possibility of a withdrawal of a deposit of HK$100. The reserve ratio is quite low in comparison with that in other countries. It reflects the absence of legal reserve requirements and the absence of a need for cash reserves on the part of note-issuing banks, since they rely on the Exchange Fund. If a program of control over the growth of CIs were implemented, this ratio could be expected to rise as note-issuing banks would want to increase their holdings of vault cash.

The end of January 1990 data from Tables 13.1 and 13.2 give the following figures:

$$M = 92,014 \qquad C = 41,811 \qquad D = 50,203$$

$$S = 135,758 \qquad T = 173,250 \qquad V = 6,752$$

$$D + S + T = 359,211.$$

Thus:

$$k = \frac{C}{D} = 0.833$$

$$s = \frac{S}{D} = 2.704$$

$$r = \frac{V}{D + S + T} = 0.019$$

$$t = \frac{T}{D} = 3.451$$

$$m = \frac{M}{B} = \frac{C + D}{C + V} = 1.89.$$

Therefore $M = 1.89B$, where B is the monetary base and M is the money supply. If the base multiplier, m, stays more or less steady, a steady rate of growth in B will be followed by a steady rate of growth in M.

The ratio m will, of course, be subject to change whenever the other ratios change. For example, if banks become more restrictive they may increase r. This will reduce m and lead to a reduction in M. The ratios are such that an increase in k will cause m to decline, and, therefore, cause M to decline as well. Similar concerns are relevant to the other ratios in the equation for m.

Notes

1. In July 1988, the Monetary Affairs Branch instituted a system for buying and selling Hong Kong dollars in the Hong Kong Inter-bank Borrowing market, the effect of which is to put pressure on interest rates in this short-term bell-wether market.
2. Thomas Mayer presents an excellent review of Hume's work in 'David Hume and Monetarism', *Quarterly Journal of Economics*, Volume 92, August 1980, pp. 89–101.
3. For a review of the Quantity Theory see Thomas M. Humphrey, 'The Quantity Theory of Money', *Essays on Inflation*, Federal Reserve Bank of Richmond, 1981.
4. Many statistical studies contain estimates of the demand for money function. For example, one study using cross-section data and a long-linear form of equation reports that the income elasticity of demand for money is near 0.80. This is interpreted to mean

that if family income increased by 10 per cent, the amount of money families would hold would increase 8 per cent. It also showed that the interest elasticity of demand for money was near −0.40. This means that if interest rates doubled (a 100 per cent increase in interest rates) families would hold 40 per cent less money. Eight other X variables were examined as well. See Lawrence J. Radecki and Cecily C. Garver, 'The Household Demand for Money: Estimates from Cross-sectional Data', *Quarterly Review*, Federal Reserve Bank of New York, Spring 1987, pp. 29–34.

5. A Monetary Statistics Ordinance was implemented in 1980. See reviews of it in *Asian Monetary Monitor*, September–October 1981 and November–December 1982.

6. See John Greenwood, 'Hong Kong Authorities Keep a Big Secret', *Wall Street Journal*, 7 December 1988.

7. The balance sheet items described above are simple summaries of the outcome. Space limitations do not allow complete descriptions. Until 1974, banks were required to give the Fund assets such as gold for the CIs. Later, from 1974 to 1983, the Fund accepted a Hong Kong dollar deposit account in the note-issuing bank instead. Thus, the bank balance sheet above would show a liability to the Exchange Fund of +100 rather than a reduction in gold or other assets. However, the Fund can use the extra 100 however it chooses, and when it buys gold or assets from the market, the Fund's assets shift from a deposit in the bank to the holding of the asset. The only difference is that the Fund need not take assets directly from the note-issuing bank itself. As of 17 October 1984, the Fund began to require that it be given a United States dollar account instead of a Hong Kong dollar account.

8. See Milton Friedman, *A Program for Monetary Stability* (New York, Fordham University Press, 1959), p. 98.

9. The principal architect was John Greenwood — an outstanding economist who should be highly commended for his efforts.

10. The *Economic Report* of the HongkongBank in January 1988 reported buying rates for overnight deposits at 0.06 per cent and selling at 0.0%! For six months the interbank money market rates were 3.0 per cent and 2.75 per cent respectively. On bank deposits customers got 0.5 per cent on 24-hour to two-week call deposits and 1.5 per cent on savings deposits. The issue of the *Economic Report* contained an article on 'Economic Misconceptions and the Linked Exchange Rate System', arguing that the system should not permit adjustments, especially when under pressure from speculators. The article also acknowledged the problem of interest rate volatility associated with the linked exchange rate system. 'It has been argued that the cost of maintaining the link is higher interest rate volatility, especially in real terms.' Then it showed a table of average annual time deposit rates from 1976 through 1987, and interest rates appear to be no more unstable after the linking of 1983 than before. However, it is important to remember that before 1983 there was no control over money supply growth. Also, annual averages cover up the considerable volatility in interest rates that occurs during the course of a year.

11. *Monetary Statistics*, Monetary Affairs Branch, Hong Kong Government, August 1988.

12. The author's views expressed here differ from those of other contributors. See, for example, Chapter 9, pp. 208–10.

References

Cheng, Hang-Sheng (ed.), *Monetary Policy in Pacific Basin Countries*, (Boston, Kluwer Academic Publishers, 1988).

Glick, Reuven, 'Interest Rate Linkages in the Pacific Basin', *Economic Review*, Federal Reserve Bank of San Francisco, Summer 1987, pp. 31–7. In this article Mr Reuven examines the data for links between interest rates in the United States and Pacific economies including Hong Kong. He finds linkages similar to those with Europe, but not close linkages.

—— 'Financial Market Changes and Monetary Policy in Pacific Basin Countries', in Hang Sheng Cheng (ed.), *Monetary Policy in Pacific Basin Countries*, (Boston, Kluwere Academic Publishers, 1988), pp. 17–42.

Goodhart, Charles A. E., *The Evolution of Central Banks*, (Cambridge, Mass., the MIT Press, 1988). Professor Goodhart of the London School of Economics served many years as adviser to Bank of England and currently is adviser to the Monetary Affairs Branch of the Government of Hong Kong. This small volume includes brief histories of eleven different central banks world wide. It also contains an examination of the case for free banking but concludes that both banks and the public need a non-profit central bank. The conclusion is based upon careful reasoning that applies modern asymmetric information theory in a non-mathematical fashion. He argues that private deposit insurance is impractical and that depositors are unable to evaluate risk because it is impossible to calculate value of a bank's loan portfolio. The book is highly recommended reading for everyone interested in the question of the need for a central bank.

Greenwood, John G., 'The Operation of the New Exchange Rate Mechanism', *Asian Monetary Monitor*, Volume 8, No. 1, January–February 1984, pp. 2–12.

—— 'Why the HK$/US$ Linked Rate System Should Not be Changed', *Asian Monetary Monitor*, Volume 8, No. 6, November–December 1984, pp. 2–17.

—— 'Forum on the Negative Interest Rate Scheme', *Hong Kong Economic Papers*, No. 19, 1989, pp. 67–70. In these remarks the Swiss experience with a similar scheme is reviewed.

Hildebrand, John R., *Monetary Integration: Key Currencies Contributing Equitably to Development* (Bristol, Indiana, Whyndham Hall Press, Inc., 1987). Panama and Liberia are the only two countries outside the United States in which the United States dollar circulates. Professor Hildebrand feels that economic development in Latin countries and other developing economies could benefit from similar arrangements. Since Hong Kong has fixed its exchange rate to the United States dollar, the arguments for an integrated currency may apply to Hong Kong as well. The distribution of seigniorage would need to be negotiated, but otherwise there is little difference between the 'linked' exchange system and an integrated currency system.

Ho, Y. K., 'Forum on the Negative Interest Rate Scheme', *Hong Kong Economic Papers*, No. 19, 1989, pp. 71–3. In these remarks Dr Ho suggests that a Financial Authority of Hong Kong be established in order to centralize all the central banking functions in Hong Kong and to launch research studies on all aspects of the territory's financial markets and institutions.

Hsu, John C., 'Hong Kong Exchange Rate System and Money Supply', *Hong Kong Economic Papers*, Hong Kong Economic Association, No. 18, 1988, pp. 45–52. Mr Hsu constructs a model with money demand and supply tied to a monetary base, and an exchange rate that fluctuates because the value of the United States dollar fluctuates against other currencies. He recommends linking the Hong Kong dollar to a basket of currencies or to varying arbitrage costs to permit some flexibility in the exchange rate through differences in the official and free foreign exchange markets.

—— 'Exchange Rate Management without a Central Bank: the Hong Kong Experience', *Hong Kong Economic Papers*, No. 16, 1985, pp. 14–26.

Jao, Y. C., 'A Comparative Analysis of Banking Crises in Hong Kong and Taiwan', *Journal of Economics and International Relations*, Asian Research Service, Volume 3, 1989.

Law, C. K., 'The Negative Interest Rate Scheme: Is It Necessary?', remarks before the Hong Kong Economic Association, 1 March 1988. Dr Law points up the volatility of interest rates on Hong Kong deposits that follows the fixed exchange rate system, and suggests that Hong Kong might benefit from adopting a basket-peg exchange rate system similar to that of Singapore. These remarks were published in 'Forum on the Negative Interest Rate Scheme', *Hong Kong Economic Papers*, No. 19, 1989, pp. 75–8.

Macfarlane, Ian J., 'Policy Targets and Operating Procedures: The Australian Case', *Monetary Policy Issues in the 1990s: A Symposium*, (Federal Reserve Bank of Kansas City, 1990), pp. 143–59.

Moreno, Ramon, 'Monetary Control Without a Central Bank: The Case of Hong Kong', *Economic Review*, Federal Reserve Bank of San Francisco, Spring 1986, pp. 17–37. In this article Mr Ramon reviews the flexible and fixed exchange rates systems — as real bills doctrine oriented. He also proposes a monetary base and money multiplier presumed to operate under a fixed exchange rate system, in which banks hold some reserves in foreign currency deposits. On p. 35 he writes: '. . . it would be desirable to spell out explicitly what determines the proportion of foreign currency deposits banks will convert for note issuance under fixed exchange rates. Such exercises would clarify the process by which a market-determined money supply in an open economy achieves stability, given the profit-maximizing behavior of banks.'

—— 'Exchange Rates and Monetary Policy in Singapore and Hong Kong', in Hang-Sheng Cheng (ed.), *Monetary Policy in Pacific Basin Countries*, (Boston, Kluwer Academic Publishers, 1988), pp. 173–200.

—— 'Exchange Rates and Monetary Policy in Singapore and Hong Kong', *Hong Kong Economic Papers*, Hong Kong Economic Association, No. 19, 1989, pp. 21–42. This paper provides an excellent review and comparison of monetary policies in the two communities. It should be required reading for those interested in the subject of this chapter. It does not, however, address the merits of any alternative monetary system for Hong Kong.

Scott, Robert Haney, *Saving Hong Kong's Dollar*, (Hong Kong, University Publisher and Printer, 1984).

Selgin, George A., *The Theory of Free Banking: Money Supply Under Competitive Note Issue*, (Totowa, New Jersey, Rowman & Littlefield, 1988).

—— 'Central Banking: Myth and Reality', *Hong Kong Economic Papers*, Hong Kong Economic Association, No. 18, 1988, pp. 1–13.

Suzuki, Yoshio, 'Policy Targets and Operating Procedures: The Case of Japan', *Monetary Policy Issues in the 1990s: A Symposium*, (Federal Reserve Bank of Kansas City, 1990), pp. 161–73.

14. Information Technology in Banking and Finance

Simon S. M. Ho

Introduction

Advances in computer micro-electronics and telecommunications technology have revolutionized the financial industry all over the world. In fact, one of the major contributing factors to the rapid development of Hong Kong as a major international financial centre is that Information Technology (IT) has been used extensively in the finance sector. This development has offered solutions to many old banking problems as well as offering new financial products, and thus widens the scope of financial business. Financial institutions must therefore maintain long-run perspectives and develop long-run strategies to deal with these technological challenges.

This chapter provides an overview of the applications of information technology in the local banking sector. It covers the features and the state-of-the-art of various Electronic Banking (EB) services that have come to be known collectively as Electronic Fund Transfer Systems (EFTSs), with particular attention to their financial, economic, legal, and social implications.

Some of this material is based on informal discussions with more than 16 banking executives during 1989. A comparison between local and overseas development will be made wherever appropriate. Although national factors may influence the pace and characteristics of some developments in an individual country, in general all countries move along a broadly similar path. Despite attempts to keep up-to-date, difficulties are inevitable with such a rapidly changing IT environment. Wherever possible, the latest statistics are provided, but it should be noted that what might be current at the time of writing might no longer be so in a matter of months.

This chapter should be useful in understanding and appraising local and international fund transfer mechanisms. The discussions should also be of interest to corporate managers, bankers, computer professionals, regulators, and others interested in the development of the financial industry.

EFTS and Electronic Banking

In Hong Kong, financial activity has been booming in recent years. From Tables 14.1 and 14.2 we see that there is a continuous increase in deposits, loans, share trading volume, number of financial institutions, and cheques cleared. Nowadays, banks and other financial institutions are faced with the challenges of brisk financial activities, transaction backlogs, deregulation, intense competition, globalization, growing customer sophistication, product diversification, and industry consolidation.

Efforts have been made in all major developed countries to introduce electronic media to cope with these trends. Although competition in the local finance sector has always been intense, it will become even more so as it becomes global. Also, with the time value of money increasing, the importance of speed in financial transactions has caused many financial controllers and fund managers to demand faster, more

Table 14.1 A Summary of Recent Financial Activities, 1984–1988

Year	Total Deposit (HK$m)	Total Loans (HK$m)	Share Trading Volume	No. of Financial Institutions	No. of People Employed
1984	354,695	421,049	48,787	3,960	75,723
1985	430,811	439,964	75,808	4,050	78,440
1986	550,651	500,596	123,128	4,066	82,612
1987	703,609	778,781	371,406	4,218	90,299
1988	845,520	962,177	198,569	4,848	97,885

Source: *Hong Kong Monthly Digest of Statistics* (Hong Kong, Census and Statistics Department), January 1990.

Table 14.2 HongkongBank Cheque Transactions, 1977–1988

Year	Number of Items Cleared	Increase Per cent	Total Value (HK$ million)	Average Increase Per cent	Value per Item (HK$ thousand)
1977	41,450,772	—	647,487	—	15.62
1978	49,621,611	19.7	1,006,598	55.50	20.29
1979	56,958,063	14.8	1,605,812	59.50	28.19
1980	67,669,491	18.8	3,019,546	88.00	44.62
1981	73,536,630	8.7	4,807,863	59.20	65.38
1982	74,832,800	1.8	5,792,607	20.50	77.41
1983	77,252,000	3.2	6,040,255	4.28	78.19
1984	82,346,706	6.5	7,099,064	17.53	86.21
1985	86,654,000	5.2	7,334,287	3.31	84.64
1986	94,127,000	8.6	9,691,488	32.14	102.96
1987	110,819,000	17.7	15,533,342	60.28	140.17
1988	117,311,000	5.9	18,702,748	20.40	159.43

Source: *Hong Kong Monthly Digest of Statistics* (Hong Kong, Census and Statistics Department), January 1990.

accurate, and more accessible account information to make global fund transfer decisions. The business of banking has been, and is still, rapidly and profoundly changing. The major ingredients for this change include the development of new technological capabilities for processing and transmitting data, and removal of the barrier between investment/loan products and non-loan products.

The growing importance of IT in today's business is reflected in banks' enormous investments in computer systems. The Bank of America spends over US$500 million and Citicorp US$1.5 billion a year on IT. In fact, among all businesses, banks comprise the largest group of computer users in Hong Kong, and they were the first in Hong Kong to experience the large cost savings of computerization. Few areas of business have benefited more from the recent technological advances than banking. Financial institutions are now increasingly using IT as a 'competitive weapon' (Ives and Learmouth, 1984; Porter and Millar, 1985), often with telling results. This is a change from the time when computers were used largely for back-office support. For instance, Merrill Lynch's innovative Cash Management Account (CMA) provides three appealing services to investors under one umbrella: investment in a Merrill-managed money market fund; cash withdrawn by cheque or Visa debit card; and credit through a standard margin account. Merrill makes over US$60 million per year in CMA-associated fees. It took competitors four years to develop comparable computer-based services. IT is therefore essential, actually indispensable, for many financial institutions to gain a competitive advantage.

Perhaps the most significant impact of IT on banks and their customers is the introduction of new payment methods. While it is unlikely that our society will be completely chequeless and paperless, a number of effective ways to transfer funds electronically are being developed.

The United States National Commission on Electronic Fund Transfer (NCEFT) defined an Electronic Fund Transfer System as 'a payment system in which the processing and communications necessary to effect economic exchange and the processing and distribution of services incidental or related to economical exchange are dependent wholly or in large part on the use of electronics'. As a new way of collecting and processing transaction data, EFTSs perform three basic functions: (1) transaction initiation and authorization, (2) fund transfer, and (3) generation of information for record keeping and decision making.

In general, banks have developed EFTSs for three main reasons: (1) to protect (and possibly increase) market share and remain competitive; (2) to reduce operating costs (including 'float' costs, that is, funds that have been dispatched by a payer but are not in a form that can be spent by the payee, and error costs) and increase efficiency; and (3) to generate new revenues by creating new products and services. Nevertheless most bank officials interviewed revealed that, in general, they considered the first two objectives more important than the last.

The technology of EFTS is basically in existence. The essence of

EFTS is effecting transactions by customers 'without the intervention of bank staff' (Revell, 1984). It also allows financial institutions to transfer funds instantly internally as well as with other financial institutions in a real-time mode. By bringing together the point of initiation of a transaction and the point of posting it, an EFTS can reduce many paper processing, labour, and float costs. Electronic banking offers individuals and firms access to the bank's services and allows them to use these services at their own convenience. Individual and corporate customers therefore have greater control over their financial affairs, as well as having more convenient service. In principle, EFTS is designed to help customers use both their money and their time as efficiently as possible.

Although the EFTS revolution began in the United States, it has affected banking and shopping habits, corporate fund management, and wage and other payment methods throughout the world. The diffusion of technological advances from abroad to Hong Kong's banking sector has taken place quickly. The first sign of these changes in Hong Kong occurred in 1980 when Automated Teller Machines (ATMs) were first installed by the two largest banks in Hong Kong — the Hongkong and Shanghai Banking Corporation and the Standard Chartered Bank. Since then various electronic banking services have been introduced through the combined efforts of financial institutions, merchants, employers, the Government, computer suppliers, system auditors, and the general public.

Components of EFTSs

To speak of 'the EFTSs' is an over-simplification. In its early days, many people viewed an EFTS as a monolithic integrated system in which all related computer systems, remote terminals, telephone systems, and switching centres were connected. Obviously, such a totally integrated national system does not yet exist and it will take many years to appear. Therefore 'EFTS' should be viewed as a generic term, referring to various computer-based technologies for delivering electronic banking services. There is as yet no such thing as a fixed and standard system of EFTS which applies in all countries. We are almost certain to be faced in the future with many different types of EFTSs, each combining elements in a different way and in different proportions. It is to be hoped that these transitional fragmented EFTS components will eventually form a fully integrated EFTS.

Both bankers and computer vendors agree that an EFTS should include at least the following physical components:

(1) Plastic and 'Smart' Cards,
(2) Computer Terminals,
(3) Communication Networks,
(4) Local Switching Centres and EFTS Intermediaries,
(5) Bank Computer Centres,
(6) Card Verification Centres, and

Fig. 14.1   The Structure and Components of a Full EFTS

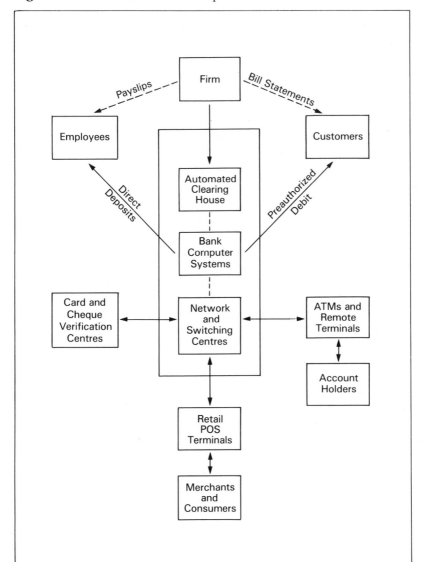

(7)   Automated Clearing Houses.

Each of these components is briefly described below. Fig. 14.1 shows diagrammatically the parties involved and the components in a full EFTS.

1.   Plastic Cards.   Magnetically striped plastic cards, in the form of ATM, debit, or credit cards, have had a significant impact on retail banking and the delivery system mechanisms. These cards can be used to pay for goods or services, and they have changed the way products offered by banks can be utilized. With over 900 million cards in

circulation throughout the world in 1987, it is clearly an accepted part of everyday life. Reports indicate that Hong Kong has about 2.5 million card holders and over 800,000 credit cards in circulation. Perhaps the existing technologies the banks are now experimenting with most are the memory cards or 'smart' cards. Large amounts of information, such as account details, transaction data, and balance data can be stored on the cards, reducing the need for passbooks and statement distribution, and greatly enhancing security. If the production cost can be sufficiently reduced, these cards will become much more widely used.

2.   Computer Terminals.   These can be in the form of an ATM, a terminal for Electronic Fund Transfer at Point-of-Sale (EFTPOS), or a microcomputer terminal. They all offer users access to the bank's services and allow them to use these services at their own convenience. The use of different terminals for various electronic banking services will be discussed in further detail later.

3.   Communication Networks.   This refers to the pattern or 'line' over which data are communicated at high speed between computers or between terminals and computers. Data communication 'lines' may be ordinary dial-up or leased telephone lines, microwave channels, or satellite paths. In the future, there could be competition from specialized communications carriers or cable television companies for a secure, high speed data service. In the United States, there are several high speed, high accuracy national financial data networks which inter-connect the automated clearing houses and credit verification systems.

4.   Local Switch Centres and EFTS Intermediaries.   Different parties to an EFTS transaction have different bank accounts. Direct communication between each party's bank is virtually impossible because of the almost unlimited potential for combinations of parties. EFTS intermediaries or switches have been established to handle these communications. Such centres are able to handle thousands of simultaneous transactions almost instantaneously. They will route or relay transaction messages to terminals or computers, via a communication network, to the appropriate financial institution's processor or the credit validation system servicing the card account.

5.   Bank Computer Centres.   Banks participating in an EFTS will either own or, through service companies, have access to an on-line, 24-hour-a-day computer system that is capable of verifying and processing transaction messages, debiting customers' accounts, storing transaction data for billing, and issuing credits to vendors' accounts.

6.   Card Verification Centres.   A POS (Point-of-Sale) terminal will have rapid access to computer files in a verification centre for a fast initial check of card validity, credit standing, transaction limits, and frequency of use pattern checks. Such centres can be associated with national or local switching centers. If the card is valid at the time of checking, the transaction is 'guaranteed' and liability for loss is assumed by the financial institution offering the card service.

7.   Automated Clearing Houses.   A clearing house is a system used by banks for clearing or exchanging paper items and cheques drawn

on each other. In a traditional clearing house, bundles of paper cheques are exchanged. The corner-stone of the EFTS is the Automated Clearing House (ACH) system. It is part of the back office inter-bank clearing system to transmit debit and credit items among financial institutions electronically rather than manually. ACHs are very efficient at handling recurring transactions such as direct deposits or preauthorized payments (known as 'auto-pay' in Hong Kong). Such preauthorized items are made automatically according to an agreed procedure and schedule. In an ACH, computer images or tapes are exchanged. Thus an ACH replaces the often burdensome physical processing of a paper cheque, and may make funds available to the receiving party more quickly.[1]

ACHs are generally operated by central banks (in Hong Kong by the Committee of Hong Kong Clearing Banks) and they use rules, procedures, and programs agreed upon by their members. In the United States, current ACH membership includes more than 13,000 financial institutions and 9,000 private corporations that initiate more than 15 million items per month. However, ACH volume in the United States is dominated by transfers from the Government to the private sector, with about 75 per cent of that volume due to social security payments. In Hong Kong, of the over 100 million or so cheques cleared annually, only a small per cent are ACH transactions. As mentioned earlier, at present the chequeless society is a long way from reality.

The Evolution of Electronic Fund Transfer Systems

Although an EFTS is often considered a revolutionary development with far-reaching effects, it can also be viewed as just another step in the evolution of the payment mechanism. In fact, EFTS development in different countries is in various phases. Generally, the development of EFTS in Hong Kong can be divided into the following four phases:

(a) Phase 1 (end-1960s to mid-1970s) was led mainly by the technologists and aimed at computerizing standard operations of banks for improved efficiency. Applications include: cheque processing, on-line current and saving accounts, bill paying, commercial loans, credit card administration, stock and bond management, and other internal accounting and administration applications. Most of these applications are limited to back office functions and offer few direct services to customers.

(b) Phase 2 (mid-1970s to mid-1980s) introduced basic electronic banking services: an automated clearing house, on-line ATM networks, regional inter-bank EFTS networks, and joining a world-wide message and fund transmission systems.

(c) Phase 3 (mid-1980s to date) involves the use of on-line systems to connect financial institutions with their corporate and private customers. It includes EFTPOS terminals, home and office banking, sophisticated Cash Management Services (CMS), on-line financial information services, and Decision Support Systems (DSS).

(d)   Phase 4 (year 2000?) will be a totally integrated nation-wide system with all of the above features.

The world's major financial institutions have reached the third (and possibly final) phase in their struggle to exploit fully electronic technology. Like other countries, Hong Kong's jump from 'cash-only' to EFTS has taken place over the first two distinct stages, with the third one just beginning. It is estimated that Japan, Hong Kong, and Singapore are leading the race to full electronic banking in Asia. The 1980s was thus a period of tremendous change in the banking industry. IT is giving rise to convenience and efficiency hardly imaginable a decade ago. There is in fact a tremendous concentration of potential electronic banking customers in Hong Kong, with many world corporations having their Asian headquarters here. These factors, coupled with the adaptability of the Hong Kong business community, place Hong Kong well in the forefront of this revolution for the foreseeable future.

With phase three, however, some problems have emerged and these must be handled carefully. Bankers now not only know the importance of utilizing IT in their business but also have a better understanding of its frequently profound implications. Though EFTS offers many advantages to both banks and customers, a number of unresolved issues block the complete and rapid implementation of the existing technology. These concerns include consumer acceptance, costs, system reliability, crime and fraud, privacy protection, control difficulties, and so on. These problems will be further explored in later sections of this chapter.

Fig. 14.1 depicts the general structure and components of a relatively integrated EFTS. It also indicates that an EFTS involves several 'players' or participants. To reap the full benefit of EFTS, all the basic economic units in society (that is, households, firms, financial institutions, and governments) must participate. For the sake of clarity in the further discussion of local EFTS progress, the various EFTS services are grouped into five major categories:

(a)   Automated Teller Machines (ATMs) and shared networks.
(b)   Electronic Fund Transfer at Point-of-Sale (EFTPOS).
(c)   Home banking systems.
(d)   Payment system wire networks.
(e)   Corporate Cash Management Services (CMS).

The first three are used for such customer-related transactions as retail purchases, bill payments, and individual transactions involving relatively small dollar amounts. The last two are generally used for business or commercial fund transfers and involve larger dollar amounts. These EFTS services together have raised the Hong Kong financial system off a paper base and on to an electronic foundation. The following pages will discuss the state-of-the-art of each of these major EFTS services in Hong Kong and the supportive forces behind their development in greater detail. We first see how IT relates to the corporate level, then we advance to 'street-level' business.

Payment Wire Systems

The most familiar form of electronic banking today — certainly in the streets of Hong Kong — is the ATM. But while ATMs are well accepted, the most dynamic area of electronic banking is now to be found in the offices of banks and other major corporations.

Today, the core of wholesale banking lies in the payment or money wire transfer system, which is vital to the movement of funds, both nationally and internationally. These payment networks are designed to replace many services that were previously performed by telegraph, telex, telephone, and mail, and they can achieve significant reductions in tedious and burdensome manual processing. On the operation side, these networks use standard message format. Such standardization facilitates information flow and avoids misunderstanding between parties. These networks are characterized by their high volume of transactions, large monetary values, payments to third parties, and the immediate availability of the funds transferred. It it these conditions, however, which make the system vulnerable to costly errors and also to potential fraud.

Payment networks fall into two categories: local networks and international networks. Local inter-bank payment networks are now well established in the world's major financial centres: New York was first, with its Clearing House Interbank Payment System (CHIPS) developed in 1970, followed by Tokyo, Hong Kong, and the United Kingdom. Before we discuss the local Clearing House Automated Transfer System (CHATS), it may be useful to summarize the features of some major world-wide EFTS networks below:

1. Fedwire (Federal Reserve Wire System)
   - Fedwire is the dominant public funds transfer system in the United States.
   - It handles 60 per cent of total transaction volume and a higher percentage of dollar volume.
   - Fedwire allows over 850 banks to move both funds and administrative messages from one member to another.
   - Fedwire also handles transactions in the United States Government securities.
   - It has 38 regional ACH associations, 37 of which (excluding the New York City ACH) are subsidized by the FED.
2. BankWire II
   - BankWire II is a private network owned co-operatively by 190 commercial banks in the United States.
3. CHIPS (The Clearing House Interbank Payment System)
   - CHIPS is a private network system owned by the New York Clearing House Association (NYCHA).
   - It has same-day clearing of transactions through NYCHA members' reserve accounts.
   - CHIPS is responsible for 90 per cent of all inter-bank international dollar transfers.

- While all 99 participating banks are located in New York, 56 of them represent the New York branches or agencies of foreign banks.
- CHIPS provides a settlement mechanism over members' accounts at the Federal Reserve Bank.
4. CHAPS (The Clearing House Automated Payment System)
- CHAPS is the London clearing system.
- It is moving towards distributed processing.
- CHAPS has largely replaced the manual London Town Clearing since 1984.
- Its formats are derived from SWIFT, and the clearing banks intend to encourage actively their banking customers to use SWIFT to send instruction for CHAPS transfer.
- CHAPS permits the United Kindgom clearing banks to offer a wide range of new services via customer terminals in a way currently being developed by their United States counterparts.
5. SWIFT (Society for World-wide Interbank Financial Telecommunications)
- SWIFT is the standard international network that enables financial institutions in different countries to transmit payment instructions, statements, and messages between themselves.
- Formed in 1973 by 293 bankers in 15 countries, it became operational in 1977.
- Current members include over 1,400 banks in 50 countries.
- SWIFT operates 24 hours a day, seven days a week.
- All messages passing through the system are stored for 10 days but will extend to four months.
- 1987 daily volume was about 900,000 messages per day, but more than half of the business comes from only 50 banks.
- SWIFT is cheap, with guaranteed delivery within a matter of a few minutes.
- SWIFT maintains a complex, multi-level security and control system.
- A new improved SWIFT II was implemented in 1989 with extended capability, flexibility, and ease of use.

Like BankWire II and CHIPS, SWIFT is a privately owned and operated transfer system. These private systems not only provide the basic function of transmitting messages, but also provide other services such as data base information and accounting. In 1980 Hong Kong's 13 major banks joined SWIFT, a service that has proved to be a success. Expansion into the foreign market is becoming progressively easier as these payment networks reduce the economic distance between banking offices and their customers. Rather than using SWIFT, large banks may also use their own telecommunication networks or that of a large international communications agency (for example, GEISCD, ADP, Telerate, Reuters, and SIT), although SWIFT services are still very popular. Another issue to be resolved is that very few non-banks and brokers can currently join SWIFT. It is expected that the international credit card networks (for example, Visa and MasterCard) may soon link with SWIFT for quick authorization and processing of transactions. However, the restrictions on the flow of data across national borders cause political threats to SWIFT's operations.

As pressure to ease the amount of paper work in cheque payments grew, banks in Hong Kong co-operated to automate the clearing of debit and credit transactions among themselves. In 1984, an on-line real-time Clearing House Automated Transfer System (CHATS) was inaugurated in Hong Kong, a system comparable to the national networks. It initially processed inter-bank fund transfer and other transactions on a same-day basis, and will eventually include cheque-clearing as well. Proposed by the Hongkong and Shanghai Banking Corporation to the Hong Kong Association of Banks in 1982, CHATS allows local banks to transmit and settle accounts with each other in same-day funds quickly, efficiently, and with maximum security (Borland, 1983).

The CHATS will almost certainly take over a substantial part of the role fulfilled in the past by the town clearing house and by telephonic transfers. Under this system all the major settlement banks provide their own 'gateway' through which payment messages are exchanged via the packet switching services. Other banks can arrange to share a gateway. Settlement is effected by each debtor bank sending a payment message to the HongkongBank, which acts as banker to all the participating banks. Under CHATS, the clearing process is initiated by the payer. Instructions may be given to the payer's bank by personal visit, telephone, telex, mail, or electronic communication links. Of personal transactions, a home purchase payment may become an ideal CHATS application, especially in large conveyancing practices, as there have been many problems in the past in arranging same-day transfer of funds.

It is believed that the future of the international banks will be inextricably tied to their ability to exploit technology.

Corporate Cash Management Services

The cash management problem faced by most multinational companies today requires an overwhelming combination of timely information, reliable forecasting, and immediate execution. With the advent of efficient payment network systems, developments in IT bring opportunities to banks by providing new products for corporate customers for money management and transfer. While some banks concentrate on automating their retail operations, some electronic office banking products, for example, the Cash Management System (CMS), have been offered by some major banks to their corporate clients.

Corporate electronic banking services are designed to benefit both the clients and the banks. From the clients' point of view, these services provide them with an electronic 'window' into the bank so that corporate treasurers can have all data on cash balances in one location, and can know where they have an excess and mobilize their funds more effectively. Before the advent of these cash management services, companies had to collect their world-wide balances by themselves. With CMS, corporate managers can also have access to their account status in the bank, make on-line transfers, and retrieve a range of financial quotations and services directly for investment purposes.

Bank managers also want all the information on their corporate customers in one place so that they can make better loan or investment decisions. From the banks' point of view, these services accomplish two objectives. First, they can process customers' messages to the bank more efficiently and accurately. Second, they keep profitable accounts which generate cash balances and new fee incomes.

Many major international banks have developed highly comprehensive CMSs. Table 14.3 illustrates the extent of developments in this area. Some of these services have been introduced to Hong Kong and provide a level of global cash management that few other local bank products can match. They are also seen by some as direct competitors to SWIFT.

Table 14.3   Proprietary Corporate CMSs

Bank	System
Merrill Lynch	Cash Management Account
Bank of America	Bantrac
Bankers Trust	Cash Connector
Chase Manhattan	Infocash
Chemical	Chemlink
Citibank	Citicash Manager
Continental	Confirm
European American	Earlicash
First National Bank of Chicago	First cash
Manufacturers Hanover	Transend
Morgan Guaranty	MARS
National Data Corporation	NordiCash

Source: The Banker, various issues.

In sum, by placing a CMS terminal in a customer's premises and linking it to a bank's local network, a typical CMS combines a variety of banking products into a new plastic-card-based package. CMS services include:
(a)   Facilities to enable corporate customers to make world-wide account balance enquiries directly, and to establish the identity of payers and the currency and location of outstanding receivables.
(b)   'Lock-box' services which immediately pool all of a customer's deposits into one single account.

(c)World-wide electronic fund transfer between accounts directly through the customers' terminals.

(d)   Traditional broking services such as brokerage margin account or sweep account, broker's loans secured by a customer's securities held by the brokers, shares trading, and a variety of money market investment funds.

(e)   On-line real-time information and decision support products, which allow customers to conduct cash flow analysis, and interest rates and foreign exchange forecasts. Better decision making comes via spreadsheet interfaces (such as Lotus 1-2-3) which allow pro forma analysis of balance sheets, profit and loss accounts, and so on.

After about five years of development, the Hongkong and Shanghai Banking Corporation has also been providing a Hong Kong-based electronic cash management system, named Hexagon, since 1987. This electronic banking system is expected to compete vigorously with those already being offered in Asia by the large American banks. Since Hexagon's major clients are mainly based in Asia, the bank decided to develop its own system rather than to use proprietary products from the United States. The bank's local customers were involved in the design of the system and consequently the system shall suit local conditions and users' needs better than any of the American ones.

Specifically, Hexagon provides three broad types of service. The first is the retrieval of information relating to a user company's global portfolio with the HongkongBank Group, including account statements, forex contracts outstanding, import/export trade position, and so on. Moreover, through an interface with SWIFT, users can also display details of accounts held with banks outside the Group. Secondly, up-dated market information on a broad range of subjects can be retrieved from Hexagon. Lastly, having seen their positions and opportunities, executives can then initiate transactions through Hexagon, for example, electronic funds movements in different countries, time-deposit, application for letters of credit, securities trading, and so on. The system allows single or repetitive payments, transfer, and electronic messages between Hexagon centres and customers.

In the long run, the HongkongBank plans to offer decision support software to assist Hexagon users in day-to-day decision making. This will certainly include the ability to download raw data from the bank's computer systems into customers' personal computers for integration with software packages such as Lotus 1-2-3 and Symphony. The number of Hexagon users world-wide is increasing as the demand for the system grows. Up to now the emphasis has been on mainly large business users, but there are already plans for small business or home users.

To promote the use of CMS by customers, banks are initially aggressive by absorbing the investment costs of the equipment and application development themselves. By offering CMS, the banks can transfer floats and idle balances to the corporate treasurers. In its early stages, corporate customers are usually provided with free or low-cost terminals for CMS. In return customers are required either to keep a compensating minimum balance and/or to pay a nominal fee for the service. But, now that lending margins are decreasing and balances disappearing, the industry is being forced to reappraise its approach to charging for electronic banking products. As CMS becomes more popular, corporate customers will increasingly manage their own funds, and banks will have to turn increasingly to technical and fee-charging services for revenue and profit.

Experience to date has shown that the demand for CMS in Hong Kong is gradually increasing. Currently, CMS users are mainly large companies. Although many of them found the information services useful, the use of CMS to transfer funds for investment is infrequent. One of the major problems that the corporate cash management concept has encountered is that many managers lack experience or confidence in operating their computer terminals or personal computers directly. There are also concerns about the security of these systems. It is expected that the clients with highest volume of transactions will probably get the most out of these facilities. It will take several more years for corporate customers to accept CMS concepts completely, but bankers are confident that their clients will find such services invaluable and cost effective.

Automated Teller Machines

A recent development that has achieved phenomenal success in electronic banking is the setting up of ATM networks. Perhaps the greatest boost in electronic banking came from the widespread Automated Teller Machines (ATMs). Hong Kong was among the first in Southeast Asia to provide widespread ATM services. In terms of the breadth of services, electronic banking in Hong Kong may lag behind some western countries. However, in terms of ATM market density Hong Kong is ahead of many other advanced countries: Hong Kong ranked fourth in the world in terms of ATMs per 10,000 persons, and thirteenth in terms of cards per 10,000 persons in 1985. With over 1,000 ATMs in Hong Kong serving about 2 million ATM card holders, with transactions for each ATM amounting to 1,000 per day while the international average is just 7,000 per month, Hong Kong probably boasts the highest usage rate in the world (Austin, 1988).

Unattended and remotely controlled ATMs which provide 24-hour retail banking services are being installed by almost all local retail banks. But ATMs are no longer necessarily sited in the wall of a bank; increasingly, they are being installed in high-traffic public areas — railway stations, airports, and factories. Nevertheless, for most ATMs installed, maintenance of a customer base and potential cost reductions are prime considerations. In fact, very few ATM systems can be employed as 'offensive' weapons to increase market share and thereby to generate revenue.

The pooling of resources to form a shared ATM network is cost justified. Shared networks allow an institution to expand the geographical coverage and range of its services, and offer products it might not be able to afford on its own. Smaller banks also find it advantageous to join a shared ATM network and expand their market area at a much lower cost than with a conventional branch (Metzker, 1982). At present, there are two major ATM networks in Hong Kong. The first is the HongkongBank and Hang Seng Bank groups' Electronic Teller Card (ETC) network, which has 550 ATMs. The second is the Joint Electronic Teller Services Company Ltd. (JETCO) network, which has a total of 710 ATMs. The ETC network is probably the most heavily utilized system in the world, in terms of the number of transactions performed per day.

JETCO was formed in 1982 by four independent local banks, the Bank of East Asia, Chekiang First Bank, Shanghai Commercial Bank, and Wing Lung Bank. The Bank of China Group, Chase Manhattan Bank, Nan Tung Bank, Tai Fung Bank of Macau, Standard Chartered Bank, and a number of other banks later joined the network, resulting in a total of over 40 member banks in Hong Kong and Macau. Card holders of JETCO may make use of over 710 ATMs now installed all over Hong Kong, Macau, Shenzhen, and Zhuhai. All the ATMs in this large shared network are accessible via one card, and all the switching and settlement of accounts between member banks is handled by a centralized Joint Electronic Teller Services (JETS) data processing centre (see Kan, 1984). Other independent networks are operated by Citibank and the Bank of Canton, while a shared network is operated by the Banque Nationale de Paris and the Banque Indosuez.

First generation ATMs were designed to dispense cash and therefore were quite basic. Current ATMs also provide services such as off-line deposit, transfer of money between accounts in the same bank, account balance enquiries, cheque book and bank statement requests, change of password, world-wide credit card cash advance, and give offical transaction receipts. Future innovations in ATM design could offer more efficient, flexible, and attractive features, with touch-screen, color video, and voice responses. The new generation of machines would employ laser-disk technology and offer a wide selection of value-added services. These new functions can include counting notes for immediate deposit; updating passbooks; paying bills and loans; issuance of loans, mortgages, and insurance policies; buying and selling of stocks and bonds; providing service-related information; displaying financial information; showing detailed account statements; dispensing retail negotiable certificates of deposit, gift cheques, and traveller's cheques; transferring funds to third party accounts; and other banking activities. Each machine can be programmed for specific functions which can be changed at any given time to suit the bank's needs. There is even the potential for cross-selling, linking with other companies and financial institutions, so that, for example, cars and holidays might be promoted and sold through the ATMs in a bank lobby.

However, not all of these advanced facilities are likely to be available in the near future in Hong Kong. Given the substantial investment cost of ATM networks, bankers have based their justification in the high transaction volume per ATM. What customers find most attractive about ATMs is a predictably short queuing time, and therefore time or speed would be a key factor in the design of ATM services. How banks in Hong Kong will exploit the use of ATM systems in the future also depends on the level of risk they are willing to bear. These factors could restrict the types of transactions that will be made available to customers. Since current ATMs are used primarily as cash dispensers, future ATM development will tend to divide into two extremes: (1) specialist type, that is, pure and simple cash dispensers; and (2) general purpose multi-function type. Recently, several banks have made extensive promotional efforts in order to draw more attention to the different functions provided by their machines.

It was found that ATMs seldom increase market share and do not trim the demand for tellers significantly. Additionally, ATMs alone cannot significantly reduce the massive volume of cheques written. In 1988, the HongkongBank was short about 400 tellers out of a required number of 2,400. In order to relieve the workload of its tellers, the Bank is now employing the Customers Operated Passbook Update Terminals (COPUTs), which automatically records for customers all of their transactions on their passbooks. ATMs will never totally replace human tellers, but they have helped banks to maintain their market without needing to employ large numbers of additional tellers.

The growth of ATM networks has been so rapid during the past decade that the market (in terms of the number of ATMs installed) may approach the saturation point in a few years. Obviously, there will still be a demand for replacement and upgraded machines. Also, the participants of the shared network are not limited to banks. In the future, other institutions such as department stores and insurance companies may install ATMs in their own premises if they find ATM services are profitable. Furthermore, a shared network input is not limited to ATMs: other possible input media include the teller machines inside bank branches, the POS terminals of retail stores, the electronic gasoline pumps in petrol stations, the reservation systems of travel agents, home banking terminals, and other similar media. All these possibilities can become a reality in a shared network. Some people also speculate whether future ATM networks will be merged into giant ATM networks, reducing the number of ATM networks. The major barriers to this development are strategic and political rather than technological issues. It is believed that any further step will represent a great leap forward in the co-operation among banks.

There are other issues related to ATMs that have yet to be resolved, including cost sharing, competition versus co-operation, network member banks' individual image and identity, customer base, security, and legal liability. Some of these will be discussed in later sections of this chapter.

Electronic Fund Transfer at Point-of-Sale

Hong Kong is probably the only place in the world to operate a single coordinated Electronic Fund Transfer at Point-of-Sale (EFTPOS) system shared by all the major banks. Although EFTPOS may be one of the less successful EFTSs in terms of cost effectiveness, it has caused marked changes in the relationships among financial institutions, retailers, and consumers.

An EFTPOS system allows a customer to pay for goods and services at the merchant's location (for example a camera shop) by transferring funds from the customer's bank account to the shop's account either immediately or at the end of the day. Any account holder with a debit card and Personal Identification Number (PIN) can effect an EFTPOS transaction. By entering transaction data into the electronic payment network at the time and place of sale, the system promotes the paperless transfer of funds in transactions between customers and business.

Such retail EFTPOS systems are being tried in France, Canada, the United States, Belgium, and Holland. Nevertheless, no EFTPOS system in the United States appears to have achieved a sufficient level of use to justify its set-up costs. In Europe, Belgium is probably the most advanced with well over 3,000 terminals installed. Recently, two competing EFTPOS networks, Bancontact and Mr. Cash, agreed to integrate their systems so that a card holder can pay through either network. The Far East is also very much in the forefront of development (*Asian Business*, 1985). In 1985 a United Kingdom computing services company, CAP, built two EFTPOS networks, one in Bangkok, and a second, NETS, in Singapore which supports over 1,000 terminals. A similar system on a larger scale was launched almost simultaneously in Hong Kong.

In Hong Kong, the Easy Pay System (EPS) was introduced to the public in June 1985. Developed mainly by the Hong Kong Association of Banks in conjunction with the HongkongBank, the EPS system is a natural development of CHATS. Electronic Payment Services Co. (HK) Ltd. (EPSCO) manages the system on behalf of 33 banks. The system enables authorized banks to connect their computers to a shared network of POS terminals at shops, through a POS central switching computer. By the end of 1988, 700 merchants were participating in the EPS system, with 1,860 terminals installed. As for ATM services, the huge population, the compact society, the lack of red tape interfering in the use of telecommunications, and the close co-operation between all major banks have contributed to make Hong Kong among the first to establish a cashless shopping system nation-wide. Hong Kong now has a large-scale operational EFTPOS while many other countries are still in the experimental stage. Study groups from other countries have visited here to learn how EPS functions (*Asian Finance*, 1986).

The primary aim of the EPS system is to allow retailers to accept about two million local ATM-type debit cards. If the customer's account has sufficient funds, it is debited for the amount of the purchase in favour of the merchant. For the over a million credit card holders, credit card checking and over-credit limit referrals will also be accepted by the same terminals, to be sent to a POS central computer for routing to the card-issuing institution for approval. The retailer must maintain an account with one authorized bank which issues debit cards and one member of a credit institution, in order to collect the proceeds of all its card transactions. Shoppers are offered the choice of purchase on credit or on-line payment.

The notion of cashless shopping holds many advantages for banks, retailers, and shoppers alike. With EFTPOS, paperwork for both banks and retailers is reduced to a minimum, and 'float time', the period between debiting and crediting different accounts in a transaction, is eliminated. The banks also benefit, as they will get less fraud and fewer delinquent accounts.

From a retailer's point of view, the EFTPOS would guarantee payment, require less cash for daily transactions, and speed up their counter service (provided that the cashier and customer are familiar with the system). According to a survey by Marti and Zeilinger (1982), the transaction time for EFTPOS (usually under 30 seconds) is faster than those for cheques and credit cards. Merchants can also reduce handling costs, cheque float, bad debt losses from bad cheques, and the risk of credit extension or excessive use. Detailed accounting and inventory data can also be recorded instantly, thus allowing the merchant to maximize the efficiency of the sales force, increase control over inventories, and monitor the characteristics of the store's clientele.

The customer seems to derive fewer benefits from EFTPOS although it does offer some advantages and convenience to certain groups of customers. Customers do not need to carry large amounts of cash, and they will write fewer cheques. By using debit cards, they will not have to risk over-reaching their credit limit each time they purchase or require cash from an ATM. It is to be hoped that with EFTPOS consumers will get better speedier transactions. But how many customers will prefer using direct debit to cash or credit is still uncertain.

The technological principle underlying EFTPOS is well proven and its operation is quite simple. However, the world-wide spread of cashless shopping is still quite slow and some key problems remain. Many bankers and retailers have begun seriously to question and reassess the basic arguments of EFTPOS. For instance, the idealized EFTPOS is designed to debit a customer's account instantaneously at point-of-sale. But who really needs such instant fund transfer? Certainly not the banks, nor the credit card companies and department stores who are making substantial profits out of their credit business. Customers will also prefer to pay by credit card if they can get a long interest-free payment period. The issue of loss of float for customers must also be properly addressed before EFTPOS can be significantly developed. Therefore EFTPOS has been frustrated by a lack of economic incentive to both customers and merchants.

Another factor that has delayed the introduction of electronic payment system has been its high cost, despite the fact that POS machines are getting progressively cheaper. A related question is who will bear this cost: the banks, the retailers, or the customers? It is obviously difficult to apportion its cost among these different parties. There have been debates over who stands to gain most from implementation of EFTPOS systems and who should pay for what. The system developers and investors expect a return on their investment. On the other hand, consumers will only use the EFTPOS system if they are assured that they will not be asked to contribute to the large capital investment which the system requires. Indeed, some consumers expect the EFTPOS system to reduce bank charges or prices eventually. If banks are the major beneficiaries, it is reasonable that banks should absorb a large portion of the cost, although retailers should be responsible for part of the installation fee and the operating costs. Under the present EPS charge scheme, the EPS company will charge the retailers for every transaction on a sliding scale according to the value of the transaction. The company will also charge the card-issuing institutions for credit card purchases, so that consumers may not have to pay any charge for using EPS services.

In Hong Kong, sales efforts of EPS were concentrated on high volume retail areas such as department stores and supermarket chains. Nevertheless, because of their low profit margin business, the supermarket chains do not realize significant benefits of EPS in terms of sales increases, as customers who used bank debit cards to pay for their groceries accounted for less 0.5 per cent of monthly sales. For example, the Wellcome supermarket officials disagreed with a fee arrangement that was recently imposed (merchants will pay either 0.75 per cent or $2 per transaction, whichever they prefer), and stopped accepting bank debit cards as a method of payment at their stores, following a lengthy period of experiment without charge. Whether other store chains will keep the EPS services permanently is hard to tell at this moment.

To summarize, the technology used in EFTPOS systems is not new. Some pilot experiments conducted overseas failed, while others achieved a marginal measure of success. The handling of the issues of cost sharing and economic incentive will determine how fast debit cards become popular.

Home Banking

The central thrust of development is now towards screen-based home banking systems that allow a customer to carry out electronic shopping and banking functions at home. Home banking is sometimes described as the personal consumer market equivalent of the corporate cash management system. In the United States and Europe, several pilot schemes are in progress. In some of these countries a home banking system is attractive because a relatively small investment is required in order to offer regular banking services to distant households (Altschul, 1984). However, the wide publicity given to these various systems might disguise the fact that home banking is very much in the experimental stages.

Many people, however, doubt that home banking will be successful in Hong Kong. At the time of writing there seems to be little interest in or need for screen-based home banking in Hong Kong. Several large local banks provide home banking services on an as-requested basis, and do not publicly advertise. The HongkongBank is promoting Hexagon, but most of its users are from the business sector. Despite its potential benefits, home banking is not popular in Hong Kong.

In its primitive, non-screen-based form, home banking systems that use only telephones rather than computer terminals or television sets have been used in several Asian countries, such as Japan, Singapore, and Hong Kong. Services are normally limited to paying personal bills, ordering cheque books, transferring funds between accounts, account status and foreign exchange rates enquiries, and purchasing foreign currency and gold. In Hong Kong, the Chase Manhattan Bank started a voice-response telephone banking service in 1982 which had some characteristics of home banking. In such systems, a customer only needs to dial a certain number and tell the bank staff his name, account number, and secret PIN. The customer then gives the instructions to an employee, or the message is recorded and later transcribed by an employee. A paper document is then prepared for actual entry into the payment system, but very few of them can generate a magnetic tape to be delivered through the ACH network. Given the high cost of telephone operators, voice-response telephone banking will sustain considerable pressure in the future as the customer base becomes larger. At present several banks in Hong Kong have promoted extensive 'telematic' services. In telematic banking service, the customer can make use of a 'touch tone' telephone to enter transaction details and will be given verbal instructions by a computer step by step. Hence the efficient and effective handling of personal finance is available.

A further step in the development of home banking is screen-based, linking the bank's computer systems with the telephone lines and microcomputers of individual customers. Direct access to the bank's computer can provide customers with the services that an ATM offers, except for cash deposits and withdrawals. Alternatively, as developed in the United Kingdom, home banking can be an interactive two-way home terminal system using videotext via public telephone networks or cable television broadcasting systems. The customers may use touch tone telephones or special compact keyboards to enter transaction details.

In addition to the many CMS and ATM-type banking services, videotext is expected to offer electronic versions of both the Yellow and White Pages, sports, news, financial information, weather, classified ads, retailers' catalogues, a community bulletin board, security trading, and a host of other services. However, it will take some time for electronic shopping to become popular because of its still high cost. Today, videotext services are available in most of western Europe and America, and a few of these services exist in other parts of the world including Japan, Hong Kong, and Singapore. In Hong Kong, Viewdata, a form of videotext, is provided by Hong Kong Telephone. No doubt, much of the success of Viewdata as an information provider lies in its ability to meet customers' needs for access to various data bases in the current complex financial environment. However, at present, information provision facilities are rather limited. Nevertheless, the present absolute distinction between Viewdata systems and other public database systems is being broken down by the introduction of the 'Gateway' software. Gateway enables all Viewdata users to obtain access to information stored in external private computer files, including those of the sponsoring bank. In the future, it is 'Viewdata plus Gateway' which will provide the power behind home banking.

In the United States, screen-based banking services are available in most states (DeCotiis, 1984). The largest of these is Covidea, a joint venture between Bank of America, Chemical Bank, Time Inc., and AT & T, with over 50,000 subscribers. Together there are more than 40 other operational screen-based services in the United States, but despite the fact that there are more than 23 million personal computers in use in the United States, there are little more than 100,000 subscribers to these services. Home banking systems have hardly touched in Europe either. There is little activity in Germany, France, and the United Kingdom, despite the rapidly expanding market for home banking hardware. While United States banks have tended to use home computers as their terminal, the European banks have opted for the cheaper Viewdata services based on the domestic television set. These include Credit Commercial de France (CCF)'s Vediocompte in France, the Bank of Scotland's Home and Office Banking Service (HOBS) in the United Kingdom, and the Verbraaucherbank operation in Germany. The first and only country to have a large-scale major screen-based system has been France, and there the government supplied over 2,500,000 free Videotext terminals (called Minitels) to telephone subscribers. However, Vediocompte in France so far offers only a limited number of services (*The Banker*, February 1984). Other rival products, such as Banque Nationale de Paris's Teleservice B and Credit Lyonnais's Telelion have similar experience. Similarly, the major problem with Bank of Scotland's HOBS is that Prestel (a viewdata system in the United Kingdom) only has around 85,000 subscribers in the United Kingdom and this limits the market. Japan is also preparing for a revolution in the home, building a service economy based on home banking, home shopping, videotext information services, advanced telecommunication services, and local community cable. But there are few data concerning their recent progress.

Not surprisingly, screen-based remote banking service has been always more attractive to corporate than private customers. In Hong

Kong, most screen-based services have concentrated their sales efforts on the business sector. At present, screen-based home banking is moving very slowly in Hong Kong, despite several favourable factors such as the high frequency of bank usage, large numbers of households, and high penetration of readily accessible delivery channels such as the telephone line and TV. There are, of course, several reasons for this unpopularity. The problems and limitations include that:

(a) It is not compatible with existing banking services, delivery systems, and customers' banking habits.
(b) The target market represents only a small percentage of the total number of households.
(c) There are questions of relative advantage: bank branches and ATMs are readily accessible to the whole population.
(d) The number of subscribers to Viewdata is very limited.
(e) It is difficult for customers to test on a brief trial or experimental basis.
(f) The cost is unknown — who bears the costs?

At present, as the infrastructure is not available, there seems to be little incentive for customers to change to screen-based home banking, so its fate in Hong Kong is uncertain. Factors that will determine its future development include the availability of proper and cost-effective delivery channels, product design and features, and pricing and acceptance by customers. Greater acceptance is likely when banking is just one of many services, which will include electronic shopping, on-line database access, and electronic mail delivered into the home terminal, and the cost is thus spread. There is also a need to extend the quality and scope of information provided. It seems that the young, educated, wealthier section of the population is most likely to use home banking. However, these people are likely to use home banking only if new, high value financial services are added beyond the regular services currently offered. The exact marketing mix and timing for its introduction has yet to be determined.

Screen-based home banking has yet to prove itself the success many people thought it would be. After a few years of trial it is now clear that such a system is not likely to be offered as a normal banking service in the next several years, and the year 2000 or later seems to be a more realistic prediction. Telephone-based systems may hold the key to the future.

Impact on Financial Systems and Transactions

The development of EFTS is dramatically changing the payment system and basic ideas about money. As Martin (1978) once described: 'Money is merely information, and as such can reside in computer storages with payments consisting of data transfer between one machine and another.' In fact, banking itself is evolving into what one can describe as the 'financial information service industry'.

It is possible to view EFTS services as a means to effect the instantaneous transfer of the ownership of assets. One example is United States Treasury securities, which are now often sold only on a book-entry basis — that is, the bills or bonds are not printed and issued to the lender, but are only registered and numbered and kept on record in the memory of a computer. When a lender sells a bond, numbers are transferred — not pieces of paper. More and more individuals and firms are moving toward the ownership of various divisible and indivisible financial and non-financial assets that can be exchanged by debits and credits to computerized accounts.

For example, assume that a person places his or her house up for mortgage with a lender (not necessarily a bank). Instead of receiving the mortgage funds and starting a system of repayments, the borrower would accept a line of credit against the mortgaged property. The house owner could then essentially 'sell' a part of the house by drawing against the line of credit offered by the lender. Eventually the borrower would be able to exchange a part of a house for a package of securities owned by some other person with similarly computerized facilities. This would be a form of barter by electronic transfer. It would not be necessary to use money as a medium of exchange, although money would still be used as a unit of account.

The possibility of eventual direct barter transactions by electronic transfer of asset ownership obviously causes concern among the authorities who regulate banks and control the money supply. The widespread use of electronic barter may weaken the constraining effect on inflationary and deflationary pressures that control over money presently exerts. With the implementation of EFTPOS, money cards used by individuals shopping in retail stores will transfer funds between accounts instantly. The demand for bank notes and coins will thus gradually decline. EFTS also causes tremendous speeding up of movement of funds on money markets and greater fluctuation in the level of interest and foreign exchange rates. This will give central banks far less time to make decisions and to intervene. EFTS would therefore make the operation of monetary policy considerably more difficult.

Also as a result of EFTS and reducing floats, the management of a firm's cash position will become increasingly sensitive to changing money market conditions and exchange rates. Semi-legal transactions, such as borrowing overdraft loans and duplicating financial investments in two countries over the weekend, will therefore become increasingly difficult. In short, the need for cash balances by corporations will probably decline, and, simultaneously, they will become more responsive to short-term yields around the world.

Evaluation of EFTS Economics

Technological breakthrough in recent years has drastically changed and improved the services banks can offer to their customers. At the same time, customers are aware of the limitation of services currently offered by the banks. Some of the services desired by customers will be detrimental to banks as they are not profitable, diminish float, increase the operating costs, increase the risk of error and fraud, and increase the risk of non-bank competition. In fact, the banks in their drive for banking automation have faced many problems. These include: a change in the competitive basis, but its implication is not known; a lack of clear legal responsibility for both banks and users; and increased potential for high-loss errors and electronic fraud. The choice of an effective marketing policy and corporate strategy is now possible, but the economics of EFTs remain to be proven.

Many related questions can not be solved easily, since they depend on many technological, economic, social, and institutional factors for which there are little data. The economic issues are discussed here, while other issues will be examined in later sections.

Since EFTS requires massive capital investment, the economic issues must be monitored and evaluated carefully. However, to assess the benefits and costs of EFTS is a complex task because it is difficult to analyse more than a small segment of the complex EFTS matrix at one time. The multi-dimensional analyses of the benefits and costs of EFTS have focused upon such issues as utilization level, cost sharing, pricing, and so on.

Most banking executives the author interviewed admitted that cost effectiveness was extremely hard to quantify. This is because many of the objectives do not lend themselves to ready quantification of benefits (either directly or indirectly). In addition, since many banks are not willing to disclose EFTS transaction data, which they classify as confidential, data on benefits gained by banks from EFTS are largely unavailable. It is therefore difficult to compare the savings or benefits of EFTSs to traditional paper payment methods (*Economic Review*, 1983, 1984). The constraints posed by lack of published data on cost items, transaction volume, and difficulties of measurement of benefits deter our evaluation of the results of electronic banking.

As a result, some EFTS installations have simply been defended on the grounds of long-term market competition. Some EFTSs are implemented without a valid assessment of whether or not they are profitable. EFTS services are also likely to be priced without an adequate understanding of their costs. This section attempts to analyse several economics issues that deserve bank management's particular attention.

Understanding the cost characteristics of EFTS is important. It is obvious that an EFTS involves a large fixed cost for expensive computer resources but relatively small variable costs. Thus, as volume expands, average cost declines (that is, scale economies exist). The basic problem is generating sufficient volume to make the specific EFTS service cost effective. It is a fact that the huge cost of processing paper cheques is at present largely subsidized by the banking system, and the cost to account holders of writing an additional cheque is usually less than the marginal cost of handling a cheque. As a result, too many cheques are written, and more resources than is desirable are allocated to cheque processing. Not until banks start to charge full fees for cheque services will it be easy to induce customers to convert to EFTS services such as EFTPOS. It is expected that appropriate pricing policies will provide economic incentives for the continuing growth of EFTS services during the 1990s.

In the future, banks expect that high utilization of other ATM services can be achieved, and that the marginal costs of an ATM transaction will be lower than those of cheque transactions. However, it is interesting that the changes in consumer behaviour due to ATMs do not always favour the banks. Some banks which have installed ATMs have had a large increase in the number of small accounts. Survey results have also shown that the use of ATMs has increased the volume of transactions, for example, balance enquiries and cash withdrawals. However, it is quite expensive to process a large number of accounts with small dollar amounts. Besides, the reduction in transactions over the counter is small. These changes in consumer behaviour have, therefore, an unfavourable influence on the operating costs of the banks. Many ATMs have not paid for themselves by either offsetting costs or generating additional revenue. In the next decade, transaction volumes are expected to grow faster than increases in accounts, and interest-free account balances will grow more slowly than money transmission costs. With reduced margins and progressively increasing operating costs, banks, especially the smaller ones, should exercise considerable care in looking at the economics of ATM installation and future market trends.

Another problem associated with increased cost is the pricing problem. As mentioned earlier, the set-up and operating costs for some electronic banking services are very high. As a result, some banks have started to collect annual fees from the ATM users and credit card holders. However, this action may cause other problems and alienate some potential customers. Improper pricing sometimes makes differentiating the services of competing banks difficult and often results in losses. A number of errors have been made in implementing EFTS in the United States, which could have been avoided if the costs and the pricing schemes had been subjected to more careful analysis. As the price of services is often set at a competitive level, banks tend to differentiate their services through promotion while trying to maintain their competitiveness at the same time.

Whatever the overall cost of electronic banking services such as CMS and EFTPOS, banks will probably change their traditional policy on charging customers for banking services. Banks will begin to charge more for the less profitable retail banking services they provide as soon as they believe that their retail customers can absorb part of the visible costs. For example, most banks have levied an annual charge for credit cards since 1983. Some banks also charge a fee for current accounts with an average balance below a minimum level. EFTS services, such as ATM transactions, are also likely to be priced at a figure that will, in the long term, favour EFTS transactions over teller-assisted or paper transactions.

It is therefore crucial to provide long-term economic justification for EFTS services which combines cost savings with value-added benefits. It seems that an adjustment of the banking fee schedule is inevitable, and a differential pricing strategy is likely to be used in order to encourage EFTS use. In addition, fee income from innovative EFTS services will be an important source of bank revenue, especially since interest margins can be expected to remain small because of competition. As electronic cash management services become more popular, corporate customers will increasingly manage their own funds, and banks will have to turn increasingly to technical and fee-related services for revenue and profit.

Competition with Non-Bank Institutions

The banking laws of most countries require the accepting of deposits and the making of loans before an institution is classified as a bank, so that the provision of payment services on its own, with balances being settled periodically by a cheque drawn on a bank account, is quite possible for institutions that escape the full rigours of regulation as banks. In this way, banks that formerly controlled certain markets now face competition from outsiders. Among the non-bank institutions that take over some of the roles formerly played by banks are the credit card networks such as Visa and MasterCard.

Similarly, once it was only the banks that could provide electronic banking services, but now deposit and loan companies, insurance companies, credit card companies, and even computer manufacturers and retailers can take part. Anybody, in fact, subject to the regulations, with access both to financial expertise and to modern micro-electronic technology, can offer EFTS-type services. One example is the services offered by American Express Co. which has purchased Warner Communications. The acquisition gave it a two-way cable system (QUBE) which allows two-way communication between the users and American Express through TV sets, used as a terminal. This development has placed American Express well to compete with banks in card and traveler's cheque operations. In another example, a finance company in Japan has established a network of ATMs through which consumers can obtain loans.

Many Hong Kong banks are already facing stiff competition for customer deposits from money market funds, credit card companies, and other non-banking institutions. There is certainly greater competition as non-banks can also transmit messages and funds. The relatively low cost of new technology and improved communications seems set to increase the pressure. At the very least, the spread of EFTSs can only weaken the banks' control of money transfer systems.

Furthermore, some retailers today are also using in-store credit cards and automated systems to extend their operations into the financial field. One example is the Sears Roebuck retail store group in the United States, which has more than 850 stores locally and over 100 abroad, and has more than 25 million active credit cards. It owns an insurance company, a real estate firm, and a brokerage firm. Sears uses IT extensively and has already launched an asset management account (Nicholas, 1982).

All these examples show that distinctions between banks and other financial institutions are becoming blurred, and marketing functions will assume even greater importance as banks seek to differentiate their products from those of their competitors. Whatever the eventual outcome, it is clear that the rapid development of EFTS facilities has provided an efficient technological base for the evolving competitive structure.

Impact of EFTSs on Bank Marketing Policy and Strategy

In the innovation of products and services, banks must make sure that the benefits derived are greater than the costs incurred, especially in the introduction of electronic banking services which involve high initial capital investment and cannot quickly be abandoned if found unnecessary later. Thus, innovation must be geared to market needs. Clearly, banks must adopt new marketing policies appropriate to the new environment in which they operate.

In the future, highly competitive EFTS environment, consumers will find it increasingly difficult to distinguish one financial institution from another. It may also become more difficult to differentiate the services provided by one bank from those of another, as any technological advantage gained will be short-lived. Banks must carefully segment their markets and use both branches and automated delivery systems to tailor products to selected consumer groups. Through market segmentation, providing each category of customers with ready access to a range of services and calibre of people to serve their needs, pleasant and rewarding bank-customer relationships can be maintained. Banks should also try to differentiate their products from those of their competitors in order to remain competitive. In addition, although various electronic banking technologies are available, most banks will have to specialize because few have the resources to cover all areas. However, in certain situations, banks may find themselves competitively bound to introduce a service which they know will be unprofitable. Certainly, each bank has to know its own strengths and weaknesses as well as its position in the market-place. Market and product research should be conducted continuously, to introduce new products or improve existing ones in order to compete effectively in the electronic banking market.

Last but not least, banks should have a clear strategy for their EFTS development. As mentioned earlier, many banks considered electronic banking products primarily as instruments for promoting efficient operations. Consequently, they tend less to evaluate IT on the basis of its ability to provide competitive advantages. In the future, financial institutions should view IT more as a competitive weapon by offering innovative services. This is especially true in the growing competitive and reduced margins environment.

For instance, some banks have considered amalgamating current accounts and saving accounts into single interest-bearing accounts. An increasing proportion of consumer lending will probably be in the form of low-cost overdrafts made available by the use of an ATM card. Using the large volume of local and international financial data stored in a bank's computer system, financial institutions may begin to offer profitable information services to their customers, either through a link with, or in direct competition with, the Viewdata service. Bankers expect that their income will be derived in the future more from fees for specialist services.

Banks are facing many challenges, particularly in the retail market and delivery systems. How well a bank is able to manage the risk-return trade-offs of the new EFTS environment will determine its financial success.

Problems for Users and Customers

When the idea of an EFTS was first conceived in the 1960s, many experts predicted that the technology would have profound effects on the economy and ultimately lead to a cashless and chequeless society. Yet only a small fraction of payment volume today is electronic. The early predictions have not been borne out in any society using an EFTS. For the most part, what exists today is a greatly improved paper-based financial system.

Research has revealed that overall EFTS development has slowed, because of soaring costs, consumer resistance, and some legal constraints (Benton, 1977). EFTS, like other technology, has its own costs and benefits. Only when the benefits derived from EFTS are greater than its costs will users be likely to adopt it. Earlier sections of this chapter have revealed the problems of electronic banking for the providers. This section focuses on problems related to EFTS users and consumers, which include: resistance to change; loss of the benefit of a float; an increase in cost, and problems of cost sharing; inadequate product design and features; loss of control of their finances; invasion of personal privacy; system security and risk; problems related to legal issues; and lack of consumer awareness, education, and participation.

It is for these reasons that many financial institutions have proceeded very slowly and carefully in installing home banking and EFTPOS terminals. Consumer acceptance will depend on how consumers perceive the impact of EFTS on them. A key question is whether consumers really want and accept EFTS. Are customers willing to pay for the value added and on what basis? One major problem associated with EFTS development is human resistance to change. Some consumers and institutions are satisfied with the present system, which they think can handle existing (and projected) transaction flows. Some people have no confidence in machines, and the lack of inter-personal communication also discourages some people from using ATMs.

Another main reason that customers have been reluctant to accept some electronic banking services is that there is no economic incentive to offset the loss of credit card and cheque float, and consumers are unwilling to pay an extra cost to use EFTS services. Many electronic banking products (for example, EFTPOS) must also compete with cash in both convenience and costs. Customers would prefer existing procedures and will resist using POS terminals if they feel that the systems are too complicated. Product designs need to be upgraded continuously, and only services that are fast, convenient, easy to use, and reliable will accelerate the use of electronic banking activities. Furthermore, whereas preauthorized payment may be a convenience, some consumers may consider the service to be a threat to their control of their own finances. It removes flexibility in meeting monthly bills. Another important consideration is the provision of leverage against a merchant or vendor in case of a dispute. Cheques offer the advantage of being able to stop payment. Similar safeguards that allow the reversal of the instantaneous transfer of funds to the merchant must be provided in the electronic systems. Laws will be needed that will guarantee consumer protection in seller-buyer disputes.

Personal privacy is increasingly important in an EFTS installation. An EFTS can capture details of an individual's financial activities instantaneously. A large volume of important and sensitive personal data, such as where transactions are conducted, property owned, and buying habits are stored in the system. Improper entry to these computer files could enable the creation of a black market in confidential information such as selling mailing lists. A major concern is the protection of consumer privacy and the need to prevent unauthorized access to and storage of these data. Privacy of customer information is not only important to a bank's market position but also involves legal binding responsibility of the bank to its customers.

There is also increased potential for infrequent but high-loss incidents. Possible failures or irregularities in the security or reliability of EFTS services could cause serious damage to participants in the system, and the operation of a shared EFTS network could cause further complications (AICPA, 1978). Personal identification numbers (PINs) have not been a particularly effective form of protection; and many consumers are reluctant to accept a payments system with an invisible audit trail. Plastic card fraud is now a quickly growing industry in many countries. Moreover, the embezzlement and manipulation of electronic financial records could be more difficult to detect, unless proper controls can be developed for EFTS.

Research has shown that there is no clear definition of legal responsibilities and liabilities for EFTS fraud, errors, or irregularities. Bankers may not have fully appreciated that the new electronic banking systems in Hong Kong may expose banks to significantly greater degrees of potential legal liability. Regulations have also not provided enough safeguards for consumers. For example, legislation remains ambiguous on the liability sharing between the financial institution and the consumer in the case of a handling discrepancy during an ATM transaction. Also, there is no legally binding liability of the financial institution of the ATM transaction receipt at present. A shared ATM network would further complicate the matters. To protect the public interest, it is believed that regulations are needed that, at the very least, specify clearly the kind of information which providers of the services must give to their customers. Such information includes the liabilities and responsibilities associated with the improper use of plastic cards; the means of stopping a payment or reversing a transaction; and the methods used to calculate interest charges or other fees for using the services. Banks now also should take steps themselves to define their legal and contractual positions related to EFTS.

While the future of EFTS services seems assured, businesses and consumers at present lack adequate knowledge of EFTS capabilities, the options for different types of EFTS development, and their economic and social implications. In fact, the effectiveness of EFTS services is also limited by consumers' limited awareness and knowledge of the development. A well co-ordinated public education programme is needed, involving the financial institutions, the Government, the Consumer Council, and the mass media, to ensure the protection of the public.

Moreover, the development of EFTS services should not be left to technical experts and computer vendors. EFTS developments deserve attention at the highest policy making level within the financial institutions. Involvement of different interested parties such as the Consumer Councils, retailers, manufacturers, and Government regulatory agencies (such as the Banking Commission and the Banking Advisory Committee) in critical nation-wide EFTS decisions is also important. In fact, some people have complained that the EFTPOS was planned for Hong Kong without the participation and support of its chief users, namely the retailers and their customers. This is in agreement with a special report published by OECD (Revell, 1983) which has warned that electronic methods of payment touch on so many aspects of public policy that governments will have to play a part in their regulation and control. It was argued that a 'national payments council' should be set up, with a mission to inform and educate the general public, where the various issues can be debated among the different interested parties.

Concluding Remarks

This chapter explores the principal trends in electronic banking, and provides a critical review of the future of 'electronic money'. It develops a broad perspective and sketches a scenario of the development of EFTS, indicating the major influence that this is likely to exert upon local business.

We have already seen how information technology was at first used to reduce the volume of transactions and the cost of operations, and how more recently financial institutions have come to regard themselves as being in the financial information business. Overall, it seems safe to predict that, by the mid-1990s, Hong Kong will have a rather sophisticated shared electronic payment network, along with traditional paper-based systems. The payment network system will enable a high proportion of large inter-bank payments to be handled automatically. The development of EFTPOS, CMS, and home banking projects will require greater co-operation between the banks that share the network system. Individual customers will have access to a wide variety of electronic banking facilities with a micro-processor memory card. The growth rate of currency and cheques will continue to decline. The number of bank branches will be more stable, and a large proportion of banking transactions will be initiated by customers away from bank premises. We should not, however, be limited by the pace of these individual developments. In the foreseeable future, we are likely to continue to use cash, cheques, and other established media of payment.

Finally, it should be stressed that financial institutions must be cautious in their approach to EFTS and should not blindly be led by technology or market forces. An EFTS should be introduced only as a part of an institution's long-term corporate business strategy. Banks should carefully analyse their markets and tailor products to meet the needs of selected consumer groups.

There are some terms that appropriately describe Hong Kong business community: aggressive, responsive, and innovative. However, it takes time to implement electronic banking. Despite all the difficulties associated with EFTS, information technology has been vital to the successful growth of financial institutions in Hong Kong and continues to be an integral part of the banking industry. Nevertheless, a number of issues still have to be resolved before the EFTS revolution dream becomes a reality.

Note

1. For an example of how an ACH processes a direct payroll deposit and a preauthorized insurance premium, see Ho (1986, pp. 158–61).

References

Altschul. J., 'No Real Need for Home Banking', *Asia Banking*, May 1984, pp. 96–8.

American Institute of Certified Public Accountants (AICPA), *Audit Considerations in Electronic Funds Transfer Systems* (New York, AICPA, 1978).

Armstrong, N., 'The Headlong Invasion of Electronic Banking', *Asian Finance*, 15 September 1983, pp. 58–62.

Asian Finance, 'Electronic Banking: Technology Creates a Class Apart', 15 March 1984, pp. 73–86.

—— 'Hong Kong EFTPOS poised for a big Leap', January 1986, pp. 80–81.

—— 'Asian Banks Start Trial Run for Cashless Shopping Plan', August 1985, pp. 43–5.

Austin, H., 'The Ubiquitous ATM', *Hong Kong Business*, June 1988, pp. 46–8.

The Banker, 'Banking Tomorrow: CLF Offers Home Banking', February 1984, pp. 65–6.

Bedwell, D. E., 'Payments in the Financial Services Industry of the 1980s', *Economic Review*, Federal Reserve Bank of Atlanta, December 1983, pp. 4–10.

Benton, J. B., 'Electronic Fund Transfer: Pitfalls and Payoffs', *Harvard Business Review*, July–August 1977, pp. 16–32.

Borland, A. G. 'CHATS — Clearing House Automated Transfer System', *Hong Kong Computer Society Yearbook 1983* (Hong Kong, Hong Kong Computer Society, 1983).

Communications of the ACM, Vol. 22, Special Issue on EFT Symposium, No. 12, December 1979, pp. 639–71.

Crampton, R. and Mofat, L., 'Corporate Cash Management', *Australian Accountants*, March 1986, pp. 22–3; 25–6.

DeCotiis, A. R., 'The Business Plan for Home Banking', *Economic Review* (Federal Reserve Bank of Atlanta, July/August 1984), p. 42.

Economic Review, Special Issue: Displacing the Check (Federal Reserve Bank of Atlanta, August 1983).

—— Special Issue on the Revolution in Retail Payment (Federal Reserve Bank of Atlanta, July/August 1984).

Greene, Peter G. H., 'Hexagon — HongkongBank's Corporate Electronic Banking System', *Hong Kong Computer Journal*, July 1986, pp. 6–9.

Ho, S. S. M., 'The Computerization of the Bank Industry in Hong Kong: Implications and Prospects'. *The Hong Kong Economic Journal Monthly*, Vol. 8, No. 10, January 1984, pp. 24–7.

—— 'Electronic Funds Transfer Systems: Special Problems in Hong Kong', *Asian Banking*, May 1984, pp. 91–2, 101.

—— 'Electronic Fund Transfer Systems' in R. H. Scott, K. A. Wong, and Y. K. Ho (eds.), *Hong Kong's Financial Institutions and Markets*, (Hong Kong, Oxford University Press, 1986), pp. 153–79.

The Institute of Banks, *The Banks and Technology in the 1980s* (London, September, 1982).

Ives, B., and Learmouth, P., 'The Information System as a Competitive Weapon', *Communication of the ACM*, December 1984, pp. 1193–201.

Jones, D., 'Leading the World in Cash Management Systems', *Banking World*, August 1983, pp. 40–1.

Kan, M., 'JETCO — The Banking Network in Hong Kong', *Proceedings of SEARCC 84 Conference* (Hong Kong, Hong Kong Computer Society,

September 1984), pp. 35.1–35.13.

Marti, J. and Zeilinger, A., 'Micro and Money: New Technology in Banking and Shopping', *Policy Studies Institute*, 1982.

Martin, J., *The Wired Society* (Englewood Cliffs, NJ, Prentice-Hall, 1978), pp. 89–103.

Metzker, P. F., 'Future Payments System Technology: Can Small Financial Institutions Compete?', *Economic Review*, (Federal Reserve Bank of Atlanta, November 1982), pp. 58–67.

National Commission on Electronic Fund Transfer, *EFT in the United States: Policy Recommendations and the Public Interest* (Washington, DC, NCEFT, 28 October 1977).

Nicholas, T., 'Effects on Retail Banking', in *The Banks and Technology in the 1980s*, September 1982.

Porter, M. E. and Millar, V. E., 'How Information Gives You Competitive Advantages', *Harvard Business Review*, July–August 1985, pp. 149–160.

Revell, J. R. S., 'Banking and Electronic Fund Transfer: A Study of Its Implications', (Paris, OECD, 1983).

—— 'The New Technology and Financial Institutions', *Managerial Finance*, Vol. 10, No. 1, 1984, pp. 1–5.

Schaller, C. A., 'The Revolution of EFTS', *Journal of Accountancy* (New York, The American Institute of Certified Public Accountants, October 1978), pp. 74–80.

Solomon, E. H., (ed.), *Electronic Funds Transfer and Payments: The Public Policy Issues* (Boston, Kluwer Nijhoff Publishing, 1987).

Todd, P. C., 'Technology will Change Face of Banking', *Asian Money Manager*, October 1981, pp. 25–6.

Wild, R. J., 'Electronic Banking: The Only Way Out', *Hong Kong Review*, (Hong Kong, South China Morning Post, January 1982), pp. 32–3.

Williams, M., 'Electronic Streamline Cash Management', *Management Review*, May 1986.

15. Bank Marketing

ALLAN K. K. CHAN AND HELEN W. M. HO

Introduction

Just like any other type of business, a bank's resources include trained labour/management and capital assets (ranging from automated teller Machines to the desk-top computers commonly used nowadays for financial analysis). Another resource, unique to a bank, is lending funds which can simply be termed deposits. These three make up the integral parts or the supply side of a banking system.

A bank will not simply let these resources sit, generating no profit. Instead, the bank will turn its resources into products such as loans, investment products, and other services such as gift cheques and safe deposit boxes at market demand. This relationship is depicted in Fig. 15.1, and it helps explain the dual marketing role of a bank.

Fig. 15.1 Resources (Supply) of and Demand for Banking Services

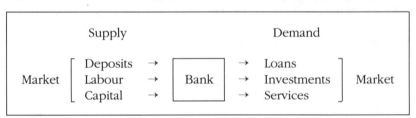

The American Marketing Association officially defined 'marketing' as the 'process of planning and executing the conception, pricing, promotion, and distribution of ideas, goods, and services to create exchanges that satisfy individual and organizational objectives.'[1] Included in this definition are marketing activities not only for physical products, but also for intangible ones such as ideas and services. Banking services, which are partly tangible and partly intangible, should be no exception.

Hodges and Tillman (1986) suggested that, in the banking context, marketing is 'the creation and delivery of customer-satisfying services at a profit to the bank.'[2] This calls for an understanding of banking's so-called 'dual marketing task.' A bank must be doubly marketing-oriented: on one hand a bank needs marketing programmes designed to attract funds; on the other hand it must then transform these funds into customer-satisfying services and create marketing programmes to attract customers for these services. This dual task is shown diagrammatically in Fig. 15.2.

Fig. 15.2 Banking's Dual Marketing Task

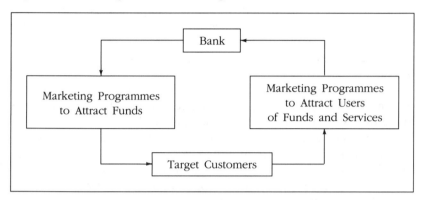

Source: Adapted from Arthur Meidan, *Bank Marketing Management* (London, Macmillan, 1984), p. 17.

Several important points should be noted here. First of all, the delivery of existing services is important, but the creation of new products should not be neglected. In addition, bank marketing is similar to marketing other products in the sense that it too is consumer-oriented. The consumer's needs and wants have to be fulfilled by the products and services that a bank offers. Furthermore, marketing is not merely promotion and advertising, as is often mistakenly thought. Marketing is a process, starting from the conception of a product to selling it finally, to the benefit of both the seller and the consumer.

The Adoption of Bank Marketing Concepts

It is difficult to trace the evolution or development of bank marketing, both locally and internationally. For example, in the United Kingdom, there has been a growing interest in applying marketing techniques and tools in the field of banking (Meidan, 1984), but 'even today it [the term "marketing"] is resisted by many traditionally oriented bank managers.'[3] In Hong Kong, banking is thought 'to have lagged behind the consumer products industry with regard to the adoption of the "marketing concept".'[4] Among many reasons that banks lagged, the major one is that the concepts of marketing were not fully understood by banks — banks traditionally attracted management people with an interest in finance, and they 'acted, looked like, and smelled like bankers . . . not creative, aggressive marketing types.'[5]

However, intense competition in the banking industry has made marketing necessary for banks to survive (Meidan, 1984). The competition comes not just from other banks, but also from other types of financial institutions. It is not hard at all to appreciate the severe competitive situation for banks operating in Hong Kong, given the presence of, at the end of 1988, 158 licensed banks with 1,397 local bank branches, together with 148 local representative offices of overseas banks, and 35 licensed deposit-taking companies as well as 216 registered deposit-taking companies. In order to compete for a better market share position, banks have to engage in some form of marketing, targeting either potential depositors, potential loan makers, or both.

Since the purpose of this chapter is to provide a basic understanding of bank marketing in Hong Kong, the rest of the chapter is devoted to the discussion of the key functional areas of bank marketing, which include product and service development, branching, and promotional activities. According to McCarthy and Perreault (1987), there are four basic controllable functional elements in marketing, known as the Four Ps: product, price, place (distribution), and promotion. However, as far as bank marketing is concerned, price is not really a controllable element, as it is of other consumer products, because of regulatory constraints. The interest rates are basically governed by the Hong Kong Association of Banks, and banks seldom use price (interest rates in particular) as a marketing tool (Ng and So, 1981), though interest rates for deposits with maturity longer than 12 months or larger than HK$500,000 are not controlled. We therefore focus our attention on the other controllable areas, that is, products and services, branch banking, and promotional activities. The final section in this chapter will discuss bank marketing strategies in Hong Kong.

Branch Banking

Banks' branching movement in Hong Kong can be traced back to the late 1950s, with two factors behind it: (a), the efforts of the whole banking system at saving mobilization; and (b), inter-bank competition.[6]

The branching movement is clearly shown in Table 15.1. During the period between 1954 and 1958, there was a decrease in the total number of banking offices as well as in banking density. However, we can observe an enormous increase in the number of branches from 1959 to 1964. While the number of licensed banks was increased by only six from 1959–64, the total number of offices was increased by 197, bringing the banking density up to 0.81 in 1964 in contrast to 0.33 in 1959. The increasing trend, from 1965 to 1968, slowed down due to the run on banks in 1965 and the riot in 1967.[7] Another point to note is that in 1966 the Government imposed a moratorium on the issue of new bank licences, mainly as a result of the 1965 bank runs, and the moratorium was not lifted until March 1978.[8] This is probably why the number of licensed banks in the period 1966–77 remained more or less at the same level.

Table 15.1 Banks' Branching Movement (1954–1988)

Year	No. of Licensed Banks	No. of Branches	Total No. of Offices*	Banking Density**
1954	94	3	97	0.42
1955	91	3	94	0.40
1956	86	4	90	0.36
1957	83	5	88	0.33
1958	81	8	89	0.32
1959	82	13	95	0.33
1960	86	38	124	0.42
1961	85	101	186	0.58
1962	92	121	213	0.64
1963	87	144	231	0.64
1964	88	204	292	0.81
1965	86	215	301	0.82
1966	76	242	318	0.85
1967	75	256	331	0.86
1968	75	274	349	0.89
1969	73	289	362	0.94
1970	73	326	399	1.01
1971	73	358	431	1.06
1972	74	404	478	1.17
1973	74	469	542	1.27
1974	74	557	631	1.44
1975	74	629	703	1.59
1976	74	685	759	1.70
1977	74	719	803	1.76
1978	88	790	878	1.86
1979	105	906	1,011	2.02
1980	113	1,032	1,145	2.22
1981	121	1,181	1,302	2.55
1982	131	1,343	1,474	2.79
1983	136	1,395	1,531	2.87
1984	140	1,407	1,547	2.87
1985	143	1,251	1,394	2.56
1986	151	1,235	1,386	2.51
1987	154	1,233	1,387	2.45
1988	158	1,239	1,397	2.44

Notes: * No. of branches plus head offices.
         ** No. of banking offices per 10,000 population.

Sources: V.F.S. Sit (1983), p. 642; *Hong Kong Annual Report*, (Hong Kong, Census and Statistics Department), various issues.

Although the increase in the number of the licensed banks was hindered by the Government's moratorium, there was another high period in the branching movement in the eight years between 1969 and 1977. The total number of bank offices was increased drastically from 362 to 803, and the banking density nearly doubled in the same period.

Although the Government imposed the moratorium again in August 1979 for more than a year, until May 1981, the number of banks increased quite smoothly afterwards, and at the end of 1988 there were 158 licensed banks, more than twice the number in 1977. The total number of bank offices also nearly doubled from 1977–88, bringing the banking density up to 2.45 in 1987 and 2.44 in 1988, implying that on average there is one bank office serving every 4,000 population.

With regard to branch banking, several points deserve further examination.

1. Roles of Branch Managers. In view of the fact that competition amongst banks is becoming more and more acute, banks have to continuously adjust themselves to the marketing environment and bring forth innovations to meet the various needs of their customers. Since opening branches has become a popular strategy for expanding the network of distribution, a branch manager, who is the key to the success of this strategy, plays an unprecedentedly important role. In reaction to this marketing change, the scope of duties of branch managers is generally widened to include not only traditional lending and administrative work but also the tasks of compiling customer profiles, estimating target sales, profit and cost figures for different financial products, monitoring the state of the market in the local area, and actively marketing the growing range of additional services offered by the banks (Turnbull, 1982).

However, a study in the United Kingdom on the role of branch managers revealed that managers are not yet either thinking or acting in an accepted customer-oriented style. Three reasons are identified to explain the phenomenon of poor marketing orientation among branch managers: lack of motivation, lack of ability, and lack of time (Turnbull, 1982). Although a similar study has not been carried out in Hong Kong, the same conclusion is perhaps also applicable to the Hong Kong situation. If it is for branch managers to cope effectively with the ever increasing competition, they especially need more training to update their knowledge and improve their ability to deal with the ever-changing marketing environment, for training in the context of banking world was traditionally reserved for operational rather than managerial level staff. Even the Bank of China Group, usually regarded as a conservative bank group, has begun to place more emphasis on staff training at managerial and senior levels.[9]

2. Locating Branch Offices. Locations of bank offices are extremely important as they affect distribution of the bank products and services. Decisions on branch location also involve economic consideration, such as land prices and rentals of individual locations, which may lead to considerable expenditure of resources on a long-term scale (Meidan,

1984). Branch location is an especially important decision in Hong Kong. Because it is such a tiny place (Hong Kong is only 1,071 square kilometers in area), land prices and rentals are extremely high compared with most other countries. In addition, one unique characteristic of the Hong Kong retail banking scene is that once a branch has opened, it is seldom closed regardless of its profit level (Lee, 1986). Taking these factors into consideration, banks in Hong Kong need better mechanisms for exploring profitable branch locations instead of simply making ad hoc decisions in the conventional way. As reported by Lee (1986), there has been a rigorous attempt to develop a systematic procedure to search for profitable retail locations for commercial banks in Hong Kong.

Branching, in addition to serving as a weapon in inter-bank competition, brings the banking services closer to the consumer and facilitates adaptation of the product mix to the particular needs of the local market. For instance, to serve firms in Hong Kong's Central District effectively, a bank would require a product mix very different from the mix that a firm in Tsuen Wan or Tuen Mun finds satisfactory. Local branches can therefore serve the local clientele better as they know the needs of the customers better.

Overseas banks and small local banks are often typical of small branch networks. They either have to go after highly selected segments (Golden Circle of Chase Manhattan Bank, for example, is a service developed particularly for high net worth individuals) or compete on the basis of price.

Overseas banks usually opt for the strategy of concentrated marketing simply because their small number of branches makes it impossible for them to appeal to the mass market and the costs needed to expand the network are not justified. If small local banks choose to compete on price, again this is not easy because the market has demonstrated that price alone is not a very effective tool in attracting more customers.

3. The Emergence of Automated Teller Machines. A look at Table 15.1 tells us that from 1985 onwards the number of bank branches shows an obvious decrease. This is not necessarily a reflection of business decline in the retail banking industry, but can probably be explained as a change in retail banking environment, typified by the extensive adoption of self-service Automated Teller Machines (ATMs) (Ho, 1986; Tai, 1986; Russell, 1987). In 1981, the definition of a bank branch in Hong Kong was clarified to distinguish between a branch and an ATM. A bank installing an ATM is not considered to be opening a branch and hence need not apply to the Government nor pay an annual fee of HK$10,000 for a branch.[10] In view of this, banks may choose to cut down the number (or slow the increase) of branches and replace them with ATMs in order to save the annual fee and the operating costs,[11] even though they have instead to invest for the installation of ATMs (Tai, 1986). The development of ATMs (and also Electronic Fund Transfer Systems) is discussed in Chapter 14 above.

4.   Telebanking.   Citibank and Chase Manhattan Bank, two banks well known for their innovativeness, recently introduced the concept of telebanking in Hong Kong. Under this product idea, customers can check their account balances, make transfers, check exchange rates, order cheque books, stop payment on cheques, request the monthly statements, and pay electricity bills, school fees, credit card bills, and so on, simply by calling a hot line and stating their passwords. This represents a revolutionary change from the conventional banking practice under which customers have to physically visit the bank or the ATMs. It is, therefore, not surprising that the product received a warm welcome immediately. After all, this also represents a major reduction in operating costs for the banks. Undoubtedly, staff must be employed to receive these phone calls, but with a savings of eight dollars per transaction (a claim made by a HongkongBank spokesperson when the Bank held a lucky draw for the users of its ATMs), telebanking may provide an even greater savings.

It was therefore not surprising that (after the market was proved to be receptive), banks in the Bank of China Group (BOCG) also followed suit. Kincheng Banking Corporation carried the idea even further by providing the convenience of carrying out foreign exchange transactions, stock transactions, and many others, all on a telephone line.

Products and Services

Traditionally bank products are broadly classified into deposit-taking instruments and lending instruments, stemming from the basic dual role of banks in deposit taking and lending. The deposit-taking instruments are offered basically in terms of accounts, for example, savings accounts, current accounts, time deposit accounts, and so on. Within these individual types of accounts, there are often further classifications. The following are some examples:
1.   Classification by Currency. Hong Kong dollar savings accounts, United States dollar savings accounts, renminbi savings accounts, and so on.
2.   Classification by the Length of Deposit Period. Seven-day call deposit, one-month time deposit, six-month time deposit, and so on.
3.   Classification by the Identity of Depositors. Children's accounts, joint accounts, company accounts, and so on.

The deposit-taking business of banks and financial institutions has been strictly regulated by the three-tier financial system. Under this system, licensed banks benefit the most because they are allowed to monopolize deposits of less than HK$50,000.

As far as lending instruments are concerned, banks conventionally direct the greatest effort to corporate clients. In the past (before 1945 for example), personal loans could be obtained only from some quasi-finance institutions like 'Ngan Ho' and 'Tsin Chong' or self-organized credit unions (Lok and Loke, 1983). However, the personal lending market was gradually emphasized, and we can now see a variety of products tailor-made for individual clients. The lending instruments are generally offered in the following classifications:

1. Classification by Purpose. In the corporate sector there are loans for trade financing, building mortgages, factoring, and so on. In the personal lending sector there are property mortgages, car mortgages, personal overdraft accounts, tax loans, travel loans, and so on.

But today's lending instruments are far more sophisticated than the conventional ones. One example is the graduated repayment method for housing loans recently introduced by Standard Chartered Bank. Under their Mortgage Plus' Graduated Repayment Method, some buyers can gear their monthly instalment to their annual salary increases. As a result, customers can save interest while shortening the mortgage repayment period. An added benefit of this new loan scheme is that customers can now rely on the pre-approved mortgage service to choose their homes.

2. Classification by Collateral. Those loans without collateral include clean overdraft accounts, credit cards, and so on, whereas most corporate lending, especially those of larger amounts, require some form of collateral.

The personal loan market is typical of lending without collateral. For example, both the Flexiline Personal Overdraft Plan of Standard Chartered Bank and the Personal Instalment Loan of HongkongBank are personal loans with no tangible security.

In the recent decade, there have been great innovations in banks' products and services. For people using a bank deposit as an investment, a great variety of choices is available. Flexibility is also allowed in the terms and conditions of lending. For example, in the past only real estate was counted as collateral for loans, but now all kinds of balance sheet assets and personal guarantees are acceptable (Lok and Loke, 1983).

It is not the purpose of this chapter to examine banking products and services in detail. Rather, we examine the recent development of banking products and services from a strategic marketing perspective. Several things become apparent from this perspective:

1. Product Combinations. Banking products have been changed from purely deposit or lending instruments into product combinations. For example, some banks offer overdraft facilities to current account holders. The Electronic Fund Transfer System (EFTS) also makes it convenient for customers to operate different accounts simultaneously, including savings accounts, current accounts, and credit card accounts. Therefore, to those EFTS users, accounts in the bank are no longer separated but rather in the form of a package closely linked together. The 'TripleAccess' of the HongkongBank is a good example. Triple-Access allows managing three accounts, which may include a savings account, current accounts, Super ETC accounts, or any HongkongBank credit card account, by using a single HongkongBank card.[12]

Only a short time ago, Citibank introduced the CitiOne Money System which featured compound daily interest, 'no-bounce-check' protection, telebanking, and one consolidated monthly statement for all accounts, all in one product. The concept of product combination is thereby not limited to just a handful of accounts.

2. Product Modifications. Banks have made a great effort to modify traditional products to be more convenient and beneficial to customers. One of the obvious examples is the modification of time deposits into Certificates of Deposit (CDs) which, under the interest rate ruling and within the framework of CDs, offer a range of benefits to customers such as higher interest yields, automatic renewal at maturity, and automatic transfer of principal and/or interest into another of the depositor's accounts (Lok and Loke, 1983).

The swap deposit is another example. Owing to the difference in interest taxes between deposits in Hong Kong currency and foreign currencies, banks allow investors to pay in Hong Kong dollars for the banks to convert into, say, a United States dollars time deposit account. Upon maturity, the investor will receive principal and interest in Hong Kong dollars at a predetermined exchange rate under a forward exchange contract (Lok and Loke, 1983).

A further example is the modification of non-interest bearing current accounts into interest bearing accounts. In this regard, banks allow customers to maintain deposits in savings accounts, but whenever cheques are drawn on a customer's current account, the same amount of money will be automatically transferred from his savings account to his current account. This transference is made possible by pre-signed withdrawal and pay-in vouchers. Under this arrangement, customers enjoy the benefits of holding current accounts without unnecessarily losing interest and without the trouble of handling the necessary transfers themselves (Lok and Loke, 1983).

3. Product Identification. It has been said that the most prominent problem for financial institutions today is the failure to establish a clear identity for their products, one that is immediately and easily recognizable by consumers (Selame and Kolligan, 1985). Banks in Hong Kong do make an effort to create product identification. There have been many cases in which banks attempt to associate their products with their names such as the Citifunds,[13] Citideposits,[14] and so on of the Citibank; and the Chase Dollarmaker, Chase Bank-By-Phone, Chase/CAC Furnishings Plan, and so on of the Chase Manhattan Bank (Tai, 1986).

4. Personalization of Banking Services. In order to capture a better market share in this highly competitive banking industry, many banks, especially foreign banks in Hong Kong, tailor their services for selected customers. The common belief is that 80 per cent of the profit comes from the top 20 per cent of customers, so it is profit-justified to emphasize 'private, executive, personal' banking (Lok and Loke, 1983). The Citibank, for example, redecorated some of its branches to reflect the bank's image as a bank for well-educated executives. The Chase

Manhattan Bank also launched a private and personal banking service, named the 'Chase Golden Circle,' to serve the money management needs of upper-middle income professionals (Chan, 1986a). Since the target customers are carefully selected and well defined, the bank can afford to provide personalized services. For example, the marketing staff of Chase Manhattan Bank's 'Chase Golden Circle' will call on clients at their homes or businesses on a one-to-one basis for a long-term personal banking relationship, instead of requiring customers to go to the bank for their banking needs. Chase has also specially designed and decorated four branch offices located in major commercial areas (Central, Tsimshatsui East, Wanchai, and Shatin) for this purpose (Chan, 1986a).

5. Credit Card Business. Since the introduction of credit cards in Hong Kong by Diners Club International in 1959, there has been a rapid growth in possession and use of credit cards in Hong Kong (Sin, Hsu, and Ho, 1987). Banks and card agencies have been promoting bank credit cards aggressively, and nowadays it appears that banks can no longer afford to neglect the credit card market. It is estimated that in 1987 nearly 600,000 people in Hong Kong held Visa cards, with another 200,000 or more carrying American Express cards. People in the industry estimate that the potential market is double this size.[15]

Promotional Activities

Advertising expenditures for general banking services in Hong Kong in 1978 were estimated to be HK$18.9 million; in 1986, it rose almost four times to HK$73.3 million; in 1987, it came up further to HK$86.5 million (Sin and Pang, 1986; Cabatit, 1988a). In the first six months of 1988, the banking industry spent as much as HK$41.1 million in advertising for general banking services, and was included in the top 10 advertisers by category in that time period, as shown in Table 15.2. It is quite obvious that banks in Hong Kong are spending much more than they did in the past to promote their services and their corporate images.

Traditionally, banks in Hong Kong did not place much emphasis on promotion. Perhaps the major reason was that the demand for banking services was, then, greater than the supply, and it was unnecessary for banks to compete for business. Customers had to come to the banks to request loans, credit, and other services. Therefore, banks seldom needed to promote their services. On the other hand, efforts were made by banks to promote their corporate images, and so the early promotion efforts of banks in Hong Kong focused on building up their goodwill. The promotional tools commonly used were well-designed pamphlets for introducing banks' services, good manners of the front-line staff (for example, receptionists and tellers), a free pocket diary at year end, free red packet envelopes and year picture before the coming of Chinese Lunar New Year, personalized service for 'big' clients,

Table 15.2   Top 10 Advertisers in Hong Kong by Category, January
             to June 1988

Categories	Advertising Expenditures (in HK$ million)
Cigarettes	142.6
Travel/accommodation overseas	139.1
Movie/concert/drama	96.3
Watches	76.2
Residential estates	60.8
Brandy	50.6
Department stores	45.2
Miscellaneous	43.1
Bank — general services	41.1
Airlines	41.0

Source: *Media*, 14 October 1988.

banquets for the officers of corporate clients during the Chinese Lunar
New Year period, and so on.

Another characteristic of early bank promotion was its didacticism.
The theme of bank advertising often centred on some didactic statement
such as 'save for a rainy day.' The Hang Seng Bank has been adopting
this strategy of promotion for many years. A jingle used by the bank
to encourage savings habits sings 'Little drops of water, little grains of
sand, make the mighty ocean and the pleasant land.'[16] To cultivate the
habit of saving, many banks also issue coin savings boxes for their
customers. Again, the Hang Seng Bank launched altogether 46 different
types of coin savings boxes from 1960 to 1987, including designs of
the Twelve Animals in the Chinese horoscope.

Some banks also promote their corporate image by involving
themselves in educational activities. Perhaps the most obvious example
is again the Hang Seng Bank. The bank initiated an Elementary Banking
Program in 1963, for those who were interested in a banking career.
The program, which was offered free of charge, finally led to the
official establishment of the Hang Seng School of Commerce in 1979.
As its predecessor did, the school, supported by a School Fund formed
by the donations from the Hang Seng Bank, the S. H. Ho Foundation,
Dah Chong Hong, and many founding shareholders of the Hang Seng
Bank, offers free educational opportunities to students (Ngan, 1983).

Recent Bank Advertising

As already mentioned, keen competition has made it necessary for
banks to emphasize marketing. As more and more banks and other
kinds of financial institutions established themselves in Hong Kong,

banks gradually realized the need for product advertising in addition to the image promotion they used to practice. Even the relatively conservative Bank of China Group launched a major advertising campaign for the first time in late 1983 (Chan, 1986b). Banks now devote a great deal of effort to promotional activities. Two important aspects of this trend can be observed. First, the promotional activities are usually launched in the form of a campaign, with a well-defined promotional objective and a variety of promotional tools. Second, professional advertising agencies are involved to a greater extent than before. Listed below are some of the major recent bank advertising campaigns.

(a) The Hongkong and Shanghai Banking Corporation, which spent an estimated HK$20 million on advertising in 1987, launched an advertising campaign in 1988 with the slogan 'HongkongBank and you, the Winning Team' focusing on the young population with middle or upper incomes. The campaign was handled by Ted Bates, a major advertising agency in Hong Kong (Cabatit, 1988c).

(b) The Security Pacific Asian Bank, previously known as the Bank of Canton, spent HK$5 million through its agency McCann-Erickson in a campaign to attract customers and announce its new name. It was reported that about 60 per cent of the budget was channelled into TV commercials while the rest was reserved for advertisements in print media (Cabatit, 1988a). The International Bank of Asia, previously known as the Sun Hung Kai Bank, went through a similar exercise when changing its name (Arsan, 1987).

(c) The Chase Manhattan Bank started a campaign with Leo Burnett in 1988 to advertise its Golden Circle concept (mentioned above). The budget of the campaign was between HK$1.5 million and HK$2 million, and included TV commercials, print advertisements, selective direct mail, and follow-up personal visits (Moy, 1987a).

Sales Promotion

Besides advertising, the following promotional tools have been employed by banks in Hong Kong:

1. Direct Marketing. Direct marketing refers to a strategy of making direct contact with potential customers in such a way that the advertiser strives to talk 'only to the most qualified audience possible, in many instances, calling them by name — as individuals — especially when . . . using direct mail as a medium.'[17] The purpose of direct marketing is to build a favourable impression and a predisposition in potential customers to buy, by giving them all the information they need to act and the means to take that action, such as telephone number, coupon, reply envelope, or all of these (Mitchell, 1987). Banks in Hong Kong are using direct marketing more and more extensively. The Standard Chartered Bank, for example, started using direct mail in a concerted manner in 1984 to promote products such as personal overdraft

schemes, credit cards, tax loans, insurance schemes, equity mortgages, and time deposits. It sends out, on average, one direct mail package a month. Response rate is reported to vary from 1 to 10 per cent. All information mailed out was professionally tailored to appeal to its carefully chosen target audience. The Gold Visa cards direct mail package, for example, was so well-designed that some recipients, even though they did not respond, kept the package as souvenir (Moy, 1987b).

2.   Promotion in Co-operation with Related Business Institutions. Some banks attempt to promote their products in co-operation with business partners for mutual benefit. The promotion of credit cards is an example. The American Express Bank launched a prize-winning joint promotion campaign with selected restaurants in Hong Kong to encourage greater use of the American Express credit card in those restaurants during the restaurant off season.[18] The number of restaurants which joined the scheme was 37 in 1986, its first year, and jumped to 103 in 1987. In 1986, the American Express bank spent about HK$0.9 million on its promotion with the restaurants, on print, direct mail, and support advertising. This campaign, handled by the world-renowned advertising agency Ogilvy and Mather, was considered so successful that it was later implemented in Korea, and will probably be launched also in Europe and America (Cabatit, 1988b; Woodall, 1988).

3.   Promotion With Lucky Draws.   Traditionally, major elements of promotion are personal selling and advertising, with sales promotion as a supporting element. In Hong Kong, banks are adopting more sales promotion tools in addition to advertising. Among these tools, lucky draws are particularly mentioned here because this is an innovative practice in the banking industry, and the promotional expenditure involved is substantial. The Standard Chartered Bank, for example, promoted the 'Tax Pleaser' (a tax loan) during the tax paying period in early 1989 with 'Gold-for-Tax' lucky draws where loan applicants may win the tax loan amount in Gold Maple Leaf coins.[19]

In promoting the use of ATMs, the HongkongBank and Hang Seng Bank (whose joint ATM network is the second largest in Hong Kong, next to the JETCO (Joint Electronic Teller Services Co. Ltd.) network)[20] jointly launched the 'Grand Porsche Giveaway' in January 1989, in which ATM users could win the grand prize of a Porsche 944. The prizes in this campaign are claimed to be worth more than HK$1.5 million in total.[21] The promotion of bank credit cards is also usually supported by lucky draws. For example, the HongkongBank launched a 'HK$1,000,000 + Super Draws' for new applicants and users of the HongkongBank Credit Cards in 1988, with grand prizes of two Volvo GLEs and free business class air tickets.[22]

4.   Free Publications.   Some large banks publish magazines or research reports for interested parties as a means of developing public relations. These include the *Hang Seng Economic Monthly* published by the Hang Seng Bank and the *Monthly Economic Report* published by the HongkongBank.

Bank Marketing Strategies

Studies on bank marketing strategies in Hong Kong usually point out that there are three groups of banks and the strategies they employ are different (for example, Wu, 1985; Chan, 1986a). The three groups are the HongkongBank Group (the HongkongBank and Hang Seng Bank), the Bank of China Group (Bank of China and the 13 sister banks), and foreign banks operating in Hong Kong. Inter-bank competition, especially between these groups, is severe.

Wu (1985) studied the emphasis of each bank group in terms of the four elements of marketing. The Bank of China Group was found to be emphasizing distribution, as the formation of JETCO clearly shows. The HongkongBank Group also emphasized an intensive distribution policy, supported by a wide range of services and efficient operations. The foreign banks, however, emphasized product differentiation, followed by credit management, quality of account officers, image, and operational efficiency.[23]

Chan's study (1986a) of the marketing tactics of the foreign banks was based on personal interviews with bank executives. His findings are in line with Wu's: that foreign banks can hardly compete with local banks in terms of branching. As shown in Table 15.3, the Hongkong-Bank, the Standard Chartered Bank, the Bank of China Group, and the Hang Seng Bank accounted for over 50 per cent of the total number of bank branches, and this high concentration made it very difficult for the foreign banks to compete. The foreign banks therefore have to adopt a marketing strategy which focuses on the provision of specialized services to selected customer segments. The major marketing tactics, according to Chan's study, are: (a) speeding up the offering of electronic banking services and slowing down the opening of branches to achieve tight control on cost management; (b) improving the quality and delivery of services to selected segments of consumer financing, such as credit card facilities, mortgages, and personal loans; and (c) focusing more on opportunities in wholesale and investment banking and treasury activities.[24]

In implementing their strategies, banks are involved in both price

Table 15.3 Distribution of Bank Branches of the Top Four Banks (April 1986)

Bank	Number of Branches
The HongkongBank	276
The Bank of China Group	240
The Standard Chartered Bank	109
The Hang Seng Bank	104

Source: T. S. Chan, (1986a), Table 3, p. 310.

and non-price competition, even though the former was found to be far less important than the latter (Wu, 1985; Tai, 1986; Chan, 1986a). The pricing aspect has become an industry practice to reduce the high overhead cost rather than a competitive tool (Tai, 1986). For example, many banks now collect service charges for banking services such as issuing gift cheques, bank drafts, and sometimes for unused overdraft facilities. Pricing is used as a competitive tool only in exceptional cases, one example of which may be the credit card business where application (joining) fees and annual fees vary. The particulars of different credit cards in Hong Kong are shown in Table 15.4. The application fees vary considerably, from no charge to HK$250, and annual fees vary from HK$120 to.HK$325. The Chase Manhattan Bank promoted its Visa Card in 1987 with an aggressive campaign, and the annual fee of HK$150 was then waived for those who applied before the end of June. Although waiving (or reducing) fees can be an attractive marketing ploy, it is not an offer easily made. A bank with 60,000 card holders that waived its HK$150 annual fee would lose HK$9 million a year. In this highly competitive banking industry, it is quite unlikely that fee waiving will become a standard practice.

Many factors account for the increasing popularity and use of credit cards. The most significant of these is that market behaviour and social attitudes have changed. Ten years ago, there were not as many frequent travellers as there are nowadays. A few years ago, overseas travel became nothing unusual or extraordinary. When people travel overseas, they discover the convenience of credit cards.

People's attitudes towards credit have changed dramatically in the recent decade. In the 1970s, people were very resistant to the idea of

Table 15.4 Particulars of Different Credit Cards in Hong Kong

Card	Application Fee (HK$)	Annual Fee (HK$)	Minimum Payment on Balance	Monthly Interest on Unpaid Balance	Number of Interest-free Days for Purchases
American Express	$250	$325	pay in full	2.5 per cent	45
Chase Visa	none	$150	5 per cent	5.0 per cent	25
Diners Club	$252	$300	pay in full	2.5 per cent	25
Hang Seng Visa	none	$120	5 per cent or $50	2.0 per cent	14
HongkongBank Mastercard and Visa	none	$120	5 per cent or $50	2.0 per cent	14
Standard Chartered Visa	none	$120	5 per cent or $50	0.067 per cent daily	20

Source: Communication Management Ltd., 'Credit Card War Fuels Spending Boom,' *Hong Kong Business Annual 1988* (Hong Kong), p. 76.

spending future money — which was what credit cards were all about. But this is no longer the case. Many credit card holders have more than one card (all have different payment due dates) and use different cards at different time intervals in order to get maximum credit from different card-issuing institutions.

Not only has the number of credit card holders experienced a tremendous increase in recent years, the number of different credit cards available on market has also increased. Competition for market share intensifies, though the credit card market is far from saturated. Since many customers are multi-card holders and there is a maximum number of credit cards one can hold in a wallet, banks have to ensure that their card is one of those in the wallet and also the first one to be used. Sales and marketing managers of HongkongBank's Card Centre have sometimes called this 'the battle of the wallet.' One way to appeal to customers is to add benefits, tangible (such as sweepstakes) and intangible (such as status symbol), to the card. At the same time, a bank has to attract more merchants to use its card system. This is important because a bank deducts a charge from the amount of purchase made on its credit card to make its profit. As far as the credit card market is concerned, the goal is to increase the market penetration, both in terms of number of customers and number of merchants.

In order to cope with competition, banks have been alert for market niches. A market, which has been recently discovered and exploited, is that of women. In 1988 the International Bank of Asia found that a large number of women who held credit cards held them as supplementary cards, and the principal card holders were men. So, in July 1988, the bank launched MyCard, a credit card just for women. 'Being a woman is special, carry the card that confirms it' is the slogan for the campaign. The idea is highly successful. And in fact, the idea is so innovative that it has been nominated as a finalist in a world-wide contest for financial ideas, the Golden Coin Award, set up by the Bank Marketing Association of the United States.

Another way to promote greater use of credit cards is to launch private label cards. These are cards issued by a bank on behalf of merchants — usually large, upmarket retail chains. Examples of chains with private label cards are Tokyo Department Store, China Arts and Crafts, and Dragon Seed. Each card carries different and exclusive benefits. The CAC Card of China Arts and Crafts (HK) Limited, for instance, has a guaranteed 10 per cent discount on all items, the ease of instant credit, and free international gift service.[25] These cards have good potential in Hong Kong, and more aggressive promotional efforts are needed to fully exploit the market (Cheung and Chan, 1989).

As far as non-price competition is concerned, banks employ a variety of tactics ranging from packages of products and services, branch banking, and promotional activities, as we have already discussed. It is worth mentioning here that promotional activities, as one of the marketing mix elements, both build up a bank's corporate image and make known to the public its products, services, and distribution.

Hsu and Ho (1988) have utilized content analysis techniques to look into 80 bank advertisements by the three groups of banks in newspapers in a period of 18 months from 1985 to 1986. It can be observed from Table 15.5 that the promotional emphasis among the three groups of banks is generally consistent with their comparative strengths and weaknesses. The local banks, according to this study, heavily emphasized full-service banking for their clients as well as service quality. Foreign banks, on the other hand, placed more emphasis on their years of experience in the industry, their international status, and their financial capabilities. This may reflect the intention of foreign banks to build up their credibility, and to avoid comparing their range of products and distribution network with those of their local competitors. The focus of the banks of mainland Chinese origin was their membership in the Bank of China Group, thus highlighting their financial strength.

Table 15.5 Content Analysis of Advertisements Placed by Banks in Hong Kong

Attributes	Number of Mentions		
	Local Banks	Foreign and Joint Venture Banks	Mainland Chinese Banks
History	4	13	1
Full-service banking	6	2	4
One particular service	14	13	3
Service quality	12	5	2
Named services	2	6	4
Local network	5	4	4
Global/regional network	4	22	0
China Trade	3	5	2
International banking	2	5	0
Financial strength	1	16	8
Technical strength	2	5	2

Source: Hsu and Ho (1988), Table 2, p. 65.

Conclusion

The banking industry in Hong Kong is now highly competitive, and intensified competition will probably continue in the foreseeable future. To be successful, therefore, banks should not only minimize the costs of operation, but invest courageously in marketing strategies for a higher return. Each bank should make sure that marketing efforts are integrated with the organization and its staff is well equiped with strategic ideas in addition to basic banking knowledge.

Notes

1. AMA Board (1985), p. 1.
2. Hodges and Tillman (1986), p. 2.
3. Turnbull and Lewis (1982), p. 1.
4. Steilen (1987), p. 4.
5. Steilen (1987), p. 4.
6. For an excellent discussion on branch banking, especially that of the Hongkong and Shanghai Banking Corporation, see Sit (1983).
7. The 1965 crisis involved runs on a large number of banks, namely Ming Tak Bank, Canton Trust and Commercial Bank, Far East Bank Ltd., Yau Yue Bank Ltd., and even Hang Seng Bank Ltd. Although it was generally believed that the real estate slump was the main reason behind the bank runs, management incompetence on the part of some of the banks was another factor forcing the banking system into difficulty.
The 1967 riot was a massive wave of rioters led by local communists in May 1967. They intended to question British rule over the territory. This outbreak had shaken public confidence to such a great extent that deposits dropped drastically in all banks.
For more detailed discussion, please see Jao (1974).
8. The only exception during this period was the issue of a licence to Barclays Bank International in 1972 (Hong Kong Government, 1973).
9. See the *Newspaper Supplement* in 'Celebrating the Silver Jubilee of the Hong Kong Institute of Bankers', *Ming Pao*, 27 June 1988, p. 5.
10. *Economic Digest*, 14 September 1981, p. 13.
11. A high percentage of the operating costs is staff expenses (Quinton, 1982).
12. See 'TripleAccess — Manage Three Accounts with One Card', a promotional leaflet issued by the HongkongBank.
13. Citifunds are a range of unit trusts, each tailored to different investment objectives: equity funds for capital growth and bond funds for income.
14. Citideposit is a Hong Kong dollar swap deposit account with flexible maturity periods of from one to twelve months.
15. See 'Credit Card War Fuels Spending Boom', *Hong Kong Business Annual 1988*, (Hong Kong, Communication Management Ltd., 1988), pp. 76–9.
16. Hang Seng Bank Ltd. Annual Report 1987, p. 8. This is apparently an adaptation from a nineteenth-century poem, 'Little Things' by Julia A. Carney, that was reprinted in *Juvenile Missionary Magazine* in 1853.
17. Mitchell (1987), p. 3.
18. This campaign won the Hong Kong Management Association's Golden Arrow Award in 1988 for an outstanding campaign in the financial category, as reported in Cabatit (1988b).
19. See 'Tax Pleaser — Win Gold for Tax', a promotional leaflet issued by the Standard Chartered Bank.
20. See the *Newspaper Supplement* in 'Celebrating the Silver Jubilee of the Hong Kong Institute of Bankers', *Ming Pao*, 27 June 1988, p. 4.
21. See 'Win a Porsche by using ETC Machines,' a promotional leaflet issued by the Hang Seng Bank and HongkongBank.
22. See 'HK$1,000,000 + Super Draws', a promotional leaflet issued by the Hongkong-Bank.
23. In Wu's study (1985), only three American banks are included in this category. They are Citibank, Chase Manhattan Bank, and the Bank of America.
24. Chan (1986a), p. 311.
25. See 'Special Report on HongkongBank, 500,000th Cardmember', Sunday Money, *South China Morning Post*, 24 September 1989.

References

AMA board, 'AMA Approves New Marketing Definition', *Marketing News*, 1 March 1985.

Arsan, A. D., 'Building a New Corporate Image', paper presented at the *Third Asia-Pacific Conference on Bank Marketing*, Hong Kong, 2–4 March 1987.

Cabatit, A., 'Bank in Ad Spree', *Media and Marketing*, 22 April 1988a.

—— 'Amex Plays Its Cards Right', *Media and Marketing*, 24 June 1988b.

—— 'Bank Follows up on "Winning Team" Drive', *Media and Marketing*, 5 August 1988c.

Chan, T. S, 'Intensified Competition in the Hong Kong Banking Industry: Changing Marketing Tactics of Foreign Bank', in Hsieh, R. T. and Scherling, S. A. (eds.), *Proceedings of the Academy of International Business Southeast Asia Regional Conference*, Vol. 1, Taipei, 26–8 June 1986a, pp. 305–14.

—— 'Management Perceptions of Marketing Effectiveness: A Study of the Bank of China Group in Hong Kong', paper presented at the *International Conference on Chinese Banking and Nation Building in Southeast Asia*, 10–11 October, The Chinese University of Hong Kong, 1986b.

Cheung, W. L. and Chan, A. K. K., 'A Profile Comparison of Retailer Credit Card Holders and Non-holders in Hong Kong', *Proceedings of the Conference on Marketing and International Business into the 90's: China, Hong Kong and the Pacific Rim*, (Hong Kong, 1989), pp. 133–42.

Communication Management Ltd., 'Credit Card War Fuels Spending Boom', *Hong Kong Business Annual 1988*, Hong Kong.

Ho, S. S. M., 'Electronic Fund Transfer Systems', in R. H. Scott, K. A. Wong, and Y. K. Ho (eds.), *Hong Kong's Financial Institutions and Markets* (Hong Kong, Oxford University Press, 1986), pp. 153–79.

Hodges, L. H. Jr and Tillman, R. Jr, *Bank Marketing: Text and Cases* (Reading, Massachusetts, Addison–Wesley, 1968).

Hong Kong Government, *Hong Kong Annual Report* (Hong Kong, Hong Kong Government Printer), various issues.

Hsu, D. L. and Ho, S. C., 'Advertising by Banks in Hong Kong: A Content Analysis', *International Journal of Bank Marketing*, Vol. 6, No. 2, 1988, pp. 62–7.

Jao, Y. C., *Banking and Currency in Hong Kong* (Hong Kong, Macmillan, 1974).

Lee, K. H. 'A Research Design for Exploring Retail Locations for Commercial Banks in Hong Kong', *International Journal of Bank Marketing*, Vol. 4, No. 3, 1986, pp. 19–30.

Lok, L. K. W. and Loke, P. S. Y., 'Current Development in Banking Products and Services in Hong Kong', unpublished M.B.A. Thesis, The Chinese University of Hong Kong, 1983.

McCarthy, E. J. and Perreault, W. D. Jr, *Basic Marketing: A Managerial Approach* (Homewood, Illinois, Irwin, ninth edition, 1987).

Media, 14 October 1988.

Meidan, A., *Bank Marketing Management*, (London, Macmillan, 1984).

Mitchell, D. W., 'Effective Direct Marketing for Financial Institutions', paper presented at the *Third Asia-Pacific Conference on Bank Marketing*, Hong Kong, 2–4 March 1987.

Moy, J. 'Bank Chases After "First Business Class" ', *Media and Marketing*, 9 October 1987a.

—— 'Banking on the Direct Mail-out "Magic" ', *Media and Marketing*, 6 November 1987b.

Ng, K. H. and So, H., 'A Study on New Product Development in Consumer Finance', unpublished M.B.A. Thesis, The Chinese University of Hong Kong, 1981.

Ngan, Y. P. 'Hang Seng Bank Limited: A Brief History', in F. H. H. King (ed.),

Eastern Banking: Essays in the History of the Hongkong and Shanghai Banking Corporation (London, The Athlone Press, 1983), pp. 709–16.

Quinton, J., 'Banking in the 1980s: Key Strategic Issues', *Journal of the Institute of Bankers*, October 1982, pp. 155–7.

Russell, J., 'Scenario for Banking Facilities of Tomorrow — Branches and Electronics', paper presented at the *Third Asia-Pacific Conference on Bank Marketing*, Hong Kong, 2–4 March 1987.

Selame, E., and Kolligan, G., 'Financial Marketing Enhanced with Indentity Program', *Marketing News*, (American Marketing Association), 12 April 1985, p. 21.

Sin, Y. M., Hsu, D. L., and Ho., S. C., 'Prospective Credit Card Holders in Hong Kong', in O. H. M. Yau (ed.), *Proceedings of the Conference on the Changing Environment of Management in Hong Kong*, Hong Kong Baptist College, 28 April 1987, pp. 52–6.

Sin, Y. M. and Pang, M. K. 'How Hong Kong Bankers Set Advertising Budgets', in Y. M. Sin and H. M. Yau (eds.), *Advertising in Hong Kong: Economic, Social, Legal and Managerial Perspectives* (Hong Kong, University Publisher and Printer, 1986), pp. 156–64.

Sit, V. F. S., 'Branching of the Hongkong and Shanghai Banking Corporation in Hong Kong: A Spatial Analysis', in F. H. H. King (ed.), *Eastern Banking: Essays in the History of the Hong Kong and Shanghai Banking Corporation* (London, The Athlone Press, 1983), pp. 629–54.

Steilen, C. F., 'Evolution of Bank Marketing in the Asia–Pacific Region', paper presented at the *Third Asia-Pacific Conference on Bank Marketing*, Hong Kong, 2–4 March 1987.

Tai, L. S. T., 'Price and Non-price Competition of Commercial Banks Services in Hong Kong: Implications for Bank Marketing', *The Hong Kong Manager*, August/September 1986, pp. 33–4.

Turnbull, P. W. and Lewis, B. (eds.), *The Marketing of Bank Services* (Bradford, England, MCB Publications, 1982).

Woodall, S., 'O & M tops, Burnett topples', *Media and Marketing*, 1 April 1988.

Wu, E. K. F., 'Competitive Strategies of Selected Banks in International Banking in Hong Kong', unpublished M.B.A. Thesis, The Chinese University of Hong Kong, 1985.

16. Protection of Investors in Hong Kong

CLEMENT SHUM

THERE are a number of ordinances in Hong Kong that contain provisions relating to the protection of investors. These include the Companies Ordinance, the Protection of Investors Ordinance, the Securities Ordinance, the Securities (Disclosure of Interests) Ordinance, and the Securities and Futures Commission Ordinance (these ordinances are abbreviated as CO, PIO, SO, SDIO, and SFCO respectively, whenever appropriate). The Government has also published the Securities (Insider Dealing) Bill of 1989, which has yet to be enacted and may well be subject to substantial amendment.

The Securities (Stock Exchange Listing) Rules of 1989 is also relevant. Further, there is the Listing Agreement entered into between The Stock Exchange of Hong Kong Ltd. ('the Stock Exchange') and the listed company and the undertakings given to the Stock Exchange by the directors of the listed company. Finally, the Stock Exchange has its own rules governing the listing of securities.

Investors are also protected by the general principles of law enshrined in cases decided by the courts — the common law.

This chapter deals with the relevant statutory provisions and the common law principles. It does not cover the listing rules which have been commented upon elsewhere in this book. Whenever appropriate, relevant provisions are quoted verbatim. This has the added advantage of providing a useful reference for current Hong Kong law. The legal convention of the citation has been retained, so that s.1(1) (a) refers to section 1, subsection (1), paragraph (a). Words and expressions importing the masculine gender include the female, words and expressions in the singular include the plural, and words and expressions in the plural include the singular. Any amount mentioned refers to the amount of Hong Kong dollars.

The Companies Ordinance

Whenever a public company invites the public to subscribe for shares or debentures, it must issue a prospectus. A private company is not allowed to issue a prospectus. The expression 'private company' means a company which by its articles restricts the right to transfer its shares, limits the number of its members to 50, and prohibits any invitation to the public to subscribe for any shares or debentures of the company (s.29(1) CO). Any company which is not a private company is a public company.

Section 2 of the CO defines a prospectus as any prospectus, notice, circular, brochure, advertisement, or other document, (a) offering any shares or debentures of a company to the public for subscription or purchase for cash or other consideration; or (b) calculated to invite offers by the public to subscribe for or purchase for cash or other consideration any shares or debentures of a company. A prospectus does not usually constitute an offer in the strict sense of the law of contract. Rather, it is an invitation to treat: the investor is invited to make an offer to subscribe for shares or debentures. If the company accepts the offer, it will then allot the securities to the investor.

A prospectus issued must include all information necessary for the public to form a correct and justified opinion of the securities offered to it, and of the financial condition and profitability of the company whose securities are being offered publicly or are sought to be admitted to the Stock Exchange listing.

Section 38 of the CO provides among other things that every prospectus issued by or on behalf of a company must be in the English language and contain a Chinese translation and must state the matters specified in Part I of the Third Schedule and set out the reports specified in Part II of that Schedule to the CO.

The matters specified in Part I of the Third Schedule are summarized as follows:

1. The general nature of the business of the company;
2. The authorized share capital and the description and nominal value of the shares into which it is divided, the amount of share capital issued or agreed to be issued and the amount paid up on the shares which have been issued;
3. Sufficient particulars and information to enable a reasonable person to form as a result thereof a valid and justifiable opinion of the shares or debentures and the financial condition and profitability of the company at the time of the issue of the prospectus;
4. The number of founders or management or deferred shares, if any, and the nature and extent of the interest of the holders in the property and profits of the company;
5. The number of shares, if any, fixed by the articles as the qualification of a director, and any provision in the articles as to the remuneration of the directors;
6. The names, descriptions and addresses of the directors or proposed directors;
7. Upon an offer of shares for public subscription, the minimum amount (known as the minimum subscription) which must be raised in cash from the issue, to provide for the purchase price of any property to be paid for out of the proceeds of the issue, preliminary expenses payable by the company, commissions payable by the company in respect of subscriptions for shares, repayment of money borrowed by the company in respect of any of the foregoing matters, and working capital; also the amounts to be provided in respect of the foregoing matters otherwise than out of the proceeds of the issue, and the sources out of which they are to be provided;

8. The date and time of the opening of the subscription lists;

9. The amount payable on application and allotment on each share, and, in the case of a second or subsequent offer of shares, the amount offered for subscription on each previous allotment made within the 2 preceding years, the amount actually allotted, and the amount, if any, paid on the shares so allotted;

10. The number, description and amount of any shares in or debentures of the company which any person has, or is entitled to be given, an option to subscribe for, together with the following particulars of the option, that is to say —
    (a) the period during which it is exercisable;
    (b) the price to be paid for shares or debentures subscribed for under it;
    (c) the consideration (if any) given or to be given for it or for the right to it;
    (d) the names and addresses of the persons to whom it or the right to it was given or, if given to existing shareholders or debenture holders as such, the relevant shares or debentures;

11. The number and amount of shares and debentures which within the 2 preceding years have been issued, or agreed to be issued, as fully or partly paid up otherwise than in cash, and in the latter case the extent to which they are so paid up, and in either case the consideration for which those shares or debentures have been issued or are proposed or intended to be issued;

12. The names and addresses of the vendors who are to be paid out of the proceeds of the issue, and the amount payable to each; and short particulars of any transaction within the 2 preceding years relating to the property, in which any vendor, promoter, director, or proposed director, had any interest;

13. The amount, if any, paid within the 2 preceding years, or payable, as commission (but not including commission to sub-underwriters) for subscribing or agreeing to subscribe, or procuring or agreeing to procure subscriptions, for any shares in or debentures of the company, or the rate of any such commission;

14. The amount or estimated amount of preliminary expenses and the persons by whom any of those expenses have been paid or are payable, and the amount or estimated amount of the expenses of the issue and the persons by whom any of those expenses have been paid or are payable;

15. Any amount or benefit paid or given within the 2 preceding years or intended to be paid or given to any promoter, and the consideration for the payment or the giving of the benefit;

16. The dates of, parties to and general nature of every material contract, unless made in the ordinary course of business or more than 2 years previously, and a statement that a copy of every such material contract has been delivered to the Registrar for registration;

17. The names and addresses of the auditors of the company;

18. Full particulars of the nature and extent of the interest, if any, of every director in the promotion of, or in the property proposed to be acquired by, the company;

19. The right of voting at meetings of the company conferred by, and the rights in respect of capital and dividends attached to, the shares;

20. In the case of a company which has been carrying on business, or of a business which has been carried on for less than 3 years, the length of

time during which the business of the company or the business to be acquired, as the case may be, has been carried on;

21. The contents or a sufficient summary of the contents of the articles of the company with regard to any borrowing powers exercisable by the directors and the manner of variation of such powers;

22. Particulars of any bank overdrafts or other similar indebtedness of the company and its subsidiaries, if any, as at the latest practicable date or, if there are no bank overdrafts or other similar indebtedness, a statement to that effect;

23. Particulars of any hire purchase commitments, guarantees or other material contingent liabilities of the company and its subsidiaries, if any, or, if there are none such, a statement to that effect;

24. Particulars of the authorized debentures of the company and its subsidiaries, if any, the amount issued and outstanding or agreed to be issued, or if no debentures are outstanding a statement to that effect;

25. If the prospectus invites the public to subscribe for debentures of the company —
    (a) the rights conferred upon the holders thereof, including rights in respect of interest and redemption, and particulars of the security, if any, therefor;
    (b) the designation of such debentures;
    (c) particulars of any guarantee subsisting in respect of the debentures;

26. A statement as to the gross trading income or sales turnover (as may be appropriate) of the company during the 5 preceding years including an explanation of the method used for the computation of such income or turnover, and a reasonable break-down between the more important trading activities;

27. If the prospectus offers shares in the company for sale to the public —
    (a) the names, addresses and descriptions of the vendor or vendors of the shares;
    (b) particulars of any beneficial interest possessed by any director of the company in any shares so offered for sale;

28. The name, date and country of incorporation, whether public or private (if applicable), the general nature of the business, the issued capital and the proportion thereof held or intended to be held, of every company the whole of the capital of which or a substantial proportion thereof is held or intended to be held, or whose profits or assets make or will make a material contribution to the figures in the auditors' report or to the next accounts of the company;

29. A statement of the persons holding or beneficially interested in any substantial part of the share capital of the company and the amounts of the holdings in question.

The reports specified in Part II of the Third Schedule are as follows:

1. A report by the auditors of the company as to —
    (a) The company's profits or losses in each of the preceding financial years;
    (b) The rates of dividends paid on each class of shares in each of those years;
    (c) The classes of shares on which such dividends have been paid;
    (d) The cases in which no dividend has been paid on any class of shares in any of such years;

(e) The company's assets and liabilities at the last date to which the accounts were made up;

(f) The fact that no accounts have been made up for any part of the 5 years ending 3 months before the issue of the prospectus, if such be the case.

If the company has subsidiaries, the report must state the profits or losses of the subsidiaries, separately or together so far as they concern members of the company; and must state the assets and liabilities of the subsidiaries, together or separately, indicating the allowance to be made for such other shareholders.

2. If all or part of the proceeds of the issue are to be applied in the purchase of a business, a report by accountants named in the prospectus as to the profits or losses of the business in each of the 5 preceding financial years, and the assets and liabilities of the business at the last date to which the accounts of such business were made up;

3. If all or part of the proceeds of the issue is to be applied, directly or indirectly, in the acquisition by the company of shares in another corporate body, so that such corporate body will become a subsidiary of the company, a similar report by named accountants as to the profits and losses, assets and liabilities of such body, stating in addition how the amounts would have concerned the acquiring company and other shareholders respectively. If the body has subsidiaries, like particulars as in the auditors' report must also be given.

If in any case the company or business has been carried on for less than 5 years, then 4, 3 or 2 years or 1 year must be substituted for the five years mentioned above.

If figures of profits, losses, assets or liabilities require adjustment for the purposes of the report, the report must either indicate the adjustments required, or make them and state that they have been made.

4. In the case of a company whose accounts at the last date to which the accounts have been made up disclose that either a value exceeding 10 per cent of the value of the assets of the company or a value of not less than $3,000,000 is placed on the company's interests in land or buildings, a valuation report made by a professionally qualified valuation surveyor with respect to all the company's interests in land or buildings which shall include the following particulars of each property —

(a) the address;

(b) a brief description;

(c) the use at the date of the report;

(d) the nature of the tenure;

(e) a summary of the terms of any sub-leases or tenancies, including repair obligations, granted by the company;

(f) the approximate age of buildings;

(g) the present capital value;

(h) the estimated current net rental, being the estimated average net annual income from the property accruing to the company over a long period of years (not being less than 3 years) before taking into account tax and any interest or mortgage expenses but after taking into account management and maintenance expenses.

The report should state

(a) whether the valuation —

    (i)   is the current value in the open market, stating whether —
          (A) on an investment basis, or
          (B) on a development basis, or
          (C) on a future capital realization basis;
    (ii) is the current value as an asset of a going concern;
    (iii) is the value after development has been completed; or
    (iv) has any other basis (which should be stated);
  (b) where the valuation is based on value after development has been
      completed —
      (i)   the date when the development is expected to be completed;
      (ii) the estimated cost of carrying out the development or (where part
            of the development has already been carried out) the estimated
            cost of completing the development; and
      (iii) the estimated value of the property in the open market in its
            present condition.
If the company has obtained more than one valuation report regarding any of
the company's interests in land or buildings within 6 months before the issue
of the prospectus then all other such reports shall be included.

There are also provisions in the CO relating to the appointment of
inspectors of companies (ss. 142–3). The Financial Secretary may
appoint one or more inspectors to investigate the affairs of a company
on the application of a certain number of members of the company,
or if the court by order declares that its affairs ought to be investigated,
or if there are circumstances suggesting:

(i)   that the business of the company has been or is being conducted with
      intent to defraud its creditors or the creditors of any other person or
      otherwise for a fraudulent or unlawful purpose or in a manner oppressive
      of any part of its members or that it was formed for any fraudulent or
      unlawful purpose; or
(ii) that persons concerned with its formation or the management of its affairs
      have in connection therewith been guilty of fraud, misfeasance or other
      misconduct towards it or towards its members; or
(iii) that its members have not been given all the information with respect to
      its affairs that they might reasonably expect.

An inspector appointed has wide powers of investigation including
the right to require production of books and documents and bank
account records, and may be required to prepare a report for the
Financial Secretary, which report may be delivered to members of the
company or made public. In addition, the officers of the company
concerned must assist the Attorney General in connection with any
prosecutions which may arise from the investigation.
    Where a prospectus includes any untrue statements, any person who
authorized the issue shall be criminally liable, unless he proves either
that the statement was immaterial or that he had reasonable grounds
to believe, and did up to the time of the issue of the prospectus
believe, that the statement was true (s.40A CO).
    It is unlawful for any person to publish or cause to be published

by way of newspaper, radio, television or cinematograph advertisement, or advertisement in any other manner, any extract from or abridged version of a prospectus whether in English or in any other language in relation to shares or debentures of a company whether incorporated in or outside Hong Kong (s.38B(1) CO). It is also unlawful to issue any form of application for shares in or debentures of a company unless it is issued with a prospectus (s.38(3) CO).

If there are mis-statements in or omissions from the prospectus, the investor may sue the company or the persons individually responsible for it. He may be entitled to (a) rescission of the contract of allotment; (b) damages for deceit (and possibly for negligence) at common law against the company or persons responsible for the issue of the prospectus or its contents; (c) damages for misrepresentation against the issuing company under the Misrepresentation Ordinance; (d) compensation (under section 40(1) CO) against persons responsible (for example, directors and promoters) for untrue statements and possibly for omission of matters that should have been included in the prospectus.

Companies which wish to have their securities admitted to listing on the Stock Exchange must comply with the listing requirements of the Stock Exchange and the Securities (Stock Exchange Listing) Rules.

There are also provisions in the CO governing the issue, circulation, or distribution in Hong Kong of any prospectus offering for subscription of shares in or debentures of a company incorporated outside Hong Kong, whether the company has or has not established a place of business in Hong Kong (part XII CO).

Protection of Investors Ordinance

The Protection of Investors Ordinance (PIO) provides that any person who, by any fraudulent or reckless misrepresentation, induces another person to enter into or offer to enter into any agreement:

(a) for or with a view to acquiring, disposing of, subscribing for or underwriting securities; or
(b) the purpose or effect, or pretended purpose or effect, of which is to secure to any of the parties to the agreement a profit from the yield of securities or by reference to fluctuations in the value of securities

is guilty of an offence and is liable on conviction on indictment to a fine of $1,000,000 and to imprisonment for 7 years [s.3(1), (3) PIO].

'Fraudulent or reckless misrepresentation' is defined as:

(a) any statement
    (i) which to the knowledge of its maker was false, misleading, or deceptive; or
    (ii) which is false, misleading, or deceptive and was made recklessly;
(b) any promise
    (i) which the maker of the promise had no intention of fulfilling; or

    (ii) which, to the knowledge of the maker of the promise, was not capable of being fulfilled; or

    (iii) which was made recklessly;

(c) any forecast

    (i) which, to the knowledge of the maker of the forecast, was not justified on the facts known to him at the time when he made it; or

    (ii) which was not justified on the facts known to the maker of the forecast at the time when he made it and was made recklessly; or

(d) any statement or forecast from which the maker of the statement intentionally or recklessly omitted a material fact, with the result that the statement was thereby rendered untrue, misleading, or deceptive, or, as the case may be, the forecast was thereby not capable of being justified or was thereby rendered misleading or deceptive [s.3(2) PIO].

If a person issues or possesses for the purposes of issue an advertisement or invitation which to his knowledge is or contains an invitation to the public to do any of the acts referred to above; or issues or possesses for the purposes of issue a document which to his knowledge contains an advertisement or invitation to the public to do any of those acts, he shall be guilty of an offence and shall be liable on conviction on indictment to a fine of $500,000 and to imprisonment for 3 years (s.4(1), (4) PIO). But this does not apply in relation to the issue of a prospectus which complies with the provisions of the CO, as well as the issue or possession of any advertisement, invitation or document by or on behalf of a dealer or investment adviser who is registered under the Securities Ordinance (SO) or who is a dealer or investment adviser exempted from registration under that Ordinance (s.4(2), (3) PIO).

Where an offence against the PIO committed by a company or other body corporate is proved to have been committed with the consent or connivance of, or to be attributable to any neglect on the part of, any director, manager, secretary, or other similar officer of the company or body corporate or any person who was purporting to act in any such capacity, he, as well as the company or body, shall be guilty of the offence and shall be liable to be proceeded against and punished accordingly (s.7(1) PIO). The PIO empowers a magistrate to grant search warrants to obtain information in relation to suspected offences.

Section 8(1) of the PIO makes the wrongdoer liable to pay compensation to the injured person for any pecuniary loss that the latter has sustained by reason of his reliance on the misrepresentation.

The Securities Ordinance

The Securities Ordinance contains, among other things, provisions relating to stock-markets, registration of dealers, investment advisers and representatives trading in securities, the compensation fund, prevention of improper trading practices, insider dealing, and the Insider Dealing Tribunal.

Registration of Dealers, Investment Advisers, and Representatives

One of the purposes of the SO is to protect investors. Under Part VI of this ordinance, no one can act, on pain of a fine, as a dealer, or an investment adviser, a dealer's representative or an investment representative in Hong Kong unless he is registered as such.

There are special provisions relating to dealers in the SO. It is worth setting out the relevant provisions in full:

65A.(1) No person, being an individual, may be registered as a dealer unless he can show that —
　(a) he has sufficient qualifications or experience in dealing in securities;
　(b) [note: repealed by the SFCO which came into force on 1 May 1989].
　(c) he is able to comply with the requirements of section 65B.
　(2) No person shall be regarded as having sufficient qualifications or experience for the purpose of subsection (1)(a) unless he has —
　(a) not less than 3 years' experience in dealing in securities —
　　(i) in Hong Kong; or
　　(ii) on any other stock market recognized by the Commission for the purposes of this paragraph by notice in the Gazette; or
　(b) passed an examination approved for the purposes of this paragraph by the Commission by notice in the Gazette.
　(3) No corporation may be registered as a dealer unless —
　(a) it is —
　　(i) a registered company; or
　　(ii) an oversea company to which Part XI of the Companies Ordinance applies and which has complied with the provisions of that Part relating to the registration of documents [note: an oversea company is a company incorporated outside Hong Kong that establishes a place of business in Hong Kong].
　(b) every person who will be a dealing director is a registered dealer; and
　(c) it is able to comply with the requirements of section 65B.
　(4) No partnership may be registered as a dealing partnership unless —
　(a) all the partners, in the case of a general partnership; or
　(b) all the general partners, in the case of a limited partnership, are able to comply with the requirements of section 65B.

65B.(1) A registered dealer shall provide and at all times maintain in his business as a dealer —
　(a) if he is a company, a net capital of not less than $5,000,000; or
　(b) subject to subsection (2), in any other case a net capital of not less than $1,000,000.
　(2) A registered dealing partnership shall provide and at all times maintain in their business as a dealer a net capital which in aggregate amounts to not less than —
　(a) $5,000,000 for each corporation which is a partner; and
　(b) $1,000,000 for any other person who is a partner,

being in either case, a partner who is required by this Ordinance to be a registered dealer.

(3) A registered dealer or dealing partnership shall at all times maintain in his or their business as a dealer a liquidity margin of not less than 10 per centum of the minimum net capital requirement specified in subsections (1) and (2).

(4) Nothing in this section shall apply to a registered dealer who is a dealing director.

'Liquidity margin' means the excess of liquid assets over ranking liabilities (such liabilities as are specified to be ranking liabilities by the Commission by notice in the *Gazette*).

The Securities and Futures Commission shall refuse to issue a certificate of registration if the applicant for registration does not satisfy the Commission that he is a fit and proper person to be so registered (s.23(1)(a) SFCO). In considering whether an applicant for registration is a 'fit and proper person', the Commission shall, in addition to any other matter that the Commission may think relevant, have regard to the matters set out below in respect of —

(a) the applicant if he is an individual;
(b) where the applicant is a company, each of its directors and officers; or
(c) where the applicant is a partnership, each of the partners [s.23(2) SFCO].

The matters referred to are in the case of an applicant and any other person:

(a) his financial status;
(b) his educational or other qualifications or experience having regard to the nature of the functions which, if the application is allowed, he will perform;
(c) his ability to perform such functions efficiently, honestly and fairly; and
(d) his reputation, character, financial integrity and reliability [s.23(3) SFCO].

The Commission may have regard to any information in its possession, whether furnished by the applicant or not (s.23(4) SFCO). It may take into account any decision relating to authorization made in relation to the applicant by the Commissioner for Banking or the Insurance Authority or any other authority (whether in Hong Kong or elsewhere), which in the opinion of the Commission performs any function similar to a function conferred on the Commission (s.23(5) SFCO).

The Commission may —
(a) take into account any matter relating to —
    (i) any person who is or is to be employed by, or associated with, the applicant for the purposes of the proposed business to which the application relates;
    (ii) any person who will be acting as a representative in relation to such business;
    (iii) where the applicant is a company, any substantial shareholder, director or officer of the company, any other company in the same group of companies or to any director or officer of any such other company; and

(iv) where the applicant is a partnership or a firm, any of the partners; and

(b) have regard to any other business which the applicant carries on or proposes to carry on [s.23(6) SFCO].

A 'substantial shareholder', in relation to a company, means a person who has an interest in shares in the company —

(a) the nominal value of which is equal to more than 10% of the issued share capital of the company; or
(b) which entitle the person to exercise or control the exercise of more than 10% of the voting power at any general meeting of the company [s.23(8) SFCO].

The Hawking of Securities

Hawking securities is a criminal offence. According to section 74(1) of the SO, a person should not, whether on his own behalf or otherwise and whether by appointment or otherwise, call from place to place —

(a) making or offering to make with any person —
  (i) an agreement for or with a view to having that other person purchase specific securities; or
  (ii) an agreement the purpose or pretended purpose of which is to secure a profit to that other person from the yield of specific securities or by reference to fluctuations in the value of specific securities; or
(b) inducing or attempting to induce any other person to enter into an agreement of the type referred to in sub-paragraph (i) or sub-paragraph (ii) of paragraph (a).

'To call' includes to visit in person and to communicate by telephone (s.74(6) SO). Any person who contravenes the law is guilty of an offence and is liable on conviction to a fine of $50,000 and to imprisonment for 2 years (s.74(4) SO).

Short Selling

A person should not sell securities at or through the Stock Exchange unless, at the time he sells them (a) he has or, where he is selling as agent, his principal has; or (b) he reasonably and honestly believes that he has or, where he is selling as agent, that his principal has, a presently exercisable and unconditional right to vest the securities in the purchaser of them (s.80(1) SO). Any person who contravenes this is guilty of an offence and is liable on conviction to a fine of $10,000 and to imprisonment for 6 months (s.80(2) SO).

Disclosure of Certain Interests

Where, in a circular or other written communication issued in Hong Kong by him to more than one person, a dealer or an investment adviser makes a recommendation, whether expressly or by implication with respect of any securities or any class of securities of a corporation, he should include in the circular or other communication a statement as to whether or not he has, at the date specified in the circular or communication an interest in any of the securities of that corporation (s.79(1) SO). A person who contravenes this is quality of an offence and is liable on conviction to a fine of $5,000 (s.79(10) SO).

Improper Trading Practices

1. False Markets and Trading.   There are provisions in the SO which are aimed primarily at proscribing manufactured sale, wash sales, matched orders, and other market fictions. Section 135(1) of the SO provides that a person should not intentionally create or cause to be created, or do anything with the intention of creating a false or misleading appearance of active trading in any securities or a false market in respect of any securities on the Stock Exchange.

In an English case known as *De Berenger* (1814), a man dressed in military uniform arrived in Winchester declaring that Napoleon had been killed and the Allies were in Paris. This rumour caused the prices on the stock-market to rise dramatically. De Berenger and others then sold their holdings in government securities, making a handsome profit. He and others were found guilty of conspiracy to spread false rumours and, thereby, to injure the investing public.

It is also provided in the SO that a person shall not with the intention of depressing, raising, or causing fluctuations in the market price of any securities effect any purchase or sale of any such securities which involves no change in the beneficial ownership of those securities (s.135(3) SO). Further, a person is prohibited from disseminating information to the effect that the price of a security will or is likely to rise or fall because of the market operations which, to his knowledge, are conducted in contravention of section 135(1) of the SO (s.135(5) SO).

2. Employment of Fraudulent or Deceptive Devices.   Section 136 of the SO is a general anti-fraud provision which states:

A person shall not, directly or indirectly, in connexion with any transaction with any other person involving the purchase, sale, or exchange of securities —
(a) employ any device, scheme, or artifice to defraud that other person; or
(b) engage in any act, practice, or course of business which operates as a fraud or deception, or is likely to operate as a fraud or deception, of that other person.

It seems that 'fraud' involves dishonesty and infliction of financial loss, and 'to defraud' is to deprive a person dishonestly of something which is his or of something to which he is or would or might, but for the perpetration of the fraud, be entitled. To invoke this section the injured party must prove that he was in a contractual or fiduciary relationship with the defendant or his conspirators.

3. False or Misleading Statements.   Section 138 of the SO provides that a person shall not, directly or indirectly, for the purposes of inducing the sale of the securities of any corporation, make with respect

to those securities, or with respect to the operations or the past or future performance of the corporation —

(a)   any statement which is, at the time and in the light of the circumstances in which it is made, false or misleading with respect to any material fact and which he knows or has reasonable ground to believe to be false or misleading; or

(b)   any statement which is, by reason of the omission of a material fact, rendered false or misleading and which he knows or has reasonable grounds for knowing is rendered false or misleading by reason of the omission of that fact.

It should be noted that the provision only relates to false or misleading statements made for the purpose of inducing the sale and not the purchase of securities. It is confined to false or misleading statements relating to a corporation or its securities and does not cover political and economic rumour. For a statement to constitute an offence under the section, it must be false or misleading with respect to any material fact. A fact is material if a reasonable person would attach importance to it as a factor that would influence him to sell the security.
4.   Consequences of Breach.   Any person who contravenes any of the provisions of section 135, section 136, or section 138 of the SO (those sections described above) is guilty of an offence and is liable on conviction on indictment to a fine of $50,000 and to imprisonment for 2 years (s.139 SO).

In addition, he is liable to pay compensation by way of damages to any person who has sustained pecuniary loss as a result of having purchased or sold securities at a price affected by the act or transaction which comprises or is the subject of the contravention (s.141(1) SO).

Compensation Fund

The Securities Compensation Fund Committee is responsible for the administration of the compensation fund. The Committee consists of five persons appointed by the Commission, of whom at least two are directors of the Commission and two are persons nominated by the Stock Exchange. Section 109(1) of the SO provides that where, in consequence of any act done in the course of or in connection with the stockbroking business of a stockbroker, a person has a cause of action against that stockbroker in relation to any money, securities or other property entrusted to or received by the stockbroker or any partner of the stockbroker or any person employed by the stockbroker, that person shall be entitled to claim compensation from the compensation fund in respect of the actual pecuniary loss suffered by him, including the reasonable costs of and incidental to the making and proving of his claim (s.109(5) SO). In the Australian case *Daly v. Sydney Stock Exchange Ltd.* (1987), the court held that money lent to a broker by an investor is not money entrusted to or received by the broker on behalf of the investor. The total amount payable to all investors suffering losses through one default by one broker is limited to

HK$2,000,000. 'Default', in relation to the failure of a stockbroker to perform a legal obligation, means a default arising from

(a) the bankruptcy, winding up or insolvency of the stockbroker;
(b) any breach of trust committed by the stockbroker; or
(c) any defalcation, fraud or misfeasance committed by the stockbroker or partner, being a partner in a dealing partnership, or by the servant of the stockbroker or of a dealing partnership in which he is a partner (s.98(1) SO).

The claim is assessed as at the date upon which the cause of action arises. In addition, interest is payable out of the compensation fund on the amount of the compensation (s.109(6) SO).

Insider Dealing in Hong Kong

The practice of what is known in the United States as 'insider trading' in Britain is called 'insider dealing'. The appropriate term in Hong Kong is 'culpable insider dealing'. The question still under discussion in Hong Kong is whether culpable insider dealing should be made a crime, subject to normal criminal process, or the present Insider Dealing Tribunal of Hong Kong should be retained, but with extended powers.

The Historical Development of Insider Dealing

In 1973 The Companies Law Revision Committee recommended that insider dealing be made a criminal offence and that any person acting on insider information be liable to compensate anyone who suffers from that action unless the information was also known to the injured party.

On 3 January 1973 Phillip Haddon-Cave, then the Financial Secretary, announced the creation of the post of Commissioner for Securities and the formation of a Securities Advisory Council (SAC) to deal with the innumerable problems generated by the stock-market boom. On 6 January, James Selwyn was appointed Commissioner for Securities. Selwyn was a former Bank of England employee who, in late 1972, had already been working on draft securities legislation in conjunction with the Attorney General's office. To work with Selwyn, Haddon-Cave announced the membership of the SAC. Y. H. Kan, former chief of the Bank of East Asia, was named Council Chairman. Other members included Y. K. Pao, the shipping magnate, and Michael Sandberg, General Manager of the Hongkong and Shanghai Banking Corporation. The members were selected to represent a spectrum of financial and business interests and to contribute expertise in various fields. By official intent, none of the members had experience in or strong ties to the securities industry. On 28 September 1973, the Government *Gazette* published the final text of the Securities Bill. In 1974, the bill became the present SO.

Parts of the Ordinance were drawn from the United Kingdom Act and parts from the London City Code. Parts of the Ordinance reflect the Australian approach. The gaps were then filled in with provisions drafted without precedent.

Section 140 of the SO of 1974 dealt with insider dealing. It provided for both criminal penalty and civil remedy for the other party to the transaction and for the company which issued the securities. Although enacted, section 140 was never brought into operation. It was eventually repealed by the Securities (Amendment) Ordinance of 1978. The main effects of the amendments were summarized in the explanatory memorandum to the bill as being:

(a) to enact a definition of insider dealing;
(b) to establish a Tribunal with jurisdiction to inquire into cases where insider
     dealing is alleged to have occurred, to determine the extent to which the
     persons involved are culpable, and to publish a report of its findings; and
(c) to provide the Tribunal and the Commissioner for Securities with powers
     to investigate such cases.

These new provisions inserted a Part XII A containing new sections 141A to 141L which constitute the current legislation on insider dealing in Hong Kong. The mischief with which Part XII A is concerned is the practice of insider dealing which is detrimental to an orderly market in securities because (a) it gives to insiders an unfair advantage over the investing public at large and over the shareholders who may be paying them; and (b) it undermines confidence in the integrity of the market-place.

The legislation does not contain any criminal sanctions or civil remedy. The Financial Secretary told the Legislative Council why this was so when he moved the second reading of the 1977 bill:

Section 140 of the Securities Ordinance, which has not been brought into operation, makes a person liable in criminal and civil law if he deals in securities on information not available to the public or discloses such information to another for the purpose of dealing. The government now considers that criminal or civil sanctions would not be effective in preventing insider dealing in Hong Kong, since it would often be impossible to obtain sufficient evidence for the courts. So the first point to be made is that clause 7 of the Bill repeals section 140 of the principal Ordinance.

Now whereas insider dealing is essentially fraudulent behaviour, it is difficult to combat it using the sanction of the criminal law because, by its very nature, the evidence required to secure a conviction is difficult, if not impossible, to obtain [see *Legislative Council Proceedings* 1977–8, pp. 64–5].

Salient Features of Insider Dealing Legislation

The Definition of Insider Dealing

Part XII A of the SO applies to the securities of a company if they are listed on the Stock Exchange or have been so listed at any time in the preceding five years.

Insider dealing takes place:

(a) When a dealing in the securities is made, procured or occasioned by a
     person connected with that corporation who is in possession of relevant
     information concerning the securities [note: relevant information means

information that is not generally available but, if it were, would be likely to bring about a material change in the price of these securities].

(b) When relevant information concerning the securities is disclosed by a person connected with that corporation, directly or indirectly, to another person and the first-mentioned person knows or has reasonable grounds for believing that the other person will make use of the information for the purpose of dealing, or procuring another to deal, in those securities [s.141B(1)].

Culpability of Insider Dealing

The crucial question in Hong Kong is not simply whether or not the dealing is insider dealing as defined within section 141B but also, if so, whether or not the insider dealing in question is culpable.

Section 141B, which defines insider dealing, provides that insider dealing may, pursuant to section 141C, be culpable for the purposes of Part XII A of the Ordinance. Section 141C does not contain any exhaustive definition of what constitutes culpable insider dealing. Subsections (1) to (4) of section 141C merely specify a number of eventualities where insider dealing is not culpable; and subsection (5) requires the Insider Dealing Tribunal to consider, in determining the culpability of a person in relation to insider dealing, whether or not such person has disclosed the dealing promptly or otherwise to the Commission of his own initiative, and to the reasonableness of any explanation offered by such person if he has made no disclosure to the Commission of his own initiative.

In the case of *Re Applications by Chow Chin-wo and others for Judicial Review* (1987), the court held that 'culpable' in the context of the SO and of culpable insider dealing means no more than 'blameworthy'. Executive directors, who did not themselves actually procure the relevant dealing, can be found to be involved in culpable insider dealing if it can be shown that they were implicated or concerned in events which led up to or induced the relevant dealing, particularly where a situation had arisen where they were aware, or ought to have been aware, of a real risk that their company might embark on culpable insider dealing but they took no action to prevent such dealing.

Insider Dealing Tribunal

If it appears to the Financial Secretary, whether following representations by the Commission or otherwise, that insider dealing in relation to the securities of a corporation has taken place or may have taken place, he may require the Insider Dealing Tribunal to inquire into the matter (s.141H(1)). The object of an inquiry is (a) to determine whether culpable insider dealing in relation to the securities of a corporation has taken place; and (b) to determine the identity of the persons involved therein and the extent of their culpability (s.141H(3)).

In making a determination, the Tribunal is not limited to the identity and culpability of an immediate party to an insider dealing but may (a) include any other person connected with the dealing; and (b) in the case of a body corporate, include the individuals who exercised control in the management thereof (s.141H(4)).

The Tribunal consists of a chairman and two other members, all of whom are appointed by the Governor. The chairman must be a judge of the Supreme Court and the other two members must not be public officers (s.141G(2), (3)).

The Third Schedule of the SO includes important procedural provisions concerning the sittings of the Tribunal and representation. Paragraph 14 provides that the chairman is to determine questions of law, and all other questions are to be determined by the opinion of the majority of the members. Paragraph 15 stipulates that every sitting of the Tribunal is to be in camera and that the Tribunal is to determine which persons may be present. However, this provision is subject to paragraph 16 which provides that a person whose conduct is the subject of an inquiry, or who is implicated or concerned in the subject matter of an inquiry, is entitled to be present in person at any sitting of the Tribunal relating to that inquiry and to be represented by a barrister or solicitor. The Tribunal may appoint a legal officer, barrister, or solicitor to act as counsel for the Tribunal.

Wide powers are conferred on the Tribunal. It is empowered to receive and consider any material notwithstanding that such material would not be admissible as evidence in civil or criminal proceedings, to summon witnesses, to examine witnesses on oath or affirmation, to issue search warrants, to regulate its own procedures, and to exercise such other powers as may be necessary for the purposes of the inquiry and to deal summarily with contempt in the face of the Tribunal (s.141J). It is also empowered to authorize the Commission to inspect, and to make copies of and take extracts from books or documents from any person where it has reasonable grounds to believe or suspect that those books or documents may contain information relevant to the inquiry (141K). It is given to the Tribunal's power of discovery by section 141L which excludes any claim of privilege, other than the privilege of a client in respect of disclosure of privileged information to his solicitor or counsel, as a justification for non-compliance by any person with a requirement for disclosure under section 141K or on appearance before the Tribunal.

The inquiry is not an ordinary civil or criminal litigation, although it is deemed to be a judicial proceeding. The proceedings are inquisitorial or investigative. Counsel of the Tribunal are not prosecutors: their role is to advise and assist the Tribunal in conducting the inquiry. All questions are determined by the Tribunal save that the chairman determines questions of law. The witnesses are the Tribunal's witnesses and the function of the Tribunal is to determine whether or not culpable insider dealing has taken place and to determine the other matters for determination under section 141H(3) of the Ordinance.

Even if the Tribunal has found that culpable insider dealing has taken place, no disqualification, penalty or other consequence, criminal or civil, results from such determination. Indeed, s.141A(2) expressly provides that 'No transaction shall be void or voidable by reason only that it is an insider dealing within the meaning of this Part.'

The members of the Insider Dealing Tribunal of Hong Kong are amenable to the process of judicial review at the instance, at least, of persons affected by their determinations in circumstances where no alternative remedy exists. Review is not to be equated with an appeal. The High Court can only interfere if it be shown that in the discharge of its statutory obligations the Tribunal exceeded its jurisdiction, erred in law, came to wholly unsupportable conclusions, or acted unfairly.

Securities (Insider Dealing) Bill of 1989

The Government published the Securities (Insider Dealing) Bill of 1989 on 30 June 1989. It aims to provide a more comprehensive definition of insider dealing and to authorize the Insider Dealing Tribunal to impose sanctions on persons it has identified as having been involved in insider dealing. It repeals Part XII A of the SO. It seems that the Government do not intend to make insider dealing a criminal offence, and do not intend to abolish the Insider Dealing Tribunal. The Bill was severely criticized for containing provisions that were onerous and ambiguous.

The Securities (Disclosure of Interests) Ordinance

The Legislative Council passed the Securities (Disclosure of Interests) Bill on 14 July 1988, which requires certain persons holding shares in or debentures of listed companies to disclose their interests in those shares or debentures.

The Ordinance, not yet in effect,

follows closely the relevant provisions of the United Kingdom Companies Act. It has five main features. First, it forces disclosure of shareholdings of 10 per cent or more within five days of the duty arising. Once a substantial shareholding has been notified, any change of 1 per cent or more must also be notified. The aim is to look through corporate interests to get at the reality of controlling shareholders. Failure to comply with the disclosure obligations attracts heavy penalties upon conviction.

Second, it gives listed companies the right to require a shareholder to provide information about his holding. If a person fails without good reason to give the necessary information, the company may apply to the High Court for restrictions to be placed on the shares in question. Similarly, a listed company may be required by 10 per cent of its shareholders, upon demonstration of good cause, to investigate into the ownership of its shares.

Third, it forces the directors and the chief executive of a listed company to disclose their shareholdings in the company and in any associated company and any dealings they may have in the relevant shares.

Fourth, it enables the Financial Secretary to appoint inspectors to investigate the ownership of a listed company or any breach of the duty of disclosure by directors and chief executives. The cost of any such investigation will be recoverable in certain circumstances from the parties involved. Where an investigation encounters difficulties in finding out relevant facts, the Financial Secretary may impose restrictions on the shares concerned.

Finally, it enables the courts or, in certain cases, the Financial Secretary to place restrictions on the transfer or disposal of shares. Where a freezing order is made, any transfer of the shares concerned is void. In addition, no voting rights are exercisable in respect of the shares and no dividends are payable. An order may only be lifted by the relevant authority when certain conditions have been met [see *Legislative Council Proceedings* 8 June 1988, pp. 1561–2].

Securities and Futures Commission Ordinance

The Legislative Council on 12 April 1989 passed the Securities and Futures Commission Ordinance, which established the Securities and Futures Commission and amended the law about dealing in securities and trading in futures contracts. The Commission is a body corporate with power to sue and be sued. It consists of a chairman appointed by the Governor and an uneven number, not less than seven, of other directors so appointed as the Governor may determine. Half of the directors (including the chairman) are appointed to be executive directors and the remainder are appointed to be non-executive directors. The Commission exercises the following functions:

(a) to advise the Financial Secretary on all matters relating to securities, futures contracts, and property investment arrangements;

(b) without prejudice to any duties imposed or powers conferred on any other person in regard to the enforcement of the law relating to securities, futures contracts, and property investment arrangements, to be responsible for ensuring that the provisions of the relevant Ordinances, and the provisions of any other Ordinance so far as they relate to securities, futures contracts and property investment arrangements, are complied with;

(c) to report to the Financial Secretary the occurrence of any dealing in relation to securities which it reasonably believes or suspects to be an insider dealing within the meaning of section 141B of the Securities Ordinance;

(d) to be responsible for supervising and monitoring the activities of the Exchange Companies and clearing houses;

(e) to take all reasonable steps to safeguard the interests of persons dealing in securities or trading in futures contracts or entering into property investment arrangements;

(f) to promote and encourage proper conduct amongst members of the Exchange Companies and clearing houses, and other registered persons;

(g) to suppress illegal, dishonorable and improper practices in dealing in securities, trading in futures contracts, entering into property investment arrangements, and the provision of investment advice or other services relating to securities, futures contracts and property investment arrangements;

(h) to promote and maintain the integrity of registered persons and encourage the promulgation by registered persons of balanced and informed advice to their clients and to the public generally;

(i) to consider and suggest reforms of the law relating to securities, futures contracts and property investment arrangements;

(j) to encourage the development of securities and futures markets in Hong Kong and the increased use of such markets by investors in Hong Kong and elsewhere;

(k) to promote and develop self-regulation by market bodies in the securities and futures industries;

(l) to perform any other functions conferred by or under any other Ordinance.

Where the Commission has reason to believe that:

(a) an offence under any of the relevant securities legislation may have been committed; or

(b) a person may have committed a defalcation or other breach of trust, fraud or misfeasance —
    (i) in dealing in securities or trading in futures contracts;
    (ii) in the management of investment in securities or in futures contracts;
    (iii) in making property investment arrangements; or
    (iv) in giving advice as regards the acquisition, disposal, purchase or sale, or otherwise investing in, any security or futures contract or as regards any property investment arrangement; or

(c) insider dealing may have taken place; or

(d) the manner in which a person has engaged or is engaging in any of the activities referred to above in paragraph (b),

the Commission may in writing direct one or more of its employees or, with the consent of the Financial Secretary, appoint one or more other persons to be an investigator ('the investigator') to investigate any matter referred to in paragraphs (a) to (d) above and report to the Commission thereon.

The person under investigation or any person who is reasonably believed or suspected by the investigator to have in his possession or under his control any record or other document which contains, or which is likely to contain, information relevant to an investigation under this section, or who is so believed or suspected of otherwise having such information in his possession or under his control, must —

(a) produce to the investigator, within such time and at such place as he may reasonably require, any record or other document specified by the investigator which is, or may be, relevant to the investigator which is, or may be, relevant to the investigation, and which is in his possession or under his control;

(b) if so required by the investigator, give to him such explanation or future particulars in respect of a record or other document produced as the investigator shall specify;

(c) attend before the investigator at such time and place as he may require in writing, and answer truthfully and to the best of his ability such questions relating to the matters under investigation as the investigator may put to him; and

(d) give to the investigator all assistance in connection with the investigation which he is reasonably able to give.

Failure to comply with the requirement of the investigator is a criminal offence. Further, the investigator may certify the failure to the High Court and the High Court may thereupon inquire into the case and:

(a) order such person to comply with the requirement within such period as may be fixed by the High Court; or
(b) if the High Court is satisfied that such person has failed without reasonable excuse to comply with such requirement, punish him in the same manner as if he had been guilty of contempt of court.

If a magistrate is satisfied on information on oath laid by the chairman or other director of the Commission, or by an employee of the Commission authorized by the Commission, that there are reasonable grounds for suspecting that there is, or is likely to be, on premises specified in the information any record or other document which is relevant to an investigation, the magistrate may issue a warrant authorizing any such person ('specified person') and any police officer, and such other persons as may be necessary to assist in the execution of the warrant:

(a) to enter the premises so specified, if necessary by force, at any time within the period of 7 days beginning on the date of the warrant; and
(b) to search for, seize and remove any record or other document which any such specified person or police officer has reasonable cause to believe may be required for the purposes of the investigation.

A specified person or a police officer or other persons authorized by a warrant under this section may:

(a) require any person on the premises specified in the warrant whom he reasonably believes to have employed in connection with a business which is, or which has been, conducted on such premises to produce for examination any record or other document which such specified person or police officer has reasonable cause to believe may be required for the purposes of the investigation and which is in his possession or under his control;
(b) prohibit any person mentioned in paragraph (a) from —
    (i) removing from the premises so specified any record or other document produced;
    (ii) erasing, adding to or otherwise altering any entry or other particular contained in, or otherwise interfering in any manner whatsoever with, or causing or permitting any other person to interfere with, any such record or other document;
(c) take, in relation to any such record or other document, any other step which may appear necessary for preserving it and preventing interference with it.

Conclusion

From the description above of recent developments and future intentions, it may be seen that Hong Kong has enacted or will enact legislation which is meant to lead to an orderly, efficient, fair, and informed market; to protect investors from being defrauded by the unscrupulous; and to ensure that all investors in the market are placed on an equal footing by requiring timely and adequate disclosure by companies of price-sensitive information and by prohibiting dealing on any such information which is undisclosed. It is not justified to claim that the stock-market in Hong Kong is under-regulated. But it is appropriate to ask whether the existing legislation or the proposed new legislation is appropriate for Hong Kong.

The Securities (Disclosure of Interests) Ordinance closely follows the relevant provisions of the United Kingdom Companies Act. It is extremely complicated and difficult to understand, even for the practitioners. It may not be the sort of legislation which Hong Kong investors would like to have. In Hong Kong, investors are on the whole much less sophisticated than those in the United States or Britain. To a much greater extent than in Britain, quoted companies in Hong Kong are controlled, or at least de facto controlled, by individuals, or by small groups of individuals associated by family or other ties, or by other companies or groups of companies. In fact, there are very few quoted companies in Hong Kong that are not so controlled. The individuals controlling a company, or some of the directors of a controlling company, are almost invariably also directors of the company controlled. In such cases, therefore, it is possible without much difficulty to ascertain who controls the company, and there is no need to follow the United Kingdom Companies Act so closely.

The Securities (Insider Dealing) Bill of 1989 has been severely criticized since its publication for being too onerous and ambiguous in some of the provisions. It may affect those who are honest and innocent. More importantly, it may have little deterrent effect, as it will not make insider dealing a criminal offence. Insider dealing is essentially fraudulent behaviour. In Australia, the United States, and the United Kingdom, contravention of the provisions of the respective legislation makes the individual guilty of a criminal offence resulting in imprisonment or a fine, or both. This is no convincing reason why the offender in Hong Kong can go free with impunity. Further there is no provision in the Bill for civil remedies whether for the other party to the transaction or for the company itself. Provision of civil remedies is particularly necessary because the common law is unable to develop civil remedies adequate to the task. The law of contract does not in general impose a duty of disclosure of material information. Even if the insider is a director of the company in question, it is well established that there is no duty of disclosure to shareholders with whom a director deals.

For political reasons, mainly, a number of Hong Kong listed companies have relocated their domicile to other British colonies such as Bermuda and the Cayman Islands over the past two years. These overseas companies will not, therefore, have to follow certain provisions relating to the protection of investors under the CO, which defines a 'company' as a company formed and registered under the CO or an existing company. Consequently, there is a need to amend the CO.

Dealers in Hong Kong are registered and not licensed. Licensing generally involves a measure of quality control, whereas registration is more a process of knowing who the players are. It is pertinent to ask whether at this stage there should be any change in the law, and whether there should be established a code of conduct for the dealers if the existing law is to remain intact.

There is also a need to consolidate and simplify the various ordinances relating to securities. They are lacking in order and full of overlapping powers among the Financial Secretary, the Securities and Futures Commission, the Registrar of Companies, and the Stock Exchange. The Stock Exchange has not been given statutory power to administer the listing rules and to investigate a possible breach of the rules. The only express sanction that the Stock Exchange may impose is cancellation or suspension of listing, a course of action which may not benefit the investors. It may now be the right time to have second thoughts on the respective powers and functions of the various regulatory bodies, with a view to achieving a balance between controls designed to maintain market integrity and freedom to encourage market development.

References

Farrar, J. H., Furey, N., and Hannigan, B., *Farrar's Company Law* (London, Butterworths, second edition, 1988).

Gower, L. C. B., *Gower's Principles of Modern Company Law* (London, Stevens, 1979).

Hahlo, H. R. and Farrar, J. H., *Hahlo's Cases and Materials on Company Law* (London, Sweet & Maxwell, third edition, 1987).

Hazen, T. L., *The Law of Securities Regulation* (Minneapolis, West Publishing Co., first edition, 1985).

Higgins, M. F., *Securities Regulation in Hong Kong 1972–1977* (Netherlands, Sijthoff & Noordhoff, 1978).

Hong Kong Government, *First Report of The Companies Law Revision Committee* (Hong Kong, Hong Kong Government Printer, 1971).

—— *Second Report of The Companies Law Revision Committee* (Hong Kong, Hong Kong Government Printer, 1973).

Review of Investor Protection Report: Part 1 (London, Her Majesty's Stationery Office, 1984).

17. Hong Kong as an International Financial Centre

RICHARD YAN-KI HO

Introduction

Hong Kong is continually referred to as an important international financial centre. What actually is a financial centre? Every person on the street seems to have a pretty good idea of what it is. They would probably say that a financial centre should have many banks, especially multinational banks; a very active foreign exchange market; a very large equity market; and a variety of other financial institutions and markets. They can keep adding to the list but they have just described the many characteristics of a financial centre, which is a generic term like 'business centre' or 'trade centre'. In a broad sense, a financial centre is a place where financial intermediation services are provided.

In Chapter 1 we discussed the evolution of financial institutions in intermediating funds between fund surplus units and fund deficit units. People with excess funds go to banks to deposit their money, while people in need of funds go to banks to borrow. The bank is thus a location, a focal point or a 'centre', where people use intermediation services. This basic concept also applies to a financial centre.

Within a country, fund surplus units and fund deficit units may not be geographically evenly distributed. Some surplus units may be concentrated in one location and some deficit units may be concentrated in another. The evolution of a financial centre requires that the fund surplus units and the fund deficit units be located in different areas. Funds are thus flowing from one area to another, that is, from fund surplus areas to fund deficit areas. Such a flow of funds across different geographical areas is intermediated through banks in one or a few locations. Thus, the bulk of the funds that are channelled within a country must go through certain areas where most of the big banks are located and where people have the most sophisticated financial know-how. Such locations are called 'financial centres' — examples are New York and San Francisco in the United States. Since they provide intermediation services for people within a country, such centres are usually referred to as domestic financial centres and the funds involved are usually demoninated in local currency.

The concept of domestic financial intermediation can be extended to the international context. In many countries or regions, some borrowers or investors may choose to go overseas to fulfil their financial needs because of insufficient domestic demand for or supply of funds (and hence too high or too low interest rates), inefficient financial markets, or stringent government regulations. Their needs have to be accommodated through financial institutions and markets located elsewhere. Some cities have thus emerged to provide intermediation services for other countries. In this sense, financial centres link different domestic financial markets and institutions. In these centres, people wishing to purchase or issue foreign securities need to purchase or sell foreign currencies, and the foreign exchange market becomes the important link. However, in some cases the participants are really supranational in that they may not need to go through the foreign currency market, for example, a British borrower may borrow United States dollars in order to make payment in United States dollars.

There may be many reasons that a certain area or city evolves into a financial centre in general, or into an international financial centre in particular. Such reasons include:

1. Foreign Exchange Control.   A large amount of foreign exchange flows in and out of an international financial centre. Governments that impose foreign exchange control may greatly impede the functioning of the centre.

2. Supply of Funds.   The country in which the centre is located may have a huge supply of funds, such as Switzerland or Japan. Although the existence of a trade surplus on the external current account is not a necessary condition for becoming an international financial centre, it will facilitate its formation. In the case of Switzerland, Swiss capital exports developed partly because domestic savings exceeded domestic needs and Switzerland continues to have a very high saving propensity compared with other industrial countries, such as Germany, the United Kingdom, and the United States. Tokyo, Japan, which also has a very high propensity to save, will also naturally evolve into a major international financial centre.

3. Financial Executives.   The centre has highly efficient, trained, and experienced financial executives.

4. Environment.   The political and economic environment is stable.

5. Communication Systems.   There exists an efficient communications system and good air transportation to neighbouring countries.

6. Time Zone and Geographical Location.   The centre is located in an appropriate time zone for it to enable certain financial markets, for example, the foreign exchange market or the gold market, to continue trading when the other markets are closed. Physical location is also important. Proximity to potential borrowers is essential for bankers to market their loans and to negotiate with borrowers. Thus, it would be beneficial to the development of a financial centre to be near to countries that have a very high growth rate, are industralizing very rapidly, and have a huge demand for funds.

7. Regulations.   Regulations and prudential supervision of the banking system are not unduly stringent, especially to foreign financial institutions.

8. Number of Financial Institutions.   There exists a sufficient number of banking and financial institutions to provide a critical mass

for the provision of services to international clients in a highly effective and efficient way. Moreover, most of the syndication loans volume is huge and the sharing of risk among different banks is thus crucial.

9.   Inter-bank Money Market.   There exists an active inter-bank money market to facilitate an efficient flow of funds among financial institutions within the centre and between centres. Such a market also provides an opportunity for efficiency with minimal amount of risk.

10.   Universal Banking Practice.   The practice of universal banking, as in the Swiss system, may help in the functioning of a financial centre because banks, under such a system, are able to perform all kinds of banking transactions.

Some Terminology of Financial Centres

As mentioned earlier, the term 'financial centre' is a generic term. There are a number of other terms that need further clarification.

1.   Domestic Financial Centres.   Domestic financial centres provide intermediation services for local residents in local currency. Good examples include San Francisco in the United States, and Shanghai in China.

2.   Global Financial Centres.   Global financial centres provide inter-mediation services for people within their region and also for people outside of their region. The host country of the centre may also have a huge supply of funds. Examples may include London in the United Kingdom and New York in the United States.

3.   Regional Financial Centres.   Regional financial centres may only provide financial intermediation services for people who live within their region.

4.   Offshore Financial Centre.   'Offshore' financial centre is probably the most widely used term. Fig. 17.1 illustrates the difference between a domestic financial centre and an offshore financial centre. An offshore financial centre usually has two features: (1) it usually deals with overseas clients, that is, neither the borrowers (users of funds) nor the lenders (sources of funds) are residents of the country where the financial centre is located, and (2) the transactions are usually denominated in foreign currencies.

London is referred to as one of the most important offshore centres or, in banking terms, one of the most important *Eurocurrency Centres*. The term 'Eurocurrency' is not specific to London. A Eurocurrency transaction is one that is denominated in a currency other than the domestic currency of the place where the transaction is executed. Thus, a United States dollar transaction carried out in London is called a 'Eurodollar deal.' If it is denominated in Japanese yen, it is called 'Euroyen'. One the reasons for the evolution of London into a Eurocurrency centre is the Cold War of the 1950s, which made Russia think that the United States Government would impound its United States dollar holdings in banks in the United States. Russia therefore

Fig. 17.1   Schematic View of Transactions in an International Financial Centre

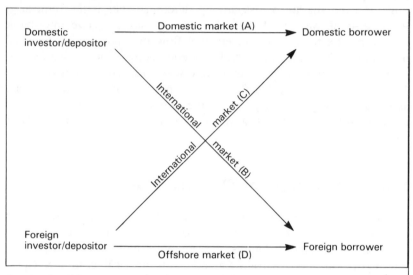

Source: David K. Eiteman and Arthur I. Stonehill, *Multinational Business Finance*, 5th ed. (Reading, Mass., Addison-Wesley, 1989), p. 253. Reprinted by permission of the publisher.

began to deposit its dollars in London, starting the Eurodollar market. Another reason is that, because of the stringent government regulations of the United States banking sector, many United States dollars were transferred to London in the 1950s, making London the most important Eurodollar centre in the world.

Within the family of offshore financial centres, Professor Y. S. Park (1982) delineates four types: primary centres, booking centres, funding centres, and collection centres. A primary centre serves world-wide clients, but the most important uses and sources of funds are within its major market area. These clients both supply funds to and withdraw funds from the centre. Good examples of primary centres are the global centres, that is, London and New York. A booking centre is usually a tax haven. It serves as a centre for booking both Eurocurrency deposits and international loans, but the actual operations and executions are not done there. Such a centre is just used for accounting entries, to capture favourable tax treatment. Nassau and Cayman Island are examples of booking centres. A funding centre plays the role of an inward financial intermediary, channelling funds from outside its market area toward regional uses. Hong Kong and Singapore fall into this category because they usually collect funds from London and lend them to other Asian countries. A collection centre such as Bahrain performs outward financial intermediation functions. There are excess savings generated from the region and the centre collects the funds and invests them efficiently.

Features and Development in International Financial Markets in the 1970s and 1980s

Since banking is the major activity carried out by international financial centres, we highlight here some features of international banking. One of the commonly used measurements of international banking activity is the size of the external claims of the Bank for International Settlements (BIS) reporting banks.[1]

Table 17.1 shows the total cross-border claims of reporting banks. These claims increased from US$1,671.4 billion in 1982 to US$4,485.3

Table 17.1   International Banking Activities (US$ billion)

Year	Total Cross-border Claims	Inside Area Inter-bank Claims	Total Net International Bank Credit
1982	1,671.4	931.8	1,015.0
1983	1,753.9	1,007.3	1,085.0
1984	2,153.5	1,268.5	1,265.0
1985	2,512.7	1,504.9	1,480.0
1986	3,221.1	2,063.3	1,770.0
1987	4,157.2	2,780.2	2,220.0
1988	4,485.3	3,068.1	2,390.0

Source: *International Banking and Financial Market Development*, Bank for International Settlements, various issues.

Fig. 17.2   International Banking Activities

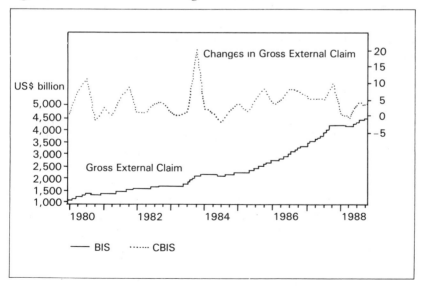

billion in 1988. One of the most striking features is that inter-bank assets within the reporting area contribute a significant share of the total assets, and the share rose from 55.7 per cent in 1982 to 68.4 per cent in 1988. Claims on countries outside the reporting area contribute only about 20 per cent of the share.

Fig. 17.2 shows the gross external assets of the reporting banks from the fourth quarter of 1979 to the fourth quarter of 1988. On the whole, the growth rate was relatively rapid with a compound annual growth rate of 17.2 per cent. However, the growth path was not that smooth. The years 1980 to 1982 and late 1983 to early 1985 were periods of relatively slow growth, but the growth rate picked up in 1985 to late 1987. However, activities began to level off in the first quarter of 1988. While international banking activities moved broadly in line with economic fluctuations, there were some basic structural changes in the international financial market which deserve further elaboration.

Structural Changes in the International Financial Markets

International banking enjoyed tremendous growth during the 1970s. This was due mainly to the two oil crises that occurred during that time. The oil crises created huge surpluses on the part of the oil-exporting countries, that is, the OPEC countries. The developing countries, especially those in Latin America and Asia, also had a huge demand for funds to finance their current account deficit. A concentration of funds in the hands of a few oil exporters initiated the demand for investment opportunities. Financial markets in those OPEC countries were not developed, and those countries had to invest their surplus funds as bank deposits and, as Table 17.2 indicates, a great majority of the current account surpluses of oil-exporting countries were placed with banks in the industrial countries and in the Eurocurrency market, which was then dominated by the United States multinational banks. Developing countries, on the other hand, had to borrow heavily from commercial banks to finance their current account deficit (Tables 17.3 and 17.4). It was thus said that commercial banks, especially United States banks, were 'recycling the oil money' from oil exporters to oil importers. This recycling process made international banking a booming business.

In the 1980s, there was a basic change in the trade pattern (Table 17.5). There was a decline in the demand for oil and in oil prices, and thus a gradual removal of OPEC country surpluses. Two distinct phenomena emerged that shaped the basic change in the financial markets in the 1980s. First, starting from 1983, current account imbalances occurred within the developed countries group, and these were more acute between the United States (the deficit country) and Japan (the surplus country). Second, there was a rapid decline in the

Table 17.2 Oil-exporting Countries: Estimated Disposition of Current Account Surplus, 1974–1983 (US$ billion)

	1974	1975	1976	1977	1978	1979	1980	1981	1982	1983	Total 1974–1983
Current Account Surplus	69	35	39	29	6	63	111	53	-12	-16	377
Plus: Oil sector capital transactions (outflow –)[1]	-12	1	-6	-1	2	-9	-2	3	6	3	-15
Net borrowing[2]	2	3	9	11	16	10	7	7	15	16	96
Equals: Cash surplus available for disposition	59	39	42	39	24	64	116	63	9	3	458
Disposition of Cash Surplus											
International Monetary Fund (IMF) and World Bank[3]	4	3	2	—	-1	-1	1	3	3	6	20
Loans and grants to non-oil-exporting, developing countries[4]	5	7	7	8	9	9	11	10	8	7	81
Bank deposits in industrial countries (net)[5]	30	11	13	13	5	40	42	2	-16	-15	125
Direct placement	7	2	1	2	2	8	6	—	4	—	32
Eurocurrency deposits	23	9	12	11	3	32	36	2	-20	-15	93
Other placements[6]	20	18	20	18	11	16	62	48	14	5	232

Notes: 1. Mainly changes in accounts receivable from oil exports.
2. Total net increase in external liabilities of public and private sectors (including banks). Includes a small amount of money in official transfer, inward non-oil direct investment capital, and miscellaneous capital items. Excludes borrowing from other oil-exporting countries.
3. Includes lending to the IMF, other changes in the reserve position in the IMF, and direct purchases of World Bank bonds.
4. Includes contributions and capital subscriptions to multilateral development agencies (other than the World Bank). Estimates are based on highly uncertain information.
5. Includes deposits in Eurocurrency markets.
6. Includes net acquisitions of government securities, corporate stocks and bonds, bilateral lending (except to non-oil-exporting, developing countries), real estate and other direct investments, and prepayments for imports. Also includes unidentified placements and statistical discrepancies.

Source: International Monetary Fund, *World Economic Outlook*, various issues.

388

THE HONG KONG FINANCIAL SYSTEM

Table 17.3 Non-oil-exporting, Developing Countries: Financing of Current Account Deficits and Reserve Accretions, 1977–1984 (US$ billion)

	1977	1978	1979	1980	1981	1982	1983	1984
Current Account Deficit	30.4	42.3	62.0	87.7	109.1	82.2	56.4	50.0
Increase in official reserves	11.5	16.3	11.8	6.8	5.4	-3.8	6.1	13.3
Total	41.9	58.6	73.8	94.5	114.5	78.4	62.5	63.3
Financed by								
Non-debt-creating flows, net	14.1	17.0	23.7	24.1	27.2	23.9	21.3	23.0
Long-term borrowing from official creditors, net	13.1	13.8	17.0	20.0	22.6	21.6	22.6	23.1
Borrowing from private creditors, net	18.4	32.8	36.5	60.6	70.5	36.2	20.2	21.2
Reserve-related liabilities	2.9	2.0	-0.5	5.3	9.8	15.4	8.4	1.0
Errors and omissions	-6.5	-6.9	-3.0	-15.4	-15.5	-18.8	-10.0	-5.0
				(In Per cent)				
Distribution of Financing Flows								
Non-debt-creating flows, net	33.6	28.9	32.2	25.5	23.8	30.6	34.1	36.3
Long-term borrowing from official creditors, net	31.3	23.5	23.0	21.1	19.7	27.5	36.1	36.5
Borrowing from private creditors, net	43.8	55.9	49.5	64.1	61.6	46.2	32.3	33.5
Reserve-related liabilities	6.9	3.4	-0.6	5.7	8.5	19.6	13.4	1.6
Errors and omissions	-15.5	-11.8	-4.1	-16.3	-13.6	-24.0	-15.9	-7.9

Note: Figures are rounded to the nearest tenth.

Source: International Monetary Fund, *World Economic Outlook*, various issues.

Table 17.4 Developing Countries: External Debt Outstanding, 1977–1984 (US$ billion)

	1977	1978	1979	1980	1981	1982	1983	1984
Total External Debt*	329.3	398.2	472.0	559.9	646.5	724.8	767.6	812.4
Short-term debt	51.7	63.7	75.8	106.5	128.1	148.2	126.2	97.6
Long-term debt	277.7	334.5	396.3	453.4	518.4	576.6	641.4	714.8
By Type of Creditor								
Official creditors	111.0	130.6	148.5	169.1	186.0	205.4	229.6	254.4
Governments	79.1	91.8	102.2	114.3	123.6	134.9	150.8	166.4
International institutions	31.9	38.8	46.4	54.8	62.4	70.5	78.9	88.0
Private Creditors	166.7	203.9	247.7	284.3	332.4	371.2	411.8	460.4
Unguaranteed debt	55.1	56.6	67.8	81.0	100.8	108.4	110.5	112.3
Guaranteed debt	111.6	147.3	179.9	203.2	231.6	262.8	301.3	348.1
Financial institutions	78.9	107.4	137.5	160.0	185.5	212.4	250.0	296.3
Other private creditors	32.7	39.9	42.4	43.2	46.1	50.4	51.3	51.8

Note: *Figures are rounded to the nearest tenth.

Source: International Monetary Fund, *World Economic Outlook*, various issues.

Table 17.5 Summary of Payment Balances on Current Account, 1979–1988* (US$ billion)

	1979	1980	1981	1982	1983	1984	1985	1986	1987	1988
Industrial Countries	-23.1	-60.5	-18.7	-22.3	-19.5	-58.5	-51.4	-18.1	-38.9	-44.2
United States	-1.0	1.9	6.9	-8.7	-46.3	-107.0	-116.4	-141.4	-152.1	-140.6
Other industrial countries	-22.1	-62.4	-25.6	-13.6	26.7	48.5	64.9	123.3	113.2	96.4
Japan	-8.8	-10.7	4.8	6.9	20.8	35.0	49.3	85.8	85.1	83.2
Germany, Fed. Rep. of	-6.0	-15.7	-5.2	4.1	4.2	8.4	15.2	37.2	40.7	32.5
Developing Countries	6.4	30.4	-48.5	-87.1	-64.2	-33.8	-23.9	-47.0	-19.6	-19.3
Africa	-3.4	-1.9	-22.4	-21.5	-12.3	-8.0	-0.1	-9.4	-7.5	-6.1
Asia	-9.7	-14.4	-19.0	-17.4	-14.9	-4.2	-14.0	4.9	15.3	10.0
Europe	-13.6	-15.6	-14.3	-8.7	-5.9	-3.2	-3.3	-1.7	-2.3	-2.5
Middle East	54.2	92.5	50.0	3.0	-20.1	-15.8	-2.2	-23.3	-12.1	-7.0
Western Hemisphere	-21.1	-30.2	-42.7	-42.5	-10.9	-2.6	-4.3	-17.5	-13.1	-13.8

Notes: * Includes official transfers.
Figures are rounded to the nearest tenth.

Source: International Monetary Fund, *World Economic Outlook*, various issues.

current account deficit in developing countries, and the Asian developing countries (especially Hong Kong, Singapore, Taiwan, and Korea) actually enjoyed a current account surplus starting from 1986, indicating that there was a corresponding decrease in fund demand. Since both the major deficit and surplus countries were developed countries where matured financial markets existed, the 'recycling of trade money' did not have to be carried out by commercial banks alone. Indeed, because of the expertise that the surplus countries had in portfolio investment, they could directly buy securities, that is, bonds, stocks, commercial paper, and various notes issued directly by the deficit countries. Thus, the Japanese have been a major buyer of United States securities, bringing life to the direct securities market in the 1980s.

As shown in Table 17.6, international bond issues increased from US$34 billion in 1976 to a peak of US$227 billion in 1986 (net international bond issues also increased from US$26 billion to US$87 billion). During the same period, net international lending (net of redepositing) increased from US$70 billion in 1976, peaked at US$165 billion in 1981, then declined to a low of US$90 billion in 1984 but recovered to US$165 billion in 1986. Thus, the ratio of bond issues to imports decreased from 2.8 per cent in 1976 to a historical low of 1.0 per cent in 1980, but then picked up rapidly to reach 4.1 per cent in 1986. The ratio of bond issues to bank lending followed roughly the same trend, but the ratio peaked in 1985 and declined in 1986, showing a recovery in the international lending market. However, a slow-down occurred in 1987, especially after the stock-market crash in October of that year.

There were three factors affecting the development of the international bond market during the past few years. The first is the rise in the market interest rate, which affected the fixed-rate securities market the most. The weakness of the United States dollar and the expectation of further depreciation also dampened the issue of United States dollar denominated bonds. Before the 1987 October Crash, one of the driving forces behind the activity in equity-related issues, mostly in the form of equity warrants, was the buoyancy of the stock-market. Such equity-related issues declined tremendously during the fourth quarter of 1987. Moreover, the collapse of the perpetual Floating-rate Notes (FRNs) market in late 1986 also affected 1987 activities. Since their first appearance in 1984 up to 1986, the total perpetual FRNs issued was US$18 billion, and US$7.4 billion was issued in 1986. In late 1986, it was perceived that such perpetual FRNs were severely underpriced and in December 1986 no investors wanted to purchase any perpetual FRNs and the price dropped sharply. Because of a drop in the bond market activities, 1987 saw a rapid recovery in the syndication loan market, the volume of which increased from US$24.8 billion in 1986 to US$53.2 billion in 1987. In early 1988, the international bond market staged a strong recovery owing to a stable interest rate and exchange rate environment.

Table 17.6 Size of International Financial Markets, 1976–1986 (US$ billion)

	1976	1977	1978	1979	1980	1981	1982	1983	1984	1985	1986
Total gross international bond issues	34	36	36	39	38	52	76	77	110	168	227
International bond issues (net)[1]	26	27	24	23	19	29	49	46	62	77	87
International bank lending (net of redepositing)	70	68	90	125	160	165	95	85	90	105	165
International bond issues (net) deflated by U.S. GNP deflator	24	24	20	17	13	18	29	26	34	41	45.2
International bank lending (net) deflated by U.S. GNP deflator	66	60	74	94	111	105	56	49	50	56	86
(In Per cent)											
Bond issues as ratio to world imports (in U.S. dollars)	2.8	2.5	1.9	1.5	1.0	1.5	2.7	2.6	3.3	4.0	4.1
International bank lending (net) as ratio to world imports (in U.S. dollars)	7.5	4.6	7.2	7.8	8.6	8.7	5.2	4.9	4.9	5.6	7.8
International bond issues (net) as ratio to international bank lending (net)	37.1	39.7	26.7	18.4	11.9	17.6	51.6	54.1	68.9	73.3	52.7

Note: 1. New international bond issues less redemptions, repurchases, and bank purchases of bonds.

Sources: International Monetary Fund, *World Economic Outlook* and *International Financial Statistics*; Organization for Economic Co-operation and Development, *Financial Market Trends*; and Bank for International Settlements.

Table 17.7 The Presence of the World's 500 Largest Banks in Hong Kong

World Ranking[1]	Licensed Overseas Banks in Hong Kong		Licensed Deposit-taking Companies Owned by Overseas Banks[2]		Registered Deposit-taking Companies Owned by Overseas Banks[2]		Local Representative Offices	
	1987	1989	1987	1989	1987	1989	1987	1989
1–20	18	19	3	6	18	17	1	0
21–50	25	26	5	2	21	16	3	0
51–100	33	32	4	4	22	22	6	7
101–200	15	24	1	1	16	19	29	24
201–500	11	16	5	4	22	23	41	50
Others	18	17	2	3	34	31	63	79
Total	120	134	20	20	133	128	143	160

Notes: 1. Top 500 banks/banking groups in the world ranked by total assets less contra items.

2. Figures in these columns represent the number of deposit-taking companies which are branches or subsidiaries of overseas banks, classified in accordance with the world ranking of these overseas banks.

Sources: Figures for 1987 and 1989 are extracted from *The Banker*, July 1987 and 1989 issues.

The Position of Hong Kong in the World Financial Market

People like to call Hong Kong the third largest financial centre in the world. Does Hong Kong really qualify for the third rank in the world financial scene? This is a very difficult question, and the rank will change under different criteria. According to an estimate by Jao (1988a), by world standards Hong Kong is the fourth largest loan syndication centre, the fifth largest foreign exchange trading centre, the fourth largest foreign bank centre (in terms of number), and the eleventh largest centre in terms of external assets of banks.[2]

Indeed, Hong Kong is an international banking centre. As indicated in Table 17.7, there was an increase in the representation of the world's largest banks in Hong Kong. Nineteen of the twenty largest banks in the world maintained a full-fledged licensed bank in Hong Kong in 1989. It is natural that most of these banks come from Japan and the United States. However, there was no increase in representation in the form of licensed DTCs, and there was even a decrease in the number of registered DTCs owned by overseas banks, while there was an increase in branches of foreign banks. This indicates that DTCs, especially registered DTCs, have limited usefulness to overseas financial institutions.

Table 17.8 shows the amount of foreign currency deposits in the Hong Kong banking system (including licensed banks and DTCs) which is another indication of the development of Hong Kong as a financial centre. There was an increase in foreign currency deposits from 1980 to 1989 and the share of foreign currency deposits in total deposits increased from 12.2 per cent to 60.1 per cent. The most dramatic rise occurred in 1982 when the Hong Kong Government abolished the

Table 17.8 Customer Foreign Currency Deposit

Year	Amount (HK$ million)	Per cent in Total Deposits
1980	10,621	12.2
1981	18,588	17.8
1982	82,384	43.3
1983	115,200	48.0
1984	138,099	46.6
1985	193,104	52.6
1986	278,016	56.6
1987	363,192	56.6
1988	498,766	59.0
1989	620,017	61.5

Note: These figures include deposits of both licensed banks and DTCs.

Source: *Hong Kong Monthly Digest of Statistics* (Hong Kong, Census and Statistics Department), various issues.

withholding tax on the interest earned from foreign currency deposits. Of course, due to the depreciating Hong Kong currency, the increase in the shares during the period of 1980 to 1983 was partly due to the exchange rate valuation effect. However, since the linked exchange rate was established in late 1983, such a currency valuation effect was minimal.[3]

Functions Performed by the Hong Kong Financial Centre

As a financial centre or an international banking centre, Hong Kong performs three main functions: financial intermediation, clearing, and maturity transformation.

Financial Intermediation

Table 17.9 gives the total net claim position (total assets minus total liabilities) of the Hong Kong banking system (including licensed banks, LDTCs, and RDTCs) *vis-à-vis* other countries or regions. Some of the most salient features of the net position from 1979 to 1988 are described here. Please note that a positive net claim means that Hong Kong is a net creditor to other countries or regions, while a negative net claim means that Hong Kong is a net debtor to other countries or regions.

On the whole, Hong Kong is a net creditor to the rest of the world. In 1979, Hong Kong had a net claim of US$3,872 million *vis-à-vis* the rest of the world and this net claim increased very rapidly to US$40,218 million in 1988 with a compound annual growth of 29.7 per cent. This indicates that Hong Kong also provides funds to the rest of the world. Hong Kong was also a net creditor to the rest of the Asia Pacific region and there was a consistent increase in the net position, from US$5.7 billion in 1979 to US$42.0 billion in 1988, an annual increase of 24.8 per cent. In the Asia Pacific region, the major net debtor countries are Japan, China, Taiwan, South Korea, and Australia. China used to be a net creditor *vis-à-vis* Hong Kong, from 1982 to 1984, but started to take a net debtor position in 1985. This net debt increased to US$5.2 billion in 1988. This was mainly due to the need for financing China's trade deficit and its huge modernization programme. South Korea used to be Hong Kong's largest net debtor, as demonstrated by the fact that Korea's net debt reached a high of US$7.1 billion in 1986, but due to an improvement in its current account, its net debt was gradually reduced to US$4.1 billion, indicating that South Korea was retiring some of its debt.

The increase in net claims of Hong Kong on both Japan and Taiwan was also very rapid (47.5 per cent for Japan and 21.6 per cent for Taiwan), but such an increase did not seem to relate to their trade deficit financing because both these countries have enjoyed huge trade surpluses over the years. There is a general trend for Taiwan to borrow

Table 17.9 Net Claims of the Hong Kong Financial System *vis-à-vis* Other Countries (US$ million)

	1979	1980	1981	1982	1983	1984	1985	1986	1987	1988
International Organizations	0	0	0	0	0	0	0	135	143	313
Asia Pacific	5,741	5,101	1,946	6,353	8,269	11,135	12,121	28,083	42,010	41,972
Australia	197	183	443	733	1,166	1,224	1,122	1,663	1,651	3,430
Bangladesh	0	6	5	12	8	12	25	23	54	25
Brunei	-2	0	1	7	27	30	16	-18	-71	-75
Burma	-59	21	9	9	5	2	-14	0	13	0
China	1,156	1,297	346	-838	-1,178	-1,366	1,098	1,921	2,235	5,237
Taiwan	727	1,167	1,026	972	1,244	432	53	1,833	4,379	4,219
Fiji	8	4	11	12	14	16	-3	3	4	-2
French Polynesia	0				0	0	-1	4	11	-1
India	119	102	73	111	227	344	748	629	916	1,343
Indonesia	955	831	441	1,008	1,139	948	820	1,202	970	1,159
Japan	693	187	537	1,591	356	2,947	2,589	14,291	26,514	22,938
Kampuchea	0	0	0		0	0	0	0	-1	-1
Laos	0	0	0		0	0	-1	0	-1	0
Macau	-226	-464	-390	-209	-95	84	172	269	472	-141
Malaysia	237	295	616	651	1,513	888	800	813	754	655
Nepal	11	12	8	-1	0	-2	0	2	-3	-1
New Zealand	165	276	310	558	510	536	436	467	1,200	2,466
North Korea	2	62	-6	4	8	1	12	41	-45	-11
Pakistan	8	9	20	24	44	40	86	109	34	77
Papua New Guinea	-13	31	99	137	163	188	187	139	123	84
Philippines	1,033	1,722	2,001	2,255	2,365	2,224	2,289	2,182	2,351	1,765
Singapore	-3,227	-4,686	-6,437	-5,082	-4,610	-3,882	-5,701	-6,021	-5,170	-5,101
Solomon Islands	0	0	3	-3	-5	75	227	329	-18	-6
South Korea	1,858	2,307	3,324	4,480	5,538	6,131	6,924	7,135	5,757	4,148
Sri Lanka	-17	6	22	163	146	188	102	201	70	59
Thailand	518	670	1,282	1,150	1,245	1,402	1,428	1,182	1,535	1,748
Vanuatu	1,475	1,180	-960	-1,113	-1,058	-935	-956	-1,258	-1,570	-1,911
Vietnam	80	57	48	37	28	26	33	30	27	22
Others	42	-171	-889	-317	-530	-418	-369	-594	-210	-155
Africa	1,691	1,929	1,958	1,752	1,607	1,829	1,851	1,859	2,087	2,034
North America	-995	-243	-44	-1,851	-2,207	-2,085	323	194	1,782	2,170
Latin America	630	805	1,139	1,111	1,170	1,149	1,108	923	942	791
Caribbean	198	-261	1,841	1,468	1,104	3,169	4,330	5,341	5,893	4,052
Middle East	-732	-805	-938	-571	-519	-1,111	-1,888	-2,330	-2,435	-2,616
Western Europe	-2,893	-5,009	-5,269	-4,543	-1,837	-1,558	-317	-3,749	14,519	-9,452
Eastern Europe	191	283	282	341	306	268	245	383	507	941
Unallocated	0	0	0	0	0	0	0	70	53	89
Total	3,872	1,924	959	4,103	7,953	12,834	17,867	29,466	36,462	40,216

Source: Hong Kong Monthly Digest of Statistics (Hong Kong, Census and Statistics Department), various issues.

in the international financial market because of the expected appreciation of the New Taiwan dollar.[4]

Between 1979 and 1988 Hong Kong consistently remained a net debtor *vis-à-vis* western Europe and the Middle East, indicating that these two regions were net suppliers of funds to the Hong Kong financial centre. Within western Europe, the great bulk of funds were supplied through the London centre. North America used to be another net fund supplier up until 1984 but turned into a net debtor *vis-à-vis* Hong Kong in 1985, and this net debt has increased tremendously since, at an annual rate of 88.7 per cent. Obviously, this is consistent with the world trend that the United States has also turned into a net debtor *vis-à-vis* the rest of the world in view of its rapidly increasing trade and budget deficits.

Inter-bank Activities[5]

Inter-bank borrowing and lending are an integral part of the international financial intermediation process. Indeed, in the offshore markets, wholesale inter-bank activities tend to dominate. The international inter-bank market is basically an informal market for banks lending to each other. The amount of transactions is usually very large (at least US$1 million) and of relatively short maturity (usually shorter than six months). All transactions are done through telecommunication networks between the banks' dealers or through money brokers. The major currency for international inter-bank deals is United States dollars, but other currencies such as the Deutschemark, Swiss franc, and Japanese yen are gaining importance. Since inter-bank loans are unsecured, banks participating in the market have to have good credit ranking. Banks with different credit standings are granted different credit limits, and their borrowings are also priced differently.

There are several reasons for the use of the inter-bank market:

1. Balancing Uses and Sources of Funds.   At a certain point in time, some banks may find that they have more deposits than they can use, while other banks may find themselves in the opposite position. Thus, the inter-bank market serves as a central market for banks to handle their surpluses and deficits. Non-bank depositors and end-users of funds can be matched more efficiently, though indirectly, through such a market. In the international arena, the picture is more complicated because some banks may have more expertise in dealing in certain currencies and with certain regions or countries. Thus, some banks may need to go through the inter-bank market to deal in currencies or regions and countries that are not familiar to them.

2. Risk Management.   The inter-bank market can also be used to manage interest rate risk and exchange rate risk by lending or borrowing funds with similar maturities or currencies.

3. Profit Making.   Banks may use the inter-bank market to generate profit, a transaction that may not be related to the ultimate needs of their customers. Banks, for example, may borrow three-month funds

and place them for six months when the yield curve is positive and the banks are expecting a fall in the interest rate. The banks are thus trying to generate profit by taking additional risk. Transactions such as interest rate arbitrage and currency swaps also provide sources of income.

Table 17.10 shows the external claims of the Hong Kong financial system (including banks and DTCs) *vis-à-vis* banks and non-banks. It shows that claims on banks account for 64.5 per cent of total external assets and claims on non-banks account for 35.5 per cent of the total in 1979. However, in recent years, (from 1985 to 1988), claims on banks usually account for more than 80 per cent of the total external claims. No corresponding data exist on the liability side. However, the external position of the BIS reporting banks *vis-à-vis* Hong Kong is available, and Table 17.11 indicates that the contribution of inter-bank transactions between Hong Kong and the BIS reporting countries is even more pronounced. In both 1987 and 1988, inter-bank transactions are shown to account for more than 90 per cent of the transactions. In both cases, the trend for inter-bank activities is generally upward, indicating the increasing dominance of wholesale business in the financial centre of Hong Kong.

Maturity Transformation

Banks are usually said to implement maturity transformation by borrowing short and lending long. Thus, banks can be said to manufacture liquidity, which is important in the functioning of the economy. This is because borrowers can have access to a stable source of funds while holders of funds can invest in highly liquid assets.

Since there are no published data on the maturity structure of the asset and liability items of the Hong Kong banking system, it is impossible to demonstrate the maturity transformation process of the Hong Kong centre. However, Hong Kong and Singapore are very similar, and it may be useful to look at the maturity distribution of the Singapore Asian dollar market (Table 17.12). It is obvious that the Asian dollar market has a larger proportion of short-term liabilities and a relatively larger proportion of long-term assets. It is believed that in the late 1960s and early 1970s, the Asian dollar market served as a conduit of funds from the Asian region to Europe and North America because of the higher interest rates and the lack of investment opportunities in the Southeast Asia region. At that time, the main borrowers were banks. Thus, the maturities of assets and liabilities of banks in the Asian dollar market were carefully matched. Starting in the mid-1970s, funds began to flow from Europe and the United States back to the developing countries in Asia (especially South-east Asia). This has changed the maturity structure of assets and liabilities in the market, with relatively longer term assets and shorter term liabilities. Thus, the function of maturity transformation has been carried out more effectively since the mid-1970s.[6]

Table 17.10   External Claims *vis-à-vis* Banks and Non-banks of the Hong Kong Financial System (US$ million)

Year	Bank		Non-Bank		Total Claims
1979	16,124	(64.5)	8,865	(35.5)	24,990
1980	23,303	(67.5)	11,215	(32.5)	34,518
1981	32,335	(69.8)	13,968	(30.2)	46,193
1982	42,443	(72.9)	15,783	(27.1)	58,225
1983	50,345	(74.3)	17,404	(25.7)	67,749
1984	59,869	(75.8)	19,062	(24.2)	78,931
1985	81,670	(80.6)	19,617	(19.4)	101,288
1986	132,678	(85.4)	22,596	(14.6)	155,274
1987	217,696	(82.2)	47,163	(17.8)	264,859
1988	252,808	(81.5)	57,370	(18.5)	310,178

Note: Figures in parentheses are proportions (in percentage) of the total.

Source: *Hong Kong Monthly Digest of Statistics* (Hong Kong, Census and Statistics Department), various issues.

Table 17.11   External Position of Banks in Twelve Reporting Countries *vis-à-vis* Hong Kong (US$ million)

	Assets			Liabilities		
	Bank	Non-Bank	Total	Bank	Non-Bank	Total
1982	23,948 (84.5)	4,393 (15.5)	28,341	16,802 (71.0)	6,876 (29.0)	23,678
1983	30,443 (85.4)	5,200 (14.6)	35,643	22,922 (74.2)	7,974 (25.8)	30,896
1984	54,273 (90.0)	6,049 (10.0)	60,322	52,127 (82.5)	11,062 (17.5)	63,189
1985	70,307 (90.3)	7,550 (9.7)	77,857	69,179 (84.1)	13,114 (15.9)	82,293
1986	110,697 (92.1)	9,452 (7.9)	120,149	115,599 (88.4)	15,153 (11.6)	130,752
1987	216,647 (95.9)	9,305 (4.1)	225,952	208,119 (92.3)	17,271 (7.7)	225,390
1988	249,643 (96.2)	9,771 (3.8)	259,414	243,024 (92.5)	19,626 (7.5)	262,650

Note: Figures in parentheses are proportions (in percentage) of the total.

Source: Bank for International Settlements, *International Banking Developments*, various issues.

Table 17.12 Maturity Structure of Assets and Liabilities of the Singapore Asian Dollar Market (in percentages)

	1976		1980		1984		1988	
	Assets	Liabilities	Assets	Liabilities	Assets	Liabilities	Assets	Liabilities
≤ 1 month	35.1	49.2	32.6	44.4	35.6	46.1	42.8	54.8
> 1–3 months	27.3	28.0	26.8	30.1	23.9	30.0	24.3	22.8
> 3–12 months	20.9	19.4	21.6	20.5	20.4	21.1	17.4	16.1
> 1–3 years	3.2	1.6	5.5	3.0	4.1	1.3	4.4	2.0
> 3 years	13.5	1.9	13.5	2.0	16.0	1.6	10.9	4.3

Source: Monetary Authority of Singapore, *Monthly Statistical Bulletin*, various issues.

Prospects and Problems[7]

There are now five offshore banking centres in Asia.[7] They are Hong Kong, Manila, Taipei, Singapore, and Tokyo. However, the development of Manila's Offshore Banking Units is not very successful because its telecommunication system is underdeveloped, its inter-bank market is inactive, and its political environment is very unstable. The Taiwan Offshore Banking Units were set up in 1984. However, the Taiwan banking system is less sophisticated and more heavily regulated than that of Hong Kong. Thus, Hong Kong's real competitors seem to be Singapore and Tokyo.

Jao (1988a) provides a detailed comparison of these three centres in his book, which is summarized briefly here.

Hong Kong Versus Singapore

Advantages

(a) Hong Kong is an integrated financial centre in that foreign banks as well as DTCs can engage in offshore and domestic business.
(b) The policy of the Hong Kong Government is more liberal than that of Singapore, and financial regulations are more lenient.
(c) The tax rate is very low and the tax system is very simple.[8] Moreover, overseas income is generally exempt from taxation.
(d) Hong Kong has a longer tradition of being a syndication and fund management centre than does Singapore.
(e) Hong Kong's economy is bigger than Singapore's. Thus, both business and financial transactions are more active in Hong Kong than in Singapore.
(f) The gold and equity markets in Hong Kong are much larger and more active than those of Singapore, and this is more attractive to foreign investors and fund managers.
(g) Because of its proximity to and traditional ties with China, Hong Kong is likely to benefit from the positive effects of the China's open door policy especially in terms of financing China trade and China's financial needs.

Disadvantages

(a) Because of the political uncertainty surrounding the resumption of sovereignty by China in 1997, the political risk of Hong Kong is higher than that of Singapore.
(b) Hong Kong seems to be less stable financially as demonstrated by the frequency of banking or financial crises.
(c) Hong Kong seems to lag behind Singapore in developing financial markets and instruments. Obvious examples include the Asian dollar market, the Asian bond market, the financial futures market (the Simex), and the discount houses.
(d) The Hong Kong Government does not have a long-term and

consciously formulated plan to foster the development of Hong Kong as a financial centre.

Hong Kong Versus Tokyo

Advantages

(a) Again, Hong Kong is an integrated financial centre while the Tokyo Offshore Banking Units are segregated from the domestic market.
(b) The policy of the Hong Kong Government is more liberal and financial regulations are more lenient than Tokyo's.
(c) The Hong Kong tax rate is very low, the tax system is simple, and overseas income is exempt.
(d) The Hong Kong legal system is based on that of the United Kingdom, and English is more widely used than in Tokyo.
(e) The cost of operating an office in Hong Kong is cheaper than it is in Tokyo.
(f) Again, proximity to China may also benefit Hong Kong.

Disadvantages

(a) The Hong Kong political risk may be higher than that of Tokyo, again because of the problem posed by the political changes of 1997.
(b) Hong Kong may be more unstable financially than Tokyo, as seen by its record of financial crises.
(c) The size of the Hong Kong economy is much smaller than that of Japan and Hong Kong itself cannot generate as many funds (and denominated in a stable and strong currency) as Japan.
(d) The capital market of Hong Kong is much less developed than that of Tokyo.

Discussion

In addition to their competitive relationship, the Hong Kong, Singapore, and Tokyo centres complement each other. It has long been recognized that Singapore is a funding centre while Hong Kong is a lending centre, because the countries surrounding Singapore, for example, Malaysia and Indonesia, are not able to absorb all the funds in the Asian dollar market. Hong Kong can thus serve as a conduit of funds from the Asian dollar market to South Korea, Taiwan, Australia, China, and Hong Kong itself.

The establishment of the Offshore Banking Units in Tokyo has not diverted business from Hong Kong. Hong Kong may, in fact, benefit from Japan's financial liberalization because more business is generated in foreign exchange and securities dealings. Moreover, the nature of the two markets is different. The Tokyo market is more efficient in long-term financing, while the Hong Kong market (and the Singapore one) are more efficient in short- to medium-term financing.

Indeed, in a survey done by this author in late 1986 on ten major Japanese banks in Hong Kong, it was confirmed that the prospect for Hong Kong as a centre for short- to medium-term financing as well as a place for arranging China-related financing packages was very good. In the survey, 60 per cent of the respondents believed that the prospects of Hong Kong remaining a market for medium-term syndication loans and a market for arranging short- to medium-term financial instruments (including certificates of deposit, commercial paper, note-issuing facilities, and revolving underwriting facilities) in the next ten years was 'very good' to 'extremely good'. Seventy per cent of the respondents believed that the prospects of Hong Kong remaining a market for arranging China financing packages in the next ten years were 'very good' to 'extremely good'. However, the prospects for being a market for long-term financing does not seem to be as promising as short- to medium-term financing.

Until May 1989, the China factor seemed to be working in favour of Hong Kong's development. However, the political turmoil in China in May to June of 1989 shook the confidence of Hong Kong people very badly. The Hang Seng Index dropped from the post-crash high of 3,310 points (on 15 May 1989) to a low of 2,094 points (on 5 June 1989). In August 1989, the dust seemed to settle. Activities in the property market started to pick up, and the Hang Seng Index recovered very rapidly and reached a level of around 2,900 by the end of 1989.

After the June 4th events, many multilateral lenders such as the World Bank and the ADB and foreign commercial banks suspended new loans to China. Hong Kong may be affected by such movements because China has become one of Hong Kong's major borrowers, and also one of Asia's biggest borrowers, since the mid-1980s. Hong Kong would definitely earn less on fees and interest by arranging loans to China. However, according to a report published in the *Asian Wall Street Journal*, China would have no difficulties in meeting scheduled repayments for its debt and China's debt service ratio is still considered to be low by world standards.[9] Thus, given that China can contain its economic problems of quickening inflation and a widening trade deficit, China's credit ranking would remain fairly good. If a go-ahead is given by both the World Bank and the ADB, the commercial banks would still continue to lend money to China. Moreover, Australia and other rapidly industrializing Asian countries, such as Thailand and Malaysia, still have a great demand for funds. In the future, we can see Tokyo develop into a global financial centre of the same status as New York and London. Hong Kong and Singapore will perform the functions of 'satellite' centres, complementary to the Tokyo one, which also functions as a fund-supplying centre. Although Singapore has been trying very hard to promote its fund management business, Hong Kong remains superior because of its excellent telecommunications system and financial expertise. There is no doubt that Singapore would capitalize on the growth potential of countries such as Indonesia, Malaysia, and Thailand, but such countries may not be able to absorb all the funds deposited in Singapore. Hong Kong would remain a natural centre for absorbing Singapore's excess funds. Moreover, although Taiwan has also been promoting its role as a financial centre by establishing the Offshore Banking Units in 1984, its financial markets are still underdeveloped. This author envisages that Taiwan would still require the financial intermediation services provided by the Hong Kong centre. All these elements together with the recovery of China's relationship with western countries would further strengthen the role of Hong Kong as an international financial centre.

Notes

1. The BIS reporting banks include banks in the group of ten countries (Belgium, Canada, France, Germany, Italy, Japan, the Netherlands, Sweden, the United Kingdom, and the United States) plus Luxemburg, Austria, Denmark, Finland, Ireland, Norway, and Spain, as well as banks engaged in international business in the Bahamas, the Cayman Islands, Hong Kong, and Singapore, all offshore units in Bahrain, all offshore banks operating in the Netherlands Antilles, and the branches of United States banks in Panama.

2. Y. C. Jao (ed.), *Hong Kong's Banking System in Transition: Problems, Prospects, and Policies*, (Hong Kong, Chinese Banks Association Ltd., 1988).

3. However, due to the rapid depreciating United States dollar *vis-à-vis* other currencies, there was a rapid increase in other non-United States dollar foreign currency deposits in Hong Kong in 1987 and 1988 (notably the Australian dollar and the New Zealand dollar). Thus, the exchange rate movement has affected the share of foreign currency deposits in these two years.

4. See 'International Banking and Financial Developments', Bank for International Settlements, May 1988.

5. This section is partly taken from 'The International Interbank Market: A Descriptive Study', *BIS Economic Papers*, No. 8, July 1983.

6. This is the observation made by Kenneth Bernauer, 'The Asian Dollar Market', *Economic Review*, No. 1, FRB-San Francisco, Winter 1983.

7. This section draws heavily from Y. C. Jao (ed.), *Hong Kong's Banking System in Transition: Problems, Prospects, and Policies*, (Hong Kong, Chinese Banks Association Ltd., 1988).

8. The current tax rate for personal income is 15 per cent and the current profit tax is 16.5 per cent.

9. See Christopher Hunt, 'China's Rising Debt Isn't Yet a Problem', *Asian Wall Street Journal*, 14–15 July 1989.

References

Bank for International Settlements, 'The International Interbank Market, a Descriptive Study, *BIS Economic Papers*, No. 8, July 1983.

—— *International Banking Developments*, various issues.

Bernauer, Kenneth, 'The Asian Dollar Market', *Economic Review*, No. 1, FRB-San Francisco, Winter 1983.

Ho, Y. K., 'The Role of Hong Kong and Singapore in the International Financial Intermediation Process', paper presented at the *Conference on Research in International Finance*, Centre HEC-ISA, Jouy-en-Josas, France, June 19–20, 1986.

Jao, Y. C., *Banking and Currency in Hong Kong*, (London, Macmillan Press, 1974).

—— 'Financial Structure and Monetary Policy in Hong Kong', in S. Y. Lee and

Y. C. Jao (eds.), *Financial Structures and Monetary Policies in Southeast Asia*, (London, Macmillan Press, 1982).

—— 'The Rise of Hong Kong as a Regional Financial Centre', *Asian Survey*, July 1979, pp. 674–94.

—— 'Hong Kong as a Regional Financial Centre: Evolution and Prospects', in C. K. Leung, J. W. Cushman, and Wang Gungwu (eds.), *Hong Kong: Dilemmas of Growth*, (Canberra, Australian National University Press, 1980), pp. 161–94.

—— (ed.), *Hong Kong's Banking System in Transition: Problems, Prospects, and Policies*, (Hong Kong, Chinese Banks Association, 1988a).

—— 'Monetary System and Banking Structure', in H. C. Y. Ho and L. C. Chau (eds.), *The Economic System of Hong Kong*, (Hong Kong, Asian Research Service, 1988b).

Park, Y. S., 'The Economics of Offshore Financial Centres', *Columbia Journal of World Business*, Winter 1982, pp. 31–5.

Scott, R. H., Wong K. A., and Ho Y. K. (eds.), *Hong Kong's Financial Institutions and Markets*, (Hong Kong, Oxford University Press, 1986).

Index